Global Text

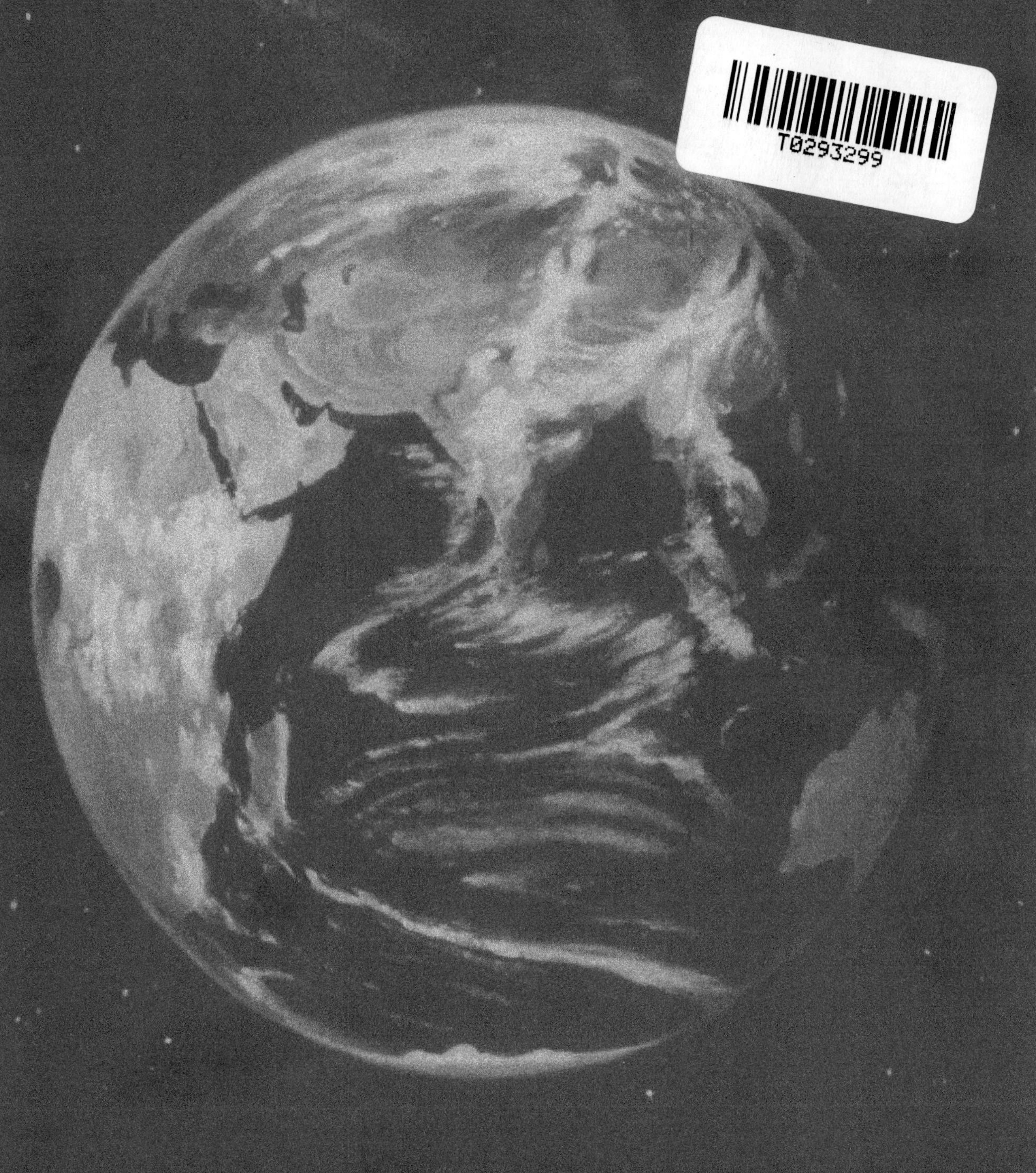

Business Processes and Information Technology

Business Processes and Information Technology

Ulric J. Gelinas, Jr.

Steve G. Sutton

Jane Federowicz

For any questions about this text, please email: drexel@uga.edu

The Global Text Project is funded by the Jacobs Foundation, Zurich, Switzerland

This edition is in the .pdf format provided to us by the author. We are in the process of converting this edition into the Global Text Project standard format. When this is complete, a new edition will be posted on the Global Text Project website and will be available in a variety of formats upon request.

BUSINESS PROCESSES AND INFORMATION TECHNOLOGY

Ulric J. Gelinas, Jr.

Bentley College

Steve G. Sutton

University of Connecticut

Jane Fedorowicz

Bentley College

Business Processes and Information Technology

Ulric J. Gelinas, Jr., Steve G. Sutton, Jane Fedorowicz

Vice President/Editorial Director: Jack Calhoun

Editor-in-Chief: George Werthman

Senior Publisher: Melissa Acuña

Acquisitions Editor: Sharon Oblinger

Developmental Editor: Mardell Toomey

Marketing Manager: Mignon Tucker

Production Editor: Cliff Kallemeyn

Manufacturing Coordinator: Doug Wilke

Media Technology Editor: Sally Neiman

Internal and Cover Designer: Rik Moore

Production House: Litten Editing and Production, Inc.GGS Information Services, Inc.

Printer: QuebecorWorldVersailles, KY

Cover Art: Digital Stock

Printed in the United States of America1 2 3 4 5 06 05 04 03

For more informationcontact South-Western,5191 Natorp Boulevard,Mason, Ohio 45040.Or you can visit our Internet site at: http://www.swlearning.com

of Congress

Gelinas FM-iii

Control Number:

2003100005

ISBN: 1-616-10146-6

Dedication

To our spouses Roxanne, Vicky, and Michael and to Jane's sons Andrew and Billy, with grateful appreciation for their patience and support throughout this project.

AUTHORS

Ulric J. (Joe) Gelinas, Jr., Ph.D., is Associate Professor of Accountancy and Davis Educational Foundation Fellow at Bentley College, Waltham, Massachusetts. He received his A.B. in Economics from St. Michael's College, Winooski Park, Vermont, and his M.B.A. and Ph.D. from the University of Massachusetts, Amherst. Professor Gelinas has also taught at the University of Tennessee and at Vesalius College, Vrije Universtiteit Brussel in Brussels, Belgium. As a Captain in the United States Air Force, he was Officer-in-Charge of IT Operations. Professor Gelinas was the founding editor of the *Journal of Accounting and Computers* (formerly the *Kent/Bentley Journal of Accounting and Computers* and the *Kent/Bentley Review*). Professor Gelinas has published articles on accounting information systems, computers in accounting education, technical communications, and information privacy. In 2000 he received the John W. Beveridge Achievement Award from the New England Chapter of the Information Systems Audit and Control Association for outstanding contributions to the IS Audit and Control profession. He has made presentations and conducted workshops at the International Conference of the Information Systems Audit & Control Association (ISACA), ISACA's Computer Audit, Control and Security (CACS) conferences, as well as other professional groups. He is a member of the American Accounting Association, the Information Systems Audit & Control Association, Beta Alpha Psi, and Beta Gamma Sigma. Professor Gelinas was a member of the U.S. expert panel that reviewed *Control Objectives for Information and Related Technology* (COBIT) and has conducted COBIT workshops in North America and Europe. He was the author of a portion of *Implementation Tool Set*, a volume that accompanies the second and third editions of COBIT. In his spare time, Professor Gelinas is engaged in his favorite activities: sailing, scuba diving, and bird watching.

Steve G. Sutton, Ph.D., CPA, is Professor of Accounting Information Systems at the University of Connecticut, Storrs, Connecticut and Professorial Fellow in Business Information Systems at the University of Melbourne, Victoria, Australia. He received his BSA, MA and Ph.D. from the University of Missouri—Columbia. Professor Sutton has taught at the University of Calgary, Arizona State University West, Texas Tech University, Oklahoma State University, and Bryant College. His audit and information systems consulting experience with Mayer Hoffman McCann, CPAs, and KPMG (and a pre-merger KMG Main Hurdman), along with experience as a computer operator with Deere & Co., support his teaching and research interests in information systems, auditing, and business education. Professor Sutton is the founding and continuing editor of the *International Journal of Accounting Information Systems* and its predecessor publication, *Advances in Accounting Information Systems.* In addition, he is a founding and continuing co-chair of the annual Accounting Information Systems Research Symposium and the sponsoring journal editor for the International Research Symposium on Accounting Information Systems. Professor Sutton is also a co-author of the monograph, *Productivity and Quality Measurement Systems for Internal Auditing* (Institute of Internal Auditors Research Foundation) and co-editor of two American Accounting Association monographs, *Behavioral Accounting Research: Foundations and Frontiers* and *Researching Accounting as an Information Systems Discipline*. Professor Sutton has published over 70 journal articles and made over 70 conference presentations on accounting information systems, auditing, and computers in accounting education. He has made continuing education presentations for both the international association and Phoenix Chapter of the Institute of Internal Auditors and the American Public Power Association, as well as several public accounting firms. Professor Sutton is a member of the Association for Information Systems, American Accounting Association, Canadian Academic Accounting Association, Accounting and Finance Association of Australia and New Zealand, European Accounting Association, American Institute of CPAs, Decision Sciences Institute, Beta Alpha Psi, and Beta Gamma Sigma. He is a past chair of the Information Systems Section of the American Accounting Association. Among Professor Sutton's hobbies are 3-on-3 basketball tournaments, travel, skiing, and hiking.

Jane Fedorowicz, the Rae D. Anderson Chair of Accounting and Information Systems, holds appointments in both the Accountancy and Computer Information Systems departments at Bentley College. Her expertise in integrating IT into business degree programs has been instrumental in launching several initiatives at the College, notably, undergraduate and graduate programs in Accounting Information Systems and the e-business concentration in the MBA program. She took a leading role in developing Bentley's Accounting Center for Electronic Learning and Business Measurement (ACELAB), a hands-on, state-of-the-art technology facility. Professor Fedorowicz holds MS and Ph.D. degrees in Systems Sciences from Carnegie Mellon University and a BS from the University of Connecticut. Before joining the Bentley faculty in 1994, she taught at Carnegie Mellon University, Northwestern University, Boston University, and the University of Massachusetts at Boston. She is a member of the AICPA Precertification Education Executive Committee. She is Vice President of Affiliated Organizations for the Association for Information Systems (AIS), Northeast regional representative for the Emerging Technologies Section of the American Accounting Association, and co-general chair for the 2001 Americas Conference for Information Systems of AIS. Professor Fedorowicz has published over 60 articles in refereed journals and conference proceedings. Her research spans a wide range of IT issues and technologies impacting individual and organizational effectiveness. The American Accounting Association recognized Professor Fedorowicz with the 1997 Notable Contribution to the Information Systems Literature Award, and she was recently selected as Bentley College's Scholar of the Year for 2000.

PREFACE

Business Processes and Information Technology prepares students to effectively use, manage, and participate in the development of information technology applications in support of common business processes. The text focuses on the interconnections among an organization's management, business processes, information systems, and information technology. An emphasis is given throughout the text to the governance, control, and security of business processes and information systems, especially underlying financial information systems. After studying this text, a student will walk away with an understanding of the foundation tools and knowledge required for the analysis, design, and control of IT-driven business processes using current and emergent technologies.

Unique Features of the Book

Business Processes and Information Technology takes a business process focus towards understanding and managing operations, information systems, and management/decision making in contemporary organizations. A wide range of information technologies in business processes are integrated throughout.

Three Themes Three themes connect our discussions to topics that are currently of great interest to business professionals. These themes are *enterprise systems*—such as those sold by SAP, JD Edwards, Oracle, and PeopleSoft; *E-Business*—including retail (Business-to-Consumer, or B2C) e-businesses such as Amazon.com and Business-to-Business (B2B) marketplaces such as Covisint.com (operated by auto manufacturers); and *information technology*—state-of-the-art hardware and software applications that keep an organization heading toward achievement of its objectives. Icons have been added to the text to identify discussions of these themes.

Enterprise systems are software packages designed to provide complete integration of an organization's business information processing systems and all related data. Data is shared across the systems to support the operation and management of the organization. Enterprise systems are introduced in Chapter 3 and then discussed throughout the remainder of the text. For example, in Chapter 10 you will find a diagram that depicts how the order fulfillment process would be implemented with an enterprise system. Similar diagrams are also in the other business process chapters. Additionally, examples of screens from enterprise systems have been included throughout the text to demonstrate business process information acquisition and presentation in contemporary organizations.

E-Business is the application of electronic networks (including the Internet) to undertake business processes between organizations and either individuals or other organizations. E-business has created entirely new ways of working within and across organizations. For example, organizations are buying and selling goods and services at virtual marketplaces. This changes how organizations identify customers and select vendors. It changes the cost of acquiring goods from a vendor and the price they should charge their customers for their products. E-business and its closely related concept, e-commerce, are explained more fully in Chapter 4 and discussed throughout the remainder of the book.

Information Technology, indicated by the Technology icon at left, encompasses any hardware, software, or communications technology that might be adopted by an organization to support or control a business process, enable management decisions, or provide a competitive advantage. Technology icons signal that an electronic mechanism is being discussed that is either in wide use, representative of the state of the art, or advocated for business adoption in the near future.

We present emerging technology examples and other current topics in sidebars, which are typeset to make them stand out from the text. Since the unique design allows you to easily locate the sidebars within each chapter, you can read about a particular technology separate from the remainder of the chapter. There are three types of sidebars:

1. *Technology Insights* define and discuss a major topic. For example, Technology Insight 4.1 describes Extensible Markup Language (XML), a Web-based language that enables information to be easily shared over the Web.
2. *Technology Applications* present short examples—taken from actual practice—of technology in use. For example, Technology

Application 10.2 describes real-world examples of e-business in global markets.

3. *Technology Excerpts* contain article reprints. For example, Technology Excerpt 7.2 summarizes experts' criteria for selecting an application service provider (ASP). ASPs are external organizations that host, manage, and provide access to application software over the Internet to multiple customers.

The issues of **governance, internal control, and security** have received greater attention in the last few years as management has realized the importance of internal control to the effective governance of organizations and the IT that drives organizations. Enron, WorldCom, and 9/11 have brought these issues into the homes and offices of many of us. Chapter 8 introduces these topics, including such control frameworks as COSO and COBIT*, and pervasive exposures such as hacking and denial of service attacks. Chapter 9 introduces a specific control framework for use in analyzing business processes and discusses technology-related controls that are key to well-controlled business processes. The framework and controls from Chapters 8 and 9 are then applied in the business process chapters—Chapters 10 through 14.

* The *Committee of Sponsoring Organizations of the Treadway Commission* (COSO) supports a framework for structuring control objectives. *Control Objectives for Information and Related*

Technology (COBIT) is a framework for control of advanced technology-based business information systems.

Documentation Tools Chapter 2 includes a comprehensive coverage of how to read and prepare data flow diagrams (DFDs) and systems flowcharts. The chapter also describes how to read entity-relationship (E-R) diagrams (the drawing of E-R diagrams is covered in Chapter 3).

Case Studies and Capsule Cases Several short cases describe typical business processes at the end of Chapters 2, 10, 11, and 12. These process narratives provide ample opportunity for students to practice application of the various tools and techniques discussed in the book. Several capsule cases, adapted from actual real-world systems, may be found at the end of Chapters 10–12. These system descriptions are shorter than those in the short cases, to provide another vehicle for students to acquire proficiency in documenting systems.

How This Textbook Presents Information Systems

This textbook is divided into five parts. Part I, *Business Processes and IS Foundations,* introduces IS, basic systems concepts, and documentation tools. Part II, *Technology for Business Processes and IS*, introduces the design and use of database management systems and reviews current advances in e-business and decision-making support technologies. Part III, *Development of IS*, presents the tools and techniques used to develop and implement information systems.

Part IV, *Internal Control for Business Processes and IS,* introduces control concepts, pervasive controls, IT control processes, and technology-related application controls. Part V, *Core Business Processes,* presents views of IS application to support key business activities.

Part I Chapter 1 introduces information systems and relates them to key business process concepts with emphasis on the importance of these subjects to today's business professional. Information systems are described as key enablers of an organization's successful operation of its important business processes. Chapter 2 shows how to read and prepare documentation to portray aspects of a business process, including operational and information systems processes. The chapter consists of modular discussions that compartmentalize the coverage of reading versus preparing each type of documentation.

Part II Chapter 3 focuses on the issues surrounding the management of data storage, retrieval, and security in contemporary organizations. While the chapter includes an overview of traditional data file structures and data storage management, the primary emphasis of the chapter material is on relational database management systems. Chapter 4 describes the emergence of electronic business (e-business) and the radical change in organizational thinking that has resulted. The evolution of information processing to its contemporary emphasis on instantaneous recording, reporting, and accessibility of business information is described. Enabling technologies such as XML and advanced data communications networks are also explored. Chapter 5 examines the evolution of business intelligence and knowledge management and their role in supporting information systems initiatives. The nature of each of these strategic initiatives is explored as well as the development and use of each to support decision making.

Part III Chapter 6 introduces the systems development process as an activity that must be undertaken successfully for an organization to effectively reengineer its business processes and make effective use of information technology. The initial phases in systems development—the feasibility study and systems analysis—are described. Chapter 7 explores several alternative sources for the development and acquisition of hardware and software. In addition, the final phases in systems development process—design and implementation—are described.

Part IV Chapter 8 explores the importance of effective management and control of IT in contemporary corporate governance. Control frameworks such as COSO and COBIT are introduced. These can provide management, business process owners, and other interested parties assurance that an organization's essential business processes and information technology resources are directed at achieving organizational objectives. Chapter 9 presents a detailed framework for the analysis of internal control. Physical implementations are used as contexts for discussing controls that are typically applied in business processes.

Part V Chapters 10 through 14 describe the typical business processes found in a variety of organizations. For each process, there is a description of the organizational context (e.g., departments, managers), the business operations being performed (e.g., order fulfillment, revenue collection), information for decision making, and IT typically applied in support of these elements. In addition, these chapters also describe the management processes that will ensure achievement of the organization's objectives for each process, including the nature, functions, purpose, control goals, and control plans for both the *operations* process and its *information* process.

To The Student

To be successful in this course and with this text, we ask you to accept that in this field there are no right and wrong answers. You will be asked to solve problems—that is, to identify what the problem is, to consider alternative solutions, to select a solution, and then to defend your choice.

Another measure of success will be your ability and willingness to accept change as the only real constant in life and to prepare yourself to deal with change in your career. Because technology is rapidly outdated, learning facts about the current state of affairs will pay dividends only in the short run. What's important for your long-term success is that, at the university, you "learn how to learn," and that you continue to learn for the rest of your life. This text can help you to learn *how to learn* about information technology and business processes.

Instructional Supplements

Our text includes the following supplemental materials to assist the student and the instructor:

- The ***Instructor's Resource Manual*** includes chapter overview, outline, and teaching suggestions.
- The ***Test Bank*** will include a variety of types of questions including true/false, multiple-choice, short answer, and problems. An electronic test bank, *ExamView*, is also available so that instructors can easily customize their tests.
- A ***Solutions Manual*** providing all answers to in-text problems is available to instructors.
- ***PowerPoint*** slides cover all major concepts and key terms and are presented in an appealing way designed to hold students' interest.
- We also invite you to visit the Web site for this text at

http://gelinas.swlearning.com. Here you will find additional materials as well as the ***Instructor's Resource Manual*, the *Solutions Manual***, and the ***PowerPoint*** slides.

We trust that you will find the teaching package both flexible and enjoyable to use. We earnestly solicit your feedback on both the text and the ancillaries and appreciate knowing your criticisms and suggestions for improving the materials. In turn, we stand ready to respond to any questions or problems you may encounter. Please feel free to contact us through Thomson Learning/South-Western, directly through our academic institutions, or through our respective e-mail addresses: ugelinas@bentley.edu, steve.sutton@business.uconn.edu, and jfedorowicz@bentley.edu. We wish you success. Enjoy!

Acknowledgments

To our families, to whom we dedicate this book, we thank you for your infinite patience throughout this project. Without your support and encouragement, the completion of this project would not have been possible.

To Thomson/Learning South-Western, we would like to thank acquisitions editor, Sharon Oblinger, developmental editor, Mardell Toomey, marketing manager, Mignon Tucker, production editor, Cliff Kallemeyn, and our designer, Rik Moore.

Finally, we wish to thank our reviewers whose feedback helped shape the final product:

- Jagdish Gangolly, *State University of New York at Albany*
- Kevin Kobelsky, *University of Southern California*
- Jane Mutchler, *Georgia State University*
- Leslie Porter, *University of Southern California*
- Curt Westbrook, *California State University, San Bernardino*

Ulric J. Gelinas, Jr.

Steve G. Sutton

Jane Fedorowicz

BRIEF CONTENTS

CONTENTS

Part I

Gelinas FM-xx

Chapter 4

E-Business 106

Part I

Business Processes and Information Systems Foundations

[Insert UNF-p.1-1 here]

1

Introduction to Information Systems

As “Pottermania” reached epidemic proportions recently, it provided a good example of how a single business event can strain critical information systems in even the most advanced organizations. When each Harry Potter book was due for release, pre-orders for the book swamped bookstores and Internet booksellers. This demand had an impact on the supply chain, from the publisher who needed to predict how many copies to produce, to booksellers who accepted pre-orders at a record pace, to the Fedex drivers charged with getting books delivered on the official release date. As the fourth book neared release, Amazon.com received over 275,000 advance orders for the single volume, exceeding its previous record-setting preorder of 43,000 copies of John Grisham’s *The Brethren.*

This large number of orders challenged Amazon's information systems in many ways. Although advance orders were accepted, for example, the book's title was not made public until shortly before the release date, leaving Web developers scrambling to update the many Web screens on which *Harry Potter and the Goblet of Fire* needed to appear. Amazon also made careful arrangements with Fedex to ship the first 250,000 preordered copies on the announced delivery date, which happened to fall on a Saturday. Fedex scheduled 100 flights and 9,000 delivery specialists to meet the deadline.

But perhaps the biggest challenge of all fell to the Information Systems staff at Amazon.com. Because the orders were received weeks or even months ahead of time, data on each customer needed to be confirmed and stored for the future shipment. Billing information for the shipment had to be verified ahead of time, even though billing could not be completed until the shipment was released. Then the data was updated as each delivery was packaged and kept in a warehouse until Fedex shipped. These proved to be challenging data quality issues for Amazon. Each order was confirmed by sending e-mail to customers to make sure that delivery information was correct. Customer credit card charges were readied to enable billing as soon as legally possible on the Saturday of the shipment.[1]

[1] Julia King, "Pottermania Strains the Supply Chain," *Computerworld* (July 3, 2000): Vol. 34, Issue 27, 1 and 16.

Did it work? Well, Harry Potter fans around the world returned vicariously to Hogwart's on July 8. As the parent of a voracious Harry Potter fan, one of the authors of your text can attest that Amazon's information system worked well in handling this highly publicized business event.

Many business professionals at Amazon.com had to work together to be able to plan and implement the successful Harry Potter release. They had to address Information Systems issues across several business processes as part of this effort. These business processes in organizations, including management, operations, and information functions, are assisted by—and sometimes operated by—large, complex enterprise systems that govern the collection and sharing of data by various groups. Sometimes business processes extend to business partners through the Internet, permitting electronic business relationships to flourish. In the case of Amazon.com, the Internet is not an alternative communications channel, but the lifeblood of its business. Amazon's e-business systems had to be highly reliable even when faced with unprecedented levels of demand.

To be successful, business professionals must understand their roles and responsibilities in the context of the surrounding business processes and information technologies. In this text we help you to connect your business knowledge to business processes and information technologies to which professional activities are inextricably linked. This book will teach you to evaluate and understand what the impacts of technology are on your organization's operations and success, and how new technologies may change your business and job performance in the future.

Synopsis

This chapter introduces Information Systems (IS) and describes its importance. Be sure to become comfortable with fundamental concepts in this chapter. Key among these are the components of information systems, business processes, and information qualities.

This chapter connects discussion of Information Systems to three themes having a major impact on modern business. These themes are enterprise systems—such as those sold by SAP, J. D. Edwards, Oracle, and PeopleSoft; e-business—including retail e-business such as Amazon.com and Business-to-Business (B2B) marketplaces such as Covisint.com (operated by auto manufacturers); and information technology—state-of-the-art hardware and software applications that keep an organization heading toward achievement of its objectives. We define these three themes in this chapter.

LEARNING OBJECTIVES

- To describe an information system's integration with business processes and the organization
- To describe the business professional's role in the current information technology-driven environment
- To illustrate the attributes of information and the importance of data quality

Introduction

This textbook asks you to focus on a set of elements broader than that introduced in a typical Information Systems course. Becoming comfortable in dealing with these elements can bring rewards in terms of professional success and the competitive edge you gain in the marketplace. An information system is a major part of the business processes of an organization performing the critical functions for it. The Information System function is doubly crucial to an organization's success because it provides useful information for management and because it supports the organization's strategic plan.

Some of the terms in this chapter may not be familiar. The text contains definitions and illustrations to facilitate your familiarization with these terms.

The Textbook's Three Themes

This text revolves around the influence of three themes on contemporary business practices: (1) enterprise systems, (2) electronic business (e-business), and (3) information technology.

Enterprise systems are integrated software packages designed to provide complete integration of an organization's business information processing systems and all related data. Data is shared across systems to support the operation and management of the organization. Modules within these packages are named for the functions that they support and include logistics (sales and distribution, procurement, inventory management), accounting (financial accounting, treasury, controlling), manufacturing (planning and scheduling, cost accounting, capacity planning), and human resources (payroll, employee tracking, tax compliance). It is critical that business professionals understand these systems because they are members of teams that install and operate them in their organizations, and they require access to information captured within these systems to be effective managers. Installing an enterprise system requires that the business processes of an organization be understood and documented. Sometimes, the business processes must be changed and then mapped to the enterprise system. A major part of installation is configuring the enterprise system to tailor it to the business processes. Consultants, business process owners, system users, and evaluators must understand these systems and be able to install, use, and assess them. Chapter 2 describes a tool set for diagramming business processes that will help us analyze those processes. Chapter 3 describes enterprise systems more fully and these systems in their business context appear throughout the remainder of the book.

E-business is the application of electronic networks (including the Internet) to undertake business processes between individuals and organizations. These processes include interaction between back-office processes (internal processes such as distribution, manufacturing, and accounting) and front-office processes (external processes such as those that connect an organization to its customers and suppliers). Electronic networks include the Internet and electronic data interchange (EDI), both described in Chapter 4. E-business has created entirely new ways of working within and across organizations. For example, organizations are buying and selling goods and services at virtual marketplaces, changing the way organizations identify customers and select vendors. E-business is also changing how to determine what it costs to acquire goods from a vendor and what price(s) to charge customers for products. Obviously, business professionals should be aware of the opportunities and risks associated with this new way of doing business. Chapter 4 explains e-business and a closely related concept, Internet commerce, more fully, and instances appear throughout the reminder of the text.[2]

[2] See Andrew Bartels, "The Difference Between E-Business and E-

Commerce," *Computerworld* (October 30, 2000): 41, for a discussion of e-business and e-commerce.

Information Technology, or simply, Technology, is the third theme reflected in the side panel icons. This concept is more broadly defined than the other two, as it encompasses any hardware, software, or communications technology that might be adopted by an organization to support or control a business process, enable management decisions, or provide a competitive advantage. The side-panel technology icons signal discussion of an electronic mechanism that is either in wide use, represents the state of the art, or may be adopted by business in the near future. Chapters 8 and 9 introduce the use of technology to provide security, privacy, or internal control of operations. Technology can be used to support enterprise systems and e-business applications as well. Business professionals need to be aware of the availability of new technologies, and be able to evaluate the costs, benefits, and usefulness of each.

Challenges and Opportunities for the Business Professional

Are you preparing yourself to be effective in the future? Will you be able to adapt to advances in technology? Are you equipped to take advantage of technology improvements? You should prepare yourself to use the available technology and to participate in planning for and growing with the technology. For example, Chapter

5 introduces *business intelligence systems* and explains why the use of such systems is a competitive imperative for many organizations. These are not conditions of the distant future; most of these changes are already underway. For example, the Radio Frequency ID tags described in Technology Insight 1.1 (page 6)will have a major impact on how material is acquired, warehoused, assembled into products, and distributed to customers. The people, activities, and technologies involved in all processes within the supply chain will change because of the impact of RFID.

[Insert TECHNOLOGY INSIGHT 1.1 box here]

Components of the Study of Information Systems

Figure 1.1 (page 7) depicts the elements central to our study of Information Systems (IS). Many may be familiar, and some have been introduced earlier in this chapter.

[Insert Figure 1.1]

Hardware and Software The ability to plan and manage business operations depends partly on knowledge of the hardware and software available. For instance, is production manageable without knowledge of robotics? It goes without saying that technological developments have a profound effect on information systems; enterprise systems, e-business, databases, and business intelligence systems are but a few examples. Hardware and software technology provides the foundation on which IS and business operations rest.

Databases Important to a complete understanding of IS are databases, both internal and external to the company; the quantity and type of data available in these databases; and methods of retrieving those data. To perform analysis or to prepare information for management decision making, a business professional must be able to access and use data from internal and external databases. Chapter 3 explores the design and use of an organization's own databases.

Reporting To design reports generated by an information system, the business professional must know what outputs are required or desirable. A user might prepare a report on an occasional basis using powerful report-generating tools or a database query language (discussed in Chapter 3). Scheduled reports appear periodically as part of normal IS function. Government agencies such as the Internal Revenue Service and the Securities and Exchange Commission require some reports. Other reports, such as sales analysis, are useful internally.

Review Question

What 10 elements are included in the study of IS?

Control Traditionally, internal auditors and IS professionals have been charged with controlling business processes. However, this responsibility has expanded to others because of the difficulty of controlling modern, complex business processes. Today's business process owners need to work with internal auditing and the IS staff, and also business process owners in partnering companies, to ensure that the activities in their business processes are secure and reliable. Chapters 8 and 9 discuss control, the means by which one assures that the intended actually happens. Business process Chapters 10 through 14 further demonstrate controls in action that facilitate development and implementation of well-controlled business processes.

The next three elements of Information Systems study, business operations, events processing, and management decision making, comprise a major focus of this text, *business processes.* A **business process** is a set of business events that together enable the creation and delivery of an organization's products or services to its customers. It was the successful interaction among business processes that enabled Amazon.com to fill all those Harry Potter book orders during peak demand periods. Knowledge of these processes is essential for success as a technology user, consultant, business process owner, or Information Technology (IT) specialist.

Business Operations Organizations engage in activities or operations, such as hiring employees, purchasing inventory, and collecting cash from customers. An IS operates in concert with these business operations. Many IS inputs are prepared by operating departments—the *action* or *work centers* of the organization—and many IS outputs are used to manage these operations. Managers must analyze an IS in light of the work the organization performs. For example, to advise management and to prepare reports for management decision making, a marketing manager must understand the organization's product cycles.

Events Processing As organizations undertake their business operations, events, such as sales and purchases, occur. Data about these events must be captured and recorded to mirror and monitor business operations. The events have operational, managerial, and IS aspects. To design and use the IS, the business professional must know what event data are needed and how they are processed.

Management Decision Making The information used for a decision must be tailored to the type of decision under consideration. Furthermore, information is more useful if it recognizes the personal management styles and preferences of the decision maker. For example, the manager of Department A prefers to receive a monthly cash flow statement that groups receipts and payments into broad categories. The manager of Department B, on the other hand, wants to see more detailed information in the form of an analysis of payments by vendors. Chapter 5 examines decision making and the business intelligence systems that support it.

Systems Development and Operation Information Systems that process business events and provide information for management decision making must be designed, implemented, and effectively operated. Business professionals often participate in systems development projects. They may be users or business process owners contributing requests for certain functions, or auditors advancing controls for the new system. Choosing the data for a report, designing that report, or configuring an enterprise system are examples of systems development tasks that can be accomplished by a business professional. Chapters 6 and 7 examine systems development and operation, and the business professional's role in those processes.

Communications To present the results of their endeavors effectively, business professionals must possess strong oral and written communication skills. Have your professors been drumming this message into you? If not, you'll become acutely aware of its importance when you enter the job market. There are few easy answers in the study of IS. Professionals must evaluate alternatives, choose solutions, and defend their choices. Technical knowledge won't be enough for the last task.

Business Principles To design and operate the IS, a business professional must understand the use to which the information will be put. As an illustration, suppose you were designing an IS for the billing function at XYZ, Inc. Would you invoice customers at the time the customer's purchase order was received, or would you wait until XYZ's shipping department notified you that the goods had been shipped? You need to know the situations for which the former is normally correct (e.g., e-business retail sales) and for which the latter is correct (e.g., typical supply-chain operations for businesses).

What Is an Information System?

This section provides a definition for Information Systems (IS) and defines related terms to establish a background for later study. The section concludes by discussing how the business professional interacts with the IS and with the current business environment.

Systems and Subsystems

A **system** is a set of interdependent elements that together accomplish specific objectives. A system must have organization, interrelationships, integration, and central objectives. Figure 1.2a depicts a system consisting of four *interrelated* parts that have come together, or *integrated,* as a single system, named "system 1.0." Each part of a system—in this case, parts 1.1, 1.2, 1.3, and 1.4—is known as a **subsystem**. Within limits, any subsystem can be further divided into its component parts or subsystems. Figure 1.2b depicts subsystem 1.2 as a system consisting of three subsystems. Notice that we use the term *system* (versus *subsystem*) to describe the area of immediate focus. For example, in a typical university, the College of Business and the College of Engineering are subsystems of the university system, and the Operations Management and Marketing Departments are subsystems of the College of Business system.

Review Question

Are the terms *system* and *subsystem* synonymous? Explain your answer.

In Figure 1.2, parts a and b depict the *interrelationships* (A through H) in a system; part c depicts the hierarchical *organization* structure inherent in any system. Again, picture system 1.0 as a university and system 1.2 as the College of Business. Interrelationship F might be a finance student being sent by the Finance Department (1.2.1) to the Department of Accountancy (1.2.2) for a minor in accounting.

[Insert Figure 1.2 here]

A system's *basic objectives* depend on its type—natural, biological, or human-made—and on the particular system. For example, the human circulatory system is a biological system (a subsystem of the human body) whose purpose is to carry blood containing oxygen and carbon dioxide to and from the organs and extremities of the body.

Review Question

A system must have organization, interrelationships, integration, and central objectives. Why must each of these four components be present in a system?

Determination of the purpose of man-made systems—such as governments, schools, and business organizations—is necessary to understanding how best to create and evaluate the processes that comprise each system. Business organizations usually have relatively straightforward purposes that are normally related to the "bottom line." Many businesses, however, establish goals other than financial return to the owners. For example, a business might strive to improve the quality of life of its employees, or to use its natural resources responsibly. Here is our own bottom line: We must know a business organization's objectives to understand that business as a system and to understand the actions and interactions of that business's components or subsystems. This is a central theme of the study of IS.

The Information System

An **Information System** is a man-made system that consists of an integrated set of computer-based and manual components established to facilitate an organization's operational functions and to support management decision making by providing information that managers can use to plan and control the activities of the firm. Figure 1.3 depicts the functional components of an Information System. Imagine a simple IS used to maintain inventory balances for a shoe store. The inputs for such a system might be receipts of new shoes or sales of shoes; the process might be to update (in storage) the inventory records for the particular shoe; and the output might be a listing of all the various kinds and sizes of shoes and their respective recorded balances.

[Insert Figure 1.3 here]

Assume that, while entering data about shoe sales, we also enter data about who purchased the shoes, how they paid for the shoes, and why they decided to buy their shoes at our store. We might store those data and then periodically print reports useful in making decisions about advertising effectiveness. Or, we might decide, on the basis of analysis of our sales data, to engage in joint advertising campaigns with a credit card company whose cards are often used in the store.

The shoe store example shows that an IS often divides into components based on the organizational function being supported. For example, the IS in the shoe store supports inventory control (a logistics function) by maintaining records for each shoe stocked in the store. The shoe store IS also supports a sales and marketing function by analyzing sales in a variety of ways. Other typical IS components include personnel, production, finance, and accounting. As discussed in Chapter 3, however, integrated computer processing has blurred the distinctions among these separate systems.

Now consider the technology components of the IS model in Figure 1.3. **Input data** are data received by the Information System from the external environment or from another area within the Information System. Data input includes *capturing* data (for example, scanning a bar code on a sales item at a grocery store) and, if necessary, *conversion* of the data to *machine-readable form.* Input data are normally recorded in **business event data stores.**[3] These business events comprise the activities of the organization, such as purchasing goods from vendors and collecting cash from customers. Business event data are used often as a key source of data to *update* various master data. A **master data update** is an information processing activity whose function is to incorporate new business event data into existing master data. Updating includes adding, deleting, and replacing master data and/or records. For example, the sales event data are used to update the accounts receivable master data by adding new accounts receivable records.

3 Business event data and master data represent the relevant portions (or *views*) of the *corporate-wide database* being used for a particular application.

Master data updates are recorded on master data stores. **Master data stores** are repositories of relatively permanent data maintained over an extended period of time.[4] **Master data** contain data related to *entities*—persons (e.g., employees, customers), places (e.g., buildings), and things (e.g., inventory). Master data include such data as the accounts receivable master data, the customer master data, and the inventory master data.

[4] See note 3.

Two types of updates can be made to master data: information processing and data maintenance. **Information processing** includes data processing functions related to economic events such as financial events, and internal operations such as manufacturing. **Data maintenance**, on the other hand, includes activities related to adding, deleting, or replacing the **standing data** portions of master data. Master data **standing data** include relatively permanent portions of master data, such as the credit limit on customer master data and the selling price and warehouse location on inventory master data. This textbook emphasizes information processing, and analysis of internal controls related to master data updates is restricted to master data updates from information processing. There are references however, to controls related to data maintenance at appropriate points in the text.

Logical Components of a Business Process

A *business process* has three component processes that work together to support its logical activities. The IS supports all three processes in that it frequently embodies many of the policies and procedures that help define each process.

Review Question

What are three logical components of a business process? Define the functions of each. How do the components interact with one another?

The **information process** is that portion of the overall IS related to a particular business process. The information process plays a critical role in the way all three processes work together.

An **operations process** is a human-made system consisting of the people, equipment, organization, policies, and procedures whose objective is to accomplish the work of the organization. Operations processes typically include distribution, manufacturing, human resources, and their sub-processes.

The **management process** is a human-made system consisting of the people, authority, organization, policies, and procedures whose objective is to plan and control the operations of the organization. The three most prominent management activities are planning, controlling, and decision making. These are discussed in Chapter 5.

These processes work together to accomplish the objectives of the business process—and therefore the organization. In order to accept and fill a customer order for a Harry Potter book from Amazon.com, all three processes engage in a set of activities, as shown in Figure 1.4. The activity numbers refer to the labeled flows in Figure 1.4.

Gelinas 1-21

Flows are numbered in the order that activities occur.

[Insert Figure 1.4 here]

The management process:

(1) hires personnel and establishes the means for accomplishing the work of the organization. For example, management designs the procedures used to warehouse inventory and then to ship those goods to the customers.

(2) establishes broad marketing objectives and assigns specific sales quotas by which progress toward the long-run objectives can be measured. Also designs the information processes' procedures for facilitating operations, such as the procedures used to pick and ship goods to the customer.

The information process:

(3) receives a customer's order over the Internet for a Harry Potter book.

(4) prepares an invoice and sends it electronically to the credit card company/bank.

(5) receives an electronic payment acknowledgement from the credit card company/bank.

(6) acknowledges the customer's order by sending an e-mail message to the customer.

(7) sends to the warehouse a request to ship a Harry Potter book to the customer. This request identifies the book and its location in the warehouse. Also sends a packing slip to be attached to the book.

The operations process:

(8) attaches to the shipment a document (i.e., a packing slip) identifying the customer and the book and ships the book to the customer.

(9) reports to the IS that the book has been shipped.

The information process:

(10) sends a shipping acknowledgement to the customer via e-mail.

(11) sends management a report comparing actual sales to previously established sales quotas.

These 11 activities highlight several important concepts.

- The information process facilitates operations by maintaining inventory and customer data and by providing electronic signals (such as those used in automated warehouses) and paper documents with which to execute business events, such as shipments to customers.

- The information process provides the means by which management monitors the operations process. For example, management learns sales results only from the sales report.

- Management designs the operations and information processes and establishes these processes by providing people, equipment, other physical components, and policies.
- Information process users include operations personnel, management, and people outside the organization, such as the customer.

Figure 1.5 represents data flows related to the processing of business events. In this figure, the top three layers represent the management process. The bottom layer represents the organization's operations processes. The information process supports all layers through horizontal and vertical information flows.[5] By studying these flows more closely, we can improve our understanding of the Information System and its relationships with the operations and the management processes. At the level of operations and business events processing, the flows are horizontal as the information moves through operational units such as sales, the warehouse, and accounting. In the sales example above, the operational documents and records are the outputs of these horizontal flows.

[Insert Figure 1.5 here]

5 Because Figure 1.5 depicts data from business events, the vertical information flows upward. Other data, such as budgets, would flow downward.

The data captured at the operations and business event processing level constitute the foundation for the vertical information flows that service a multilevel management function. At the operations management level, personnel such as supervisors use information to monitor the daily functioning of their operating units. The vertical information useful to operations management is a summarized and tailored version of the information that flows horizontally. For example, horizontal flows relate to specific business events, such as one shipment, or to individual inventory items. On the other hand, information useful to operations management personnel is often an aggregate of data related to several business events. For example, a report summarizing shipments made each day might be useful to the shipping manager.

At the tactical management level, middle managers such as a warehousing or distribution manager, might want information about the timeliness of shipments each month. Such information is more summarized and broader in scope than is the information used by operations management.

Finally, at the strategic management level, senior managers such as division managers, chief financial officers (CFOs), and chief executive officers (CEOs), require information that is even more summarized and broader in scope than is the information used by tactical management. For these managers information must relate to longer time periods, be sufficiently broad in scope, and be summarized to provide a means for judging the long-term effectiveness of management policies. External financial statements, annual sales reports, and division income statements are but a few examples of strategic-level information. Note, however, that information technology facilitates access to detailed data at all management levels.

How does the IS support the multiple information uses suggested by the preceding discussion? For example, how does the IS support such users as the organization's operations units, the organization's management, and people outside the organization? How does the IS supply the information needed by three levels of management? One key component enabling the IS to meet the needs of this diverse constituency is the entitywide database. The **entitywide** database is the central repository for all of the data used by the organization. Information processes, such as order entry, billing, and inventory, update the database. Output can be obtained by other information processes and by other users such as management. When processes or other users access the entitywide database, they get a *view* of the database appropriate for their needs. For example, when entering the customer order in the earlier example, the information process had access to that *portion* of the database that was required, such as the applicable customer and inventory data.

Management Uses of Information

An IS serves two important functions within an organization. First, the IS mirrors and monitors actions in the operations process by processing, recording, and reporting business events. For example, the IS processes customer orders; records sales to customers by updating sales, accounts receivable, and inventory data; and produces invoices and sales event summaries. This event-based, operations-oriented function is depicted by the horizontal information flows shown along the bottom of Figure 1.5.

The vertical information flows shown in Figure 1.5 highlight the second major function of the IS: to support managerial activities in the management process, including management decision making. How do managers use this information? First, they monitor current operations to keep their ship on course. For example, managers need to know if enough inventory is being produced each day to meet expected demand. Managers' second use of information is to help them achieve satisfactory results for all of their stakeholders (e.g., customers, stockholders). For example, information can measure attainment of goals regarding product quality, timely deliveries, and cash flow. Finally, managers use the information system to recognize and adapt in a timely manner to trends in the organization's environment. For example, managers need answers to questions such as: "How does the time it takes us to introduce a new product compare to our competitors?" "Does our unit cost to manufacture compare to our competitors?"[6] Because information systems provide critical support to such management activities, one must understand these activities, including decision making, to understand the features of good information systems.

[6] To read more about measures of performance, see Robert S. Kaplan and David P. Norton, "The Balanced Scorecard—Measures That Drive Performance," *Harvard Business Review* (January–February 1992): 71–79, as well as subsequent articles that have appeared in the *Harvard Business Review.*

Review Question

Why is the Information System important to the organization?

Data versus Information

Information is data presented in a form that is useful in a decision-making activity. The information has value to the decision maker because it reduces uncertainty and increases knowledge about a particular area of concern. **Data** are facts or figures in raw form. Data represent the measurements or observations of objects and events. To become useful to a decision maker, data must be transformed into information. The most basic function of an IS, then, is to transform data into information that is *useful* in decision making. What attributes give information its utility value?

Review Question

What factors distinguish *data* from *information?*

Qualities of Information

To provide output useful for assisting managers and other users of information, an IS must collect data and convert them into information that possesses important qualities. Exhibit 1.1 describes qualities of information that, if attained, will help an organization achieve its business objectives. Figure 1.6 (page 18) presents an overview of information qualities depicted as a hierarchy.

[Insert Figure 1.6 here]

[Insert Exhibit 1.1 here]

Review Question

Refer to Figure 1.5 (page 14). Characterize the horizontal information flows and the vertical information flows.

You can see that *effectiveness* overlaps with other qualities as it includes such measures as "timely" (i.e., availability) and "correct" (i.e., integrity). The effectiveness of information must be evaluated in relation to the purpose to be served—decision making. Effectiveness, then, is a function of the decisions to be made, the method of decision making to be used, the information already possessed by the decision maker, and the decision maker's capacity to process information. The higher level factors in Figure 1.6, such as "users of information" and "overall quality (decision usefulness)," provide additional emphasis for these points.[7]

[7] The descriptions of many of these terms are adapted from *Statement of Financial Accounting Concepts No. 2: Qualitative Characteristics of Accounting Information,* Financial Accounting Standards Board (FASB), May 1980.

Understandability enables users to perceive the information's significance. For example, information must be in a language understood by the decision maker. By language, we mean native language, such as English or French, as well as technical language, such as one that might be used in physics or computer science. Information that makes excessive use of codes and acronyms may not be understandable by some decision makers.

Information capable of making a difference in a decision-making situation by reducing uncertainty or increasing knowledge has **relevance**. For example, a credit manager making a decision about whether to grant credit to a customer might use the customer's financial statements and credit history because that information could be relevant to the credit-granting decision. The customer's organization chart would not be relevant. The description of *reliability of information* in Exhibit 1.1 uses the term "appropriate." Relevance is a primary component of appropriateness.

Information that is available to a decision maker before it loses its capacity to influence a decision has **timeliness**. Lack of timeliness can make information irrelevant. For example, the credit manager must receive the customer's credit history before making the credit-granting decision. Otherwise, if the decision must be made without the information, the credit history becomes irrelevant. Exhibit 1.1 describes *availability* as "being available when required." Thus, availability can increase timeliness.

Predictive value and **feedback value** improve a decision maker's capacity to predict, confirm, or correct earlier expectations. Information can have both types of value. A buyer for a retail store might use a sales forecast—a prediction—to establish inventory levels. As the buyer continues to use these sales forecasts and to review past inventory shortages and overages—feedback—he or she can refine decision making concerning inventory.

If there is a high degree of consensus about the information among independent measurers using the same measurement methods, the information has **verifiability**. Real estate assets are recorded in financial records at their purchase price. Why? Because the evidence of the assets' cost provides an objective valuation for the property at that point.

Neutrality or **freedom from bias** means that the information is reliably represented. For example, the number of current members of a professional association may be overstated due to member deaths, career changers who don't bother to quit, or members listed twice because of misspellings or address changes. Notice that verifiability addresses the reliability of the measurement method (e.g., purchase price vs. current value) and neutrality addresses the reliability of the entity doing the measuring.

Comparability is the quality that enables users to identify similarities and differences in two pieces of information. If we can compare information about two similar objects or events, the information is comparable. Comparing vendor pricing estimates where one vendor gives a per unit price, and another a price per case is problematic in choosing a low-cost vendor.

If, on the other hand, we can compare information about the same object or event collected at two points in time, the information is **consistent**. Analyzing sales growth, for example, might require horizontal or trend analysis for two or more years for one company.

As noted in Exhibit 1.1, *integrity* is an information quality that can be expanded into three very important qualities: validity, accuracy, and completeness. In Figure 1.6 these are components of reliability. Information about actual events and actual objects has **validity**. For example, suppose that the IS records a sale and an account receivable for a shipment that didn't actually occur. The *recorded* information describes a fictitious event; therefore, the information lacks validity.

Accuracy is the correspondence or agreement between the information and the actual events or objects that the information represents. For example, if the quantity on hand indicated on an inventory report was 51 units, when the actual physical quantity on hand was 15 units whether the cause was a transposed number or an erroneous count, the information is inaccurate.

Completeness is the degree to which information includes data about every relevant object or event necessary to make a decision. We use *relevant* in the sense of all objects or events that we *intended* to include. For instance, suppose that a shipping department prepared 50 shipping notices for 50 actual shipments made for the day. Two of the notices fell to the floor and were discarded with the trash. As a result, the billing department prepared customer invoices for only 48 shipments, not for 50.

Review Question

What are the qualities of information presented in this chapter? Explain each quality in your own words and give an example of each.

In summary, there are many ways to measure the *effectiveness* of information. Those discussed above and included in Exhibit 1.1 and Figure 1.6 include: *understandability, relevance* (or *reliability*), *timeliness* (or *availability*), *predictive value, feedback value, verifiability, neutrality* (or *freedom from bias*), *comparability, consistency, integrity* (or *validity, accuracy,* and *completeness*). These qualities appear again, in addition to some not discussed here (*efficiency, confidentiality*, and *compliance*), in subsequent chapters.

Costs and Benefits of Information We often hear people say that, before an action is undertaken, the estimated benefits of that action should exceed the estimated costs. This is a basic expectation, as basic as the American assumption that truth, justice, and the American way will prevail. In business, we make an assumption that there is a cost associated with each improvement in the quality of information. For example, the information reflected in an inventory data store could be improved if it were checked against a physical count of inventory each week. But imagine how costly that would be! Many companies use perpetual inventory balances for most of the year, or estimate their inventory balances based on sales or past years' levels.

In practice, the benefits and sometimes the costs of information are often hard to measure. Chapter 6 provides some ideas for measuring the costs and benefits of an information system.

Conflicts Among Information Qualities It is virtually impossible to achieve a maximum level for all of the qualities of information simultaneously. In fact, for some qualities, an increased level of one requires a reduced level of another. As one instance, obtaining complete information for a decision may require delaying use of the information until all events related to the decision have taken place. That delay may sacrifice the timeliness of the information. For example, to determine all the merchandise shipments made in November, an organization may have to wait until several days into December to make sure that all shipments get recorded.

As another example, to obtain accurate information, we may carefully and methodically prepare the information, thus sacrificing its *timeliness*. To ensure the accuracy of a customer invoice, billing clerks might check the invoice for accuracy several times and then get their supervisor to initial the invoice, indicating that she also has checked the invoice for accuracy. Though ensuring accuracy, these procedures certainly hurt timeliness.

Prioritizing Information Qualities In cases where there are conflicts between qualities of information, defining a hierarchy establishes the relative importance of each quality. We could decide that accuracy is more important than any other quality. Or we could insist that timeliness be achieved even if that means that accuracy is sacrificed. For example, a marketing manager wanting to know quickly the impact of a new advertising campaign might check sales in just a few regions to get an early indication. The information may be timely, but it might be collected so hastily that it has limited reliability.

In some situations, managers choose to sacrifice maximum

attainment of individual goals or values for achievement of a higher goal. For many decision makers, relevance of information is the key quality when choosing among many viable options. Maximizing one objective, rather than obtaining the highest possible levels for individual subordinate values, is a strategic choice. Later chapters revisit these information qualities and their role in the design, control, and use of various business processes.

The Role of the Business Professional

In relation to an Information System, the business professional may assume one or more of three roles: designer, user, and evaluator.

As a *designer* of an IS, the business professional brings a knowledge of business, information systems techniques, and systems development methods. In designing the IS, the business professional might answer such questions as:

- What will be recorded (i.e., what is a recordable business event)?
- How will the event be recorded (i.e., what data stores will be used)?
- When will the event be recorded (i.e., before or after occurrence)?
- What controls will be necessary to provide valid, accurate, and complete records; to protect assets; and to ensure that the IS can be audited?
- What reports will be produced, and when will they be produced?

- How much detail will the reports include?

The business professional is also a *user* of the IS to perform functions. The business professional's effectiveness depends on how well she knows the IS and the technology used to implement it. For instance, to analyze financial information, a financial analyst must know what data are stored in the IS, how to access those data, what analysis tools exist and how to use them, and how to present the information using available report-writing facilities.

As a *user*, the business professional may also be called on to participate in the IS design process. In fact, an Information System user should insist on being involved to make sure that a new system contains required features. To be effective in the design process, the user must know how systems are developed, the techniques used to develop a system, and the technology that will be used in a new system.

Review Question

What three roles can a business professional fill in relation to the IS? Describe them.

As business process owners, business professionals are *evaluators* of the IS. They may stipulate the system's controls, assess the system's efficiency and effectiveness, and participate in the system design process. To be effective, the evaluator must possess knowledge of systems development techniques, of controls, of the technology used in the Information Systems, and of the design and operation of the IS.

Conclusions

Companies survive or fail these days based in large part on how well they conduct their business processes. In the business world, information technology and Information Systems play a pivotal role in how effectively and efficiently companies perform. It is not sufficient to have a flashy Web site or the cheapest product line. Customers expect quality service, accurate and timely delivery of orders, and a well-run organization behind the flashy Web site. This textbook is written to give you the background you need to understand how to succeed as a business professional in providing high-quality products and services while collecting and managing the data a profitable organization needs to plan, organize and control its people, processes, and systems.

Business professionals can no longer hide in a functional silo within a company. Companies do not separate product development and manufacturing into well-defined pieces; the accountants need to talk to the product development team, who need to connect with marketing people, who need to understand production cycles. All business professionals must share common information, information that is collected centrally and made available via integrated

Information Systems to all company users. Since these users need to share the output of their Information Systems, they will also have to coordinate the systems' design and control to make sure all users have access to the highest quality information possible.

As you read each chapter of this book, take with you an understanding of how topics fit together as the pieces of a puzzle whose objective is to create the best possible structure in which to run a business. The challenge of this puzzle, however, is that the pieces keep changing, and the shape of the puzzle does, too. These changes are what will make your career both challenging and rewarding. The more you know about working with interchangeable pieces, the better prepared you will be to succeed as a business professional.

REVIEW QUESTIONS

RQ1-1 What 10 elements are included in the study of IS?

RQ1-2 Are the terms *system* and *subsystem* synonymous? Explain your answer.

RQ1-3 A system must have organization, interrelationships, integration, and central objectives. Why must each of these four components be present in a system?

RQ1-4 What are three logical components of a business process? Define the functions of each. How do the components interact with one another?

RQ1-5 Why is the Information System important to the organization?

RQ1-6 What factors distinguish *data* from *information?*

RQ1-7 Refer to Figure 1.5 (page 14). Characterize the horizontal information flows and the vertical information flows.

RQ1-8 What are the qualities of information presented in this chapter? Explain each quality in your own words and give an example of each.

RQ1-9 What three roles can a business professional fill in relation to the IS? Describe them.

DISCUSSION QUESTIONS

DQ1-1 "I don't want to learn about technology; I just want to be good at my job." Comment.

DQ1-2 Examine Figure 1.1 (page 7). Based on your college education to date, with which elements are you most comfortable? With which are you least comfortable? Discuss your answers.

DQ1-3 Examine Figure 1.1. Based on any practical experience that you have had, with which elements are you most comfortable? With which are you least comfortable? Discuss your answers.

DQ1-4 Why might we have more trouble assessing the success of a federal government entitlement program than we would have judging the success of a business organization?

DQ1-5 Why must we have knowledge of a system's objectives to study that system?

DQ1-6 Can one person be a member of all three business process components: information, management, and operations? Discuss your answer.

DQ1-7 Where do you see your role(s) as a business professional—in the information, management, or operations processes? Discuss your answer.

DQ1-8 Examine Figure 1.5 (page 14). Discuss the relative importance of horizontal information flows and vertical information flows to the business professional.

DQ1-9 "When we computerize an IS, we merely change how the data are processed; we don't change what tasks are performed.'' Do you agree? Give examples to support your position.

DQ1-10 Assume that a manager can obtain information from the organization's computer in three ways: by direct inquiry using his laptop connected to the enterprise system, by a daily paper report, and by a monthly report. Using the qualities of information discussed in this chapter *(understandability, relevance, timeliness, predictive value/feedback value, neutrality/freedom from bias, comparability, consistency, validity, accuracy* and *completeness),* compare and contrast these three sources of information.

DQ1-11 Give several examples not mentioned in the chapter of potential conflicts between pairs of information qualities.

DQ1-12 What information quality is most important for decision making—relevance or reliability? Discuss your answer.

DQ1-13 Which information qualities are most important to Amazon.com's ability to fill advance orders for books? Explain your answer.

BOXES

[Start TECHNOLOGY INSIGHT 1.1 box here]

TECHNOLOGY INSIGHT 1.1

Radio Frequency ID Tags

Bar codes revolutionized the tracking of merchandise and shipments by including an easily readable label to identify a product or shipping container full of products. Bar codes dramatically cut the time needed to inventory packages, items within packages, and even truck-sized shipping containers. Because the codes were standardized, this technology also improved the accuracy with which products could be tracked and accounted for.

Now another technology is appearing that will take this revolution a step farther. Radio Frequency ID Tags (RFID) are intelligent chips that can be embedded in or attached to a product. These chips transmit descriptive data through packaging and shipping containers, so humans need not open and physically examine each item. The more advanced (and expensive) versions of RFID periodically send out signals identifying their location, reducing further the need for human intervention or time-consuming searches for particular products or shipments. They are also much faster to scan than their bar code equivalent, especially since an entire container's contents can be assessed at once, in the same time a single bar code could be scanned manually.

RFID is being used by the military to track shipments to war zones. It is also being investigated as a way to track radioactive or dangerous materials during transport. But the most widespread and commonplace applications of RFID will likely be in manufacturing and distribution, where the devices are being investigated to track everything from automobiles as they proceed through the assembly line to items of clothing in the stock room of a retail store.

RFID will improve a company's ability to track inventory throughout all processes. Savings related to reduced need for humans to track inventory, less need for excess inventory, and better awareness of supplier and customer shipment location and times will propel more companies to investigate this emerging technology.

Sources: Steve Konecki, "Sophisticated Supply," *Informationweek* (December 10, 2001), http://www.informationweek.com/story/IWK20011209S0012 (as of January 27, 2002); Cheryl Rosen, "RFID Chips Put to the Test," *Informationweek* (July 2, 2001), p. 55.

[End TECHNOLOGY INSIGHT 1.1 box here]

Gelinas 2-1

2

DOCUMENTING BUSINESS PROCESSES AND INFORMATION SYSTEMS

Wander through the offices of a group of systems analysts and you will likely see many flowcharts and other diagrams taped to the walls. These diagrams are roadmaps for the systems and processes that run the business. The analysts themselves may have created them, but more than likely business process owners or business process experts provided the description or narrative of the existing or proposed process. Business professionals who work with complex information systems can benefit greatly from knowing how to understand and create flowcharts and narratives of their business processes. These professionals may be users, designers, or evaluators of business processes, as well as systems professionals.

A recent graduate described how he has used flowcharting and other documentation techniques in his job:

> Auditors and consultants at PricewaterhouseCoopers LLP use flowcharts and systems narratives in a variety of engagements, including financial audits, business process reengineering, and security reviews. During financial audits, auditors review business applications—such as sales, billing, and purchasing—and the processes associated with those applications. To document each process, the auditor conducts interviews with the process owner, writes a narrative, and

prepares accompanying flowcharts. Then, the auditor reviews the narrative with the process owner for accuracy and completeness. These documents allow an auditor to design the audit, identify areas where controls may be needed, and prepare audit findings and recommendations.

With the increasing use of computers in business today, flowcharting is essential in financial audits to allow the auditor—as well as consultants and the business process owners—to see information flows and identify areas where information may be changed, manipulated, or even lost. In addition, with the reliance on automated processing systems for financial information, the IRS now requires flowcharts and narratives to be created and maintained for all automated processing systems used by businesses.[1]

[1] Rev. Proc. 97–22

In professional services firms, individuals may work on many different types of jobs at many different clients. It is rare that auditors and consultants work with the same systems year after year. This has made it necessary for documentation of information systems to be created and maintained for all clients serviced by such professional services firms and carried forward for each subsequent audit or other engagement. Such documentation is usually kept as part of the audit bundle and on disk, or in the automated working papers."[2]

[2] Jeffrey S. Trent, PricewaterhouseCoopers LLP, prepared this section. Jeff graduated from Bentley College with a BS in Accountancy.

Synopsis

This chapter discusses reading and preparing documentation to portray aspects of business processes and related information systems. The text describes how to read data flow diagrams, systems flowcharts, and entity-relationship diagrams and, in the appendices, how to prepare data flow diagrams and systems flowcharts. In Chapter 3 we show you how to prepare entity-relationship diagrams. Proficiency with these tools should help you to read and prepare systems documentation, which will help you understand and evaluate business processes and their information systems.

Consultants, auditors, systems analysts, business process owners, students, and others use documentation to understand, explain, and improve complex business processes and information systems, such as an *enterprise system.* First, consider a typical enterprise system. This system probably includes all of the activities associated with receiving a customer order, picking the goods off a warehouse shelf, packing and shipping the goods, and billing the customer. Further, the Information System supporting this business process is likely to be used by dozens of people within and outside the organization.

Enterprise systems have hundreds of programs that perform functions for virtually every department in the organization, process thousands of transactions and hundreds of requests for management information, and have people throughout the organization preparing inputs and receiving system outputs within the company and over the Internet.

For such complex systems, we require maps or pictures, rather than a detailed narrative description, to "see" and analyze all the activities, inputs, and outputs. Being able to draw these diagrams demonstrates that we understand the system and will be able to explain the system to someone else. For example, with a systems flowchart we can understand and analyze document flows (electronic and paper) through the business process, including its management system and information system. Perhaps our analysis will lead to system improvements. Data flow diagrams, systems flowcharts, and entity-relationship diagrams are much more efficient (and effective) than narratives for working with complex systems. The application of these tools, even to the relatively simple systems depicted in this textbook, demonstrates this fact.

In addition to using documentation to understand and improve a system, an organization can use it for other important purposes. For example, managers use documentation to explain systems and to train personnel. Auditors also use documentation to understand systems and to evaluate the systems' controls.

Review Question

Why do we need to document an Information System?

LEARNING OBJECTIVES

- To read and evaluate data flow diagrams
- To read and evaluate systems flowcharts
- To read and evaluate entity-relationship diagrams
- To prepare data flow diagrams from a narrative
- To prepare systems flowcharts from a narrative

Introduction

When you learn to read, you first learn individual letters, then string them together in words, and finally the words collectively make sentences. It is only when you practice reading that real understanding occurs, and you open up a new path to learning. These diagramming techniques are another pathway, one that gives a visual overview of complex organizational relationships.

This chapter begins by showing you how to read data flow diagrams, systems flowcharts, and entity-relationship diagrams. Then, in the appendices, you see how to prepare data flow diagrams and systems flowcharts. You will use these documentation tools throughout the remainder of the textbook. Don't be a passive observer; work along with the text and practice these tools to develop your skills.

Although we discuss drawing diagrams as if you were to draw them with pencil and paper, keep in mind that professionals using these techniques prefer using specialized flowcharting or documenting software. Specialized tools produce highly professional-looking diagrams that are much easier to update and share. You may have access to one of these tools through your instructor or workplace.

Reading Systems Documentation

This chapter shows you how to read and interpret three types of systems documentation: data flow diagrams, systems flowcharts, and entity-relationship diagrams. We will look at data flow diagrams first.

Reading Data Flow Diagrams

A **data flow diagram (DFD)** is a graphical representation of a system. A DFD depicts a system's components, the data flows among the components, and the sources, destinations, and storage of data. Figure 2.1 shows the four symbols used in a DFD.

[Insert Figure 2.1 here]

Context Diagram Figure 2.2 (page 28) is an example of our first type of DFD, the context diagram. A **context diagram** is a top-level, or least-detailed diagram of an information system. The diagram describes data flows into and out of the system and into and out of external entities. **External entities** are items such as persons, places, or things outside a system that send data to, or receive data from, a system.[3]

[3] Used in this manner, *entities* is a narrower concept than that used in Chapter 1. *External* entities must be able to send or receive data.

[Insert Figure 2.2 here]

Physical Data Flow Diagram A **physical data flow diagram** is a graphical representation of a system showing the system's internal and external entities, and the flows of data into and out of these entities. An **internal entity** is an entity (i.e., person, place, or thing) within the system that transforms data.[4] Internal entities include, for example, sales clerks (persons), departments (places), and computers (things). Therefore, physical DFDs specify *where, how,* and by *whom* a system's processes are accomplished. A physical DFD does not tell us *what* is being accomplished, though. For example, in Figure 2.3 we see that the Sales clerk receives cash from the Customer and sends cash, along with a register tape, to the Cashier. So, we see where the cash goes and how the cash receipts data are captured on the register tape, but we don't know exactly what was done by the Sales clerk.

[4] Used in this manner, *entities* is a narrower concept than that used in Chapter 1. *Internal* entities must be able to transform data.

[Insert Figure 2.3 here]

Notice that the physical DFD's bubbles are labeled with nouns and that the data flows are labeled to indicate how data are transmitted between bubbles. For example, the Sales clerk sends cash and a register tape to the Cashier. Also, see that a data store's location indicates exactly *where* (in the Computer) and a data store's label indicates *how* (in the sales data store) a system maintains sales records. Finally, while the entity boxes on the context diagram define external entities in the relevant environment, the bubbles in the physical DFD define internal entities.

Review Question

What is a physical data flow diagram (DFD)?

Logical Data Flow Diagram A **logical data flow diagram** is a graphical representation of a system showing the system's processes and the flows of data into and out of the processes. We use logical DFDs to document information systems because we can represent the logical nature of a system—what tasks the system is doing—without having to specify how, where, or by whom the tasks are accomplished. What a system is doing will change less over time than will how it is doing it. For example, a cash receipts system will typically receive customer payments and post them to the customer's account. Over time, however, the form of the payment—cash, check, electronic funds—and the method of recording—manual, computer—may change.

Review Question

What is a logical data flow diagram (DFD)?

The advantage of a *logical* DFD (versus a *physical* DFD) is that we can concentrate on the functions that a system performs. See, for example, Figure 2.4 (page 30), where the labels on the data flows describe the nature of the data, rather than how the data are transmitted. Is the "payment" in the form of a check, cash, credit card, or debit card? We don't know. Is "Sales data" a book, card, or records stored on a computer? Again, we don't know. What we do know is that customer payments are received, recorded in a sales data store, verified for accuracy, and deposited in the bank. So, a logical DFD portrays a system's activities, while a physical DFD depicts a system's infrastructure. We need both pictures to understand a system completely.

Review Question

Describe the symbols used in constructing data flow diagrams.

[Insert Figure 2.4 here]

Finally, note that the processes in Figure 2.4 are labeled with verbs that describe the actions being performed, rather than with the nouns we saw in the physical DFD.

Figure 2.4 is a top-level view of the single bubble in Figure 2.2, the context diagram. Because all of the bubbles in Figure 2.4 are numbers followed by a decimal point and a zero, this diagram is often called a "level 0" diagram.[5] You should notice that each of the data flows into and out of the context bubble in Figure 2.2 also flow into and out of the bubbles in Figure 2.4 (except for the flows between bubbles, such as "Sales record," which were contained *within* the bubble in Figure 2.2). When two DFDs—in this case, the context and the level 0—have equivalent external data flows, we say that the DFDs are **balanced**. Only balanced sets of DFDs (that is, a context diagram, a logical DFD, and a physical DFD) are correct.

[5] Even though physical DFDs are similarly numbered, we do not use the term "level 0" when referring to a physical DFD because there are no lower-level DFDs.

To derive Figure 2.4, we have "exploded" the context diagram in Figure 2.2 into its top-level components. We have looked inside the context diagram bubble to see the major subdivisions of the Cash receipts process. The successive subdividing, or "exploding," of logical DFDs is called **top-down partitioning** and, when properly performed, leads to a set of balanced DFDs.

We will use Figure 2.5 (page 31), which depicts a generic set of balanced DFDs, to study partitioning and balancing. Notice that the level 0 DFD (part b) has the same input "A" and the same output "B" as the context diagram (part a). Now look at part c, an explosion of bubble 1.0. Part c has the same input "A" and the same outputs "C" and "D" as part b. This relationship must exist because diagram 1.0 (part c) is an explosion of bubble 1.0 in part b. The same can be said for part d, the partitioning of bubble 3.0. Finally, part e shows diagram 3.1, a partitioning of bubble 3.1 in part d. Study Figure 2.5 to make sure you understand the relationships among levels in this set of DFDs. While you are studying the figure, you might also notice the convention used to number the bubbles at each level. Also, see that the entity boxes appear in the context diagram and the level 0 diagram but do not usually appear in diagrams below the level 0.

Review Question

What is the difference between a context diagram, a logical DFD, and a physical DFD?

[Insert Figure 2.5 here]

Reading Systems Flowcharts

A **systems flowchart** is a graphical representation of *information processes* (activities, logic flows, inputs, outputs, and data storage), as well as the related *operations processes* (entities, physical flows, and operations activities). Including both manual and computer activities, the systems flowchart presents a logical and physical rendering of the who, what, how, and where of business processes and Information Systems.

Systems flowcharts can be complex and cumbersome when they depict a large or complicated process. DFDs can be drawn at many levels of complexity, so someone needing only a high level view or a picture of only a part of the process doesn't need to work through the complexities of a systems flowchart. However, for detailed analysis of business processes, the complexity of a systems flowchart is invaluable.

Review Question

What is a systems flowchart?

By combining the physical and logical aspects of a system, the systems flowchart gives us a complete picture of a system. Physical and logical DFDs each depict different aspects of a system. In addition, the systems flowchart includes the business process and management context for a system, aspects ignored in DFDs. Like DFDs, systems flowcharts represent a system to identify parts that could be improved or streamlined, and to analyze a system's controls. Taken together, DFDs and flowcharts provide multiple, complementary methods for describing a system.

Review Question

What are the similarities and differences between a systems flowchart and a DFD?

Systems Flowcharting Symbols Figure 2.6 shows systems flowcharting symbols used in this textbook. This is a limited set to illustrate flowcharting principles. Use this set as a key to interpreting later diagrams.

[Insert Figure 2.6 here]

Common Systems Flowcharting Routines Figure 2.7 (pages 34–35) contains routines often found on systems flowcharts. Follow along with us as we describe each of these routines.

[Insert Figure 2.7 here]

Figure 2.7, part (a), depicts a typical two-step data entry process which might be described as follows:

> **The data entry clerk (such as a telephone sales clerk) keys a sales input document while online. The computer accesses data in data store 1 (perhaps a table of valid codes, such as customer codes) and in data store 2 (perhaps a table of open sales orders) to edit/validate the input. The computer displays the input, including any errors. The clerk compares the input document to the display, keys in corrections as necessary, and accepts the input. The computer updates the table in data store 2 and notifies the clerk that the input has**

been recorded.

Notice the following about Figure 2.7, part (a):

- The edit or validate step may be performed with one or more data stores.
- The display is implied with most, if not all, data entry processes.
- By combining the "Edit/validate input" rectangle with the "Record input" rectangle, we could depict this input process in one—rather than two—steps without losing much detail about the activities being performed.
- The manual processes undertaken by the clerk are isolated in a separate column to distinguish them from the automated processes undertaken by the computer.
- We show the input document at the bottom of the column to indicate that the document "flows" through the input process.

Figure 2.7, part (b), depicts a typical online computer query, which might be described as follows:

A user keys a query request online into a computer. The computer accesses the table(s) in one or more data stores and presents a response to the user.

Notice the following about Figure 2.7, part (b):

- The user and computer activities are again isolated in separate columns.
- The display is an implied element of the online computer.

Figure 2.7, part (c), depicts the update of master data stored in a sequential data store and might be described as follows:

New data (a customer address change, for example) previously recorded on disk are input to the computer, along with the existing (old) master data (customer master data, for example). The computer updates the existing master data and creates a new version of the master data.

Notice the following about Figure 2.7, part (c):

- When sequential master data is updated, we show two data store symbols on a flowchart. One symbol represents the existing (old) version and the other represents the new version.
- A dashed line connects the new with the old master data version to show that the new *becomes* the old version during the next update process.

Figure 2.7, part (d), depicts the input and reconciliation of computer inputs and might be described as follows:

The user collects a number of input documents in a "batch" (such as a week's worth of time cards), prepares batch

totals, and enters the documents into the computer. The computer records the inputs on a disk and notifies the user as each input is accepted. The user files the input documents in numerical sequence. At the end of the batch, the computer prepares an exception and summary report (a list of inputs accepted and rejected by the system) that includes batch totals. The user compares the computer batch totals to those prepared prior to entry of the documents to make sure the data were entered correctly.

Notice the following about Figure 2.7, part (d):

- The annotation makes it clear that the computer prepares the exception and summary report *after* the user has completed entry of the batch.
- The user's comparison of the batch totals is depicted with a dashed line—rather than a manual process.
- If the batch totals had been input with the batch, the computer—rather than the user—could compare the batch totals.

Figure 2.7, part (e), depicts entry of data to a data entry system and might be described as follows:

A data entry clerk (perhaps clerk 1) enters documents into a PC (client) connected to a data entry system. The system

records the inputs on a disk and notifies the user of the acceptance of each input. The documents are then forwarded to a *different* clerk (say clerk 2) who keys the documents *again*.[6] Differences are resolved and the transaction data are updated to reflect the verifications and corrections.

[6] The majority of data processing errors occur at the data entry stage and the majority of those errors can be attributed to misreading or miskeying the input. Because it is unlikely that two different clerks will make the same reading or keying mistake, the rekeying by a different clerk will discover the majority of these errors.

Notice the following about Figure 2.7, part (e):

- The key-to-disk unit is an offline device and should be depicted with a square—rather than a rectangle—and in a column separate from the computer.
- We show the data entry clerks in two columns to emphasize that the keying and two different clerks perform verification steps.
- Clerk 2 probably follows an established procedure to reconcile differences found during the verification step. We use the annotation about error routine to suggest the existence of these procedures.

Figure 2.7, part (f), depicts the entry and recording of an input using a scanner and might be described as follows:

A clerk scans a document (e.g., a customer's billing stub) into the computer. Using the data from the scanned document, the computer updates the data located on one or more data stores.

Notice the following about Figure 2.7, part (f):

- We represent the scanner with the offline process symbol.
- We could include a display coming from the scanner, showing the clerk the document that had just been scanned.
- To be able to read data from the document, the scanner must have optical character recognition (OCR) capabilities.[7]

[7] Document scanning and OCR are discussed in Chapter 4.

Figure 2.7, part (g), depicts the entry and recording of an input using a scanner and a keyboard and might be described as follows:

A clerk scans a document into the computer. The computer routes an image of the scanned input to a data entry clerk, who keys data from the document's image into the computer. The computer records the keyed data with the scanned document.

You should quickly become reasonably proficient in reading flowcharts if you learn these routines. You may encounter many different flowcharting methods during your career, but the principles you learn here will carry over to those techniques.

Reading Entity-Relationship Diagrams

As a professional you will likely be performing one or more of four functions. You might be (1) a business process *owner*; (2) a *designer* of an IS; (3) an IS *user*; or (4) an *evaluator* of an IS. To effectively perform these roles, you must be aware of the procedures used to develop and install an IS. Systems development procedures include two concurrent and often inseparable processes: the development of the system procedures and the design of the database. DFDs often portray system procedures, and entity-relationship diagrams often depict specifications for the database.

Review Question

Distinguish the aspects of systems depicted by DFDs from those depicted by E-R diagrams.

As you will see in Chapter 3, a *data model* depicts user requirements for data in the database. The model is expressed as a structure of entities and relationships among those entities. Figure 2.8 (page 38) depicts a data model expressed as an entity-relationship diagram. An **entity-relationship diagram** (also called an **E-R diagram**) reflects the system's key entities and the relationships among those entities and is commonly used to represent a data model. The rectangles are called "entities" and the diamonds are called "relationships." We use the E-R diagram because it helps us develop a *logical* model of the data—the entities and relationships—in a way that is independent of the way that we will physically implement the database.[8]

[8] Logical versus physical is a common theme in systems work. Earlier we introduced logical and physical DFDs. In Chapters 3, 6, and 7 (systems development), we emphasize the notion that to develop good systems—including good databases—logical design must *precede* physical design and implementation.

Review Question

What is an E-R diagram?

[Insert Figure 2.8 here]

Let's see how to read an E-R diagram. The diamond (i.e., *relationship*) on the left side of the diagram tells us that an order is received from a customer. The formal notation is ORDER *received from* CUSTOMER. We might be confused by the diagram and want to say "CUSTOMER *received from* ORDER." But we can usually interpret the diagram correctly by knowing the sense of the relationship.

In Figure 2.8, the "N" beneath the ORDER rectangle tells us that each customer may have more than one order; the "1" above the

CUSTOMER rectangle tells us that each order is from only 1 customer. This, the first of three relationship categories, is called "*one-to-N*,'' and the notation is 1:*N* (or "*N-to-one*" and noted as *N*:1).

The second relationship category is called "*M-to-N*," and the notation is *M:N*. In Figure 2.8, we see that each INVENTORY item has many ORDERs, and each ORDER has many INVENTORY items (a many-to-many relationship). Figure 2.8 also tells us that there are many SALES (shipments) for each INVENTORY item and that each SALE (shipment) can consist of many line items of inventory.

Review Question

Describe the symbols used in constructing E-R diagrams.

There is a third relationship category, called "*one-to-one*," and it uses the notation *1:1*. If, in Figure 2.8, only one SALE (shipment) filled an ORDER, there would be a 1:1 relationship between ORDER and SALE. In Chapter 3, we explore how to prepare an E-R diagram.

Conclusions

The diagramming tools introduced in this chapter illustrate common techniques business professionals encounter when seeking a pictorial representation of business processes and data relationships. Each technique has its own purpose, strengths, and weaknesses, which is why you have been shown a variety of them. After all, an architect would not use the same representation technique for house plans as a programmer would for computer code! The chapters that follow include many examples of each technique, to help you understand how to read them, when to use them, and how to create them yourself. If ever there was a good example of "practice makes perfect," this is one. The more you use the techniques, the better prepared you will be to work with them later in your professional career.

Appendix 2A

Preparing Data Flow Diagrams

We use DFDs in two main ways. We may draw them to document an existing system, or we may create them from scratch when developing a new system. Construction of DFDs for new systems will be described in the systems development chapters (Chapters 6 and 7). In this section, we explain a process for deriving a set of DFDs from a narrative that describes an existing system.

The Narrative

Figure 2.9 (page 40) contains a narrative describing the cash receipts system for the Causeway Company. The first column indicates the paragraph number; the second column contains the line number for the text of the narrative. We describe here an orderly method for drawing the DFDs for the Causeway system. You will get the most benefit from this section if you follow the instructions carefully, perform each step as directed, and don't read ahead. Draw your diagrams by hand or use the software package of your choice.

[Insert Figure 2.9 here]

Table of Entities and Activities

Our first step is to create a table of entities and activities. In the long run, this list will lead to quicker and more accurate preparation of DFDs and a systems flowchart because it clarifies the information contained in a narrative and helps us to document the system correctly.

Review Question

What is a table of entities and activities?

To begin your table, go through the narrative line-by-line and *circle* each activity being performed. An **activity** is any action being performed by an *internal entity* or an *external entity*. Activities can include actions related to data (originate, transform, file, or receive) or to a business process. Business process activities might include picking goods in the warehouse, inspecting goods at the receiving dock, or counting cash. For each activity there must be an entity that performs the activity. As you circle each activity, put a *box* around the entity that performs the activity.

Now you are ready to prepare your table. List each activity *in the order that it is performed, regardless of the sequence in which it appears in the narrative.* List the activity, along with the name of the entity that performs the activity and the paragraph number indicating the location of the activity in the narrative. After you have listed all activities, consecutively number each activity.

Compare your table to Table 2.1 (page 41). Notice that the narrative refers to some entities in more than one way. For example, we have "accounts receivable" and the "clerk" on line 16. Notice that we listed both activity 7 and activity 8. It might be that activity 7 describes activity 8 and does not need to be listed itself. However, it is better to list doubtful activities than to miss an activity. See how we listed activity 11, found on lines 23 and 24. We changed to the active form of the verb "notify" so that we could show the activity next to the entity that performs the action. Before continuing, resolve any differences between your list of entities and activities and those in Table 2.1.

Drawing the Context Diagram We are now ready to draw the context diagram. Since a context diagram consists of only one circle, we can begin our context diagram by drawing one circle in the center of our paper. Next, we must draw the external entity boxes. To do this, we must decide which of the entities in Table 2.1 are external and which are internal to the system.

[Insert Table 2.1 here]

DFD guideline 1:

Include *within* the system context (bubble) any entity that performs one or more information processing activities.

Information processing activities are those activities that retrieve data from storage, transform data, or file data. Information processing activities include document preparation, data entry, verification, classification, arrangement or sorting, calculation, summarization, and filing—both manual and automated. The sending and receiving of data between entities are not information processing activities because they do not transform data. If we send data to another entity, we do not process data. If, however, we file data, we do perform an information processing activity. Likewise, if we receive data from another entity, we do not perform an information processing activity. But, if we retrieve data from a file or table, we do perform an information processing activity. Operational, or physical, business process activities are not information processing activities.

To discover which entities perform no information processing activities, we must inspect the table of entities and activities and mark those activities that are not information processing activities.

Any entities that do not perform any information processing activities will be *external* entities; the remaining entities will be *internal*. Go through your table of entities and activities and mark all the activities that do not perform information processing activities. These marked activities—mostly sends and receives—indicate data flows.

Review Question

Which entities in a narrative are included in the context diagram as internal and which are shown as external?

At first, you should have indicated activities 1, 5, 6, 15, and 19 because these activities only send or receive data. As we mentioned earlier, activity 7 only describes activity 8 and can be marked. Finally, activity 11 can be marked because of the following guideline:

DFD guideline 2:

For now, include only *normal* processing routines, *not* exception routines or error routines, on context diagrams, physical DFDs, and level 0 logical DFDs.

Since activity 11 occurs only when the payment data contain an error, we will not consider this activity *for now.*

Your table of entities and activities, with certain non-information processing activities marked, should now indicate that the mailroom, accounts receivable, the cashier, and the computer perform information processing activities and will be included in our diagrams as internal entities. The customer, on the other hand, does not perform any such activities and is an external entity.

Are there other external entities to be included in our diagrams? To answer this question, go through the narrative one more time and put a box around those entities not yet marked. You should find the bank (line 30) and the general ledger office (line 40) that, in *this* system, do not perform information processing activities. These entities, along with the customer, are external entities and are included in the context diagram as sources or destinations of data. We now have three external entities, four internal entities, and 19 activities. *No other entities or activities are to be added* because of the following guideline:

DFD guideline 3:

Include on the systems documentation all (and only) activities and entities described in the system narrative—no more, no less.

When we say narrative, we are talking about the narratives that you will find as problem material in this book. You are to assume, in those cases, that the narrative is complete and accurate. However, when you prepare a narrative to document a real-world case, you cannot assume that your narrative is perfect. It should be reviewed and revised by working with all participating internal entity representatives. When you have verified that your narrative is complete and that it accurately reflects reality, you must then follow DFD guideline 3.

Review Question

When do we have a choice as to what will be included in a context diagram?

Because there are three entities external to the Causeway cash receipts system—the customer, the bank, and the general ledger office—you must draw three boxes surrounding the one context bubble. Next, draw and label the data flows that connect the external entities with the bubble. Because logical (versus physical) labels are usually used on a context diagram, you should do your best to derive logical labels for the flows. The final step is to label the context bubble. Write a descriptive label that encompasses the processing taking place within the system. Our label in Figure 2.10 indicates the scope of the Causeway system—namely, cash receipts from charge customers. The Causeway system does not include cash receipts from any other source.

Figure 2.10 is the completed Causeway context diagram. Compare it to your context diagram, and resolve any differences. Notice that we include a single square for many customers. Likewise, although we may use several banks, we have a single

Bank square. The following guideline applies:

[Insert Figure 2.10 here]

DFD guideline 4:

When multiple entities operate identically, depict only one to represent all.

Drawing the Current Physical Data Flow Diagram To keep the current physical DFD balanced with the context diagram, start a current physical DFD by drawing the three external entities from the context diagram near the edges of a piece of paper. Next, draw and label each data flow going into the two destinations and coming out of the single source. Leave the center of the page, into which we will sketch the rest of the diagram, as open as possible. As this is a physical DFD, the data flows should have labels that describe the means by which the flow is accomplished. For example, the "Payment" from the customer should now be labeled "Checks and remittance advices," and the "Deposit" should now be labeled "Deposit slip and checks."

Because each *internal* entity listed in the table of entities and activities (Table 2.1) becomes a bubble in our physical DFD, we know that our current physical DFD will contain four bubbles: one each for the mailroom, the cashier, accounts receivable, and the computer. We will start adding these four bubbles by first drawing the bubbles on our diagram that are connected to the sources and destinations. During this process, you must consider all "send" and "receive" activities and the implied reciprocal activities. (Many of these were marked earlier to indicate that they were not data processing activities.) For example, activity 1 indicates that the customer "sends" the checks and remittance advices. Draw and label a mailroom bubble, an accounts receivable bubble, and a cashier bubble. Use a data flow to connect each of these three bubbles to its related external entity.

To complete the physical DFD, we must go through the table of entities and activities once again and draw all the remaining entities and flows. Activity 5 indicates a connection between the mailroom and accounts receivable. Activity 6 indicates a connection between the mailroom and the cashier. Activity 8 tells us that the accounts receivable clerk enters data into the computer. Draw the computer bubble, label it "4.0," and connect it to accounts receivable. To perform activity 18, accounts receivable must receive the reports from the computer. Draw and label one or two flows (we chose two flows) from the computer to accounts receivable. To perform activity 14, the cashier must receive the deposit slip from the computer. Activity 16 implies that the table of accounts receivable master data must be read so that the open invoice record can be retrieved. Draw the data store for the accounts receivable master table and a flow from the data store to the computer bubble. Notice that the label on the data store shows that the *physical* storage medium is a disk. We draw a flow only from the data store because a data *request* is not a flow of data. Therefore, we do not show the request for the open invoice record. The movement of the record out of the data store in response to this request *is* a flow of data and is shown. Also, notice that we did not show a flow from the accounts receivable data store directly to the accounts receivable bubble. Because the accounts receivable data store is on a computer disk, only the computer can read from or write to that disk. This also excludes any direct connection between computerized data stores. To update the data on one computerized data store from another, you must go through a computer bubble.

Because the open invoice record must be read into the computer, updated, and then written back to the accounts receivable master table, activity 10 requires a data flow from *and* to the accounts receivable data store. But, since we drew a flow from the data store for activity 9, we need only draw a flow back to the data store. Activity 12 requires that we draw a data store for the cash receipts log and that we draw a data flow from the computer into that data store, whereas activity 13 requires that we draw a flow from the data store. Finally, to depict the flow of data required to print the reports indicated in activities 16 and 17, we need to draw flows from both data stores into the computer. You may think that all the flows into and out of the data stores aren't necessary. Here is a guideline:

DFD guideline 5:

For clarity, draw a data flow for each flow into and out of a data store. You may, also for clarity and to help you determine that you have included all necessary flows, label each flow with the activity number that gives rise to the flow or with a description of the flow (e.g., "retrieve accounts receivable master data").

Figure 2.11 is the completed Causeway current physical DFD. Compare it to your diagram and, before continuing, resolve any differences. You should notice that there is a data store of endorsed checks connected to the cashier. This file, not mentioned in the narrative, was added to show that the cashier must hold on to batches of checks until the deposit slip is printed on the computer terminal. This format leads to another guideline:

[Insert Figure 2.11 here]

DFD guideline 6:

If a data store is logically necessary (that is, because of a delay between processes), include a data store in the diagrams, whether or not it is mentioned in the narrative.

Should we draw a data store to show that the remittance advice batches and batch totals are retained in accounts receivable until the computer reports are received? We could. You must use DFD guideline 6 carefully, however, so that you don't draw DFDs that are cluttered with files and are therefore difficult to read. You need to use your judgment. Does this guideline contradict DFD guideline 3? No. DFD guideline 3 tells you to include in your diagrams only those activities included in your narrative; while DFD guideline 6 tells you to describe those activities completely. So, if the narrative implies an activity or data store, include it in the diagrams. How about an example that would violate DFD guideline 6? Because they are *outside the context* of this particular system, the following activities are not described in the narrative (Figure 2.9) and should not be included in the diagrams:

- The actual update of the general ledger data
- Cash receipts from cash sales
- Customer billing

Drawing the Current Logical Data Flow Diagram The current logical DFD portrays the logical activities performed within the system. Because level 0 DFDs depict a particular grouping of the logical activities, we start the level 0 DFD by enumerating the activities in the system; then, we group those activities. You already have a list of the activities to be included in the level 0 DFD. Do you know what that list is? The activities to be included in the level 0

DFD are the *unmarked* activities on the table of entities and activities, Table 2.1. Our list includes activities 2, 3, 4, 8, 9, 10, 12, 13, 14, 16, 17, and 18. Recall that, at this time, we don't consider any other activities because the other activities either are actions performed in other-than-normal situations, are actions that merely send or receive data rather than transform data, or are business process activities, such as picking goods off the shelf. Several guidelines will help us to group the activities remaining in our list:

DFD guideline 7:

Group activities if they occur in the same place and at the same time. For example, the clerk performs activities 2 and 3 in the mailroom as each payment is received.

DFD guideline 8:

Group activities if they occur at the same time but in different places. For example, the cashier performs activity 14 "immediately" after the computer prints the deposit slip in activity 13.

DFD guideline 9:

Group activities that seem to be logically related.

DFD guideline 10:

To make the DFD readable, use between five and seven bubbles.[9]

[9] For very simple systems, such as those described in the narratives in this textbook, your solutions may have fewer than five bubbles.

Review Question

Which activities can be included in the logical processes on a logical DFD?

Review Question

What are the guidelines for grouping logical activities for a logical DFD?

To start preparing your logical DFD, try bracketing the activities in Table 2.1 as you believe they should be grouped (do not consider the marked activities). For example, if we apply DFD guideline 7 (that is, same time *and* same place), we could combine activities 2 and 3; activities 9, 10, and 12; and activities 16 and 17. Although this would provide a satisfactory solution, there would be eight bubbles, and there would be several bubbles containing only one activity. Since we prefer not to have too many single-activity bubbles until we get to the lowest-level DFDs, we proceed with further groupings.

If we apply DFD guideline 8 (that is, same time but different place) to the preceding grouping, we could combine activities 8 with 9, 10, and 12; 13 with 14; and 16 and 17 with 18. This solution is also fine, and is a little better than our first solution because we now have five bubbles and we have only one single-activity bubble.

If we apply DFD guideline 9 (that is, logically related activities), we can combine activities 2, 3, and 4. Although this leaves us with only four bubbles, this solution is superior to the first two because we have no single-activity bubbles.

In summary, our groups are:

- Group 1: activities 2, 3, 4
- Group 2: activities 8, 9, 10, 12
- Group 3: activities 13, 14
- Group 4: activities 16, 17, 18

After we choose our groupings, we must give each group a name that describes the logical activities within the group. For Causeway, we chose the following labels:

- Group 1 (activities 2, 3, 4) is bubble 1.0 and is labeled "Capture cash receipts" because that bubble comprises all the activities after the payment is sent by the customer until the payment is keyed into the computer.
- Group 2 (activities 8, 9, 10, 12) is bubble 2.0 and is labeled "Record customer collections" because the activities in bubble 2.0 record the payment in the cash receipts transaction table and the accounts receivable master table.

- Group 3 (activities 13 and 14) is bubble 3.0 and is labeled "Prepare deposit" because the activities generate a deposit slip and send the deposit to the bank.
- Group 4 (activities 16, 17, 18) is bubble 4.0 and is labeled "Prepare cash receipts total" because that is the main purpose of the reporting and comparison that takes place.

Mark these groups and labels on Table 2.1.

Table 2.2 demonstrates how you should annotate your table of entities and activities. (Notice that we have not carried forward from Table 2.1 the marked activities.) Now draw the current logical DFD for Causeway. You'll need paper and pencil (or your computer), the Causeway context diagram (Figure 2.10), the Causeway current physical DFD (Figure 2.11), your annotated table of entities and activities (Table 2.2), and your original table of entities and activities (Table 2.1). To draw the logical DFD, begin in the same manner that you began to draw the current physical DFD. Draw the external entities near the edges of a piece of paper. Draw and label flows to and from the external entities, while leaving the center of the page blank to receive the remainder of the diagram. Since this is a *logical* DFD, the data flows to and from the entities must have logical descriptions (for example, the descriptions used on the context diagram).

[Insert Table 2.1 here]

After we have completed the external flows, we can begin to draw internal bubbles and flows. The "Payment" from the "Charge customer" is the input to bubble 1.0. Activities 2, 3, and 4 happen within the bubble. What are the outputs? The endorsed checks leave bubble 1.0 (see activity 6 in Table 2.1). For the logical DFD, we'll call this flow "Monetary transfers." The other data flow out from bubble 1.0 was called "Annotated remittance advices and copy of batch total" (see activity 5 on Table 2.1). For the logical DFD, let's call it "Batched customer receipts." Before moving on, compare your drawing to bubble 1.0 in Figure 2.12 (page 48).

[Insert Figure 2.12 here]

The batched customer receipts are the input to bubble 2.0. In response to the keying action (activity 8), a record is read from the accounts receivable master data store. Draw the data store for this table (remember, use a logical label) and a flow *from* the data store into bubble 2.0. Activity 9 occurs within the bubble. What are the outputs? Activity 10 indicates a flow *to* the accounts receivable master data store, and activity 12 indicates a flow *to* the cash receipts events data store. Draw the data store for the event data and the flows into that data store and into the accounts receivable data store. Before moving on, compare your drawing to bubble 2.0, Figure 2.12.

Now draw bubble 3.0. To accomplish activity 13, bubble 3.0 must obtain the records contained on the cash receipts events data store.

Draw a flow from that table's data store into bubble 3.0. To perform activity 14, bubble 3.0 must obtain the records stored in the monetary transfers data store. Draw a flow from that data store into bubble 3.0. What are the outputs from bubble 3.0? Activity 15 on Table 2.1 indicates that bubble 3.0 should be connected to the flow "Deposit" going into the Bank. Compare your drawing to bubble 3.0 in Figure 2.12.

Finally, let's draw bubble 4.0. To create a cash receipts listing (activity 16), bubble 4.0 must obtain the records contained in the cash receipts events data store. Draw a flow *from* that table's data store into bubble 4.0. To print a summary of customer accounts paid (activity 17), bubble 4.0 must obtain the records stored in the accounts receivable master data store. Draw a flow *from* that table's data store into bubble 4.0. To perform activity 18, bubble 4.0 must obtain the data contained on the RAs and batch totals. Where are those data? They are in the flow "Batched customer receipts" that went into bubble 2.0. Since bubble 4.0 must also obtain those data, we must split that flow and connect it to both bubble 2.0 and to bubble 4.0.

We have finished drawing the Causeway current logical DFD. Compare your diagram to the solution in Figure 2.12. Resolve any discrepancies. Your diagram should look like that in Figure 2.12 *if you use the groupings we described.* Many other groupings are possible within the guidelines. Each different grouping should lead to a different logical DFD.

There will be times when a *business operations* function performs information processing activities. For example, when the receiving department prepares a document indicating how many widgets have been received, the receiving department, which is primarily a business operations unit, is performing an information processing activity. The warehouse and the shipping department are other business operations units that often perform information processing activities. The following guideline applies:

DFD guideline 11:

A data flow should go to a business operations entity *square* when *only* business operations functions (that is, work-related functions such as storing goods, picking goods from the shelves, packaging the customer's order, and so on) are to be performed by that external entity. A data flow should enter an entity *bubble* if the business operations entity is to perform an information processing activity.

For example, when the business operations entity is receiving goods, a physical DFD could show either a "receiving" box or a "receiving" bubble, whereas the logical DFD might show either a receiving department box or a "Complete receiving report" bubble.

DFD guideline 12:

On a physical DFD, reading computer data stores and writing to computer data stores must go through a computer bubble.

DFD guideline 13:

On a logical DFD, data flows cannot go from higher- to lower-numbered bubbles.

Review Question

Where are error and exception routines shown on DFDs?

If, on a logical DFD, you have a data flow going back to a previous processing point (that is, to a lower-numbered bubble), you have a physical representation of the flow or process. Flows may, however, flow backwards to a data store.

Aren't there occasions when processing can't proceed as planned? Yes, and in such cases processes called exception routines or error routines handle the required actions. These are processes for out-of-the-ordinary (exceptional) or erroneous transactions. Processing that is performed in other-than-normal situations should be documented *below the level 0 DFD* with reject stubs that indicate that exceptional processing must be performed. A **reject stub** is a data flow assigned the label "Reject" that leaves a bubble but does not go to any other bubble or data store. These reject stubs, *which* *are shown only in lower-level diagrams,* may be added without bringing the set of diagrams out of balance.

Summary of Drawing DFD Diagrams

Although there are many ways to draw DFD diagrams, they all start with a careful examination of existing systems or processes, careful thinking about what really happens, and careful choices about how to accurately represent what happens using the diagrams. Our diagrams in this appendix were fairly simple, although a lot of thought went into making decisions about them.

The basic steps of the process are these:

- Create or obtain an accurate and reliable narrative.
- From the narrative, create a complete table of entities and activites.
- Draw a context diagram with external entity boxes by distinguishing carefully between internal and external entities.
- Draw current physical flow diagrams by creating bubbles for internal entities, and showing flows to and from all entities and data stores.
- Draw current logical flow diagrams by grouping activities that occur together, and naming the logical sub-processes each describes. Remember to balance this diagram with the other diagrams by matching their external entities and their data flows.

Don't let the rigor of the documentation get in the way of using the diagrams to understand the system. You have seen many guidelines, hints, and instructions to help you draw DFDs. Use your judgment in applying this information.

Appendix 2B

Preparing Systems Flowcharts

This section describes steps for preparing a systems flowchart. The following guidelines outline our basic flowcharting technique.

Systems flowcharting guideline 1:

Divide the flowchart into columns; one column for each internal entity and one for each external entity. Label each column.

Systems flowcharting guideline 2:

Flowchart columns should be laid out so that the flowchart activities flow from left to right, but you should locate columns so as to minimize crossed lines and connectors.

Systems flowcharting guideline 3:

Flowchart logic should flow from top to bottom and from left to right. For clarity, put arrows on all flow lines.

Systems flowcharting guideline 4:

Keep the flowchart on one page. If you can't, use multiple

pages and connect the pages with off-page connectors. Do not glue, tape, staple, or otherwise "extend" your flowchart page to get the flowchart onto one page.

To use an off-page connector, draw the symbol shown in Figure 2.6 (page 32) at the point where you leave one page *and* at the corresponding point where you begin again on the next page. If you leave page 1 for the first time and you are going to page 2, then the code inside the symbol should be "P. 2, A" on page 1 and "P. 1, A" on page 2. That is, you point to page 2 from page 1 and you point back to page 1 from page 2. If you draft your flowchart on paper, discipline yourself to draw flowcharts on paper of limited size, as computerized flowcharting packages will print your flowcharts only on paper that will fit in your printer!

Systems flowcharting guideline 5:

Within each column, there must be at least one manual process, keying operation, or data store between documents. That is, do not directly connect documents within the same column.

This guideline suggests that you show all processing that is taking place. For example, if two documents are being attached, include a manual process to show the matching and attaching activities.

Systems flowcharting guideline 6:

When crossing organizational lines (i.e., moving from one column to another), show a document at both ends of the flow line unless the connection is so short that the intent is unambiguous.

Systems flowcharting guideline 7:

Documents or reports printed in a computer facility should be shown in that facility's column first. You can then show the document or report going to the destination unit.

Systems flowcharting guideline 8:

Documents or reports printed by a centralized computer facility on equipment located in another organizational unit (e.g., a warehouse or a shipping department) should not be shown within the computer facility.

Systems flowcharting guideline 9:

Processing within an organizational unit on devices such as a PC or computerized cash register should be shown within the unit or as a separate column next to that unit—but *not* in the central computer facility column.

Systems flowcharting guideline 10:

Sequential processing steps (either computerized or manual) with no delay between them (and resulting from the same input) can be shown as one process or as a

sequence of processes.

Systems flowcharting guideline 11:

The only way to get data into or out of a computer data storage unit is through a computer processing rectangle.

For example, if you key-enter data from a source document, you must show a manual keying symbol, a rectangle or square, and then a computer storage unit [see, for example, part (a) of Figure 2.7 on p. 34].

Systems flowcharting guideline 12:

A manual process is not needed to show the sending of a document. The sending should be apparent from the movement of the document itself.

Systems flowcharting guideline 13:

Do not use a manual process to file a document. Just show the document going into the file.

Drawing Systems Flowcharts We are now ready to draw the Causeway flowchart. The entities in our current physical DFD (Figure 2.11, page 45) should help us to set up and label our columns. Although we set up columns for each entity (systems flowcharting guideline 1), we do not have to include columns for the customer, the bank, or the general ledger office because these entities do not perform any information processing activities. Since accounts receivable and the cashier both interact with the computer, let's locate them on either side of the "Computer" column (see systems flowcharting guideline 2). So, from left to right, your columns should be "Mailroom," "Accounts receivable," "Computer," and "Cashier."

We usually start a flowchart in the top left corner with a "start" symbol. Since we have eliminated the "Customer" column, we must start the flowchart with a start symbol labeled "Customer," followed by two documents labeled "Remittance advices" (RAs) and "Checks." To show that they are together, we can place the RAs and the checks on top of each other with the back document a little above and to the right of the front document. We place all these symbols in the "Mailroom" column because lines 3 and 4 of the narrative tell us that the customer "sends" checks and remittance advices. This technique makes it clear where the flowchart starts and the source of the document that starts the process. Draw this portion of your flowchart.

Lines 5 and 6 of the narrative tells us that the mailroom clerk "endorses" the checks, and lines 6 and 7 tells us that the clerk "writes" the amount paid and the check number on the RA. "Endorse" and "write" are manual processes that, being performed by the mailroom clerk, should be documented with a *manual process symbol* (or two symbols) placed in the "Mailroom" column. Systems flowcharting guideline 10 tells us that sequential processes may be documented in one or more process symbols. Because one action is directed at the checks and the other action at the RAs (and because our description of the actions would not fit in one process symbol), we'll use two processes. Draw these processes.

In lines 9 and 10, we find a process—preparing the batch total—that is performed "periodically" by the mailroom clerk. So, still working in the "Mailroom" column, draw another manual process for the batch total preparation. Find the *annotation* symbol on Figure 2.6 (page 32) and annotate the batch total preparation process to describe the periodic nature of the process.

Lines 11 through 15 describe the three items exiting the mailroom and their destination. All three items should exit the batch total preparation process. Since the RAs and the batch total are going to the next column, they can exit from either the right side or the bottom of the process. Systems flowcharting guideline 6 tells us that we do not need to show the RAs and the batch total in both the "Mailroom" and the "Accounts receivable" columns. Since you'll probably have more room in the "Accounts receivable" column, draw these items at the top of that column. Your flow line will require arrows because your logic flow has gone up, rather than down! Did you find the symbol for batch totals on Figure 2.6?

Send the endorsed checks to the cashier using an on-page

connector. Systems flowcharting guideline 6 dictates showing the endorsed checks in the sending and receiving columns. In the cashier column, the endorsed checks must be filed awaiting the receipt of the deposit slip. We introduced this file when we described the current physical DFD (Figure 2.11, page 45). Notice that the on-page connector is shown where the process ends and again where the process begins. The same letter is shown in both places. Use letters, starting with the letter "A," and restart with A on each page. Review the "Mailroom" column of Figure 2.13 (page 54) and compare it to your solution. Resolve any discrepancies.

[Insert Figure 2.13 here]

Let's return now to drawing Figure 2.13. Narrative paragraph 2 describes the process by which the RAs are entered into the computer by the accounts receivable clerk and are edited and posted to the accounts receivable master table. Figure 2.7, part (a), page 34, depicts a method for documenting such a process. Notice that the keying symbols, the manual process symbols, and the display symbols are located in the "Clerk" column of Figure 2.7, while the computer files and computer process are located in the "Computer" column. Figure 2.7, part (a), indicates a two-step process in which input errors are displayed on the display screen and a clerk corrects the errors and notifies the computer that the input is acceptable. Because paragraph 2 of the Causeway narrative implies, but does not directly require, a two-step process such as that in Figure 2.7, part (a) we can draw the flowchart with a one-step process. Draw the activity included in narrative paragraph 2 using a one-step input process. Send the RAs and the batch total out of the "bottom" of the input process [that is, out of the bottom of the screen, as shown in Figure 2.7, part (a)]. If the computer does not accept the input, we can assume that the accounts receivable clerk will correct and re-input the erroneous RA. To show this, connect—with a dashed line—an annotation symbol to the display screen. Include the phrase "Error routine not shown" within the symbol. Lines 31 through 33 (paragraph 4) tell us that the transactions are logged as they are input. Include a disk symbol for this data store in the computer column of your flowchart. Connect it to the same computer process block with which you updated the accounts receivable data store.

We have completed flowcharting the accounts receivable clerk's activities, *for now*. Review the upper portion of the "Accounts receivable" column in Figure 2.13 and compare it to your solution. Resolve any discrepancies.

Let's return once again to drawing Figure 2.13. Narrative paragraph 3, lines 25 through 28, describes the process by which the computer prints the deposit slip in the cashier's office. What data must be accessed to get the information for the deposit slip? The cash receipts log has the check number and the amount, and is the only table that contains *only* the most recent payments—the accounts receivable master table summarizes *all* billings and payments. Read systems flowcharting guidelines 7 and 8 and draw this section of the flowchart. We have used an annotation to indicate that this process is performed only periodically. If you have laid out your flowchart well, the file of endorsed checks—previously sent from the mailroom—and the deposit slip printed by the computer should be near each other in the "Cashier" column. Now, to flowchart lines 27 through 30, we need only a manual process for comparing these two items and then, coming out of the process, we have the endorsed checks and a copy of the deposit slip going to the bank. If we had a "Bank" column, these items would go to that column. Since we have no such column, we send these items to a *start/stop* symbol labeled "Bank." Complete your own flowchart and then review these sections of Figure 2.13.

To complete our flowchart, we need to chart the end-of-day report generation described on lines 33 through 36 and the use of these reports in accounts receivable described on lines 36 through 40. Since both reports are generated at the same time, we can depict this with one computer process symbol. Access to both computer data stores is required for the report generation, and the reports must be shown in the "Computer" column and then go to accounts receivable where they are compared to the RAs and to the batch total. A total of cash receipts must be sent to the general ledger office. Figure 2.6 shows that the symbol used for batch totals can be used for any total. However, as the narrative is not clear, you would not be wrong in using the general-purpose input-output file symbol (parallelogram). Since we're not sure how the total is prepared, just send the total to the general ledger office directly from the process where the batch totals, RAs, and reports are compared. Again, without a "General ledger" column we send the cash receipts total to a stop symbol labeled "General ledger office."

We have now completed the flowchart. Verify your work by checking through the table of entities and activities (Table 2.1, page 41) to make sure that each activity has been diagrammed. Compare your flowchart to the narrative (Figure 2.9, page 40) to see that the system has been accurately documented and compare your flowchart to the DFDs to see whether the flowchart and DFDs are consistent. Finally, compare your flowchart to the solution in Figure 2.13. Resolve any discrepancies.

Summary of Systems Flowcharting

As with DFDs, there may be numerous ways to create an accurate systems flowchart. The general process is to:

- Set up and label columns, one for each internal and one for each external entity.

- Use narratives, tables of entities and activities, and DFD physical and logical diagrams for source information for the flowchart.
- Show activities proceeding from top to bottom and left to right. Keep a flowchart as clear and simple as possible while representing activities fully. Keep the flowchart to a single page, using off-page connectors when necessary.
- Use appropriate flowcharting symbols to show all processing that occurs.
- Strike a balance between clarity and clutter by using annotation judiciously and by using on-page connectors whenever flow lines might create clutter.
- Avoid crossing lines wherever possible. If you must cross lines, use a "bridge."
- Flowchart normal routines and leave exception routines for another page of the flowchart.
- Compare the finished flowchart to narratives, activities and entities tables, and physical and logical DFDs to make sure all activities are accounted for fully.

Review Question

Where are error and exception routines shown on systems flowcharts?

Drawing flowcharts requires judgment, which you can develop

through practice. You have seen a number of guidelines to help you as you learn how to draw flowcharts. Before you get locked into the guidelines and the details of flowcharting, or of drawing DFDs, remember that the purpose of creating this documentation is to simplify and clarify a narrative. We draw these diagrams so that we can better analyze and understand a system. We want to portray a system's logic and implementation *accurately*, and there can be many correct solutions. With practice, you can learn to use these techniques to create the most appropriate one.

REVIEW QUESTIONS

RQ2-1 Why do we need to document an Information System?

RQ2-2 What is a physical data flow diagram (DFD)?

RQ2-3 What is a logical data flow diagram (DFD)?

RQ2-4 Describe the symbols used in constructing data flow diagrams.

RQ2-5 What is the difference between a context diagram, a logical DFD, and a physical DFD?

RQ2-6 What is a systems flowchart?

RQ2-7 What are the similarities and differences between a systems flowchart and a DFD?

RQ2-8 Distinguish the aspects of systems depicted by DFDs from those depicted by E-R diagrams.

RQ2-9 What is an E-R diagram?

RQ2-10 Describe the symbols used in constructing E-R diagrams.

RQ2-11 What is a table of entities and activities?

RQ2-12 Which entities in a narrative are included in the context diagram as internal and which are shown as external?

RQ2-13 When do we have a choice as to what will be included in a context diagram?

RQ2-14 Which activities can be included in the logical processes on a logical DFD?

RQ2-15 What are the guidelines for grouping logical activities for a logical DFD?

RQ2-16 Where are error and exception routines shown on DFDs?

RQ2-17 Where are error and exception routines shown on systems flowcharts?

DISCUSSION QUESTIONS

DQ2-1 "Data flow diagrams and flowcharts provide redundant pictures of an Information System. We don't need both." Discuss.

DQ2-2 "It is easier to learn to prepare data flow diagrams, which use only a few symbols, than it is to learn to prepare flowcharts, which use a number of different symbols." Discuss.

DQ2-3 Describe the *who, what, where,* and *how* of the following scenario: A customer gives his purchase to a sales clerk, who enters the sale in a cash register and puts the money in the register drawer. At the end of the day, the sales clerk gives the cash and the register tape to the cashier.

DQ2-4 Why are there *many* correct logical DFD solutions? Why is there only *one* correct physical DFD solution?

DQ2-5 Explain why a flow from a higher- to a lower-numbered bubble on a logical DFD is a physical manifestation of the system. Give an example.

DQ2-6 Compare and contrast the purpose of and techniques used in drawing physical DFDs and logical DFDs.

DQ2-7 "If we document a system with a systems flowchart, data flow diagrams, and E-R diagrams, we have over-documented the system." Discuss.

DQ2-8 "Preparing a table of entities and activities as the first step in documenting systems seems to be unnecessary and unduly cumbersome. It would be a lot easier to bypass this step and get right to the necessary business of actually drawing the diagrams." Do you agree? Why or why not?

DQ2-9 "In terms of the sequence used in documenting systems, it would be easier to prepare a systems flowchart *before* we prepare a data flow diagrams." Do you agree?

DQ2-10 "Since there are computer-based documentation products that can draw data flow diagrams and systems flowcharts, learning to draw them manually is a waste of time." Do you agree? Why or why not?

PROBLEMS

P2-1 Prepare a narrative to describe the system depicted in the physical DFD in Figure 2.14.

[Insert Figure 2.14 here]

P2-2 Prepare a narrative to describe the system depicted in the logical DFD in Figure 2.15.

[Insert Figure 2.15 here]

P2-3 Prepare a narrative to describe the system depicted in the flowchart in Figure 2.16 (page 60).

[Insert Figure 2.16 here]

P2-4 a. List the entities and activities in Figure 2.17 (page 61).

[Insert Figure 2.17 here]

b. Prepare a statement for *each* entity-relationship pair in Figure 2.17. (There are six pairs.) Each statement should explain the relationship category (e.g., "N-to-1," "1-to-N," "1-to-1," etc.). For example, to describe the order-customer relationship in Figure 2.8 on page 38, we might say: "Orders are received from customers. A customer may place many orders (N) but each order is from only one customer (1), an N-to-1 relationship."

APPENDICES 2A AND 2B.

P2-5 through P2-8. Problems 5 through 8 are based on the following two narratives. Lincoln Company describes sales and credit card billing systems. Bono Insurance describes an automobile insurance order entry and billing system. For those who wish to test their documentation skills beyond the problems below, there are narratives at the end of Chapters 10 through 12. Note that for the Lincoln case we do not discuss, and you should ignore, the handling of cash received at the time of a sale.

Lincoln Company

The Lincoln Company operates pet supply stores at many locations throughout New England. The company's headquarters are in Boston. The company accepts cash and its own Lincoln charge card (LCC). LCC billing and the treasury functions are located at headquarters.

At each store a customer presents the item(s) to be purchased along with cash or a LCC. Sales clerks prepare LCC slips and then all sales—cash and charge—are keyed into the cash register. At the end of the shift, the clerk forwards the LCC slips to the store cashier (again, as noted above, ignore the handling of the cash). The store cashier batches the LCC slips and sends the batches to the cash receipts department in Boston at 5:00 p.m. each day.

As each sale is keyed in by the sales clerks, Lincoln's central computer system captures the data and stores them on a disk ("sales data"). Each night, the computer prints a sales report summarizing each store's sales data. On the following morning, the sales report is sent to the cash receipts department, where the LCC slips for each store are reconciled to the line on the sales report that totals LCC sales for that store. The LCC slips are then sent to Lincoln's IT division, where data preparation clerks scan the LCC slips to record the charges on a disk ("credit sales data"). At 9:00 p.m. each evening, the disk containing the credit sales data is e-mailed as an attachment to the computer room, where it is used to update the accounts receivable master data (also on disk). Each month, the computer prepares customer statements that summarize the LCC charges, and sends the statements to the customers.

Bono Insurance

The Bono Insurance Company of Needham, Massachusetts, processes its automobile insurance policies on a batch-oriented computer system. Customers send requests for auto insurance into the Needham sales office where sales clerks prepare policy request forms. These documents are forwarded to the input preparation department where data entry clerks use networked PCs to key and key-verify the data contained on the documents to a disk ("policy events").

Each evening, the computer operations department retrieves the policy events data from the network and edits the data on the computer and then sorts the data in policy number sequence. Events data that do not pass the edits are deleted from the events data disk and printed on an error report. The error report is sent to the sales office where sales clerks review the report, correct the errors (contacting the customer, if necessary), and prepare another policy request form. These forms are submitted to data preparation each day along with other policy request forms.

In addition to the error report, the computer also prints a summary report listing the good events data. This report is sent to the sales office where the sales clerks compare the report to the copy of the policy request form that they had previously filed. If everything checks out, they notify computer operations to go ahead with processing. When notified, computer operations processes the correct events data against the policyholder master data to create a new policy record. Each evening, a disk, which was created during the processing run, is used to print premium notices that are sent to the customer.

P2-5 a. Prepare a table of entities and activities based on either the Lincoln Company or the Bono Insurance narrative.

b. Construct a context diagram based on the table you prepared in part a.

P2-6 Prepare a physical DFD based on the output from Problem 5.

P2-7 a. Prepare an annotated table of entities and activities based on the output from Problem 5 and Problem 6. Indicate on this table the groupings, bubble numbers, and bubble titles to be used in preparing a level 0 logical DFD.

b. Prepare a logical DFD (level 0 only) based on the table you prepared in part a.

P2-8 Construct a systems flowchart based on the narrative and the output from Problems 5 through 7.

P2-9 A description of fourteen typical information processing routines is given here, along with ten numbered excerpts from systems flowcharts (see Figure 2.18).

[Insert Figure 2.18 here]

Match the flowcharting segments with the descriptions to which they correspond. Four descriptions will be left blank.

a. Data on source documents are keyed to an offline disk.

b. A deposit slip and check are sent to a customer.

c. A printed output document is filed.

d. Output is sent to a computer screen at a remote location.

e. A clerk manually posts sales orders to the outstanding order data store.

f. A report is printed from the contents of a master data store.

g. Data stored on a disk is sorted and placed on another disk.

h. Data on a magnetic tape are printed during an offline operation.

i. Data are keyed from a terminal at a remote location.

j. A batch total is compared to the total reflected on an error and summary report.

k. Magnetic tape input is used to update master data kept on a disk.

l. The cash receipts summary report is sent by the accounts receivable department to the general ledger department.

m. Input stored on two magnetic disks is merged.

n. Programmed edits are performed on key input, the data entry clerk investigates exceptions and keys in corrections, then the master file is updated.

APPENDIX 2A P2-10 Refer to Figure 2.12 (see page 48), the level 0 DFD of Causeway's cash receipts system.

a. Construct a diagram 1, which "explodes" process 1.0, "Capture cash receipts," down to the next level.

b. Construct a diagram 2, which "explodes" process 2.0, "Record customer collections," down to the next level.

c. Construct a diagram 3, which "explodes" process 3.0, "Prepare deposit," down to the next level.

d. Construct a diagram 4, which "explodes" process 4.0, "Prepare cash receipts total," down to the next level.

TABLES

[Start Table]

Table 2.1 Table of Entities and Activities for Causeway Cash Receipts System

Entities	**Para**	**Activities**
Customers	1	1. Send checks and remittance advices.
Mailroom (clerk)	1	2. Endorses checks.
Mailroom (clerk)	1	3. Writes the amount paid and the check number on the remittance advice
Mailroom (clerk)	1	4. Prepares a batch total of the remittance advices.
Mailroom (clerk)	1	5. Sends the batch of remittance advices and the batch total to the accounts receivable clerk
Mailroom (clerk)	1	6. Sends the batch of checks to the cashier.
Accounts receivable (clerk)	2	7. Enters the batch into the computer.
Accounts receivable (clerk)	2	8. Keys the batch total, the customer number, the invoice number, the amount paid, and the check number.
Computer	2	9. Verifies that the invoice is open and that the correct amount is being paid.
Computer	2	10. Updates the accounts receivable master data.
Computer	2	11. Notifies the clerk of errors.
Computer	4	12. Logs check number and amount paid.
Computer	3	13. Prints a deposit slip.
Cashier	3	14. Compares the deposit slip with the batch of checks.
Cashier	3	15. Takes the deposit to the bank.
Computer	4	16. Creates a cash receipts listing.
Computer	4	17. Prints a summary of customer accounts paid.

Accounts receivable (clerk)	4	18. Compares the computer reports with the remittance advices and batch totals
Accounts receivable (clerk)	4	19. Sends the total of cash receipts to the general ledger office.

[End Table]

[Start Table]

Table 2.2 Table of Entities and Activities for Causeway Cash Receipts System (Annotated)

Entities	**Para**	**Activities**	
Mailroom (clerk)	1	2. Endorses checks.	*1.0 Capture cash receipts*
	1	3. Writes the amount paid and the check number on the remittance advice.	
	1	4. Prepares a batch total of the remittance advices.	
Accounts receivable (clerk)	2	8. Keys the batch total, the customer number, the invoice number, the amount paid, and the check number.	*2.0 Record customer collections*
Computer (online terminal)	2	9. Verifies that the invoice is open and that the correct amount is being paid.	
	2	10. Updates the accounts receivable master data.	
	4	12. Logs check number & amount paid.	
Computer (online terminal) Cashier	3 3	13. Prints a deposit slip. 14. Compares the deposit slip with the batch of	*3.0 Prepare deposit checks*
Computer (online terminal)	4	16. Creates a cash receipts listing.	*4.0 Prepare cash receipts total*
	4	17. Prints a summary of customer accounts paid.	
Accounts receivable (clerk)	4	18. Compares the computer reports with remittance advices and batch totals.	

[End Table]

Part II

TECHNOLOGY FOR

BUSINESS PROCESSES AND

INFORMATION SYSTEMS

3 Database Management Systems

4 E-Business

5 Business Intelligence and Knowledge Management Systems

[Insert UNF-p.65-1 here]

3

DATABASE MANAGEMENT SYSTEMS

The massive recall of Firestone Tires in the autumn of 2000, particularly those on Ford Explorer SUVs, produced a major financial impact on both Firestone (including its parent Bridgestone) and Ford Motor Company. The sweeping recall occurred as tire blowouts and related vehicle rollovers were reported at alarming rates. The tread on certain brands and sizes of Firestone tires had a tendency to separate—particularly if the tires were under-inflated, driven at high speeds in hot climates, or carrying a heavy load. The result has been numerous lawsuits filed against both Bridgestone/Firestone and Ford Motor Co.

The burning question is why didn't Ford and/or Firestone

discover the problem earlier? One reason was that Ford "lack[ed] a database it could use to determine whether incident reports on one type or brand of tire represented a deviation from those of other tires on Ford vehicles."[1] As a result, Ford did not identify the problem until the public relations damage was severe and then only after organizing a team to pore over the documentation on hand in the offices of Firestone. If a database of information related to tire problems had been available, standard data mining techniques likely would have detected the information much earlier. In this chapter, we will explore the advantages of database management systems and related analysis tools that can improve the decision support required for timely decision making.

[1] R. L. Simison, K. Lundegaard, N. Shirouzu and J. Heller, "How the Tire Problem Turned Into a Crisis for Firestone and Ford—Lack of a Database Masked the Pattern that Led To Yesterday's Big Recall," *The Wall Street Journal* (August 10, 2000), A1 and A12.

Synopsis

This chapter introduces approaches used to process data related to major business events that take place in an organization, such as purchasing materials, manufacturing products, and filling customer orders. Data from these events are recorded and processed using differing systems designs. As these business events are processed, data are recorded in files, tables, databases, and so on. The management of data comprises two distinct processes—event data processing and data maintenance. Having laid this foundation, we build your understanding by describing event-driven approaches and the various uses of databases to facilitate data management. Throughout this discussion we consider how various control procedures can enhance accuracy and safeguarding of data. Finally, in the appendices, we discuss the processes used in the design and implementation of entity-relationship (E-R) models and databases.

LEARNING OBJECTIVES

- To describe and analyze the major approaches used to process data related to business events
- To describe the major business events in merchandising, service and manufacturing firms
- To explain the complexities and limitations of using traditional data management approaches
- To recognize the advantages of using the database approach to data management
- To be able to perform the basic processes involved in database design and implementation

Introduction

An organization engages in various business processes—such as hiring employees, purchasing inventory, and collecting cash from customers—and the activities that occur during execution of these business processes are referred to as **events**. **Event data processing** is the process whereby event-related data are collected and stored. This chapter describes event data processing, discusses the major approaches employed to capture, process, and store event data, and recounts the types of data collected in event data processing systems. After introducing the major types of events, the text describes a crucial element of the Information System—the data. You need to know how data and databases will become an integral part of your day-to-day work. What data do we collect? How do we collect the data, store the data, and use the data?

Consider the importance of the groundwork laid in this chapter. In Chapters 4 and 5, we focus on advanced techniques for managing data and speeding the delivery of information. In Chapters 6 and 7, we emphasize techniques for developing good Information Systems that capture and deliver the right data. In Chapters 8 and 9, we focus on techniques to assure the reliability and security of data. Finally, in Chapters 10–14, we focus on how data are captured and processed across an organization's business processes. What's the moral to the story? If you can't access good, useful data, you can't make good business decisions.

Event Data Processing

In Chapter 2, we studied several types of diagrams in which

something happened (e.g., a customer order) that triggered a series of human and automated business activities. These business activities represent the occurrence of a *business event.* Every firm has a number of business events that link together to form a *business process.* The nature of a firm's business dictates the range of processes it can adopt to achieve its objectives. The firm's information system will collect, process, and store business event data in support of its business processes. Each of these business processes may be divided into components, or subprocesses.

Take, for instance, a merchandising firm. A **merchandising firm** is an organization (e.g., a store) that buys goods from vendors and resells those goods to customers. On the customer side, its business events within the Order-to-Sales process include:

- Capturing and recording of customer orders
- Shipment of goods and recording of sales
- Sending invoices for goods and recording the amount to be received
- Receipt and recording of payments

Figure 3.1 depicts how the physical processing of these business events is also captured in the data recorded and processed by the merchandising firm's information system. On the supplier end, business events within the Purchase-to-Pay process include:

[Insert Figure 3.1 here]

- Preparation and recording of purchase orders
- Receipt of goods into inventory and recording the receipt of inventory
- Receipt of vendor invoices and recording of the amount owed
- Preparation and recording of payments

Review Question

What business events are typically encountered by a merchandising firm?

There may be other business processes in a typical merchandising business, such as payroll processing, hiring new employees, and many more.

As another example, a **service firm** is an organization that sells services, rather than merchandise, to its customers. The business events for a service firm that parallel the Order-to-Sales process include:

- Recording of customer services performed
- Billing for services rendered
- Receipt and recording of payments

Because there is no physical exchange of goods in a service firm, its Order-to-Cash process would have a slightly modified set of events reflected in its corresponding information system, as shown in Figure 3.2. Service firms also must record other business events, including the purchase of materials used in the performance of service engagements and payroll disbursements.

[Insert Figure 3.2 here]

Review Question

How do the business events for a service firm differ from those of a merchandising firm? How are they similar for the two firms?

A **manufacturing firm** acquires raw materials, converts those materials into finished goods, and sells those goods to its customers. Its **production process** includes recording activities related to the manufacture of goods for sale. A manufacturing firm must also receive customer orders, record sales, send invoices, and receive customer payments. Its Order-to-Cash process is essentially the same as that of the merchandising firm in Figure 3.1. The events that make up these processes will be described in detail in Chapters 10–14.

As each business event occurs, a firm must record at least a minimal set of data about the event so that it can maintain records and produce reports that help assess how well it is meeting its objectives. Today, virtually all of these records are maintained by a computerized Information System.

An organization's Information System performs event data

processing to support an overall business process and its component subprocesses. For example, we describe the Information System employed to prepare and send a bill to a customer as the "billing"portion of the Order-to-Sales process. Similarly, we describe the Information System that prepares and records a purchase order as the "purchasing" portion of the Purchase-to-Pay process.

Transaction Processing Approach

Throughout the preceding discussion of event data processing, the focus was on events that take place within various business processes. Once these events have been identified, data that describe the events are collected, organized, manipulated, summarized, stored, and made available for retrieval. Traditionally, computerized Information Systems were designed around particular events called **transactions**, those business activities that have an economic impact on the firm. These include sales, payroll, accounts payable, and other typical financial transactions. The data that are recorded by a **transaction processing system** reflect the minimal information needed to represent each transaction, and are stored in a file along with the records of all of the other transactions of the same type. This transaction orientation led to the dominance of "file-centric" techniques for systems design, an approach discussed later in this chapter. This traditional approach to transaction processing worked well when technology was expensive and record keeping was not as sophisticated as it is today.

Event-Driven Approach

As society progresses in the information age, users' expectations of the information they need at their fingertips has escalated dramatically. User information demands have highlighted several fundamental weaknesses in the traditional approach of transaction processing. First, in order for data to be in a format that can be easily summarized, only data related to classification (e.g., a customer account number or an inventory part number) and quantitative descriptions can be captured. Thus, only a very narrow view of the event is portrayed by the data we collect—for instance, maybe only a financial accounting assessment or a listing of available stock in the warehouse. Second, once transaction data have been summarized, descriptions of individual transactions may be lost, with only summary information available to users.

Event-driven systems capture a complete description of each event, regardless of its economic impact on the firm, and permanently store the individual descriptions of each event. There are many business events that carry no economic impact, which would not be reflected in traditional transaction-oriented systems. Two examples are a sales representative capturing contact information about a potential customer, and a warehouse clerk updating location information when inventory items are moved from long-term storage to a place where "pickers" can get easy access to them. Neither of these events shows up on financial reports, but both are important for running the business.

Review Question

How are event-driven systems different from traditional transaction processing systems?

Of equal importance, however, is the focus on capturing a wider variety of data about each business event to meet the needs of multiple users. *Transaction processing* systems have historically been limited in the diversity of data they capture. This limitation is due to an initial focus on automating paper-driven financial processes. While these traditional systems may play an important role in meeting the financial information needs of an organization, they do not necessarily support the marketing, human resources, and manufacturing aspects of an organization very well. The nonfinancial aspects of business events are of great importance to these varied users. Event-driven systems facilitate use by multiple information users with very different needs for information about the events that have occurred within business processes.

Review Question

What is meant by the idea of "storing data at the event level"?

Storing data at the event level makes it much easier to retain data related to other nonfinancial and nonquantitative aspects of an event. Ideally, in an event-driven system, the data captured during business processes will be sufficient for someone who was not a party to the event to reconstruct every important aspect of what happened—whether he or she is in marketing, human resources, financial management, manufacturing, or any other part of the organization. Typically, this mandates that at a minimum data be collected and stored related to the *four Ws:*

- *Who* relates to all individuals and/or organizations that are involved in the event.
- *What* relates to all assets that exchange hands as a result of the event.
- *Where* relates to the locations in which (1) the event takes place, (2) exchanged assets reside before and after the event, and (3) the parties to the event are during the event and for any future correspondence.
- *When* relates to all the time periods involved in completion of the event—including future exchanges of assets (e.g., when will we need to pay a bill?) that result from the event.

Once the event data are collected and recorded, the data can be aggregated and summarized in any manner that a given user chooses.

The key is that any aggregations and summaries are temporary and only for the user's application, but the event data remain available to other users in its original form. For applications such as the generation of financial and inventory reports that are frequently required in the same format, programmed procedures can be developed within computerized systems to generate such reports automatically. Thus, the same needs for financial information fulfilled by traditional transaction processing systems are fulfilled by *event-driven systems*, but with the latter systems a host of other users' needs can also be met more efficiently and effectively.

Let us take, for example, a series of events that might take place during the course of capturing a customer's order, putting through a job order to produce the ordered goods, and delivering the goods to the customer. When setting up our *event-based* system, we will want to capture multifaceted data to track the progression of the process. To capture the *sales order* event, we need to record data related to the salesperson and customer (the *who*), the goods ordered (the *what*), the delivery location (the *where*), and the date of sale and promised delivery (the *when*). This information would then be linked with information already stored that relates to a selected supplier for goods. Based on the combined information, an order would be placed with the supplier. A *purchase order* becomes a link between the purchaser and the supplier (the *who*) already in the system, the goods (the *what*) that have already been entered, the location to which the goods will be delivered (the *where*), and the delivery date from the supplier to our company (the *when*).

Notice in our sales example that all of the *traditional* systems data are readily available. The data required for the Order-to-Sales, Purchase-to-Pay, and Business Reporting processes are all captured and available for processing. But, now if the supplier changes the delivery date, the salesperson can also have immediate access to the change and notify the customer. The salesperson can pull together the necessary data by using links between the changed order information, the sales order, and the customer, and narrow the search down to only the sales that he or she is handling. Very quickly, the salesperson can have the information needed to notify the customer immediately of any delay in shipment.

Review Question

Why is it important to capture the who, what, where, and when in describing business events?

It is important to note that *event-driven* systems may appear no different to the average user than more traditional transaction processing systems for collecting business event data. Rather, the underlying data storage and management (that is unobservable to most users) differ, while at the same time new sets of users have access to more relevant information for business decision making. In subsequent sections of this chapter, we will revisit these two approaches to Information Systems and discuss the underlying information technologies that enable their existence.

File Management Processes

File management comprises the functions that collect, organize, store, retrieve, and manipulate data maintained in traditional file-oriented data processing environments. We have already noted that business event data processing systems collect, process, and store data. So, admittedly, there is an overlap between these two environments, for data used by the system must physically reside somewhere! This section concentrates on file management. We see how data are managed—particularly how data are stored and retrieved, knowing that part of file management is undertaken by Information Systems underlying Order-to-Cash, Purchase-to-Pay, and other business processes. Thus, file management supports the generation of reports associated with traditional transaction processing systems.

Review Question

What is file management?

Managing Data Files

Let's quickly review the hierarchy of data that may already be familiar to you. A **character** is a basic unit of data such as a letter, number, or special character. A **field** is a collection of related characters, such as a customer number or a customer name. A **record** is a collection of related data fields pertaining to a particular entity (person, place, or thing, such as a customer record) or event (sale, hiring of a new employee, and so on). A **file** is a collection of related records, such as a customer file or a payroll file. A **record layout** describes the fields making up a record. These relationships are depicted in part (a) of Figure 3.3.

[Insert Figure 3.3 here]

Chapter 1 introduced you to two types of data, *master data* (entity-type files) and *business event data* (event-type files). A business event data processing system may operate on one or more files. Some of these files are used to obtain reference information, such as the warehouse location of an item of merchandise. Other files are used to organize and store the data being collected, such as sales orders or inventory data. Some companies still rely on older, legacy systems that use file structures for data storage.

A database approach is a superior data storage method. In a database approach, *tables,* not *files,* are used to organize and store data. For now, we want to discuss data management using well-known terms and concepts associated with files; we'll get to tables later.

Let's examine two flowcharts. Figure 3.3, part (b), depicts a typical data maintenance activity—the addition of a new customer record to the customer master data. Figure 3.4 (page 74)depicts a typical business event data processing activity—entering a customer's order. In this text, we use the more generic term, *data store* to distinguish the conceptual file from its physical implementation as a file or database table.

What is important about these two figures? First, the data maintenance activity (Figure 3.3, part b) does not involve a business transaction as such; however, the business event data processing activity (Figure 3.4) does.

[Insert Figure 3.3 here]

Second, the existence of the customer record—including the credit limit [see Figure 3.3, part (a)]—provides the basic authorization required to enter the customer order. Without the customer record, the computer would reject the customer order in Figure 3.4. It is important to separate authorizations for data maintenance activities from authorizations for business event data processing activities. This separation provides an important control, a topic explored in greater detail in Chapters 8 and 9.

[Insert Figure 3.4 here]

Limitations of File Processing

In Figure 3.5 (page 75) we compare and contrast the applications-based file approach found in a transaction processing system (discussed in this section) with the database approach to data management (discussed in the following section). Figure 3.6 (page 76) contains the record layouts for the files in Figure 3.5, part (a).

[Insert Figure 3.5 here]

Prior to the development of database concepts, companies tended to view data as a necessary adjunct of the program or process that used the data. As shown in part (a) of Figure 3.5, this view of data, based on the transaction processing approach to file management, concentrates on the process being performed; therefore, the data play a secondary or supportive role in each application system. Under this approach, each application collects and manages its own data, generally in dedicated, separate, physically distinguishable files for each application. For example, Figures 3.3, part (b) and 3.4 assumed a "transaction-centric" approach to file management. One outgrowth of this approach is the *data redundancy* that occurs among various files. For example, notice the redundancies (indicated by double-ended arrows) depicted in the record layouts in Figure 3.6. Data redundancy often leads to inconsistencies among the same data in different files and increases the storage cost associated with multiple versions of the same data. In addition, data residing in separate files are not shareable among applications. Now let's examine how some of these redundancies might come about.

[Insert Figure 3.6 here]

The data represented in Figure 3.6 have two purposes. The data (1) mirror and monitor the business operations (the *horizontal information flows*) and (2) provide the basis for managerial decisions (the *vertical information flows*).[2] In addition to data derived from the horizontal flows, managers use information unrelated to event data processing. These data would be collected and stored with the business event related data. Let's look at a few examples to tie this discussion together.

[2] The horizontal and vertical information flows are depicted in Figure 1.5 (page 14).

Suppose that the sales application wished to perform sales analysis, such as product sales by territory, by customer, or by salesperson. To do so, the sales application would store data for sales territory and salesperson in the sales order record shown in part (a) of Figure 3.6. But, what if the inventory application wanted to perform similar analyses? To do so, the inventory application would store similar, redundant data about territory and salesperson as depicted in part (b) of Figure 3.6. As implied by Figure 3.5, part (a), the sales data in the inventory data file—including customer territory and salesperson—could be updated by the sales application or updated separately by the inventory application. As a second example, what if the sales application wanted to know very quickly the amount of sales for a customer? Then, the summary data on the customer master data file (year-to-date sales) could be stored as shown in part (c) of Figure 3.6. Alternatively, the information could be obtained as needed by summarizing data on the sales order or in the inventory data.

As a final sales example, let's assume we would like to know all the products that a particular customer buys (perhaps so we can promote those products the customer is not buying). Given the record layouts depicted in Figure 3.6, we could obtain that information by sorting the inventory or sales order data by customer number. Alternatively, we could have collected these data in the customer master data store! In either case, the data are difficult and expensive to obtain. And, if the applications were not originally designed to give us these data, this approach to file management makes it quite difficult to add this access after the fact.

We could provide several more examples from inventory, but by now we trust that we have made our point. All of these examples consist of business event data related to the selling of merchandise. The transaction processing approach leaves us with similar problems for *standing data.* Note in Figure 3.6 the redundancies among the three data files with respect to standing data such as customer number, territory, and salesperson. Could these redundant fields become inconsistent? Again, we would have to say yes. The database approach to data management solves many of these problems. We will return to Figure 3.6 and describe what these data might look like with a database, rather than separate application files.

Database Management Systems

A **database management system** is a set of integrated programs designed to simplify the tasks of creating, accessing, and managing data. Database management systems integrate a collection of files or data *tables* that are independent of application programs and are available to satisfy a number of different processing needs. A database management system is really the means by which an organization coordinates the disparate activities of its many functional areas. The database management system, containing data related to all of an organization's applications, supports normal event data processing needs and enhances the organization's management activities by providing data useful to managers. While in its strictest sense a database is a collection of files, we will use the term **database** synonymously with database management system since this has evolved as the normal meaning intended by the vast majority of computer users and developers.

Logical vs. Physical Database Models

The concept underlying the **database approach to data management** is to decouple the data from the system applications (i.e., to make the data *independent* of the application or other users). Therefore, as reflected in part (b) of Figure 3.5 (page 75), the data become the focus of attention. Several other aspects of part (b) are noteworthy:

- The *database* is now shared by *multiple* system applications that support related business processes, as shown at the left of Figure 3.5, part (b).
- In addition to being used by application programs, the data can also be accessed through two other user interfaces: (1) *report generation,* as shown in the upper-right portion of part (b), and (2) ad hoc user inquiries, i.e., *queries* handled through *query language* software, depicted in the lower-right portion of part (b).[3]
- A "layer" of software called the database management system (DBMS) is needed to translate a user's *logical view* of the data into instructions for retrieving the data from *physical* storage. Some of the more technical design issues of database management systems are described in Technology Insight 3.1 (page 78).

[3] In many database management systems, report generation and queries may not be distinct functions.

Figure 3.7 (page 79) depicts how a database might look to us if the data were stored using a *relational* data structure. The data from our three files are now stored in four *relational tables:* CUSTOMERS (instead of customer master data), INVENTORY_ITEMS (inventory master data), SALES_ORDERS, and SALES_LINES (i.e., the last two tables store the data from the sales order master data). These tables are *logical views* of data that are *physically* stored in a database. The **logical database view** is how the data appear to the user to be stored. This view represents the structure that the user must interface with in order to extract data from the database. The **physical database storage** is how the data are actually physically stored on the storage medium used in the database management system. It has little relationship to how the data appear to be stored (e.g., the *logical view*). The user can access the data in the tables (e.g., the *logical view* in a *relational database*) by:

1. Formulating a query, or
2. Preparing a report using a report writer, or
3. Including a request for data within an application program.

These three methods are depicted in the flowchart in Figure 3.5, part (b) (page 75).

[Insert TECHNOLOGY INSIGHT 3.1 box here]

Now let's see how easily data can be obtained from the relational tables in Figure 3.7 using the database query language *SQL (structured query language)*.

[Insert Figure 3.7 here]

1. We can perform a query (the SELECT command) to find the customers assigned to salesperson Garcia.

SELECT CUST_CODE CUST_NAME CUST_CITY

FROM CUSTOMERS

WHERE SALESPERSON = 'Garcia'

[Insert UNF-p.80-3 here]

We see that there are two customers, STANS and WHEEL.

2. We can also create a listing using the SELECT command.

SELECT SO_Number INVENTORY_ITEMS.Item_Number Sales_Price Unit_Price

FROM SALES_LINES INVENTORY_ITEMS

WHERE Sales_Price • Unit_Price AND INVENTORY_ITEMS.Item_Number = SALES_LINES.Item_Number

[Insert UNF-p.80-4 here]

The SELECT command combines the SALES_LINES and INVENTORY_ITEMS tables over the list of items (Item_Number) and finds those items in the combined table that were sold at a price

(Sales_Price) other than the price contained on the INVENTORY_ITEMS table (Unit_Price). We see that there are six instances.

Review Question

How are the applications-based file and database approaches to data management the same? How are they different?

Neither the user nor the application programs have any idea that these mappings are taking place. In preparing the query, a user might formulate the SELECT command (i.e., choose the selection criteria). Alternatively, rather than being visible to the users, the SQL commands might be part of an underlying application or database structure. Finally, the user might execute these commands using drop-down menus and a mouse. In these latter two alternatives, the commands would be embedded within the application programs. *Relational data structures* are discussed in greater detail later in this chapter.

Overcoming the Limitations of File Processing

We discussed earlier some of the limitations of applications that rely on traditional file management. What are the advantages of the database approach?

- *Eliminating data redundancy.* With the database approach to data management, data need only be stored once. Applications that need data can access the data from the central database. For example, in Figure 3.5 (page 75), part (a), there are multiple versions of the inventory master data, while in part (b) of that figure there is but one. Further, Figure 3.6 (page 76) depicts the same data elements on more than one file, whereas Figure 3.7 (page 79) shows each data element only once. An organization using the applications-based file approach to data management must incur the costs and risks of storing and maintaining these duplicate files and data elements.

- *Ease of maintenance.* Because each data element is stored only once, any additions, deletions, or changes to the database are accomplished easily. Contrast this to the illustration in Figure 3.6, where a change in a salesperson, territory, or customer combination, for instance, would require a change in three different files.
- *Reduced storage costs.* By eliminating redundant data, storage space is reduced, resulting in associated cost savings. However, in most database installations, this savings is *more than offset* by the additional costs of DBMS software.
- *Data integrity.* This advantage, like several others, results from eliminating data redundancy. As mentioned earlier, storing multiple versions of the same data element is bound to produce inconsistencies among the versions. For instance, the salesperson

and sales territory data might differ among their many versions, not only because of clerical errors but because of timing differences in making data maintenance changes. We could make similar comments about inconsistent data resulting from the timing differences that might occur during *event data processing* of the inventory master data by the sales and inventory applications. With only one version of each data element stored in the database, such inconsistencies disappear.

- *Data independence.* As illustrated in part (b) of Figure 3.5, the database approach allows multiple application programs to use the data concurrently. In addition, the data can be accessed in several different ways (e.g., through applications processing, online query, and report writing programs). And, the access can be quickly changed by modifying the definition of the tables or views. With the traditional *applications-based file approach,* the programs would have to be revised to provide access to more or less data.

- *Privacy.* The security modules available through DBMS software can contain powerful features to protect the database against unauthorized disclosure, alteration, or destruction. Control over data access can typically be exercised down to the data element level. Users can be granted access to data for reading or updating (add, revise, delete) data. Other ways to implement security include *data classification* (i.e., data objects are given classification levels and users are assigned clearance levels) and *data encryption* (discussed in Chapter 9).

Review Question

What are the relative advantages of the database approach?

These advantages add greatly to the incentive for firms relying on legacy systems to move to database-supported applications.

Enabling Event-Driven Systems

Earlier we noted that file management approaches are often sufficient to support traditional transaction processing. Without question, database management systems can improve the efficiency of processing data by eliminating data redundancies, improving data integrity, and so forth. However, the big change that database management systems have enabled is the realization of event-driven data processing systems. As noted earlier, event-driven systems are oriented toward the concept that complete data describing business events should be kept in its original form, where multiple users from throughout the organization can view and aggregate event data according to their needs.

At the heart of this movement toward event-driven systems is a fundamental shift in the view of information processing in business organizations. Traditionally, organizational Information Systems have been focused first on capturing data for the purpose of generating reports, and using the reporting function to support decision making. Increasingly, management is shifting to viewing the primary purpose of organizational Information Systems as decision support while reporting is secondary. This perspective leads to a focus on aggregating and maintaining data in an original form from which reports can be derived, but users can also access and manipulate data using their own models and their own data aggregations. In Chapter 5, we will discuss Information Systems such as business intelligence and expert systems that are designed to improve decision making. If you look ahead to the figures in Technology Insights 5.2 (page 149) and 5.3 (page 152) you will notice that both types of support systems generally require access to detailed data stored in databases.

The strategic shift toward event-driven systems is further embodied in two contemporary concepts that are driving new database management systems implementations: *data warehousing* and *data mining.* **Data warehousing** is the use of Information Systems facilities to focus on the collection, organization, integration, and long-term storage of entity-wide data. Data warehousing's purpose is to provide users with easy access to large quantities of varied data from across the organization for the sole purpose of improving decision-making capabilities. **Data mining** is the complementary action to data warehousing. Data mining refers to the exploration, aggregation, and analysis of large quantities of varied data from across the organization to better understand an organization's business processes, trends within these processes, and potential opportunities to improve the effectiveness and/or efficiency of the organization. The "warehouses of data" analogy makes sense as the software to support data storage is akin to physical warehousing approaches used to store and retrieve inventory—when an item needs to be restocked on the store shelf, there must be some system whereby the item can be located in the warehouse and retrieved.

Data warehousing and data mining opportunities are enabled and enriched through the use of event-driven systems focused on capturing data that provide comprehensive views of business events. However, neither effective event-driven systems nor data warehouses are possible without effective implementation of database management systems. Both objectives are dependent on the massive data integration and data independence made possible through database technology. Both warehousing and data mining may also be limited if well-designed database models that provide for future information needs are not effectively implemented. This process starts with the information requirements analysis and successful attainment of an understanding of all users' potential data and information needs.

Review Question

What do the concepts of data warehousing and data mining mean?

Entity-Relationship (E-R) Modeling

Chapter 2 described E-R diagrams and showed you how to read them. Before moving on to developing E-R diagrams (in Appendix A), you should expand upon your knowledge of E-R diagrams to ensure a solid understanding of *entities* and *attributes.* This knowledge aids in the development of solid data models that lead to effective database structures. Although the diagrams can appear complex at first, they provide a very useful high-level tool for understanding the complicated relationships that exist among data in typical firms. E-R diagrams permit users and/or developers to communicate with a common understanding of how different types of data relate, including data about entities and business events. This understanding also permits a decision maker to interpret reports and analyses correctly based on extracts from a database.

Entities and Attributes

An **entity** is an object, event, or agent about which data are collected. As examples, objects could include such things as orders, sales, and purchases. Agents include people such as customers, employees, and vendors. Basically, an *entity* is anything that independently exists.

Review Question

What is an entity?

In order to understand which entity we are capturing in our database and, likewise, to be able to identify that unique entity when we retrieve the data, we need to describe the entity in detail. In a data model, we describe entities by recording the essential characteristics of that entity that fully describe it. In other words, we record its *attributes.* An **attribute** is an item of data that characterizes an entity or relationship. Figure 3.8 displays an attribute hierarchy for an entity CLIENT. Notice that to describe fully a CLIENT we need to record several attributes such as Name, Address, Contact_Person, and Phone_Number. Sometimes, attributes are a combination of parts that have unique meanings of their own. For instance, in Figure 3.8, Address might consist of several independent subattributes such as the Street_Address, City, State, and Zip_Code. Attributes that consist of multiple sub-attributes are referred to as *composite attributes.*

[Insert Figure 3.8 here]

Review Question

What is an attribute?

Note that an inherent assumption we have made in specifying the attributes for the entity, CLIENT, is that there is a common set of attributes for each entity of interest in our database.[4] That is, for every client we need to know the client's name, address, contact person, and phone number. To design an effective data model, you must learn to identify the complete set of entities and the common attributes that fully describe each entity. It is very important that the attributes are also sufficient to allow the user of a database to identify uniquely each entity in the database.

[4] Technically, CLIENT would be an "entity type" in that it describes a collective group of *entities* (e.g., different clients). However, most database developers use the term *entity* rather than "entity type," as it is understood that all *entities* of interest will fall into some category of similar-type *entities.* We will use this common terminology throughout the remainder of our discussion.

To achieve the objective of uniquely identifying each entity to be stored in our database, it is necessary that one or more *attributes* be identified that will always allow the user to access the entity that he or she is seeking. A **key attribute** is the attribute whose value is unique (i.e., different) for every entity that will ever appear in the database and is the most meaningful way of identifying each entity. This key attribute becomes the primary key. For our CLIENT entity, we might be able to use the Name for the key attribute; but alphabetic-based attributes like names are tricky because computers are sometimes sensitive to the use (or non-use) of capital letters. Further, spellings and full names can be tricky in that one user might view the company name as "Arnold Consultants" while another user might use the full name, "Arnold Consultants, LLP." If possible, it is preferable to use a numeric-valued or a non-naming alphabetic attribute. For instance, we could use a client number that would typically be assigned to each CLIENT. A numeric form using a sequential coding scheme might assign a number such as "12345." A non-naming alphabetic form using block coding to categorize companies by the first letter of a company's name might assign an alphanumeric such as "A1234" for the client number.

Review Questions

What is a relationship?

What is a key attribute?

Review Question

Why is it preferable to use a numeric-based attribute as the key attribute?

Figure 3.9 part (a), displays the symbols that are used to represent entities and attributes, as seen earlier in the E-R diagrams in Chapter 2. In Figure 3.9, part (b), the rectangle is accordingly used to represent the CLIENT entity. In order to map the attributes of an entity, we add oval connectors [as shown in part (a)] for each attribute. Notice in part (b) that we have added an oval for each of the attributes shown in Figure 3.8. For the composite attribute Address, we use the same oval connectors for each of the subattributes of the main attribute. Note that we have added an attribute beyond those shown in Figure 3.8—Client_Number. We have added this attribute as a key attribute, and have used an underline on the attribute name to document its selection as the *key attribute.*

[Insert Figure 3.9 here]

Relationships

Relationships are associations between entities. As we have discussed in the previous section, a database consists of several (or many) different types of entities. However, in order to make the data stored in these entities effective for users to reconstruct descriptions of various business events, the various entities must be logically linked to represent the *relationships* that exist during such business events. The ease with which a user can ultimately extract related data from a database is heavily dependent on the quality of the database's *logical design*—that is, effective identification of the relationships between different entities. These relationships map and define the way in which data can be extracted from the database in the future. The mapping of the relationships between entities (i.e., development of the E-R diagram) provides a roadmap for getting from one piece of data in the database to another related piece of data.

A three-step strategy is generally most effective in identifying all of the relationships that should be included in a model. First, consider the existing and desired information requirements of users to determine if relationships can be established within the data model to fulfill these requirements. Second, evaluate each of the entities in pairs to determine if any entity provides an improvement in the describing of an attribute contained in the other entity. Third, evaluate each entity to determine if there would be any need for two occurrences of the same *entity* type to be linked—e.g., identify *recursive relationships*. Appendix A describes the development of an E-R model in greater detail.

Review Question

Why is it important that you identify all of the important relationships when developing an entity-relationship (E-R) diagram?

A major thrust in many organizations has been a move toward completely integrating all data across an organization. These completely integrated enterprise models are the foundations for implementing *enterprise systems,* which are discussed in Technology Insight 3.2. Integration allows many users to share entity-level data by linking business events within related business processes.

[Insert TECHNOLOGY INSIGHT 3.2 box here]

Relational Databases

The **relational database model** is a logical model for a database in which data are logically organized in two-dimensional tables referred to as relations. We focus on the *relational database model* at this point because of its dominance in contemporary systems. (An alternative, the object-oriented model, is discussed in Technology Insight 3.3.) While there is a growing push toward object-oriented databases, the prevalence of large numbers of relational database-driven legacy systems makes such a switchover rather costly for most organizations. Many of these legacy systems (i.e., old systems that were developed using an organization's previous computer hardware and software platforms) have been functioning reliably for decades. As an alternative to making costly switchovers to object-oriented databases, relational database vendors provide modified versions of their software that support objects within the relational structure. We anticipate that relational-based systems will remain dominant for the foreseeable future.

[Insert TECHNOLOGY INSIGHT 3.3 box here]

Review Question

What are the relative advantages of the relational and object-oriented database models?

Basic Relational Concepts

Relational databases are often perceived to be a collection of tables. This is a reasonable perception in that the logical view of the data is a tabular type format referred to as a *relation*. A **relation** is defined as a collection of data representing multiple occurrences of an object, event, or agent. Similar to an *entity*, objects include such things as inventory, equipment, and cash. Events may include orders, sales, and purchases. Agents could include customers, employees, and vendors.

Review Question

What is a relation?

Figure 3.10 displays an example relation along with labels for each of its components. Consistent with a tabular representation, a *relation* consists of rows and columns. Rows are referred to as *tuples* and columns are referred to as *attributes*. **Tuples** are sets of data that describe an instance of the entity represented by a relation (e.g., one employee in the EMPLOYEE relation). We may think of a tuple as being akin to a record in a traditional file structure. While technically they are different, logically they are similar. Attributes, as they do in an E-R diagram, represent an item of data that characterizes an object, event, or agent. In terms of traditional file structures, we would parallel attributes (i.e., the columns in a *relation*) to fields.

[Insert Figure 3.10 here]

Review Questions

What is a tuple?

What is an attribute in a relational data model?

In viewing the relation in Figure 3.10, note that the data contained in the table do not appear to be in any particular order. In a relational database model there is no ordering of tuples contained within a relation. This is different from the traditional file structures you studied earlier in this chapter, where sequence or keyed location was usually critical. Rather, ordering of the tuples is unimportant since the tuples are recalled by the database through matching an attribute's value with some prescribed value, or through a query by which ordering could be established if desired (e.g., by sorting on one of the attributes—such as by Pay_Rate or Billing_Rate).

Review Question

Compare and contrast the data structures for data stored in a file and data stored in a relational table.

In order to uniquely identify a tuple, it is critical that each be distinct. This means that each tuple in a relation can be uniquely identified by a single attribute or some combination of multiple attributes. Similar to the rules used for constructing an E-R diagram, a primary key (which is equivalent to a key attribute in an E-R diagram) is specified to uniquely identify each tuple in the relation.

Notice in Figure 3.10 that Employee_Number is the *primary key* (the attribute name is underlined) and that it is unique for every tuple. There may be other attributes in the relation that also have the ability to serve as a key attribute, and in a relation these additional attributes can form secondary keys referred to as *candidate keys.* For any attribute specified as a key attribute, that attribute must have a unique and "non-null" value (i.e., there has to be some value assigned to the *attribute* for each tuple). Notice that Soc_Sec_No would also be unique and could possibly be used as a candidate key, but constraints would have to be put in place to ensure every tuple has a value since it is possible that an employee could, at least temporarily, not have a social security number.

Additionally, constraints should be put in place to assure that the *referential integrity* of the database is maintained. **Referential integrity** requires that for every attribute value in one relation that has been specified in order to allow reference to another relation, the tuple being referenced must remain intact. In other words, as you look at the relation, EMPLOYEE, in Figure 3.10, notice that EMPLOYEE is party to a *recursive relation* [also modeled in Appendix A in Figure 3.11, part (b), page 90]. In this *recursive relation,* Supervisor_No is used to reference the Employee_Number of the supervising employee. If the tuple for Greg Kinman were deleted from the database, note that four other employees would no longer have a valid Supervisor_No (e.g., the Supervisor_No would be referencing a tuple [A632] that no longer exists). Hence, a *referential integrity constraint* would require the user to reassign the four employees to a new supervisor before the tuple for Greg Kinman could be deleted.

Review Question

What is referential integrity?

Conclusions

As information needs and wants of users escalate, integrated databases have become the norm rather than the exception. The focus is no longer on the question, "Where can we implement databases?" But rather the focus has shifted to, "How do we integrate as much of our data as possible into a single logical database?" To retain flexibility, some organizations pursue self-developed and self-designed integrated database systems. For many organizations, the packaged solution of an enterprise system is the desired approach for data integration. Either way, the expertise of information specialists is key to successfully overcoming the challenges of implementing such integrated database systems.

With these opportunities and challenges also come huge responsibilities. The very lifeblood of an organization becomes wrapped up in a database that contains all of the organization's information. If the database is destroyed and cannot be recovered, the organization will probably not survive in today's business environment. Likewise, if competitors or others gain access to the data, the organization's ability to compete can also be seriously jeopardized.

Safeguarding data, while at the same time getting the information to users who need the information, is not a simple task. In Chapters 8 and 9, our discussion will shift to the issues surrounding data reliability, access, and security. You will learn about procedures that organizations implement to assure the reliability of information that is updated or added to the database. You will also learn about safeguarding data and maintaining backups of data so that if something should happen to the database, it can be recovered in a timely manner. These are truly challenging but exciting times for managers and other professionals who are prepared to operate in an information systems environment.

Appendix 3A

E-R Model Development

As we mentioned earlier, there is a three-step strategy to identify the relationships that should be included in a data model. First, it is very important that you study business events, and understand users' information requirements, in order to identify all of the ways in which different entities are related. This information will provide the foundation level of relationships required in the database model. The remaining two steps (i.e., evaluating each of the entities in pairs to determine if any entity provides an improvement in describing an attribute contained in the other entity, and evaluating each entity to determine if there would be any need for two occurrences of the same entity to be linked) enable you to refine and improve this foundation-level model.

The focus for our E-R model development will be on the client billing process generally used by service firms such as architecture, consulting, and legal firms. The nature of the process is that each employee in the firm keeps track of time spent working on each client's service, generally filling out a time sheet each week. The hours spent on a client are then multiplied by that employee's billable rate for each hour worked. The cumulative fees for all employees' work are used to generate the bill for the client. This way, the client only pays for the services it actually receives. The challenge here is capturing all of the information necessary to track employees' work hours and client billing information.

Examine Figure 3.11, part (a). Desirable linkages between entities will often be fairly easy to recognize when the relationship appears to define an attribute more clearly. If our billing system requires that we know for which client an employee has worked, the entity representing work completed needs to include a client number. This client number would link the WORK_COMPLETED entity to the CLIENT entity that provides us with a full description of the attribute denoted by client number in WORK_COMPLETED. Obviously, as shown in Figure 3.11, part (a), CLIENT is a separate entity and not an attribute. At the same time, CLIENT does improve the description of an attribute for the work completed—the client for whom the work was performed. This descriptive value makes it apparent there should be a relationship between the CLIENT entity and the entity capturing the completed work. Hence, we can often identify the need for defining relationships (such as Works_For) by also looking at the prescribed *entities* as pairs (in this case, we jointly examined the pair CLIENT and WORK_COMPLETED) to identify logical linkages that would improve the description of an entity's attributes.

[Insert Figure 3.11 here]

Let's look at another type of relationship that is displayed in Figure 3.11, part (b). The relationship Supervises is referred to as a *recursive relationship.* A **recursive relationship** is a relationship between two different *entities* of the same entity type. For instance, there usually are relationships between two employees, such as one employee who supervises another employee. This relationship may be important in some decision-making contexts and, therefore, should be represented in our database. We represent this relationship using the technique demonstrated in Figure 3.11, part (b). Consider the alternative: If we try to represent supervisors and their supervised employees as separate entities in our model, we end up with data redundancies when the supervisor is in fact supervised by a third employee. It is easier simply to create a recursive relationship to the entity, EMPLOYEE, whereby a link is created between one employee who is being supervised and another employee who is the supervisor. As shown in our sample diagram, the diamond is still used to represent the recursive relationship, Supervises, just as would be used to show any relationship (e.g., Works_For in part a).

Review Question

What is different about a recursive relationship in comparison to other relationships in a data model?

Model Constraints

In this section we explore the various types of relationships that can occur and discuss the constraints that are used to specify such relationships. In Chapter 2, we briefly explored three different relationship types: 1:N (one-to-many), M:N (many-to-many), and 1:1 (one-to-one). The connotations of these three relationships are what we refer to as *cardinality.* The **cardinality constraint** of a relationship relates to the specification of how many occurrences of an entity can participate in the given relationship with any one occurrence of the other entity in the relationship.

In Figure 3.12 (page 92), part (a), we demonstrate the specification of cardinality constraints for the one-to-many relationship Works. Note that the specification is done by placing the "1" above the left line of the relationship, specifying one employee performs an employee work day; and the "N" above the right line, specifying that many client work days may be performed by an employee. To determine the cardinality of a relationship, you have to ask yourself the question, "How many items (records) in this entity could be related to any one item (record) in the other entity—one or multiple?" The answer determines that half of the cardinality ratio, and then the same question is asked in the reverse direction of the relationship in order to determine the other half of the cardinality ratio. In our example, we take the relationship in Figure 3.12, part (a) and ask the question, "How many work days can an employee have on a client service engagement?" The answer is many (based on the attributes specified for WORK_COMPLETED in Figure 3.12, part (a), which indicates that a given occurrence in the WORK_COMPLETED entity relates to one employee's time spent on a given client in a single day—based on time being captured by the Date attribute). The question is then reversed and we ask, "How many employees can provide a specific employee work day?" The maximum number will be one. Hence, the cardinality of the relationship is specified as one-to-many and notated on the diagram with the “1” and “N.” For the database to maintain this relationship, a constraint must be enforced to ensure that data are never entered indicating that more than one employee is responsible for a given client work day.

[Insert Figure 3.12 here]

Cardinality is the most common constraint specified in E-R diagrams. The other meaningful constraint that may be specified is *participation.* The **participation constraint** is used to specify both the minimum and maximum participation of one entity in the relationship with the other entity. In Figure 3.12, part (b), the participation constraints are reflected in the partial E-R diagram. In our Works relationship we just discussed, not every employee will have worked on specific client service projects, but rather may have non-client service responsibilities, such as training, that he or she spends time on. The “many” in the cardinality ratio only specifies the maximum participation in the relationship, not the minimum. In specifying the participation in the relationship, the maximum is still many, but the minimum may be zero. The line on the right reflects the range of zero to many occurrences of work being completed on client projects with the notation (0,N), where the numbers reflect (minimum, maximum). On the other hand, for any given occurrence of a client workday, the maximum of one employee providing the specific service still holds. At the same time, the minimum is also one as there must be an employee who performs a particular occurrence of the completed work. Note the required participation of one, and only one, employee is shown on the left line of the relationship as (1,1).

While the participation constraint may provide more information, it is still used much less frequently than the cardinality constraint. As such, we will tend to present the diagrams in this text using cardinality constraints. It is important, however, that you are familiar with both types of constraints and the notation applied, since as a member of a team developing or using an E-R diagram, you need to be able to communicate using the methods selected by a given organization.

Review Question

What is different about the information provided through cardinality constraints versus participation constraints?

Entity Relationship (E-R) Diagrams

We have now worked our way through all the pieces necessary to develop effective E-R diagrams. If you have successfully gotten a handle on each of the concepts explored so far in this chapter, you should be ready to start developing an integrated database model. Each of the data model segments that has been displayed in Figures 3.8 through 3.12 represents part of the evolution toward our diagram.

Review Question

What is the importance of an E-R diagram in facilitating event-driven systems and the integration of data between business processes?

At this point, it may be worth recalling our discussion earlier in this chapter on event-driven systems. One of the fundamental requirements for moving toward an event-driven model was the complete integration of data related to an organization's various business events. We will use our data modeling techniques to demonstrate the integration of just two business processes: client billing and human resources.

The objective in the development of an E-R diagram is to integrate the data in a manner that allows business processes access to the data necessary for effective performance. Figure 3.13 presents the integrated data model for two business processes (i.e., the billing and human resources functions).

[Insert Figure 3.13 here]

In a service organization such as a consultancy firm, billing of clients is heavily dependent on tracking the actual person-hours put into providing service to a client. To effectively execute the client billing process, our database needs to capture data related to all employees who contributed time to client service and, at the same time, be able to tie these employees' efforts to a specific client. To further complicate matters, each employee may have a different billing rate for his or her time. To meet the needs of the billing process, we must be able to aggregate specific employees' time put into providing service to a client, each employee's billing rate, and sufficient information about the client to deliver the billing statement. Three entities are involved in the billing process: (1) EMPLOYEE, (2) CLIENT, and (3) WORK_COMPLETED. Note in Figure 3.13 that the three entities for the billing process are linked together on the right half of the diagram. The linkages allow us to pull together information related to the employees' hours worked on a specific client, their billing rates, and the contact address for sending the billing statement.

Service organizations are also interested in tracking employee work activities through the human resources process. The human resources process includes (among other activities) both payroll activities and employee education and development. To complete the payroll process, information is needed regarding work hours completed, pay rate, vacation time, sick days, and training time. Payroll activity information can be drawn from four entities (i.e., RELEASE_TIME, TRAINING_COMPLETED, EMPLOYEE, and WORK_COMPLETED) in order to aggregate the information necessary to determine the employee's pay rate, hours worked, hours in training, and hours used of allocated sick and vacation time.

Regarding employee education and development, the human resources department monitors training activities to assure the employee is receiving enough continuing education. At the same time, human resources also monitors the percentage of billable hours the employee has accumulated as a measure of job performance. To handle all of these activities, human resources needs to be able to link data related to completed work activities and training programs. This information can be drawn from three *entities* (i.e., EMPLOYEE, TRAINING_COMPLETED, and WORK_ COMPLETED) to determine a given employee's training coverage and percentage of billable hours.

Again, it is important to recognize that Figure 3.13 demonstrates only a small part of the overall enterprise model that would be required to integrate all information across an organization. The E-R diagram does effectively integrate the data required for the prescribed business processes. As other business processes are selected and integrated, the model will continue to expand through an explosion of entities and relationships.

Appendix 3B

Mapping an E-R Diagram to a Relational DBMS

In this chapter, we have discussed the development of E-R diagrams and the foundations for implementing well-constrained relational database models. It is now time to put these two concepts together. This process is referred to as mapping an E-R diagram into a logical database model—in this case a relational data model.

We introduce here a five-step process for specifying relations based on an E-R diagram. Based on the constraints we have discussed in this chapter, we will use this five-step process to develop a well-constrained relational database implementation. Follow along as we map the E-R diagram in Figure 3.13 (page 93) to the relational database schema in Figure 3.14.

1. *Create a separate relational table for each entity.*

This a logical starting point when mapping an E-R diagram into a relational database model. It is generally useful first to specify the database schema before proceeding to expansion of the relations to account for specific tuples. Notice that each of the entities in Figure 3.13 has become a relation in Figure 3.14. To complete the schema, however, steps 2 and 3 must also be completed.

[Insert Figure 3.14 here]

2. *Determine the primary key for each of the relations. The primary key must uniquely identify any row within the table.*

3. *Determine the attributes for each of the entities.*

Note in Figure 3.13 that a complete E-R diagram includes

specification of all attributes, including the key attribute. This eliminates the need to expend energy on this function during development of the relations. Rather, the focus is on step 2 and now becomes simply a manner of determining how to implement the prescribed key attribute within a relation. With a single attribute specified as the key, this is a very straightforward matching between the key attribute specified in the E-R diagram and the corresponding attribute in the relation (e.g., Employee_Number in the EMPLOYEE entity of Figure 3.13 and the EMPLOYEE relation in Figure 3.14). For a composite key, this is a little trickier—but not much. For a composite key, we can simply break it down into its component subattributes. For instance, in the implementation of the WORK_COMPLETED relation, Employee_No, Date, and Client_No would be three distinct attributes in the relation, but would also be defined as the key via a combination of the three. The completed *schema* is presented in Figure 3.14. Note the direct mapping between the entities and attributes in the E-R diagram and the relations and attributes respectively in the relational schema.

Review Question

How is a composite key implemented in a relational database model?

4. *Implement the relationships among the entities. This is accomplished by ensuring that the primary key in one table also exists as an attribute in every table (entity) for which there is a*

relationship specified in the entity-relationship diagram.

With the availability of the full E-R diagram, the mapping of the relationships in the diagram with the relationships embedded in the relational schema is again fairly straightforward. References to the key attributes in one entity are captured through the inclusion of a corresponding attribute in the other entity participating in the relationship. However, the dominance of 1:N relationships in our model simplifies this process. Let's take a quick look at how the different categories of relationships (i.e., cardinality constraints) affect the mapping to a relational schema.

- One-to-many (1:N or N:1) relationships are implemented by including the primary key of the "one" relationship as an attribute in the "many" relationship. This is the situation we have for all of the relationships in Figure 3.13. The linking between these relations in the schema are drawn in Figure 3.15. Note that Client_No in CLIENT and Employee_Number in EMPLOYEE provide the links to WORK_COMPLETED. Similarly, Employee_Number in EMPLOYEE provides links to TRAINING_ COMPLETED and RELEASE_TIME. The recursive relationship with EMPLOYEE is linked using Supervisor_No to identify the correct EMPLOYEE as the supervisor.

[Insert Figure 3.15 here]

- One-to-one (1:1) relationships are treated as a one-to-many relationship. But, to implement the one-to-one relationship, we must decide which of the entities is to be the "many" and which is to be the "one." To do this we might predict which of the "ones" might become a "many" in the future and make that the "many." If we can't decide, then either will do. For example, if at present one employee workday was sufficient to complete any client project, then a 1:1 relationship would exist between WORK_COMPLETED and CLIENT. Even in this situation we would still select the Client_No in CLIENT to establish the primary key (see Figure 3.15) in anticipation that in the future a client engagement might require more than one day to complete and more than one employee to complete (i.e., the formation of the many dimension shown in the relationship of Figure 3.13, page 93).

- Many-to-many (M:N) relationships are implemented by creating a new relation whose primary key is a composite of the primary keys of the relations to be linked. In our model we do not have any M:N relationships, but if we had not needed to record the Date and Hours in the WORK_COMPLETED entity, that entity would not have existed. Still, we would then need a relationship between the EMPLOYEE and CLIENT entities which would then be a M:N relationship. This creates problems because our relations cannot store multiple client numbers in a single EMPLOYEE tuple for all clients in which an employee provides services. Similarly, a single CLIENT tuple cannot store multiple employee numbers to record all employees working on an engagement. In that situation, we would have needed to develop a relation to link the EMPLOYEE and CLIENT relations (see Figure 3.16). This new relation would have a composite key consisting of Employee_Number from EMPLOYEE and Client_No from CLIENT—essentially the same as what we currently have with the composite key in the existing relation, WORK_COMPLETED (see Figure 3.15). Note that we wouldn't combine the columns, but rather just as we have done in the WORK_COMPLETED, TRAINING_COMPLETED, and RELEASE_TIME relations, the individual attributes making up the composite key remain independent in the corresponding relation.

Review Question

What is the difference in implementation of a one-to-many and a one-to-one relationship in a relational database model?

[Insert Figure 3.16 here]

Beyond concerns over meeting the constraint requirements for primary keys, we must also assure adherence to the referential integrity constraints. We identify the referential integrity constraints by locating the corresponding attribute in each relation that is linked via a relationship. We then determine which of the relations contain the tuple that if the reference attribute were deleted or changed would jeopardize the integrity of the database. In Figure 3.15 the referential integrity constraints are represented by arrows, with the destination of the arrow being the attribute requiring control for referential integrity. In other words, the attribute that is pointed to, if changed or deleted, could cause an attribute to have a nonmatching value at the source of the arrow. To ensure referential integrity, constraints should be put in place to assure Employee_Number is not altered or deleted for any EMPLOYEE until the referencing attribute values for the Employee_No attributes in WORK_COMPLETED, TRAINING_COMPLETED, and RELEASE_TIME have first been corrected. Likewise, a similar constraint should be placed on Client_No in CLIENT until Client_No has been corrected in WORK_COMPLETED.

5. *Determine the attributes, if any, for each of the relationship tables.*

Again, in the extended version of the E-R diagram, the attributes map directly over to the relations. The implementation of the schema is shown in Figure 3.17.

[Insert Figure 3.17 here]

REVIEW QUESTIONS

RQ3-1 What business events are typically encountered by a merchandising firm?

RQ3-2 How do the business events for a service firm differ from those of a merchandising firm? How are they similar for the two firms?

RQ3-3 How are event-driven systems different from traditional transaction processing systems?

RQ3-4 What is meant by the idea of "storing data at the event level"?

RQ3-5 Why is it important to capture the who, what, where, and when in describing business events?

RQ3-6 a. What is file management?

b. How are the applications-based file and database approaches to data management the same? How are they different?

c. What are the relative advantages of the database approach?

RQ3-7 What do the concepts of data warehousing and data mining mean?

RQ3-8 a. What is an entity?

b. What is an attribute?

c. What is a relationship?

d. What is a key attribute?

RQ3-9 Why is it preferable to use a numeric-based attribute as the key attribute?

RQ3-10 Why is it important that you identify all of the important relationships when developing an entity-relationship (E-R) diagram?

RQ3-11 What are the relative advantages of the relational and object-oriented database models (Technical Insight 3.3)?

RQ3-12 a. What is a relation?

b. What is a tuple?

c. What is an attribute in a relational data model?

d. What is referential integrity?

RQ3-13 Compare and contrast the data structures for data stored in a file and data stored in a relational table.

RQ3-14 (Appendix A) What is different about a recursive relationship in comparison to other relationships in a data model?

RQ3-15 (Appendix A) What is different about the information provided through cardinality constraints versus participation constraints?

RQ3-16 What is the importance of an E-R diagram in facilitating event-driven systems and the integration of data between business processes?

RQ3-17 (Appendix B) How is a composite key implemented in a relational database model?

RQ3-18 (Appendix B) What is the difference in implementation of a one-to-many and a one-to-one relationship in a relational database model?

DISCUSSION QUESTIONS

DQ3-1 Using the descriptions provided in Figure 3.4 (page 74), identify the key event data you would want to capture based on the 4 *W's* (who, what, where, and when).

DQ3-2 "The database approach to data management is the only approach that makes sense for most organizations in today's economic and technical environment." Do you agree? Discuss fully.

DQ3-3 "Our company's database contains some very sensitive information about our customers. Shouldn't we keep that in a separate file so that those who shouldn't have access to it (like the payroll supervisor and the receptionist) can't look through it?" Discuss.

DQ3-4 Examine Figures 3.18 (page 101) and 3.19 (page 102). Using the combination of the E-R diagram and the schema, identify each of the referential integrity constraints that should be considered. Explain why each is necessary.

[Insert Figure 3.18 here]

[Insert Figure 3.19 here]

DQ3-5 (Appendix A) Examine Figure 3.18 and the five relationships. Determine the cardinality constraints for each of the relationships. Be prepared to defend the rationale for your selection.

DQ3-6 (Appendix A) Examine Figure 3.18 and the five relationships. Determine the participation constraints for each of the relationships.

Be prepared to defend the rationale for your selection.

PROBLEMS

Notes regarding Problems 1 through 5: *These problems should be completed with a database software package, such as Microsoft Access. For Problems 1 through 3, you may use data that you (or your instructor) downloaded from a database. Problem 4 provides an alternative to Problems 1 through 3 by using the database structure and sample data from Figure 3.19 (page 102). This problem may also be completed using the software of your choosing.*

P3-1 Before starting this problem, you should consult the customer master file record layout in Figure 3.6 (page 76).

REQUIRED: Using the database software indicated by your instructor:

a. Create the "structure" for the records in the customer file. Use Figure 3.6 as a general guide to the data elements to be included in the customer records. However, observe the following specific requirements:

(1) Devise your own coding scheme for the "customer number."

(2) For the customer address, provide three separate fields, one each for street address, state, and ZIP code.

(3) Provide for two additional data elements that are not shown

in Figure 3.6 (because they normally would be accessed from other files)—open sales orders and accounts receivable balance.

b. If the software package supports a function to design input screens, create the screen format to be used for entering customer data.

c. Create hypothetical customer records and key the data into the database. The only design constraint is to use a variety of names, street addresses, states/ZIP codes, open sales order amounts, accounts receivable balances, and credit limits. (The number of records will be indicated by your instructor.)

d. Obtain a printout of the database records.

P3-2 **NOTE:** This problem is a continuation of Problem 1.

REQUIRED:

a. "Search" the database for all customers with a ZIP code of ZZZZZ (choose a code that is common to at least two, but not to all, of your customers). Obtain a printout of your search algorithm and a list of customers whose records met the search parameter.

b. "Sort" the database in the *descending* order of credit limit amounts. Obtain both a printout of your sort algorithm and the sorted list of customers.

c. Create a "Customer Status Report" (the report title). Observe the following specific requirements:

(1) Provide column headings, in left-to-right order, for customer name, credit limit, accounts receivable balance, and open orders.

(2) For each state, print subtotals of the accounts receivable balance and open orders columns.

P3-3 **NOTE:** This problem is a continuation of Problem 1.

REQUIRED:

a. Write a "program" to enter customer order *amounts* into the system and to have the system either warn the user if the new order places the customer over his or her credit limit or advise the user if the credit limit is not exceeded. Store the program in the system, and obtain a hardcopy printout of the program.

b. Test the program developed in (a) by entering the amounts of customer order transactions (use a variety of order amounts and different customers, such that you test all possible combinations of variables involved in the credit-checking algorithm). (The number of order transactions will be indicated by your instructor.) Obtain hardcopy evidence of the results of your testing.

P3-4 Using the database structure and sample data in Figure 3.19 as a starting point (rather than Figure 3.6), complete the requirements of

Problems 1 through 3 (or whatever portions of those problems your instructor may indicate).

P3-5 Use the database structure and sample data in Figure 3.19 to:

a. Combine the tables to obtain a complete record of the order and shipment. Obtain both a printout of the algorithm(s) used to combine the tables and the list of these records.

b. Select the inventory items for which there is *no* order. Obtain both a printout of the algorithm(s) used to select the items and the list of the selected records.

c. Select those orders that have not yet been shipped (i.e., open orders). Obtain both a printout of the algorithm(s) used to select the open orders and the list of the selected records.

d. Calculate the total value (price) of the inventory items that are on hand. Sort the items in descending order of value. Obtain both a printout of the algorithm(s) used to perform the calculations and to sort the records, and a list of the sorted records.

P3-6 This problem asks you to research the literature for controls that apply to database management software.

REQUIRED: Develop a paper that discusses control plans for single user PC database management systems (Microsoft Access or another of your choosing). Your paper should explain how each plan operates (with illustrations where appropriate) and how the plan helps to achieve the *information process control goals* discussed in Chapter 8 (see Table 8.1 on page 250). (The number of pages will be indicated by your instructor.) *Note:* Limit yourself to controls that apply only to database application software. Do *not* discuss PC pervasive control plans.

P3-7 Write a short paper describing the database underlying a small company enterprise system (e.g., Quickbooks®, Peachtree®, MYOB®, or another you have access to).

a. Does it appear to be integrated? When you change an item of data in one application, does it carry through to others? (For example, if a customer's billing address is changed, do all existing invoices reflect the change?)

b. How easy is it to set up the data relationships for the database?

c. Can you view the schema? Are subschemas supported?

d. Are there any controls in place to ensure that data relationships make sense? (For example, is referential integrity supported?)

P3-8 **REQUIRED:** Develop an entity-relationship diagram of the Information System that supports the purchasing process of Proware Company described below. Include the cardinality constraints.

The individual departments of Proware Company refer to various vendor catalogs when they need to purchase items. They then complete a purchase request form over the company intranet for each vendor. Once completed, the form is forwarded to the Purchasing department, where it is validated and checked against the department's budget to ensure there are still funds available in its supply budget. Each form is assigned a unique serial number, referred to as the PO number. Purchasing transmits the validated form to the vendor, or faxes it if the vendor is not online.

When the vendor fills the order, it sends an invoice to purchasing and enclose a copy of the invoice with the shipment when it is delivered to the department. The department verifies that the contents match the PO, attaches a note approving payment, and forwards the approved invoice to purchasing. An invoice may only be partially approved, if an item was missing or incorrect. A second payment authorization may be submitted at a later time when the correct item is received.

Each week purchasing generates vendor checks based on the approved authorizations from departments, and maintains a copy of the check in the computer file. Vendors may be paid for multiple orders (e.g. for several departments) in any given week.

Each month, purchasing generates a budget report for each department, which itemizes the amount paid for each invoice, the amount allocated for outstanding purchase orders, and the remaining available funds for the department.

Gelinas 3-66

P3-9 **REQUIRED:** Develop an entity-relationship diagram of the information ssystem that supports the hiring process of Proware Company described below. Include cardinality and participation constraints.

When a manager needs to hire an employee, he or she first completes an Employee Requistion form over the company intranet, which indicates the position open, the rate of pay, hours, skills needed, and whether the requisition is for a replacement or additional employee.

Once submitted, Human Resources recruits as needed to fill the position. When applications arrive, Human Resources is responsible for prescreening the applicants. Anyone who appears suitable is scheduled for an interview with the hiring manager. The interview date and time is noted on the application, and forwarded to the hiring manager.

The hiring manager completes an interview form after each interview and attaches it to the application. When all of the interviews are complete, the hiring manager gives the name of the top candidate to Human Resources, who prepares an offer letter to be sent to the applicant. The applicant signs the letter to indicate acceptance and returns it to Human Resources. An employee file for the newest member of Proware is created, and the original application, the interview form, and the offer letter are included in it.

BOXES

[Start TECHNOLOGY INSIGHT 3.1 box here]

TECHNOLOGY INSIGHT 3.1

Database Management Systems (DBMS)

A *database management system (DBMS)* is a set of integrated programs designed to simplify the tasks of creating, accessing, and managing a database. The DBMS performs several functions, such as:

defining the data.

defining the relationships among data (e.g., whether the data structure is *relational* or *object-oriented*).

mapping each user's view of the data (through *subschema* → *schema*).

In the language of DBMS, a **schema** is a complete description of the configuration of record types and data items and the relationships among them. The schema defines the *logical* structure of the database. The schema, therefore, defines the organizational view of the data.

A **subschema** is a description of a *portion* of a schema. The DBMS maps each user's view of the data from subschemas to the schema. In this way the DBMS provides flexibility in identifying and selecting records. Each of the many database users may want to access records in his or her own way. For example, the accounts receivable manager may want to access customer records by invoice number, whereas a marketing manager may want to access the customer records by geographic location. The figure below portrays the schema-subschema relationship.

[Insert UNF-p.78-2 here]

A chief advantage of a DBMS is that it contains a **query language**, which is a language much like ordinary language. A query language is used to access a database and to produce inquiry reports. These languages allow a nontechnical user to bypass the programmer and to access the database directly. Deriving data from the database using a query does not replace applications programs, which are still required to perform routine data processing tasks. However, when information is needed quickly, or when a manager wishes to "browse" through the database, combining data in unique ways, the query facility of a DBMS is a vast improvement over the traditional method of requesting that a program be written to generate a report.

A DBMS normally contains a number of security controls to protect the data from access by unauthorized users as well as from accidental or deliberate alteration or destruction. A DBMS also contains routines for ensuring that the data can be simultaneously shared by multiple users.

[End TECHNOLOGY INSIGHT 3.1 box here]

[Start TECHNOLOGY INSIGHT 3.2 box here]

TECHNOLOGY INSIGHT 3.2

Enterprise Systems

Enterprise systems are integrated software packages designed to provide complete integration of an organization's business information processing systems and all related data. These systems are based on event-driven systems concepts, which include the capturing of business data for supporting decision making, as well as integration of the underlying data to facilitate access and ad hoc analysis.

A number of enterprise systems are commercially available. The dominant player is System Application Products (SAP) R/3, which commands the largest percentage of the Fortune 500 market. Several other products are available and have established large customer bases—often through establishing excellence in certain market niches. These other vendors include JD Edwards, PeopleSoft, and Oracle. While these products are designed to offer integration of everything from accounting and human resources to manufacturing and sales staff logistics, products designed to focus on specific industries are also appearing in the marketplace. These systems are capable of extracting data from both enterprise systems' data sources and legacy systems that may still exist within an organization (or subsidiary of the organization). They can also support a Web interface to allow business partners to initiate business events directly.

Originally, the implementation of enterprise systems was predominantly targeted at large multinational manufacturers such as General Motors, IBM, and General Mills. This strategy aimed where benefits would be expected to be the greatest, in that large multilocation and multidivision companies often present the greatest challenges to managers who *mine* data from corporate databases to improve overall organizational decision making. Enterprise systems allow companies to standardize systems across multiple locations and multiple divisions in order to link data in a consistent fashion and provide organization-wide accessibility.

Large enterprises were the predominant implementers of enterprise systems, but largely due to the costs of implementation. These systems typically took a year or more to implement at a cost of up to hundreds of millions of dollars, necessitating a similarly significant return in benefits. As advances in technology underlying these systems has evolved, small and medium sized enterprises (SMEs) have driven the new implementation base. This shift has happened primarily due to two drivers: (1) the move towards *web-browser* driven systems that reduce the expense of both the technology and training; and (2) the emergence of *application service providers (ASPs)* that implement enterprise systems and then lease out use of the enterprise system to several other companies. In other words, the ASP runs the hardware and software for the company that wants its data integrated via an enterprise system, and the company saves money by essentially sharing the costs of the enterprise system implementation and maintenance with several other companies that also use the same ASP. ASPs are discussed in greater detail in Chapter 7 of the text.

[End TECHNOLOGY INSIGHT 3.2 box here]

[Start TECHNOLOGY INSIGHT 3.3 box here]

TECHNOLOGY INSIGHT 3.3

Object-Oriented Database Model

In an **object-oriented database model**, both simple and complex objects can be stored through use of abstract data types, inheritance, and encapsulation. Let's explain each of these concepts. The relational model focuses on the storage of text-based data. In *object-oriented* data models, these simple text-based data can be supplanted by non-text objects. For instance, storage of video clips or pictures could become attribute values in an object-oriented database. The use of abstract data types allows the user to define the data that will be stored in the database rather than having limitations placed during the database development process. Inheritance allows object subclasses of an object superclass (the equivalent to an entity in a relational database) to assume the same properties or attributes (attribute means the same in object-oriented terminology as it does in relational) as the object superclass, or in other words to inherit the attributes. The following figure demonstrates such an inheritance hierarchy with the superclass EMPLOYEE providing the same set of attributes to both subclasses—MANAGER and ADMIN_STAFF. In other words, every MANAGER would have a Name, Address, and Employee_No (as would every ADMIN_STAFF). Note that an object is drawn using a rectangle with rounded corners and is divided into three parts: the object name, the attributes, and any encapsulated methods (from top to bottom, respectively).

[Insert UNF-p.87-5 here]

Encapsulation is the biggest difference in *object-oriented database models.* Encapsulation refers to the ability to build into the database model, as part of an object's definition, programmed procedures that change that object's value (i.e., any of the attribute values). At the same time, no other object can change the value of a given object, as this is controlled within each object. On the other hand, part of the encapsulation may be the querying of information from another object in order to have sufficient data by which to perform encapsulated operations.

Users usually don't see much difference. Other than encapsulation, other characteristics of object-oriented models could be integrated into relational data models and are increasingly being integrated in commercial packages. The most successful integration tends to occur within relational models where attributes can be redefined to handle more complex object data.

[End TECHNOLOGY INSIGHT 3.3 box here]

4

E-BUSINESS

When speaking about innovative electronic business (e-business) organizations, we normally think of web pioneers such as Amazon.com, E*TRADE, and eBay.[1] Yet, e-business is radically changing the way many so-called brick-and-mortar companies (i.e., traditional organizations with extensive sales staffs and internally controlled business processes) conduct operations in the current business environment. Caterpillar Incorporated is typical of such evolving organizations. The 75-year-old manufacturer of construction and farming equipment is radically changing its supply-chain operations through a Web-based makeover. This initiative will allow Caterpillar's customers to order and configure heavy machinery and related products through an Internet connection. In order to facilitate timely fulfillment of the many combinations of equipment that may be ordered, Caterpillar is also opening up access to key sales and business data for use by its suppliers. These suppliers work closely with Caterpillar to ensure parts and materials are available on an as-needed basis without interruptions on assembly lines.

[1] A primary source for this vignette was Marc L. Songini, "Caterpillar Moves to Revamp Supply-Chain Operations via the Web," *Computerworld Online* (October 11, 2000).

Why would Caterpillar make such a radical change? Well, for starters, there is the anticipated savings of $100 million in costs during the first year the system is fully in place. Second, there is the newly created ability to allow customers actually to customize products and to provide them with build-to-order models not previously available.

Synopsis

This chapter introduces the concept of e-business and explores how communications technology is revolutionizing the way individuals and organizations conduct business. As organizations venture down this path, driving their business processes with electronic communications, the trail of paper including invoices, check payments, and so forth quickly disappears. E-business captures business event data at the connection with a customer or supplier. Enterprise systems store data and make it readily accessible to all who need it. The evolution to e-business had been a rather slow process before the advent of the Internet, which has switched the evolution into high gear. As you study this chapter, you will learn about the underlying technologies that facilitate e-business, the complexities of displacing paper records with electronic ones, the challenges faced in overcoming differences in technology usage and Information Systems design in order to link two companies' computer systems together, and finally the actions that must be taken to ensure that e-business conducted over the Internet is secure. All of these technologies, along with the flexible processes they allow to exist, are fundamental to providing companies like Caterpillar with the capability to implement new streamlined processes and to create build-to-order service for its customers.

LEARNING OBJECTIVES

- To describe and analyze the major approaches used to transfer electronic data during business event data processing
- To explain the complexities that are introduced as electronic document management moves us steadily toward the paperless office
- To evaluate the complexities surrounding electronic data interchange that are introduced when linking two different organizations' computer systems for joint business event data processing
- To explain the challenges faced by organizations when they pursue direct business links with customers via the Internet
- To be able to use business advantages gained through effective facilitation of e-business

Introduction

The power of computers in transforming society is perhaps most obvious today in the way communications have changed. Our society has evolved from one that relied on face-to-face communication, to one in which phones became the primary medium, to today's society that is increasingly dependent on e-mail and instant messages. In essence, the richness of older media has been sacrificed for efficiency and effectiveness. In other words, the phone took away the ability to detect emotions through an individualappearance, and e-mail took away the ability to detect emotions through voice inflection.

The Internet expanded the impact on society since it can substitute for such a wide range of personal and commercial interaction. The power of the Internet to support the sales and marketing of products efficiently has led to incredible levels of Web activity to support *electronic commerce (e-commerce)*. **E-commerce** is a commonly used term that describes the business events associated with the Order-to-Cash and Purchase-to-Pay business processes, which encompass electronically ordering goods and services, and often the associated electronic payments. Although frequently used interchangeably with e-business, e-commerce is really only one part of what e-business encompasses. As noted in Chapter 1, *e-business* is the involvement of two (or more) individuals and/or organizations in the completion of electronically based business events (i.e., the partial or complete elimination of paper documentation and human intervention during business processes in favor of more efficient electronically based communication). These electronically based business events entail the interconnection of the underlying back-office processes of both organizations. Pricewaterhouse Coopers was one of the first firms to use the term e-business to broaden the narrower view of e-commerce as support of the sales process. In 1999, the firm's Web site included a statement in its discussion of e-business that recommended looking beyond the marketing aspects of a firm to see that e-business involves "optimizing business processes, enhancing human capital, harnessing technology, and managing risk and compliance." We use the term "e-business" to refer to any interorganizational business activities conducted by electronic means, including e-commerce. We will sometimes use the term e-commerce when specifically discussing Internet-enabled sales support.

Review Question

Briefly define e-business and e-commerce. How are they related?

A by-product of e-business is often the elimination of the staff that would normally serve as the intermediary between the two parties to the business event. In e-commerce, bypassing the sales staff speeds up the business event by eliminating the interaction with a salesperson, establishing a direct and therefore immediate linkage to the vendor's own Information System (which for many organizations participating in e-business today would be their enterprise system), and facilitating the electronic transfer of funds for immediate payment. The business event is completed more quickly. Additionally, the purchaser may electronically solicit pricing and quickly determine the best priceprice efficiency as well. Often, the computer, eliminating any waste of a purchaser's time on such activities, does the price checking automatically.

It is not just big organizations that are using such technologies to speed up a process. For instance, your favorite pizza joint or sandwich shop may very well accept e-mail or fax ordering—basically allowing you to avoid being put on hold when you place your order and avoid the risk of the phone answerer getting the wrong ingredients on your pizza or sandwich. The Domino's Pizza chain allows Internet ordering in some markets. You simply enter the order yourself—reducing the business's need for people to answer the phones and take orders.

With the Internet, many more organizations now have the opportunity to reach customers directly through electronic communication. The potential of this distribution channel has led to the explosion of e-business over the Internet. In this chapter, we will explore a variety of technologies that enable e-business. We will also learn about the various forms of e-business that are used by organizations in today's business environment.

One final note before we proceed. Throughout this text we highlight the discussion of e-business as it relates to various business processes, controls, and systems development issues. Since this chapter is specifically on e-business, we will reserve use of the e-business icon to those places in the chapter where a particularly critical e-business technology or concept is discussed.

The Changing World of Business Processing

For centuries, the basic manner in which commerce transpired changed very little. In the past, a merchant would meet with a customer or another merchant and form an agreement to provide goods to customers in exchange for cash or other goods and services. The merchant would then record these exchanges in books of accounts, and periodically consolidate the entries recorded in the books to determine how much various individuals owed the merchant, how much the merchant owed other people, and the excess cash and assets that the merchant owned.

Over the past three decades, the relative change in business practice has been exponential. We have seen cottage industries springing up on the *Internet* where there are no personal contacts and face-to-face negotiations. We also see *online* catalogs that can be viewed through an *Internet browser* and where orders can immediately be placed and paid for over the Internet. Of course, the bookkeeping functions may be done much the same as the ancient merchant did them, but more likely the system will automatically trigger collection from the credit card company, automatically record the business event in the electronic database, and automatically update all of the related accounts. Indeed, many companies are using web development tools from their enterprise system vendors to build Web sites that from day one are linked into the enterprise system's processing and database.

While it may sometimes appear that we have switched from an old way of doing commerce to a brand new way, both methods are actually used by many organizations. The evolution of information technology has simply provided for alternative channels supporting business processes and business event data processing that enable some organizations to become more efficient and effective by altering the traditional means by which they have done business. To understand fully how technology can enable an organization to *reengineer* its business processes and more effectively enter into commerce activities, you first must have a solid understanding of how business event data processing can be completed. Once you understand how processing is done, then the exploration of the technologies that enable improved efficiencies in business event data processing will be more meaningful.

In this chapter, we first examine the evolution of business event data processing. Doing so will help you to understand how we got where we are and to appreciate different stages of the e-business evolution—including many organizations that still operate using essentially the same processes used three or four decades ago! We might well view this latter method as a pre–e-business stage.

Automating Manual Systems

Ever since the earliest days of business, when fairly primitive manual approaches were the only available information systems, the cheapest and most efficient way to do data processing on large volumes of similar business event data was to aggregate (i.e., batch) several events together and then periodically complete the processing on all of the event data at once. The **periodic mode** is the processing mode in which there is a delay between the various data processing steps. Although technically not the same, the *periodic mode* is heavily dependent on the use of *batch processing,* and the two terms are often used interchangeably. **Batch processing** is the aggregation of several business events over some period of time with the subsequent processing of these data as a group by the information system.

Review Question

Explain the relationship between the periodic mode and batch processing.

Almost all manual systems use the *periodic mode.* In a computerized environment, the easiest approach to automating some business processes has been to simply mirror analogous manual batch processing systems.

Batch processing systems typically require four basic subprocesses to be completed before event data is converted into informational reports that can be used by decision makers. Follow along with Figure 4.1 (page 110)as we explain how each of these four subprocesses are typically completed.

[Insert Figure 4.1 here]

- *Business event occurs:* At the point of occurrence for the business event, the information for the event is recorded on a source document (the activities of the sales department in Figure 4.1). For example, if you think of one of the small businesses you might frequent, such as a used books and CDs shop, they may often have you bring the books and CDs you wish to purchase to a clerk at the front of the store. The clerk then writes down a description of the items purchased on a sales slip (prepared in duplicate) and totals the sale. He or she returns one copy to you (often a white copy) and stuffs the other copy (generally a yellow or pink copy) into a drawer of sales receipts.
- *Record business event data:* A batch of source documents is transferred to a data entry clerk (in the data processing department in Figure 4.1) who takes the information from the source documents and enters the data in a computerized format. The business event data are usually entered using an **offline** device (i.e., one that is not directly connected to the processing

computer). The resulting computerized format becomes the event data store. In our used books and CDs store, the owner-manager or the employee closing up at the end of the day may take responsibility for keying all of the sales slips into a personal computer for storage on a disk. The personal computer becomes simply a data-entry device for keying in the sales data. Upon completing the entry, the copies of the sales receipts are clipped together and stored in a file for possible future reference.

- *Update master data:* After all of the data have been entered into the system, the data are then processed, and any calculations and summarizations completed (represented by the sales processing update symbol in Figure 4.1). This information is used to update the master data. In the sales example, this might include taking prior inventory totals and subtracting the items sold to derive the new inventory levels. The new inventory levels are accordingly written as the newly updated master data. The sales event data would also be stored in a more permanent data store. It would not be uncommon for the owner-manager of our used books and CDs store to either take the data stores home and process it on a computer at home, or perhaps take the information to a public accountant for processing.
- *Generate outputs:* After all of the calculations have been completed and the data have been updated, the system

periodically generates the applicable reports (the report generator program in Figure 4.1). For our used books and CDs store, this might include such documents as a sales report and an inventory update report. For our small store, both reports would probably go to the owner-manager.

Review Question

List and describe the four basic subprocesses completed in processing business event data using batch processing.

Note that between each step there is a time delay before the next step occurs. We might think of this form of automated system as a *pure* periodic system in that the entire process uses a *periodic mode* for processing. For instance, in our used books and CDs store, the sales documents are collected for the day before being passed on for keying. After keying, the sales data are held until the data can be transferred to the location and person where the data can be used to update the master data. After the data are updated each day, the reports may still not be generated until later—perhaps on a weekly or monthly basis.

A disadvantage of *periodic mode* systems is that the only time the master data are up to date is right after the processing has been completed. As soon as the next business event occurs, the master data are no longer up to date. As a result, there is little reason to provide a query capability (as discussed in Chapter 3) for data that are used in a *periodic mode* system. Usually, systems users will simply get a copy of the reports generated at the end of a processing run and use this information to make their decisions until the next processing run and a new set of reports is available. Only in rare situations will a query capability be provided, and then only to eliminate the needless printing of reports for occasional users of the information generated by the system.

Online Transaction Entry (OLTE)

Information technology improvements have provided a low-cost means for improving the efficiency of these traditional automated equivalents to manual systems. The most prevalent change has been the increasing use of *online transaction entry* to reduce redundancies in pure *periodic mode* processing (see Figure 4.2). In an **online transaction entry (OLTE)** system, use of data entry devices allows business event data to be entered directly into the Information System at the time and place that the business event occurs. These systems merge the traditional subprocesses of *business event occurs* (which includes completion of the source document) and *record business event data* into a single operation. At the point of the business event, a computer input device is used to enter the event data into the data entry system rather than onto a source document. Generally, the system automatically generates prices as the computer retrieves data from the system data stores. Such a system is considered **online** because the data entry device is connected to the processing computer. The input system usually also services a printer that then prints document copies to fill the still-needed role of source documents. As business events occur, the related data are usually accumulated on disk.

[Insert Figure 4.2 here]

If we go back to our used books and CDs store scenario, it may be that you prefer to buy your books and CDs at one of the chain stores such as those found in shopping malls. When you take your books and CDs to the clerk at the counter in these types of stores, the clerk generally keys the purchase straight into the cash register. As noted in Figure 4.2, what is occurring at this point is that the sales items are being entered into a computer that is recording a log of the sales event, retrieving price list information, and generating duplicate copies of the sales receipt. One copy of the sales receipt is given to you (the customer), and the other is placed in the cash register drawer (for filing in the audit file). Note the differences between Figures 4.1 and 4.2. The manual recording process (in Figure 4.1) by the sales clerk becomes a computer entry process (in Figure 4.2), and the record input process in Figure 4.1 becomes part of process sales in Figure 4.2. Other than these changes, the two flowcharts are the same.

The use of OLTE eliminates the need to have one person enter business event data on a source document and then have a second person perform the data entry to convert the business event data to a computer-ready form. In an OLTE system, one person performs both operations. In many systems, this data entry will be completed using *bar code readers* or *scanners.* The use of such technologies eliminates the human error that can result from entering data manually. Thus, in many OLTE systems the only human impact on the accuracy of the input data is the necessity to scan items properly into the system. Various control procedures that assure data accuracy are discussed in detail in Chapter 9.

It should be noted that the processing of the data in Figure 4.2 is still completed on a batch of event data at a later point in time. In the case of many systems in use by businesses today, sales event data is aggregated by cash register terminals for the entire day; and then, after the store has closed, the data is electronically transferred to the computer system where the business event data is processed. This process is reflected in Figure 4.2 by the communications line connecting the sales log in the sales department with the program procedures in data processing. The processing is completed overnight (note the reference to third shift in the column heading for data processing) while all stores in a region are closed, and updated reports are periodically generated to reflect the sales event updates to the master data.

Note here that the use of electronic communication technology does not change the traditional periodic approach, but rather makes the approach much more efficient. Thus, we encounter one of the first steps in the evolution toward e-business systems.

Periodic mode systems had long been the most common method for completing business event data processing, but in the last decade, they have become much less common for most activities. However, for some applications, periodic mode processing is almost always the preferred approach. For instance, payroll systems are a natural match with the batching of business event data, since all employees are generally paid on a periodic basis and all at the same time. It is almost unrealistic to think that such an application will eventually be processed using systems other than periodic mode.

Review Question

Explain how the use of online transaction entry (OLTE) can increase efficiency when using batch processing.

Online Real-Time (OLRT) Processing

Among the many clichés that one hears in today's harried business environment is the phrase "time is money." While a cliché by its nature is worn out, this one is quite descriptive of the current demands on Information Systems. Traditional periodic mode systems that provide information primarily through periodic reports that are hours, days, or weeks out of date can put an organization's decision makers at a disadvantage if its competitors are using up-to-date information to make the same decisions (e.g., recall the importance placed on *timeliness* and *relevance* in Chapter 1). The pressures for timely information flows coupled with significant advances in available information technologies led to a rapid migration towards *online real-time* systems. **Online real-time (OLRT)** systems gather business event data at the time of occurrence, update the master data almost instantaneously, and provide the results arising from the business event within a very short time—i.e., in *real-time.* OLRT systems complete all stages of business event data processing in *immediate mode.* **Immediate mode** is the data processing mode in which there is little or no delay between any two data processing steps (as opposed to *periodic mode,* in which there is a significant delay between two or more data processing steps).

Review Question

Explain the relationship between online real-time (OLRT) and immediate mode processing.

OLRT systems typically require three basic subprocesses to be completed before an event is converted into information that can be used by decision makers. Figure 4.3 illustrates each of these subprocesses.

[Insert Figure 4.3 here]

- *Business event occurrence and recording of event data:* At the time of the business event, related data are entered directly into the system. Source documents are almost never used, as they significantly slow the process and remove some of the advantages of nonredundant data entry. Notice that the data entry process where the sale is entered into the system is the same as in Figure 4.2 (other than the absence of an audit file). This process is consistent with the use of *online transaction entry* (OLTE) for OLRT systems.
- *Update master data:* Each business event entered into the system is processed individually and any calculations and summarizations completed. This information is then used to update the master data. Note in Figure 4.3 that the processing is now being done on-site where the sales event data are entered.[2] Because each business event is processed independently and immediately, the master data at any given time will be within seconds of being up to date. When your books and CDs store is entering your information into the computer, it may be using an OLRT system if it is important to the store to know whether a given book or CD title is in stock at a given time—perhaps to answer a customer's question.
- *Generate reports and support queries:* It is neither practical nor

desirable that reports be generated after each business event is recorded and master data have been updated. Typically, applicable reports are generated by the system on a periodic basis. At the same time, however, these reports are usually instantaneously available through access to the system on an as-needed basis, as demonstrated in Figure 4.3 with the communications links to the sales and inventory managers. One of the main advantages provided by many OLRT systems is an ability to check the current status of master data items at any given time. In the books and CDs store, it would allow the sales staff to check quickly whether a given book or CD is in stock. In many cases, rather than using pre-specified reports that may not necessarily provide information that decision makers need, these Information Systems users use a query language (as discussed in Chapter 3) to create unique reports dynamically that provide the one-time information they need to make key decisions. For instance, the store manager may want to run a report on the inventory stock for the top-ten selling CDs and books.

[2] This is one method of accomplishing *OLRT* that uses expensive, continuous direct communications to a remotely located central computer. Many organizations use a distributed processing mode that places the computer locally to avoid the costs associated with the continuous communications line; however, as in the case

shown here, the need to process information centrally for multiple locations may warrant the communications line costs of continuous direct communication.

Review Question

List and describe the three basic subprocesses completed in processing business event data using online real-time processing.

It was noted previously that OLTE systems are also increasingly used with systems that primarily use the *periodic mode.* While the data entry performed in all OLTE systems is essentially the same, the mode of processing may vary. While a pure periodic mode system still processes business event data in batches, an OLRT system using OLTE processes each recorded business event in real time. In a *real-time* system, business event data cannot be aggregated on a local computer to be transferred later to the data processing center. Rather, each business event must be communicated for processing at the time the event occurs. This results in a more expensive approach to OLTE. In essence, rather than creating a temporary electronic communications connection to download data to the data processing center, an OLRT system generally requires a continuous electronic communication connection, usually necessitating the use of some form of *network.* This arrangement will be addressed later in this chapter.

It should be noted here that automated systems that model manual systems and OLRT systems are the two extremes in business event data processing. The systems that mimic manual systems are what we might term pure *periodic mode* systems in that there is a delay between every step of the processing. On the other hand, OLRT systems represent pure *immediate mode* systems in that there is little or no delay between any steps in the processing. We note these as the extremes because many systems lie somewhere between these two extremes, exhibiting a mix of *periodic* and *immediate mode* processes at various stages. For example, OLTE used with batch processing results in an immediate mode approach for combining the business event occurrence and record event data steps, while periodic mode processing might be used for the remainder of the steps.

Online Transaction Processing (OLTP)

In an effort to reduce both the expense and delay of communicating business event data over what are sometimes great distances to complete business event data processing in real time, many entities are turning to **online transaction processing (OLTP)** systems. An OLTP system is a real-time system that performs all or part of the processing activities at the user's location. These systems use business event data processing machines that have the capability to manage data, run applications, and control communications with the central computer and data stores. By performing most of the processing at the user's location, delays caused from electronic communications between the user and the central computer are reduced or eliminated (see Figure 4.4), as is the cost associated with communicating to the central location *during* the processing of the business event. Only the results need be communicated. Two common applications for these systems have been automatic teller machines (ATMs) and computerized reservation systems. Note in Figure 4.4 that the electronic communication network in an OLTP system becomes even more complex as processing occurs at the user's end, but then data must be updated at all computers. For instance, in the case of an ATM, once an individual has withdrawn money from his or her account, the system needs to update the balance at all ATMs before additional withdrawals may be made.

[Insert Figure 4.4 here]

Many banks have only recently converted to OLTP technology. Note that in an OLTP system, the immediate updating of balances at the central location and the user locations is done with shadow data (e.g., copies of the master data used for real-time processing) which are duplicated at each site, but for control purposes, the actual master data are usually updated once a day using batch processing.

While *immediate mode*-dominated systems are becoming the most prevalent method for new business event data processing applications, they are not necessarily the end-all solution for all applications. Both periodic mode and immediate mode approaches have distinctive characteristics that make each a preferable option for certain types of applications. If periodic processing were used for ATM processing, for example, a person might withdraw the entire balance from his or her account multiple times before the system processed the event data and updated the accounts—a significant losing proposition for a bank. Clearly, any given application should be matched with the best or most applicable processing method.

Review Question

How does the use of online transaction processing (OLTP) improve the timeliness of online real-time processing?

Advances in Electronic Processing and Communication

The key enabler of the transition from primarily periodic mode systems to primarily immediate mode systems has been communications technology. Similarly, communications technology has enhanced many of the remaining periodic mode systems through enabled approaches such as online transaction entry (OLTE). Many important recent advances have relied on image-based technologies. These technologies are discussed in this section as a precursor to exploring their application in early stage e-business systems.

Communications-based systems that facilitate the processing, storage, and management of image-based data require the use of several related technologies. First are technologies that facilitate the effective capturing of data to support business information processing through the use of imaging technology. Second are communications-based systems that facilitate the storage and distribution of image-based data used in business processing and managerial decision making. Third, data communications networks are necessary for effective transmission and routing of data from the point of recording and storage to the processes or users needing the data. In this part of the chapter we take a brief look at these key communications technologies.

Automated Data Entry

While there are a variety of methods for electronic data capturing, the interest here is in image-based technologies. Increasingly, optical-based technologies eliminate the need to key in data (a major source of data entry error) as well as voluminous files of paper documents by maintaining electronic copies.

[Insert UNF-p.117-1 here]

One commonly used technology is bar coding. **Bar code readers** are devices that use light reflection to read differences in bar code patterns in order to identify a labeled item. While the most common place consumers see bar code readers is in grocery and department stores, bar coding systems are also used extensively by warehouses for inventory tracking. Similarly, delivery and courier companies frequently use such coding systems to track inventory items and packages during shipping transfers. The next time you receive a delivery from Federal Express or United Parcel Services, notice the bar codes on the package that were used to track its delivery to you.

Utility and credit card companies frequently ask customers to handwrite the amount of the payment on the remittance slip. In such cases, **optical character recognition (OCR)** is used—similar to the way bar code readers work—for pattern recognition of handwritten or printed characters. Both bar code readers and OCR are technologies designed to eliminate the need to key in data and reduce the accompanying risk of error.

A third optical input technology is the **scanner.** *Scanners* are input devices that capture printed images or documents and convert them into electronic digital signals (i.e., into binary representations of the printed image or document) that can be stored and manipulated on computer media. *Scanners* are key to the increased use of electronic digital imaging to drive business processes and facilitate management decision making.

Review Question

a. Explain how bar code readers work.

b. Explain how optical character recognition works and how it differs from bar code technology.

c.Explain how scanners are used to capture data.

Digital Image Processing

Digital image processing systems are computer-based systems for storage, retrieval, and presentation of images of real or simulated objects. In the typical business application, the images are usually documents.

After a document has been input, additional processing may take place. The user may enter additional data related to the document or that acts on data contained in, or associated with, the document. Recall that in Chapter 3 we discussed the move toward object-oriented databases that are capable of handling object data—such as images—and that we noted the move toward enabling object storage within relational databases. A major part of the demand for object-capable databases is the management of a vast array of document images. Linkages of these images into the enterprise system can make accessibility much easier as information can readily be distributed throughout the organization. In many advanced digital imaging systems, the content of the digital image may subsequently be manipulated as if it were directly entered into an application or retrieved from a database. For example, a scanned word processing document could be edited directly, or a purchase order changed to reflect the receipt of a backordered item. This is not always a desirable feature, as some business documents (e.g., contracts) should not be manipulable once they are digitally recorded.

Review Question

How is digital image processing used to support the keying in of data?

Communication Networks

The key component for electronic communication systems is the network that provides the pathways for transfer of electronic data. Communication networks come in several different levels: from those designed to link a few computers together to the *Internet,* which links all publicly networked computers in the world together.

Within organizations, a major focus of network computing has been on client-server technology. **Client-server** technology is the physical and logical division between user-oriented application programs that run at the client level (i.e., user level) and the shared data that must be available through the server (i.e., a separate computer that handles centrally shared activities—such as databases and printing queues—between multiple users). The enabling networks underlying *client-server* technologies are **local area networks (LANs)** and **wide area networks (WANs)**. LANs are communication networks that link together several different local user machines with printers, databases, and other shared devices. WANs are communication networks that link distributed users and local networks into an integrated communications network. Such systems have traditionally been the backbone of enterprise system technology, but recent advances in communications technology are rapidly changing the underlying infrastructure models to rely more on the Internet.

Review Question

Explain the difference between wide area networks and local area networks.

Network technologies are driving the evolution of e-business. These technologies allow for more simplified user interactions, and empower users to access broad arrays of data for supplementing management decision making as well as opening new avenues for direct commerce. The leading technology in this arena is the **Internet,** the massive interconnection of computer networks worldwide that enables communication between dissimilar technology platforms. The Internet is the network that connects all of the WANs to which organizations choose to have access.

To simplify access to the vast arrays of data that have suddenly become available via the Internet, *Web browsers* were developed by several vendors. **Web browsers** are software programs designed specifically to allow users to search through the various sites and data sources available on the Internet. The advent of this easy-to-use software has rippled back through organizations and caused a rethinking of how companies can set up their own networks. The result has been the development of **intranets,** which are essentially mini internal equivalents of the Internet that link an organization's internal documents and databases into a system that is accessible through Web browsers or, increasingly, through internally developed software. For instance, the use of an intranet by PricewaterhouseCoopers' *TeamMate* system to support teams of auditors will be discussed in Technology Application 5.1 (page 147).

Extranets serve the same purpose as a WAN, in that they link together a set of users (usually from the supply chain of a single company, or a professional organization), but use the Internet instead of a private communication network. Access to the extranet is restricted, so that private activities using internal data can be securely supported as part of the organization's business processes.

The by-product of the expansion in intranets, extranets, and the Internet is a rich media for e-business. These networks provide the foundation for what has been exponential growth in e-business—both at the resale level and in supplier-buyer relationships.

Stages of E-Business

To this point the discussion has focused on the modes of business event data processing and related communication technologies that underlie the ability of organizations to enter into e-business. Now the discussion moves to specific methods for conducting e-business and how these methods use alternative modes of business event data processing and available communication technologies.

The three stages of e-business discussed here are fairly diverse. First is *electronic document management* (EDM). Some might not consider EDM part of e-business because the majority of such applications support non-e-business events, but it has an integral role in supporting the last two stages. *Electronic data interchange* (EDI) is the second area discussed. It currently represents the predominant form of e-business in transactions between two businesses. The third stage is *e-commerce,* which comprises the fastest-growing segments of e-business, and where EDI is slowly being replaced by XML.

Electronic Document Management

Electronic document management (EDM) is the capture, storage, management, and control of electronic document images for the purposes of supporting management decision making and facilitating business event data processing. Capturing and storing document images typically relies on the *digital image processing* approaches discussed earlier in the chapter. The added dimensions of management and control are critical to maintaining the physical security of the documents while at the same time assuring timely distribution to users requiring the information. Technology Application 4.1 discusses some general uses of EDM.

[Insert Technology Application 4.1 box here]

In general, business applications of EDM fall into two categories:

1. *Document storage and retrieval.* For example, mortgages, deeds, and liens are archived and made available to the public for such uses as title searches.
2. *Business event data processing.* For example, loan and insurance applications must pass through several stages, such as origination, underwriting, and closing. The EDM system can manage the workflow and route the documents to the appropriate people—even if these people are geographically dispersed.

EDM systems provide a relatively inexpensive alternative to paper documentation. The ability to access and manipulate real images of business documents offers great opportunities for improving the efficiency and effectiveness of many business applications and can create significant competitive advantages for an organization. For instance, fast access to imaged documents often can translate into faster and better customer service and result in increased customer loyalty—themes we explore in some depth in Chapter 10. The typical benefits include:

- Reduced cost of handling and storing paper.
- Improved staff productivity.
- Wider use of geographically distributed virtual teams.

- Superior customer service.
- Enhanced management of operational workflow.
- Faster processing.

Review Question

Explain the advantages of using electronic document management rather than traditional paper-based document systems.

Electronic Data Interchange

Computer and communications technology have been successfully applied by organizations to improve accuracy and control and to eliminate paper *within* their Information Systems applications. However, direct, paperless business communication *between* organizations had been slowed by a lack of transmission and presentation standards. What this often meant was that an organization used its computer technology to prepare a purchase order (PO), for example, completely without paper and human intervention—an efficient, fast, and accurate process. But, the PO had to be printed and mailed or faxed to the vendor. Then, at the vendor, the PO had to be sorted from other mail in the mailroom, routed to the appropriate clerk, and entered into the vendor's computer. The efficiency, timeliness, and accuracy gained by the automated purchasing process at the originating organization were lost through the mailing and reentry of the data at the vendor.

One technology that permits streamlining data communication among organizations is that of *electronic data interchange (EDI).* **Electronic data interchange (EDI)** is the computer-to-computer exchange of business data (i.e., documents) in standardized formats that allow direct processing of those electronic documents by the receiving computer system. Technology Application 4.2 describes some general uses of EDI, and Figure 4.5 (page 123) depicts typical EDI components. The numbers in circles are cross-references to corresponding locations in the narrative description.

[Insert Technology Application 4.2 box here]

[Insert Figure 4.5 here]

Application Software (circles 1 and 7) An originating application prepares an electronic business document, such as a purchase order (PO). At the destination organization, an application processes the business data. For example, the originating application's PO would be processed as a customer order in the destination organization's Order-to-Cash process.

Translation Software (circles 2 and 6) An application's electronic business document must be translated to the structured EDI format that will be recognized by the receiving computer. Figure 4.6 (page 124) depicts the translation process. The figure shows a specimen PO as it might appear as a conventional paper document and then illustrates how the PO is transformed into an EDI transaction standard, referred to as transaction set 850. *Translation sets* are the generally accepted representation standard for EDI and are described in Appendix A.

[Insert Figure 4.6 here]

Communications Network (circles 3 and 5) One method for communicating electronic messages between business partners would be to establish a direct computer-to-computer link between the origination computer and one or more destination computers. This kind of interface could be accomplished through a leased or dedicated communication line with each trading partner, or through a communications network in which one of the partners—let's say a large manufacturer—serves as the "hub" of the network, and its suppliers and other trading partners are the network "spokes." However, communications system incompatibilities may require that one partner or the other purchase communications hardware or software, making this a costly option. Further, agreeing on such details as what time of day to send and receive data from trading partners makes this option difficult to manage.

An alternative is to use an EDI *service bureau*—an organization that acts as an intermediary between a large hub company and its suppliers. The EDI service bureau generally works with smaller suppliers reluctant to acquire in-house translation and communications software. In such a case, the *translation software* and *communications software* reside on the service bureau's computer system. For a fee, the service bureau takes EDI messages from the hub, translates the messages into formats that are usable by the suppliers' computer applications, and forwards them to the suppliers. In the other direction, the bureau translates suppliers' *paper* documents—such as shipping notices or invoices—into EDI format and sends the electronic documents to the hub. Service bureaus are declining in use due to easily accessed and relatively inexpensive Internet-based options.

Review Question

Explain how electronic data interchange is used to link two companies' business processes together.

Value-Added Network (VAN) Service (circle 4) Rather than connecting to *each* trading partner, an organization can connect to a **value-added network (VAN)** service. A VAN service acts as the EDI "postman." An organization can connect to the VAN when it wants, leave its outgoing messages and at the same time, pick up incoming messages from its "mailbox." A VAN is a network service that provides communications capabilities for organizations not wishing to obtain their own communications links. VANs are also dropping in popularity due to Internet-based options for EDI.

Review Question

Explain how value-added networks (VANs) are used to simplify electronic data interchange between two or more companies.

As shown in Figure 4.5, one of the several functions that the VAN will perform is to translate the message from one communications protocol to another, if necessary.

EDI and Business Event Data Processing If we consider the implications of EDI for business event data processing, one of the main advantages is the significant reduction in need for interaction between purchasers and salespeople, coupled with the standard implementation of online transaction entry (OLTE). With EDI, both source document capture of business event data and subsequent keying in of the source document are eliminated for the selling organization as OLTE activities are initiated and completed by the linking purchaser. This eliminates any risk of erroneous data entry from within the selling organization. Keep in mind that EDI may be completed through traditional modes using dedicated communications lines, but are increasingly moving to the Internet.

You should be careful, however, not to make assumptions as to the mode of business event data processing. You will recall from our earlier discussion that OLTE can be used with both periodic and immediate modes of processing. The same holds true for the core business processing activities in an EDI environment. The business event data are frequently processed using an online real-time system, but many organizations also choose to do the bulk of the processing steps using periodic mode as well—particularly with batching of business event data for more efficient processing. It is worth noting also that particularly when *batch* processing is being used, there may be the need for online transaction processing (OLTP) approaches to handle order and payment confirmation activities during acceptance of the externally generated OLTE transmission—in other words, the customer may need an *immediate* confirmation that the order has been accepted and the business event will be completed by the vendor.

When trading partners communicate with each other electronically, they also discover that they have to communicate *internally* in new ways to achieve the full benefit of EDI. That is, EDI forces an organization to assume that all information flows, both internally and externally, are instantaneous. Accordingly, for many, EDI—along with other enabling technologies such as electronic document management—has been the catalyst for change in a firm's basic business processes.

Technical Insight 4.1 (page 126) presents some management, operational, and control issues associated with EDI.

[Insert TECHNOLOGY INSIGHT 4.1 box here]

Internet Commerce

A mere decade or so ago, e-business basically meant EDI. The Internet has radically changed the nature of e-business so that it has become the dominant platform for not only e-business, but EDI as well. Does this mean EDI is dying? Well, not exactly. Many experts believe EDI is here to stay and currently EDI volume continues to grow at a rate of about 15% per year. Still, the Internet shows far more potential growth—primarily from the potential seen in the emerging replacement language for EDI on the web, XML (eXtensible Markup Language).[3] XML is described in Technology Insight 4.2 (page 128).

[3] Carol Sliwa, "Firms Wait on XML, Increase Use of EDI," *Computerworld Online* (May 1, 2000).

[Insert TECHNOLOGY INSIGHT 4.2 box here]

Review Question

Compare EDI and XMLtechnologies.

Today, e-business enables the computer-to-computer exchange of business event data in structured (e.g., EDI or XML) or partially structured formats, usually via the Internet, that allows the initiation and consummation of business events. In many cases, the goods or services that are contracted for through the Internet are immediately (or soon thereafter) forwarded back to the consumer via the Internet as well (i.e., when the goods or services can be provided in electronic format, such as the case with software). The Internet radically simplifies business processes by allowing the organization that is receiving and processing business event data to project template formats to business partners for easy data entry and data transmission. For instance, if you connect across the Internet with Lands' End (a direct merchandiser of clothing—particularly warm stuff!) you see an "intelligent order form." You are provided an entry box to type in the product number for the item you want to order. The Web page automatically takes the number and identifies what additional information is needed (e.g., for most clothing, it will be size, color, and quantity). The additional information appears in menu form for you to select from the options available (e.g., for color, the menu might show red, navy, black, white, and green). As you enter responses on your computer, the data are automatically captured and recorded on the Lands' End computer. Technology Insight 4.3 (page 129) provides some management, operational, and control issues associated with the use of the Internet for e-business, while Technology Application 4.3 (page 130)provides some examples of ventures into Internet commerce.

Review Question

How does the Internet simplify the world of e-business?

[Insert TECHNOLOGY INSIGHT 4.3 box here]

[Insert Technology Application 4.3 box here]

There are two primary categories of e-business over the Web: (1) business-to-consumer, or B2C (e.g., Lands' End), and (2) business-to-business, or B2B. Figure 4.7 depicts a typical type of secure B2B arrangement. Note that the numbers in the circles are cross-references to corresponding locations in the narrative description.

[Insert Figure 4.7 here]

Client-Server Relationship (circles 1 and 7) The connection created between the customer and the vendor is a Web-enabled extended form of client-server applications. The customer (circle 1) is the client node—dictating that during connection, the customer computer environment should be secure and essentially inaccessible via the network. The vendor (circle 7) is the server node and therefore must have the capability to receive the customer's transmission and translate that transmission into processable data for use in the vendor's application programs. This translation is made through *common gateway interface* (CGI) software. The vendor, acting as the server part of the relationship, then provides the necessary correspondence back to the customer *(client)* in an understandable format (i.e., an Internet-based language such as Java or XML). To use the Lands' End example again, when you place your order, your computer should be inaccessible (i.e., secure) over the Internet, and the type of computer and software you are using will be unknown on the system. The Lands' End computer receives your order and uses CGI to translate your message into a form their program can understand and process. Similar to EDI environments, once the business event data have been collected by the vendor, applications can be completed through any of the modes of business event data processing. For instance, Lands' End used a periodic mode approach to process batches of sales several times an hour.[4]

[4] Lands' End, "Security on the Lands' End Web Site," http://www.landsend.com, December 2000.

Network Providers (circles 2 and 5) As with EDI, to participate in the business event, both parties must have the capability to communicate over the Internet. For many companies and organizations (as well as some individuals), this access comes through a direct connection between the entity's computer networks (or a single server) and the Internet. For other companies and organizations, as well as the vast majority of individuals, it will be more desirable to gain access through a *network provider.*

Network providers are companies that provide a link into the Internet by making their directly connected networks available to fee-paying customers. Most network providers bring a host of other benefits along with Internet access. Common benefits include e-mail access, electronic mail boxes, space allocation for personal Web pages, and remote connection to other computer sites (e.g., telnet and FTP connection). Many organizations will also use network providers to run their servers when assuming that role in the client-server relationship. In Figure 4.7, circle 5 denotes a network provider who would be providing server management services for the CPA or CA firm denoted by circle 6. Hence, when the business event is being completed between the customer and the vendor, information from the accounting firm would be acquired from a server operated by the firm's network provider.

Review Question

What role do network providers play in the e-commerce environment?

Assurance Providers (circles 4 and 6) A major concern for most organizations and individuals participating in e-commerce has been Internet security. Security is the most critical factor that has hampered the growth of e-commerce. One early survey showed that 90% of Internet users felt increased security was necessary before they would transmit personal information (e.g., credit card information) across the Internet.[5] Many stories have circulated about the risk of credit or debit card information being pirated off the network, with large sums of money being expended by unauthorized users. Additionally, the Internet has spawned a whole array of cottage industries that have no physical storefronts, but rather are operated completely from Internet server-supported Web pages. Many Internet users are rightfully concerned about the possibility that a company may be fictitious, with the electronic storefront merely being a means by which to gather credit card and debit card information for illicit use.

[5] J. Walker Smith, "Who Are the New, Interactive Consumers?" *Commerce in Cyberspace: A Conference Report* (The Conference Board, New York, 1996): 13–15.

These concerns over security have spurred the development of a new linc of business—Internet assurance services. **Internet assurance** is a service provided for a fee to vendors in order to provide limited assurance to users of the vendor's Web site that a site is in fact reliable and data security is reasonable. Technology Application 4.4 provides a more detailed discussion of Internet certification programs and assurance services.

[Insert Technology Application 4.4 box here]

Review Question

What types of assurances are provided by Internet assurance services?

Figure 4.7 demonstrates how one common type of assurance provider operates using the WebTrust program as discussed in Technology Application 4.4. The vendor (circle 7) displays the WebTrust certification seal and a reference to the assurance provider on its server Web page. When the customer accesses the vendor's

Web page, he or she can click on the WebTrust symbol to assure it continues to be applicable. Clicking on the WebTrust symbol executes a link to the VeriSign server (circle 4) for verification of the authorized use of the symbol. VeriSign verifies the symbol's appropriate use by sending a message to the customer (circle 1). The customer can also get a report on the level of assurance provided with the certification by clicking on the Web link (contained on the vendor's web page) for the accounting firm. Clicking this link connects to the accounting firm's (circle 6) server—provided by its network provider in this case (circle 5)—and the auditor's Internet assurance report for the vendor displays on the customer's computer (circle 1).

Internet Connection (circle 3) To obtain an Internet connection you must have a link to one of the networks that connect to the Internet and indicate the Internet site with which the client wants to connect. A connection is then made between the *client* and the desired site—the *server.*

A couple of other issues related to the organization of the Internet and its impact on e-commerce should be noted. First, the nature of the Internet as a public network-based infrastructure has greatly leveled the field in e-business. Only fairly large businesses could afford EDI's communications hardware and software. The creation of a public network and the subsequent creation of XML and relatively inexpensive (or even free) software for using the network have brought the costs of e-business within the ranges of economic feasibility for most small- and medium-sized entities. This change in cost structure and ease of use are the two forces driving the strong growth in e-commerce.

Review Question

Why is EDI moving to the Internet?

Other Internet Uses for E-Business While we have focused in this chapter on the most common forms of e-commerce and the direct linkages between customer and vendor, a number of intermediaries are evolving that promise to bring costs down even further for organizations. Two forms that seem most likely to have long-term success are *auction markets* and *market exchanges.* These are explained in greater detail in Technology Insights 4.4 and 4.5.

[Insert TECHNOLOGY INSIGHT 4.4 box here]

[Insert TECHNOLOGY INSIGHT 4.5 box here]

The Internet is not only a place for completing sales, but is also an environment for improving customer support for non-Internet-based commerce. A Web page may simply be one more channel in which to advertise and market an organization's goods and services. At the next level, it may be an arena for providing ongoing customer support. For instance, Symantec is one of many companies that provides free software upgrades over the Internet—in this case, providing monthly updates for its Anti Virus software. In another example, many courier companies (such as Federal Express) use the Internet to allow customers to access information to track their packages at any given point and to know when they have reached their destination. Such examples of customer support have become a huge new market for major software vendors. These systems fall under the broader category of customer relationship management (CRM) systems. CRM systems provide customer self-service capabilities (i.e., let the customer inspect an account or get product help through a Web interface rather than through interaction with a support person), electronic catalogues, shipment update information, and aid the salesperson by storing an analyzable history of the customer and the customer's past business interactions. One of the bigger challenges has been to get the CRM systems to interact with enterprise systems to share data. In an effort to improve integration, all of the major software firms are involved in initiatives to further empower CRM extensions to their enterprise systems.

Conclusions

The future of e-business will see an increasing merge of technologies as the lines between EDI and Internet commerce become less defined. The major impediment to most organizations (and individuals) conducting business over the Internet is the concern about security. Yet the advances in Internet security have been significant in the past few years, with the potential major beneficiaries of e-commerce leading the charge. For instance, software companies like Microsoft and Netscape, along with financial providers Mastercard and Visa, have been in the forefront of development efforts to assure safe use of the Internet in commerce.

The evolution of EDI practices toward the Internet and XML will initially involve increased use of corporate intranets. Moving EDI applications to an intranet environment can help simplify processing while maintaining high levels of control and security. These intranets will be opened to business partners using programs, referred to as tunneling software (or VPNs, virtual private networks) that limit intranet access to selected business partners. As security increases, the Internet will increasingly become a viable alternative as the communications infrastructure of choice.

These increases in security will help to fuel the growth of Internet commerce. As the Internet becomes an increasingly acceptable channel for doing business, companies will experience newfound opportunities for reaching customers; and for many companies, will bring globalization of their customer bases. On the other hand, there will also be new competition from distant companies who have access to the same customers.

Entering the e-business domain is not simply a matter of switching on the connection, however. E-business is nothing less than a fundamental change in the way organizations do business and as such, is a driver of organizational change. To succeed in an e-business environment, an organization must recognize the need to embrace change and must effectively plan and manage change.

It is thought to be an ancient curse to wish upon someone "may you live in interesting times." We are certainly not wishing a curse upon you, but the reality is that we are all living in interesting times. E-business success will rely heavily on understanding how to manage and control change at a fast pace. While these are interesting times, they are also exciting times.

Appendix 4A

EDI Standards

Presently, there are two major, nonproprietary, public, translation standards:

1. In the United States and Canada, the American National Standards Institute (ANSI) X12 standard has been used.
2. EDIFACT (EDI for Administration, Commerce, and Transport) is the predominant standard for international EDI transactions.

In addition, there are several standards that are specific to particular industries, such as the Automotive Industry Action Group

(AIAG), Transportation Data Coordinating Committee (TDCC), and Chemical Industry Data eXchange (CIDX). Some of these industry standards are compatible with the public, interindustry standards (e.g., ANSI X12), while some are not compatible.

Translation standards include formats and codes for each transmission type, called a *transaction set,* as well as standards for combining several transaction sets for transmission. For example, under the ANSI X12 standard, a purchase order (PO) is a transaction set "850," a shipping notice is a transaction set "856," an invoice is a transaction set "810," and so forth. The ANSI *data dictionary* for transaction set 850 defines the length, type, and acceptable coding for each data element in an EDI purchase order. For example, ANSI X12 describes the format and location within the message of the customer name and address, the part numbers and quantities ordered, the unit of measure of the items ordered (e.g., each, dozen, ton), and so on.

Besides purchase orders, other typical EDI transaction sets include (the ANSI X12 transaction set number appears in parentheses):

- Purchase order acknowledgment (855).
- Advance shipping notice (ASN) (856). From supplier to customer, advising that the goods are on the way.

- Receiving advice (861). From customer to supplier to report late, incomplete, or incorrect shipments.
- Invoice (810).
- Payment order/remittance advice (820). From customer to supplier for payment.
- Functional acknowledgment (FA) (997). A message is sent from receiver to sender to acknowledge receipt of *each and every one* of the above transaction sets. For instance, when the seller receives a purchase order (850) from the buyer, the seller sends back an FA (997) to indicate the message was received. Then, when the buyer receives a purchase order acknowledgment (855), the buyer acknowledges that the message was received by sending the seller an FA (997).

Translation software translates outgoing messages so that they are in the standard message format (e.g., ANSI X12) and translates the incoming messages from the standard message format into the form understood by the application system. This intermediate translation to/from the EDI format precludes the need for an organization to reprogram its application so that it can communicate with *each* trading partner's application.

The translation software also performs administrative, audit, and control functions. For example, the software inserts identification and control information in front of (header) and after (trailer):

- Each transaction set, such as one purchase order.
- Each *functional group* (e.g., a group of purchase orders, a group of receiving advices, and so forth) so that several groups may be sent in one transmission.
- All components comprising one transmission.

In EDI lingo, the data sets and the headers/trailers are called "envelopes." In addition to assembling and disassembling the EDI envelopes, the translation software may log incoming and outgoing messages and route the messages from and to the proper application.

REVIEW QUESTIONS

RQ4-1 Briefly define e-business and e-commerce. How are they related?

RQ4-2 Explain the relationship between the periodic mode and batch processing.

RQ4-3 List and describe the four basic subprocesses completed in processing business event data using batch processing.

RQ4-4 Explain how the use of online transaction entry (OLTE) can increase efficiency when using batch processing.

RQ4-5 Explain the relationship between online real-time (OLRT) and immediate mode processing.

RQ4-6 List and describe the three basic subprocesses completed in processing business event data using online real-time processing.

RQ4-7 How does the use of online transaction processing (OLTP) improve the timeliness of online real-time processing?

RQ4-8 a. Explain how bar code readers work.

b. Explain how optical character recognition works and how it differs from bar code technology.

c. Explain how scanners are used to capture data.

RQ4-9 How is digital image processing used to support the keying in of data?

RQ4-10 Explain the difference between wide area networks and local area networks.

RQ4-11 Explain the advantages of using electronic document management rather than traditional paper-based document systems.

RQ4-12 Explain how electronic data interchange is used to link two companies' business processes together.

RQ4-13 Explain how value-added networks (VANs) are used to simplify electronic data interchange between two or more companies.

RQ4-14 Compare EDI and XML technologies.

RQ4-15 How does the Internet simplify the world of e-business?

RQ4-16 What role do network providers play in the e-commerce environment?

RQ4-17 What types of assurances are provided by Internet assurance services?

RQ4-18 Why is EDI moving to the Internet?

DISCUSSION QUESTIONS

DQ4-1 The business environment is increasingly demanding the use of online real-time systems for more up-to-date information. Identify one business application, and the environment in which it would be used, as an example of why immediate mode processing is so critical. Be prepared to explain your answer to the class.

DQ4-2 Take as an example your favorite fast food chain restaurant. How do you think this restaurant might use online transaction entry to improve its business event data processing activities? Explain.

DQ4-3 We noted during the chapter discussion that banks were one of the earliest adopters of online transaction processing systems. Discuss why OLTP would be so desirable for use in ATM systems.

DQ4-4 How does your university use the Internet to improve communication between students, faculty, and staff?

DQ4-5 What would you perceive to be the advantages and disadvantages of conducting business on the Internet? Be prepared to explain your answer.

DQ4-6 Why has the Internet caused such an explosion in e-business when electronic data interchange has been available for decades?

DQ4-7 Consider again the example of Lands' End and its use of Internet commerce as discussed in the text. In a business where customers want to know fairly definitive delivery dates, what are the risks of using periodic processing on orders? Does the processing of orders several times each hour negate the disadvantages of periodic processing?

DQ4-8 How can e-mail be adapted to a more structured form to aid in capturing business event data?

PROBLEMS

P4-1 Find a merchandising business on the Internet (other than the Lands' End example used in this chapter). Explore its Web page and how the order processing system works.

a. Is there any information provided on how secure the Web page is? What level of comfort do you feel with its security? Explain.

b. Does the business provide information regarding delivery time/stock-outs on purchases?

c. What methods of payment does it accept?

d. Analyze the design of the Web page in terms of usability and completeness of information content. Write a brief critique of your company's page.

P4-2 Identify a business venture that you believe could be successful solely using the Internet. Explain how you would design your Web page, how you would capture business event data, and the mode of processing you would use. Provide a report detailing support for your design decisions. (Your professor will tell you how long the report should be.)

P4-3 Develop a research paper on the growing use of the Internet to support electronic data interchange (EDI) between companies. Your paper should consider how companies set up communications over the Internet to maintain the same security and standardization that are achieved using value-added networks for non-Internet EDI (Your professor will tell you how long the paper should be.)

P4-4 Explain how electronic document management is or could be used in your Information Systems class to eliminate all paper flow between the students and professor. Include in your explanation what technologies would be necessary to facilitate your plan. (Your professor will tell you how long the paper should be.)

P4-5 Write a research paper on the issues involved in developing an XML-based alternative to EDI for use in a specific industry of your choosing. Consult the Internet to see if a standard has been proposed for that industry, and if so, evaluate its use.

BOXES

[Start Technology Application 4.1 box here]

Technology Application 4.1

Gelinas 4-56

General Uses of Electronic Document Management Systems

Case 1

The push to improve crime investigation time and accuracy, in an effort to let fewer criminals escape from the vicinity of the crime, has led to one of the biggest EDM networks to date. In August 1999, the FBI unveiled a $640 million fingerprint system that allows fingerprint scans to be compared from the cars of police officers through connection to the central EDM repository. Prior to the implementation of the new system, law enforcement agencies, security firms, child-care organizations, and other entities requiring background checks would mail more than 50,000 fingerprints to the FBI each day. Specialists would then spend months trying to match the submitted fingerprints to some 34 million cards with an average of 10 fingerprint images each. The new system digitizes the fingerprint images to make them available for electronic comparison. The rapid access to fingerprint images coupled with the ability to do electronic comparisons should vastly reduce the number of arrested individuals who are released before their fingerprints have been reviewed and tied to past criminal activities.

Case 2

European companies use EDM to cut the cost of filing regulatory documents, a practice expected to grow 42% per year over a five-year period. Certainly driving this growth has been the integration of Internet capabilities for distribution of electronic images along with recent developments that enable integrated storage of voice and video clips as well. The European trend also includes increased use of laser disk storage for faster retrieval of document images coupled with high levels of storage capacity. Finally, EDM is being perceived as a key enabler for evolving knowledge management endeavors (see Chapter 5), as much of the knowledge captured in such systems is document based.

Sources: Gary Fields, "FBI Digitizes Fingerprint System Today," *USA Today* (August 10, 1999): 1A; Jana Sanchez-Klein, "Europeans Tap Document Management to Compete," *Computerworld Online* (December 23, 1998).

[End Technology Application 4.1 box here]

[Start Technology Application 4.2 box here]

Technology Application 4.2

General Uses of Electronic Data Interchange

Case 1

Total Home Entertainment (THE) viewed the Internet as a new opportunity to expand their EDI services to the 12,000 retail outlets in the U.K., as well as some 2,000 outlets outside the U.K., that the company services. THE is a supplier of over 200,000 home entertainment products such as videos, CDs, and books. Most of the retail outlets that THE provided its products to were small, independent stores that were ill prepared to deal with the complexities of EDI. Further, these small stores also represented the biggest growth area for THE. The Web Factory, a London-based solution provider for custom EDI Internet solutions helped THE construct an Internet interface that simplified the EDI communication process for its customers (the retail stores) and became a vehicle for locking in customers to its product. The results have helped keep THE at the forefront of the retail industry in the U.K.

Case 2

Perhaps the biggest change in EDI in recent years is being driven by the Internet.

Several companies are racing toward the development of Internet services to provide links from Internet sites to EDI sites. One of the leaders in the development of such an approach has been a consortium of Netscape Communications Corp. and GE Information Services, which has launched Actra. The system uses business document gateway software (BDG) to translate EDI forms to Internet formats. The Actra system is designed to run off Netscape servers. A major challenge in building such an EDI to Internet connection is business event data security. The BDG software employs Secure Multipurpose Internet Mail Extension (S/MIME) and Secure Sockets Layer (SSL) standards to ensure adequate security is achieved.

Sources: David Baum, "Entertaining with EDI,". *Byte* (August 1997); Michael Moeller, "Partners Get Actra Together," *PC Week* (January 13, 1997).

[End Technology Application 4.2 box here]

[Start TECHNOLOGY INSIGHT 4.1 box here]

TECHNOLOGY INSIGHT 4.1

From Private EDI Networks to the Internet: Management, Operational, and Control Considerations in Computer-to-Computer Business Linkages

We use EDI in our examples but the benefits, costs, and control risks described below may apply to EDI using a VAN, when the Internet is the vehicle for EDI communication, or when XML is the standard at the heart of B2B transactions.

Benefits may include the following:

- Survival. Many organizations have been "forced" to implement EDI if they wished to continue doing business with certain customers. For instance, in the early days of

EDI, Wal-Mart Stores and Kmart Corporation told all of their suppliers to establish EDI capability by a specified deadline if they wished to continue doing business with these retail giants.

- Improved responsiveness to customers' needs. In some cases, EDI has lead to what are known as "quick response" replenishment systems, also known as vendor-managed inventory. In such systems, a large customer—Sears Roebuck, for instance—gives its suppliers access (through EDI communication links) to real-time, *point of sale (POS)* information. With that information available, the suppliers can forecast customer demand more accurately, fine-tune their production schedules accordingly, and meet that demand in a highly responsive manner.
- Elimination of data re-entry at the receiving organization reduces processing costs and accuracy is improved. To better appreciate the potential impact of this benefit, consider the fact that, according to one estimate, 70 percent of the data processed by a typical company's computer system had been output by another computer system.
- Mailroom and other document preparation and handling costs are eliminated. For example, in the automobile industry, it is estimated that $200 of the cost of each car is incurred because of the amount of paper shuffling that has to be done.

Costs may include:

- Buying or leasing hardware and software.
- Establishing relationships with VANs or other electronic marketplaces and negotiating contracts.
- Training employees.

- Reengineering affected applications.
- Implementing security, audit, and control procedures.

Control considerations:

- Because signatures will no longer evidence authorizations, controls must ensure proper authorization. And, at some point during the process, we must authenticate that the message is sent to—and received from—the party intended and is authorized by someone having the proper authority.
- Without external, visual review, some business event data can be significantly in error. For example, a payment could be off by one decimal point! Therefore, controls must *prevent* rather than *detect* such errors.
- Given that the computer will initiate and authenticate messages, controls over the computer programs and data—*program change controls* and *physical security* (see Chapter 8)—become even more important than with traditional systems.
- Security procedures and other controls must prevent compromise of sensitive data and controls must ensure correct translation and routing of all messages.

Therefore, there must be *controls* to ensure that all messages are accurate, authorized, and complete.

To attain these control goals, organizations have implemented the following control plans, among others:

- *Artificial Intelligence* applications (see Chapter 5) may be used to determine that incoming messages are reasonable—consistent with normal message patterns—to authenticate the source and authorization for the message.

- Access to EDI applications may require a *biometric security system,* a *smartcard,* or a physical key as well as a *password* (see Chapter 8).
- *Data encryption* (see Chapter 9) may be employed to protect data during transmission.
- *Digital signatures* (see Chapter 9) may be used. Much like a password or other access code, the digital signature uniquely identifies who approved a business event and also helps to ensure that the EDI message was not altered during transmission.

[End TECHNOLOGY INSIGHT 4.1 box here]

[Start TECHNOLOGY INSIGHT 4.2 box here]

TECHNOLOGY INSIGHT 4.2

XML

Extensible Markup Language (XML) is a Web-based data format that enables information to be shared over the Web. XML provides a framework within which data from any type of source can be communicated and understood by any business partner's system, independent of technology platform.

XML supports a tree structure in which labeled data items are hierarchically related. A simple example is an XML item in which a phrase labeled as a greeting might hail the world with the following XML code:

```
<?xml version="1.0" encoding="UTF-8" ?>
<!DOCTYPE greeting [
<!ELEMENT greeting (#PCDATA)>
```

]>

<greeting>Hello, world!</greeting>

Most XML standards are being established to permit common transaction processing among like-minded industries or corporate functions (e.g., buying or selling computer hardware components, or exchanging human resources data). XML-enabled transaction processing will simplify Web transaction exchanges, and may completely replace EDI as the standard of choice as soon as reliability and security problems have been adequately addressed. XML parsers (programs that can read XML) have been integrated into many Web browsers, Web-enabled enterprise systems (e.g., Oracle Applications and Great Plains), and other business applications.

In a recent Zona Research Market Report, almost half of surveyed companies reported that they plan to convert some or all of their EDI applications to XML within the near future. Of the rest, half don't use EDI presently, and the other half will stay with EDI or convert EDI dynamically to XML. XML's usage is expected to rise from 0.5% of e-commerce transactions in early 2000 to 40% by the end of 2003. The key reasons these companies see for using XML are that XML

- Makes it easier to search for business partners or products
- Lets the company use event data for other purposes once it's in XML form
- Shortens application development time
- Enables business processes to take less time from start to finish
- Makes it easier to convert business data to a more usable form
- Ties together multiple internal applications within the company

- Allows links with customers' systems
- Supports links with suppliers' and trading partners' systems
- Allows the company to join an electronic marketplace that uses XML

Although many vendors are working diligently to release XML-based products, there remain many issues and questions to be answered before the language reaches its potential. These include security, agreement on standard formats, and senior management's lack of understanding about its challenges and potential. XML encryption standards are in development and a draft was released in 2001.

Sources: Martin Marshall, "XML—Like the Air that We Breathe," *Informationweek,* March 5, 2001, pp. 47–53; http://www.w3.org/TR/REC-xml, April 2001.

[End TECHNOLOGY INSIGHT 4.2 box here]

[Start TECHNOLOGY INSIGHT 4.3 box here]

TECHNOLOGY INSIGHT 4.3

E-Business Management and Operations Considerations

Benefits of Internet commerce include the following:

- Survival. Many organizations have been "forced" to implement e-business to compete in the changing nature of their industries. If they wish to remain competitive with other companies taking advantage of the Internet for commerce, they will need to venture to the Web.
- Improved responsiveness to customers' needs. Customers expect immediate feedback and easy availability of information and help. The Internet is a useful tool

for servicing customer and client needs—forming the communications medium for distributing information and support services.

- Global penetration. The Internet is generally the easiest and least expensive way to reach customers worldwide that an organization may never have been able to reach previously.
- Reduced processing costs and improved accuracy result when data are not reentered at the receiving organization. Customers now provide most of the data entry themselves, removing the need for the selling organization to key in most of the business event data.
- Mailroom and other document preparation and handling costs are eliminated. The business event data processing side of a business can operate with virtually no human intervention until it is time to prepare and deliver goods.
- The opportunity to rethink and redesign existing business processes and controls in the course of implementing e-business.

Costs of using the Internet include:

- Organizational change to a completely different way of doing business.
- Buying equipment and maintaining connection to the Internet (or leasing through a network provider).
- Establishing connections with a new set of customers.
- Staffing and training employees to work in a technology-driven environment.
- Reengineering application systems to process data acquired through the Internet.

- Maintaining security of the Internet site.

Risks of Internet commerce include:

- Hackers attempting to access sensitive information such as customer lists or customer credit card information.
- Denial of service attacks. Denial of service attacks are expected to escalate over the next few years as individuals or organizations attempt to knock out Web sites by overloading them with site visits and preventing customers or other users from gaining access. These attacks may occur simply for the challenge or frequently due to a political or other difference with the organization that hosts the site. See Technology Insight 8.3, on page 267, for a fuller description.
- Trust. Increasingly, the success of B2B relationships necessitates the identification of business partners who are allowed access to sensitive internal information. A breakdown of that trust can have grave consequences to the organization making its information available.

[End TECHNOLOGY INSIGHT 4.3 box here]

[Start Technology Application 4.3 box here]

Technology Application 4.3

General Uses of E-Business

Case 1

Office Depot is a major player in the business to consumer (B2C) space. Its Web-based sales reached $350 million in 1999, and were estimated at $800 million for 2000, or approximately 9 percent of its revenue. It is a leader in the move from "bricks and mortar" (a traditional company structure) to "bricks-and-clicks," an organization that views the Internet as an alternative marketing channel to traditional interactions with customers. The company has garnered significant e-commerce sales agreements with many large companies such as General Electric and Procter & Gamble. In addition to permitting online sales, Office Depot also helps customers by supplying online business tools, forms, human resource handbooks, and other useful Internet links. Much of the success of the site is attributable to the integration between its distribution channels and its Order-to-Cash process (e.g., order processing and billing) in its enterprise system. The system has also formed the basis of an extranet with vendors that feeds into the Purchase-to-Pay business process. Vendors are able to set up product information in Office Depot's enterprise system and check inventory levels at each location without human intervention, speeding replenishment and reducing stockouts.

Case 2

One type of business that is particularly compatible with e-business is one in which the goods or services can be delivered across the Internet instantaneously, much the same as payment is provided by the customer. TheStreet.com is one company that has implemented such a business plan. TheStreet.com is in the business of providing financial information that is valuable, unique, and timely. The company philosophy is that if it fails in any of these three attributes for the information it delivers, customers will stop coming. Despite the many business publications on the market, TheStreet.com has quickly risen as a leading provider of financial information by being both cheaper and timelier. It is one of the few information providers able to provide subscription service solely through the

Internet. This is one form of the so-called Internet cottage industry whereby new small businesses spring up on the net to provide unique services.

Case 3

Wal-Mart is one of many retailers who are setting up electronic storefronts on the Internet to sell its goods directly to customers. Wal-Mart takes the customer's order and credit card number over the Internet, electronically processes the order, and sends the order directly to the manufacturer, who ships the product to the customer. The company's Web site becomes little more than a for-fee electronic interface between the customer and the manufacturer.

Sources: Eric Berkman, "Clicklayer," *CIO Magazine,* Volume 14, issue 8, (February 1, 2001): 92–100; Eric Hall, "Information Wants To Be Free? Not at TheStreet.com," *Infoworld* (December 8, 1997): 94–96; Linda Rosencrance, "TheStreet.com Looks for Road to Profitability," *Computerworld Online* (November 16, 2000); Todd R. Weiss, "Walmart.com Site Back Online After 28-day Overhaul," *Computerworld Online* (October 31, 2000).

[End Technology Application 4.3 box here]

[Start Technology Application 4.4 box here]

Technology Application 4.4

Internet Security Certification

Case 1: Webtrust Certification

Like many vendors of high technology products, Westek Presentation Systems made a decision to pursue opportunities for e-commerce by taking its product lines to the Web.

However, a major problem was many customers' reluctance to purchase products over the Internet because of security issues. These security issues included concerns over whether the company really existed (or was simply a front to collect credit card numbers for fraudulent use) and over the safety of transmitting credit card information over the Internet. Westek's CPA proposed a solution recommending that Westek have the CPA provide assurance services that would attest to the validation of the company and the safety of its Web site for potential customers. In late 1997, Westek became the first certification client for this new type of security service.

The WebTrust Seal of Assurance is the product of a joint venture between the American Institute of Certified Public Accountants (AICPA) and the Canadian Institute of Chartered Accountants (CICA). It is designed to provide comfort and assurance that a Web site is reasonably safe for users participating in B2C e-commerce. Once a site receives WebTrust certification, it should be reviewed at least every 90 days by the CPA/CA to assure adequate standards have remained in place and the site remains reasonably secure. Basically, the Web site must meet three standards:

- *Business practices disclosure:* The client company must disclose its business practices for conducting e-commerce to users accessing its Web page.
- *Transaction integrity:* The client company must have proper control procedures in place to assure that customers' business events data are completed and billed correctly.
- *Information protection:* The client company must have proper controls in place to ensure customer information is protected from unauthorized use.

Recently, WebTrust certification was made available in separate components rather than requiring certification on all three of the above areas. For instance, one of the available seals now covers only business practices and transaction integrity.

Case 2: ICSA Certification

An alternative to WebTrust is provided by the International Computer Security Association (ICSA) Labs—a subsidiary of TruSecure. ICSA Labs provides reduced risk to both the customer and the vendor by providing, verifying, and improving the use of appropriate security standards across a range of critical dimensions. The Anti-Virus certification helps product developers address threats from malicious programs. The Firewalls certification is based on testing of commercially available firewall packages. Crytography certification helps users identify products that effectively use cryptography to provide security services. Intrusion Detection tests the functionality and compliance of intrusion detection products. Additionally, a new product related to Public Key Infrastructure (PKI) product certification is due out around the beginning of 2003.

Case 3: TRUSTe

Another product, TRUSTe, focuses solely on privacy issues. The TRUSTe certificate is awarded only to sites that adhere to established privacy principles of disclosure, choice, access, and security. Webstites carrying the seal also agree to TRUSTe's prescribed dispute resolution processes for customers. The focus on privacy creates a nice market niche for TRUSTe as privacy concerns have been in the forefront of Internet legislation for many countries. TRUSTe has recently added services for compliance with the guidelines of the Children's Online Privacy Protection Act (COPPA). The Children's Privacy Seal Program assures Web sites are safe harbors for children to visit.

Case 4: BBB Online

The most popular certification program is the Better Business Bureau's BBB OnLine program with 10,482 active Web sites. The program confirms a company is a member of the Better Business Bureau and that there has been a review for truth in advertisement guidelines and good customer service practices. The program is likely so popular because of the broad recognition of the Better Business Bureau and the low cost of attaining certification.

Sources: Richard J. Koreto, "In CPAs We Trust," *Journal of Accountancy* (December 1997): 62–64; AICPA/CICA, "CPA/CA WebTrust^{sm} Version 2.0" http://www.cica.ca (August 2000); ICSA, "ICSA Certified Secure Web Certification Program," http://www.icsalabs.com (January 2002).

[End Technology Application 4.4 box here]

[Start TECHNOLOGY INSIGHT 4.4 box here]

TECHNOLOGY INSIGHT 4.4

Internet Auction Markets

Internet auction markets provide an Internet base for companies to either place products up for bid or for buyers to put proposed purchases up for bid. In the first case, a market participant puts an item up for bid, sets a minimum bid price, and awaits completion of the bidding process, as happens on eBay. While this market works fairly well for B2C e-commerce, it is not as effective for business-to-business commerce. For B2B e-commerce, a company may put specifications for a product out on the marketplace as a request for proposals (RFPs). Participating organizations in the market can then bid on the sales by providing a proposal that includes details on product specifications, costs, availability (i.e., timing of delivery), and logistics. The buying organization can then select the proposal that seems most desirable for meeting the organization's needs at a minimal cost and risk.

[End TECHNOLOGY INSIGHT 4.4 box here]

[Start TECHNOLOGY INSIGHT 4.5 box here]

TECHNOLOGY INSIGHT 4.5

Internet Market Exchanges

Internet market exchanges bring together a variety of suppliers in a given industry and one or more buyers in the same industry. Suppliers can put their products online, generally feeding into electronic catalogs that allow the buyer(s) to sort through alternatives from different suppliers and electronically place an order. Even if only one supplier carries a certain item, efficiencies are still gained by avoiding the purchase order process (described in detail in Chapter 12) and executing an order through selection from a Web catalog. In some cases, the buyer will make its needs known on the marketplace and suppliers will review the needs and determine whether to fill the orders. The key is to make sure the market is efficient enough to assure that the buyer will get the product purchased on a timely basis for when it is needed, for example getting purchased goods to an assembly line within an hour of when needed for production. This part can get tricky and the exchange must be set up carefully.

Internet market exchanges can be either private or public. Private exchanges limit the buyers and suppliers who can participate in the market. Public exchanges bring together suppliers and buyers and allow essentially any organization to participate, subject sometimes to credit approval and background checks. Private exchanges that have been planned or are currently operating outnumber such public exchanges 30,000 to 600. However, private exchanges have drawn the watchful eye of the Federal Trade Commission (FTC), which oversees fair trade practices and potential anti-competitive practices that may result from restricting participation in the market exchange.

Source: Steve Ulfelder, "Members Only Exchanges," *Computerworld Online* (October 23, 2000).

[End TECHNOLOGY INSIGHT 4.5 box here]

5

Business Intelligence and Knowledge Management Systems

There is a popular saying that the amount of information in the world doubles every ten years. That's a lot of information! How can the average manager or decision maker expect to keep up with the flood of data that is so easily accessible? How can this decision maker determine what data is useful, which is believable, and how much of it is even relevant to a current problem or opportunity? Information technology turns out to be both the enabler of this flood of data and a tool for sorting through and analyzing it all. When used creatively, information technology can tease out trends and opportunities from data collected for entirely different purposes.

Take, for example, Amazon.com. Amazon.com is known for being the most successful "dot-com" company doing business solely over the Internet. It is heralded for its competitive pricing, efficient transactions, and speedy delivery. What it is less well known for is its ability to collect, analyze, and reuse marketing data. Amazon.com keeps a database of every sale it makes to a customer. The company knows when and what you order, and will send you an e-mail coupon to prod you to order again if it has been a while since you last ordered anything. The coupon may be for an entirely different product line. If you bought a computer book, you might get a coupon to order some computer equipment. Buy Harry Potter, and get a discount on toys or video games.

When you look at a book on the site, you will also see a list of other books bought by customers who bought the book you are considering, which may entice you to expand your purchase. Amazon.com had been publishing a list of books bought by customers at different large employers but stopped when companies objected on the grounds of privacy. (Of course, this change doesn't mean Amazon.com can't follow trends internally to help its marketing staff.) Amazon.com can also analyze pricing, occasionally experimenting with varying purchase prices to different customers to increase revenues on its current volume of sales.

How does Amazon.com accomplish all of this? It relies on high-quality data in its database and uses business intelligence tools to analyze the data in support of business decisions. This chapter introduces several types of business intelligence tools to give you an idea of how a company combines the data that it collects with publicly available data to support decision making throughout the layers of management.

LEARNING OBJECTIVES

- To recognize how information is used for different types of decisions at various levels in the organization
- To become familiar with the support that management receives from decision aids

such as Business Intelligence systems, OLAP, groupware, expert systems, and intelligent agents

- To understand the importance and challenges of formally managing organizational knowledge, and to recognize the technologies that enable successful knowledge management

Introduction

In Chapter 1 we defined the *Information System* as a system " . . . established to facilitate an organization's operational functions and to support management decision making by providing information that managers can use to plan and control the activities of the firm." Let's pursue the meaning and importance of one of the key concepts within that definition. Very simply, **decision making** is the process of making choices. It is the central activity of all management. Managers make decisions or choices, such as what products to sell, in which markets to sell those products, what organizational structure to use, and how to direct and motivate employees. Herbert A. Simon, a Nobel-prize-winning economist, described decision making as a three-step process. His three stages have been adopted over the years as the "classic" view of decision making:

1. *Intelligence:* Searching the environment for conditions calling for a decision.
2. *Design:* Inventing, developing, and analyzing possible courses

of action.

3. *Choice:* Selecting a course of action.[1]

[1] Herbert A. Simon, *The New Science of Management Decision* (New York: Harper & Row, 1960): 2.

Review Question

What are the three steps in decision making?

Figure 5.1 depicts these three steps. Analyze the figure to see what information is required for each step. Information from and about the environment and the organization is needed to recognize situations or problems requiring decisions. For example, information about economic trends, marketing intelligence, and likely competitor actions help management recognize opportunities for new markets and products. Information about inefficient or overworked processes in the organization focus management's attention on problems in the organization. Managers use information from within and from outside the organization to design courses of action. For example, information about human resources, production capacity, and available distribution channels help management to develop alternative methods for producing and distributing a new product. Finally, a manager requires information about possible outcomes from alternative courses of action. For example, to choose from among alternative production options, a manager needs information about the costs and benefits of the alternatives and about the probability of success of each option.

[Insert Figure 5.1 here]

Once a course of action is in place, the decision needs to be implemented and the results communicated. Many people find that the most important step in the decision making process is how well it is implemented. Effective communication is a key component of this success. Technology Insight 5.1 describes the effective presentation of information in technical communications.

[Insert TECHNOLOGY INSIGHT 5.1 box here]

Management Decision Making

The nature of the information required by managers varies by management level.[2] *Strategic* level managers require information that allows them to assess the environment and to project future events and conditions. Much of the information comes from outside the organization and is used infrequently. *Tactical* management requires information that is focused on relevant operational units. Some external information is required, as well as information that is more detailed and accurate than is the information used at the strategic level. *Operational* management needs information that is narrower in scope, more detailed, more accurate, and that comes largely from within the organization.

[2] The levels of management are depicted in Figure 1.4 on page 13.

Review Question

What factors distinguish the types of information required by strategic level managers, by tactical level managers, and by operational level managers?

The kind of information required to make a decision is also heavily influenced by the decision's structure or lack thereof. *Structure* is the degree of repetition and routine in the decision. Structure implies that we have seen this very decision before and have developed procedures for making the decision. We can use the degree of structure inherent in each decision-making step to categorize the decisions as structured or unstructured. We define **structured decisions** as those for which all three decision phases (intelligence, design, and choice) are relatively routine or repetitive. In fact, many decisions are so routine that a computer can be programmed to make them. For example, many organizations have automated the decision of when and how much credit to grant a customer when an order is received. At the time the customer's order is entered, the computer compares the amount of the order to the customer's credit limit, credit history, and outstanding balances. Using this information, the computer may grant credit, deny credit, or suggest a review by the credit department. We cover this procedure in more detail in Chapter 10.

Review Question

In your own words, explain *structure* as it relates to decisions.

Consider, on the other hand, the decision-making process that managers undertake in choosing what research and development projects to pursue in the next year. This is only one example of what we classify as an **unstructured decision,** one for which none of the decision phases (intelligence, design, or choice) are routine or repetitive.

Figure 5.2 (page 146)summarizes several concepts introduced in this section and also helps us to understand the nature of the characteristics associated with information used by the three levels of management for decision making. Further, this figure indicates the proportion of structured and unstructured decisions handled by the three management levels.

[Insert Figure 5.2 here]

Information Qualities and Decision-Making Level The level of the decision maker and the type of decision to be made determines the preeminence of certain information qualities. For example, strategic management may require information high in predictive value. Information used for strategic planning should help managers "see" the future and assist them in formulating long-term plans. The strategic level manager may not be as concerned with timeliness or accuracy and would therefore prefer a quarterly sales report to a daily report containing several quarters of information so that trends could be detected more easily. Operations management must make frequent decisions, with shorter lead times, and may therefore require a daily sales report to be able to react in a timely manner to recent changes in sales patterns. Operations management may require more timely and accurate information and may not be concerned about the predictive value of the information. Without a certain level of accuracy, however, even the largest data warehouse will not be useful for forecasting or analysis of historical data. Technology Application 5.1 gives examples of the importance of high-quality data.

[Insert Technology Application 5.1 box here]

Conclusions About Management Decision Making From Figures 5.1 and 5.2 and their related discussions, we can reach the following conclusions. Information needed for decision making can differ in degree of aggregation and detail, in source, and in fundamental character. We have also seen that the required qualities of information differ by decision type and level of management.

Within the organization, managers can secure inputs to their decisions directly: from the environment or from direct observation of operations. Managers can also receive information indirectly through the IS, which retrieves and presents operational and environmental information. Environmental information is now widely available, given the ease of searching for and sharing information over the Internet. As we understand more about the decisions to be made and can better anticipate the data needed to make those decisions, the IS can be designed to provide more of the required information.

Because data requirements for structured decisions are well defined, we strive to improve our understanding of decisions so that we can make more decisions more structured, anticipate the data needed for those decisions, and regularly provide those data through the IS.

Systems For Aiding Decision Makers

As mentioned above, the IS supporting a firm's business processes focuses on information requirements that can be identified in advance: information for well-structured decision situations in which the typical information requirements can be anticipated. Perhaps we make this sound simple. However, providing information to help managers make decisions is a rather daunting task. Figure 5.3 (page 148) gives you some idea of the roadblocks facing managers when they must make decisions. This section discusses some of the information tools designed to help decision makers: *Business Intelligence systems, Online Analytical Processing systems (OLAP), group support systems, expert systems,* and *intelligent agents.*

[Insert Figure 5.3 here]

As we discussed in the preceding section, many decisions—particularly important decisions made by high-level management—are predominantly unstructured. There are four levels of expertise that can be applied to these decision situations:

- A manager can make the decision without assistance, using his or her own expertise.
- The decision maker can be assisted by problem-solving aids such as models, manuals, and checklists.
- The decision aid (e.g., models, checklists, and manuals) might be automated.
- The system itself can replace the decision maker, as when an *expert system* monitors the activity in a production line and adjusts the machinery as required.

Business Intelligence Systems, OLAP, and Group Support Systems Automated tools can assist or replace the decision maker. Technology Insight 5.2 describes Business Intelligence systems (BI) and Online Analytical Processing (OLAP) systems. BI assists the decision maker by combining current and historical facts, numerical data, and statistics—from inside and from outside the organization—and by converting these data into information useful in making the decision. BI is a broadly defined approach to supporting decision makers, and many software products provide this capability in conjunction with data warehouses and other large-scale database products. OLAP tools are software products that focus on the analytical needs of decision makers. Frequently software vendors sell OLAP tools to provide business intelligence within the client firm. We will use these terms almost interchangeably in this chapter, as they are so closely related.

[Insert TECHNOLOGY INSIGHT 5.2 box here]

Let's see how a manager uses BI. A decision maker might create a spreadsheet to identify changes in sales for several product lines and to compare them to similar figures from a previous period. This information might help the manager to determine if sales quotas have been attained for this period and if current performance is consistent with past experience. With the spreadsheet, the decision maker prepares a report in a format that is suitable for *this* decision at *this* point in time.

With a more complex BI system, screen reports could have been programmed in advance. For example, when an executive turns to her computer each morning, a screen appears containing a "dashboard"—a visual display of the company's key performance indicators. Imagine that the executive wants to examine sales trends. She might click on a "sales trends" graph. To determine what to do about a potential problem observed in the graph, the manager might successively request more detailed information, a process known as "drilling down." This sales trend information might alert the manager to some problem, i.e., the *intelligence* step in a decision. OLAP tools could then be used to analyze the trends to determine if the problem resulted from a manufacturing problem, a salesforce issue, or improvements in a competitor's product.

Figure 5.4 shows a sales analysis screen shot in which data displayed in a table can be easily converted to a graphical representation by clicking an icon. The sales data can be analyzed over a number of dimensions by drilling down by region, product, time period, and a number of other displayed fields.

[Insert Figure 5.4 here]

Examine again the figure that accompanies Technology Insight 5.2 and notice the four items entering the system: the data warehouse, external databases, World Wide Web information, and OLAP models. When the BI system is originally designed, the organization identifies the data and models that allow the managers to monitor issues of interest. By agreeing on these issues of interest, the organization develops a consensus on the key factors that will indicate success, i.e., achievement of organizational goals.[3]

[3] See the discussion of strategic planning in Chapter 6 for a discussion of developing organizational objectives and key success factors.

Once the data have been identified, the users must ensure that the data provided are relevant, timely, accurate, valid, and complete. Managers unable to identify and provide such data risk irrelevance and obsolescence in their organizations.

BI systems do not suggest to the decision maker what to do; they simply provide views for interpreting information. With BI, the knowledge and experience required to analyze information, to make judgments, and to take required actions reside with the decision maker.

BI systems help managers, who are typically working alone, to make decisions. **Group support systems (GSS),** commonly called **groupware,** are computer-based systems that support collaborative intellectual work such as idea generation, elaboration, analysis, synthesis, information sharing, and decision making. GSS use technology to solve the time and place problems associated with group work. That is, a GSS creates a “virtual meeting” for a group. While “attending” this meeting, members of the group work toward completion of their task and achievement of the group’s objective(s).

Groupware focuses on such functions as e-mail, group scheduling, and document sharing. Technology Application 5.2 describes PricewaterhouseCoopers’ use of distributed database technology to facilitate audit team work.

[Insert Technology Application 5.2 box here]

Artificial Intelligence Many decision-making situations require a high level of expertise in a deep or complicated problem area. *Artificial Intelligence* (AI) facilitates the capture of expertise in many ways. In this section, we discuss three AI techniques, expert systems, neural networks and intelligent agents.

Expert systems (ES), described in Technology Insight 5.3, may help decision makers overcome many of the roadblocks depicted in Figure 5.3 (page 148). Expert systems may be appropriate where:

[Insert TECHNOLOGY INSIGHT 5.3 box here]

- Decisions are extremely complex.
- Consistency of decision making is desirable.
- The decision maker wishes to *optimize* the decision. That is, the decision maker wants to minimize time spent making the decision while *maximizing* the quality of the decision.
- There is an expert decision maker, and his or her knowledge can be efficiently captured and effectively modeled via computer software.

Review Question

Describe the components of an *expert system*.

Technology Application 5.3 provides a real-world example of how expert systems can be used. You will find additional examples of the use of expert systems in several remaining chapters.

[Insert Technology Application 5.3 box here]

To increase competitiveness, businesses are increasingly using AI. Three trends are indicative of this increased use. First, in the process of downsizing a large percentage of an organization's experience is lost. The targets of early retirement programs are the people with the most seniority and the highest pay. These are the same people who have accumulated knowledge about the business and whose expertise will be greatly missed. The second trend is the increasing complexity of business organizations and operations. The third trend is the decentralization of business. All three explain the need for AI systems to help maintain expertise and increase a company's ability to share it among many employees.

Technology Insight 5.4 describes one of the most common contemporary development approaches in AI, called *neural networks* (NN), and Technology Application 5.4 (page 156) provides real-world examples of neural networks. The ability of NN to discover patterns in large quantities of data makes them useful in decision making, performing well in areas that can't be reached by ES or BI. Picture a neural network poring through reams of internal and external data and notifying an executive that there may be something that requires attention. For example, the NN might predict that, because ratios A, B, and C are down, there will be a decline in income next year. It might go on to tell the executive what to do to prevent the decline. An expert system could perform a similar function, but *only* if an expert had found the relationship between ratios A, B, C, and income *and* someone had entered that relationship into the knowledge base.

[Insert TECHNOLOGY INSIGHT 5.4 box here]

[Insert Technology Application 5.4 box here]

What stops us from using AI in every decision-making situation—what's the downside? If we do use AI, what does a good manager need to consider? The benefits derived in terms of increased productivity, improved decision making, competitive advantage, and so on, must exceed the costs of development *and* maintenance of the system. And, for ES in particular, we must be able to identify and extract the expertise required and to enter that expertise into our knowledge base. Therefore, we must carefully choose the areas in which we will apply AI technology.

Perhaps the area of greatest recent growth in decision-aiding systems is the development and application of *intelligent agents.* An **intelligent agent** is a software component integrated into a BI system, Web search engine, or software productivity tool (such as word-processing, spreadsheet, or database packages) that provides assistance and/or advice to the user on use of the software, decision-making attributes, or supplying of common responses by other users. Most intelligent agents are designed to learn from the actions of the system's user and to respond based on the user's responses or usage patterns. Technology Application 5.5 discusses the use of intelligent agents in a tax preparation software package—TurboTax.

[Insert Technology Application 5.5 box here]

Much of the demand for intelligent agents has arisen from two realities in the workplace. First, as productivity software (i.e., word-processing, spreadsheets, and presentation software) and data warehousing continue to increase in power—and therefore complexity—these agents become critical to explaining to many users how to use certain features. For instance, Microsoft Word analyzes your text input, recognizes if you are trying to write a letter, and offers to help format the letter. The program can analyze grammar and automatically flag errors, providing recommended corrections as well. Agents are increasingly being embedded in BI software for a host of things such as facilitation of data mining approaches with use of data warehouses.

The second driver is the sudden information explosion coming from the use of the Internet. The vast volumes of information have made it difficult for users to find information germane to their given interest. The result has been extensive work in embedding intelligent agents into browsers to recognize users' search patterns and to provide advice on searches. Many of these tools, by learning the user's behavioral patterns, facilitate the rapid access and filtering of information to provide precise searches on applicable information. Such use of intelligent agents holds the greatest promise for the future of AI-based systems.

Let's summarize what we have learned regarding systems that provide intelligence-based assistance to the management decision maker.

- To overcome the roadblocks to quality decision making, managers use Business Intelligence systems (BI), group support systems (GSS), expert systems (ES), neural networks, (NN) and intelligent agents.
- A BI system structures available data to provide information about alternative courses of action without offering a solution. BI works well with unstructured (or semi-structured, i.e., having only some structured components) problems that have a quantifiable dimension.
- A GSS facilitates group interaction and group consensus-building.
- An ES applies expertise—modeled after that acquired from an expert—to provide specific recommendations on problem resolution.
- Both BI and ES can assist a user in problem solving, but in different ways. A BI system is a *passive* tool; it depends on the

human user's knowledge and ability to provide the right data to the system's decision model. OLAP tools expect the user to know when and how to apply analytical expertise. An ES, on the other hand, is an *active* teacher or partner that can guide the user in deciding what data to enter, and in providing hints about further actions that are indicated by the analysis to date.

- Neural networks supplement the expert system in areas where expertise has not yet been captured. By examining the data, the NN can identify and replicate the patterns that exist.
- Expert systems can automate portions of decision making. They can function independently and actually make the decision. Alternatively, an ES can merely assist the decision maker and recommend a course of action. One final comment: We are not talking about replacing people with ES. These systems make it possible for valuable expertise to be available in multiple locations. The systems supplement managers in a timely manner to facilitate important decisions for maintaining an organization's competitive edge.
- Intelligent agents can provide smart assistants that simplify and/or improve effective use of software systems. Intelligent agents can adapt to the user's specific situation and provide guidance on potential errors and suggest alternatives.

Review Question

What factors distinguish a *BI system* from an *ES*? What factors distinguish *ES* from *NN*?

Knowledge Management

In a recent interview, Susan O'Neill, deputy chief knowledge officer of PricewaterhouseCoopers, noted, "Knowledge is what we're all about. All of our profitability and viability is about how good we are at leveraging the intellectual assets of our people and making that available to our clients." Indeed, a survey of 200 IT managers by *InformationWeek* shows that 94 percent of companies consider knowledge management strategic to their business or IT processes and that these companies are in the early stages of their knowledge-management efforts. Additional results reveal that on average companies are capturing only 45 percent of their intellectual capital.[4] A manager at Ernst & Young referred to knowledge management as the biggest problem faced by the firm in trying to maintain the quality of service expected by its customers.[5]

[4] "Knowledge Management: A Concept Worth Pursuing," *Information Week* (April 5, 1999).

[5] Chris Nagle, "Research Opportunities in Knowledge Management" *Mid-Year Meeting of the Auditing Section of the American Accounting Association* (January 14, 1999).

Knowledge management is the process of capturing, storing, retrieving and distributing the knowledge of the individuals in an organization for use by others in the organization to improve the quality and/or efficiency of decision making across the firm. The primary enabler of knowledge management efforts is the power of contemporary information technologies.

Review Question

Describe the purpose of a *knowledge management system.*

Effective knowledge management means that an organization must be able to connect the knowledge of one individual (e.g., capturing) with other individuals in the firm (e.g., distributing) who need the same knowledge. Distribution dictates the use of electronic communications technology—namely *groupware* systems. Advanced database management systems and AI systems technologies for orderly storage and retrieval of the captured knowledge are also critical.

Gathering Knowledge with Groupware

All of the capabilities of *groupware,* as discussed earlier in this chapter, are key to supporting *knowledge management* for organizations of virtually any size. Even the simplest components such as e-mail and document sharing are vital components. Add to these the capability of Electronic Document Management systems, and the information content of the electronically distributed messages vastly increases. Indeed, many people consider the roots of knowledge management to be in the development of Lotus Notes, a widely used *groupware* system specifically designed to facilitate sharing of documents, e-mail, and group communication. Technology Insight 5.5 (page 160) describes a new approach to groupware that provides Notes-like capabilities anywhere on the Internet.

[Insert TECHNOLOGY INSIGHT 5.5 box here]

In many organizations, when an individual is faced with a problem and is unsure of the solution, he or she will post the problem to an electronic blackboard maintained by the groupware system. Other individuals in the organization who have the knowledge to resolve the issue will note the query on the blackboard and e-mail their suggested solution approach to the original individual posting the issue—hence, sharing their knowledge.

The document component becomes a means of making the process even more efficient by having individuals within the organization transfer documents detailing their resolution to a given problem to a central repository. As shown in Figure 5.5 (page 161), the document is transmitted by the user through the *groupware* system and is transferred to the knowledge management system for storage.

Storing Knowledge in Data Warehouses

At the heart of most knowledge management systems is a series of interconnected data management systems. As shown in Figure 5.5 (page 161), these databases of information and knowledge are generally best managed by using contemporary data warehousing technologies. Data warehousing technology enables the information needed for effective support of decision making to be integrated into a searchable warehouse of knowledge (often via the use of data mining techniques).

[Insert Figure 5.5 here]

The need for data warehousing technology is driven by the vast amounts of information typically required for effective knowledge management. Not all of this so-called “knowledge” is that sophisticated. Much of the “knowledge” in such systems is what is frequently referred to as “three-ring binder knowledge” consisting of items such as standard operating procedures manuals, employee resumes, troubleshooting guides, regulatory guidelines (such as tax laws), and corporate codes (such as codes of conduct or ethics). Other documentation might include memoranda and letters written by various people within the organization. These memoranda and letters are often the best documentation of problem resolution provided customers or clients.

Given the volume of document-driven knowledge included in such systems, it should be apparent that electronic document management technologies can greatly enhance the efficiency and usability of most knowledge management systems. The most prevalent problem with such systems, however, is finding the document that has the answer to your problem. Intelligent systems are increasingly being used to help with this dilemma.

Intelligent Agents for Knowledge Retrieval

Intelligent agents (as discussed earlier in this chapter) have greatly improved the usability and efficiency of knowledge management systems. Many organizations have found electronic blackboards embedded in *groupware* to be somewhat inefficient because experts in their organizations end up spending unproductive time reviewing questions on blackboards placed by other employees. A more efficient approach has long been thought to be the centralized storage of documents such as memoranda and letters that explain problem resolutions and may be reusable with other customers and clients. The problem is how to find the right document for your problem.

Intelligent agents come to the rescue by providing software agents that learn about an individual's work tasks and search behavior to better understand the information the user is likely to be seeking. The intelligent agent is then able to better refine the search and filter out much extraneous information that may be retrieved. The intelligence in these agents generally decreases search time, and so knowledge management systems end up getting used more frequently, as information is identified easily and quickly and with reduced frustration over mounds of unrelated information.

While intelligent agents tend to be the dominant form of AI used for knowledge management, you should certainly recognize that other AI components are used in knowledge management systems. Neural networks can be very helpful in recognizing patterns within the information stored in the vast knowledge warehouses. Further, such technologies can help pull together associated documents to recognize the common threads of information between different documents and pieces of information that have been stored. Additionally, expert systems and business intelligence systems are increasingly finding a home as integrated components of the knowledge management system.

Creating A Knowledge Culture

A major challenge faced in developing effective knowledge management systems is a cultural issue. Knowledge enters the knowledge management system only if individuals within an organization develop the necessary habit of entering information into the system. There are two primary reasons that knowledge is often slow to enter such systems: (1) a reluctance to give up the power associated with being the keeper of some knowledge or expertise and (2) the failure to remember to enter information into the system when key problems have been resolved.

In many organizations, the key to success is to know more about the nature of the organization, its work, or its clients than anyone else. For some who were promoted based upon what they know and whom they know, sharing information freely is a relinquishment of power. Entering information into a knowledge management system is a formal extension to sharing—and far more of an individual's peers will have access to the information. The organization must adjust its criteria for rewarding and promoting employees to reflect the change to a shared knowledge environment. This change in compensation criteria encourages individuals within their organization to participate.

The other problem is getting employees into the habit of entering information into the knowledge management system. Some organizations have moved to the practice of recording participation in the knowledge management system and making participation a part of employees' annual personnel review. This practice provides an extrinsic reward that encourages participation, generally successfully, but also may formalize the knowledge management culture, which can actually inhibit the free flow of information among an entity's employees.

Informal organizations are frequently the most effective at knowledge management, but creating a culture of knowledge sharing remains the difficult part of making such structures work. Perhaps the greatest factor in the failure of organizations to achieve effective knowledge management is the concurrent failure to have addressed behavioral issues surrounding implementation of knowledge management systems. The company in Technology Application 5.6 tackled this problem head on and succeeded in getting its employees to participate.

[Insert Technology Application 5.6 box here]

As organizations continue to struggle with knowledge management issues, one thing that is clear is that organizations cannot afford to ignore cultural issues. Knowledge management is but one of many choices faced by organizations as they attempt to implement information technologies that support their strategic mission. The challenge is in determining a logical plan for the development of intelligent technologies that provide maximum support for the strategic mission of the organization.

Conclusions

Business organizations must be successful in increasingly competitive international markets. Not-for-profit organizations—such as those in health care, education, and government—must deliver high-quality services at a cost that is acceptable to their customers and constituents. Effectively analyzing internal data and business trends gives each organization the understanding it needs to plan for its success in the future.

As we study IS, we find that the Information System and the effective use of information by all members of the organization are central issues for organizations. Advanced information technologies and intelligent systems—such as groupware and intelligent agents—must be successfully integrated with existing Information Systems. Investigation of business intelligence systems, knowledge management systems, and other methods of assisting the management decision maker can lead to Information Systems that drive the long-term success of an organization. Developing your knowledge of decision making, information processing, and advanced technology will allow you to play an important role in the effective application of advanced technologies in your own company.

REVIEW QUESTIONS

RQ5-1 What are the three steps in decision making?

RQ5-2 What factors distinguish the types of information required by strategic level managers, by tactical level managers, and by operational level managers?

RQ5-3 In your own words, explain *structure* as it relates to decisions.

RQ5-4 Describe the components of an *expert system.*

RQ5-5 What factors distinguish a *BI system* from an *ES*? What factors distinguish *ES* from *NN*?

RQ5-6 Describe the purpose of a *knowledge management* system.

DISCUSSION QUESTIONS

DQ5-1 Describe a few structured decisions and a few unstructured decisions. Discuss the relative amount of structure in each decision.

DQ5-2 "To be of any value, an Information System must assist all levels of management." Discuss.

DQ5-3 "All managers should be willing to invest the time to learn to use the organization's BI system." Discuss.

DQ5-4 Describe an example of an organization changing in reaction to pressures in the environment. Compare your example to another example of an organization changing in anticipation of environmental opportunities. Discuss the Information System implications of these two examples.

DQ5-5 Describe how an *expert system* might have helped you to choose which colleges and universities might be best suited for you.

DQ5-6 Explain how a *Business Intelligence system (BI)*, an *expert system (ES)*, and a *neural network (NN)* can assist a decision maker in performing the three steps in decision making. Can these systems perform any of these steps independent of the human decision maker? Discuss your answer.

DQ5-7 Use two different Web search engines (such as Yahoo, Altavista,

Lycos, AskJeeves, Google, or others) to look up a term you learned in this chapter. Why do you think each search engine produces a different list of links? Shouldn't they be the same?

PROBLEMS

P5-1 Select a software package to which you have access that incorporates an intelligent agent. Describe the actions of the intelligent agent and how these actions assist in the use of this package.

P5-2 Assume that you are the owner of a small local business of your choosing. Assume further that you are trying to decide if you want to extend your business by adding an e-business component. For each of the decision-making steps—intelligence, design, and choice—describe the information that you will need and the source of that information.

P5-3 For their maintenance and repair division, Otis Elevator had a goal of not being noticed. That is, the company wanted its elevators to work all the time. They wanted to anticipate when any elevator would need repair and to get the right person, with the right parts and knowledge, to fix any elevator that is having, or may have, a problem. Describe how the company could accomplish this objective by applying the technology introduced in this chapter. For each technology application, describe how it will be used to help achieve the objective.

P5-4 While studying for your open-book final exam in biology, you daydream about having access to an expert system during the exam that would help you get all the correct answers. Based on the ES components described in Technology Insight 5.3 (page 152), describe the contents of the ES. Describe where each of the following would be found:

a) Contents of the textbook

b) Your lecture notes

c) Problem background provided on the exam

d) Your personal experience with nature

e) Your common sense

f) Answers to questions you have about the objective of a problem

Which kinds of questions (e.g., multiple choice, true/false, short essay, problem solving) would the expert system best help you to answer? For which kinds would a neural net be better?

P5-5 Many full-time students aim to complete their college education in a four-year period. Often, students join clubs, fraternities or sororities, or other campus organizations while in school. Since membership in these organizations changes radically each year, it would be very useful for the membership to create and use a knowledge management system to record the "organizational memory" of its prior officers, members, and event planners. Describe the contents of such a knowledge management system for an organization to which you belong. Discuss how your organization might design, create, use and control access to the system.

P5-6 Search the Web to locate the home page of an OLAP or business intelligence software vendor. Download a demo version of the software and try it. Is it easy to use? Does it provide a good level of flexibility? Overall, how would you evaluate the software?

BOXES

[Start TECHNOLOGY INSIGHT 5.1 box here]

TECHNOLOGY INSIGHT 5.1

Lessons About Information Effectiveness from Technical Communication Experts

To be successful providers and consumers of information, to support management decision making, and to add value to their organizations, business professionals must understand specific needs for information so that they can determine the information that best meets those needs. Experts in technical communication (TC) provide some terminology and ideas that we can use to enhance the *effectiveness* of information. This technology insight reinforces the discussion in this chapter as well as provides background for the systems development discussions in Chapters 6 and 7.

First, let's define some terms:

- At the heart of a *business situation* is a problem that needs to be solved, creating a need for information, services, products, or decisions. For example, the situation might be an insufficient quantity of raw materials to continue production of widgets.

Our problem is to decide what to do about it.

- An *activity* is a solution to the situational problem and can vary by management level. For example, a lower-level manager's activity might be to place an emergency order for raw materials; a middle manager could temporarily shift production to another product; and an upper-level manager might choose to stop making widgets altogether.
- The *scenario* defines the actions that enable the information, services, or products to be transferred or the decision to be made. In choosing the appropriate scenario, we answer such questions as: Who will be involved? When? In what way? What roles will people play? What are the types of documents, meetings, or presentations that are part of the situation? What are the values, preferences, rules of etiquette, technological considerations, and criteria that are pertinent to this interaction? For example, when we go to a restaurant we expect certain things to happen: A waiter or waitress will take our order and bring our food. And, we typically won't receive the check until after we get our food. We do *not* expect to give our order to another patron, or to cook our own food, or to get the check before we order! That is, there is a scenario appropriate for a restaurant.

To provide effective communication, we must pick the scenario that is appropriate for the situation. We must be able to say, "This is one of these situations where . . ." and know what actions this situation requires. For example, when we have run out of raw material for making widgets, the scenario for the lower-level manager might include: data about raw materials on order and due in from vendors, names of vendors who can provide the raw materials, cost of an emergency order, whether this decision may be made by a lower-level manager, etc.

- The *communication* includes documents, presentations, meetings, and electronic interaction that initiate, conduct, or interpret the activity or decision. Communication assists in solving the problem by:

    1. Defining the problem by analyzing the need for communication and the audience that must be addressed. This parallels the *intelligence* step in decision making.

    2. Generating alternative courses of action by summarizing and analyzing information. This parallels the *design* step in decision making.

    3. Making choices, negotiating the evaluation of these alternatives, and developing support for any solution. This parallels the *choice* step in decision making.

Let's summarize what we can learn from these technical communication ideas:

1. The context for problem solving (or decision making) is important. As we said when we described *relevance*, information, to be useful, must reduce uncertainty for *this* decision maker for *this* decision.

2. A communication's effectiveness (or information's effectiveness) is situational and rule-governed. For our information to be understood by the recipient, and for the communication to have its intended effect, we must have knowledge of the attitudes and expectations of the audience of the communication.

3. Information's *relevance, usability,* and *understandability*, indeed its value, depend on the audience of the communication, not on the subject being communicated.

4. The relationship of communication and problem solving is not: "(1) I have a problem, (2) I solve the problem, and (3) I communicate the results." Rather, the required communication—the required output—determines your problem-solving activities. In Technical Communications terms, we would say, "We have a business situation (a problem) that requires a solution (an activity), and the communication (the output) determines the scenario (the problem-solving actions to be taken)."

[End TECHNOLOGY INSIGHT 5.1 box here]

[Start Technology Application 5.1 box here]

TECHNOLOGY APPLICATION 5.1

Data Quality

Case 1

The information systems of the state of Montana's Department of Corrections were relying on very poor-quality data as the basis of state and federal reports. Poor data quality caused the state to lose a $1 million grant because they couldn't predict how many of a certain type of offender would be jailed over the next few years. As a result, a major overhaul of the database coupled with the hiring of a data validity officer was undertaken. By 2000, anyone responsible for entering data—from attorneys to guards—was held responsible for the quality of the data entered, and the problem has been reversed.

Case 2

The Prudential Insurance Company of America started a data warehouse project in 1996 to consolidate data from its eight separate lines of business. The goal of the project was to enable data mining to improve customer relationships. In the process, Prudential discovered that different parts of the company collected different data on each customer who might hold several types of policies. Each line of business had its own standards for encoding policy numbers, customer names, and other critical items of data. All told, the company had to define and equate 3,000 different terms describing its customer data. The result of this long data-scrubbing process is a six terabyte data warehouse with common data definitions across the eight lines of business.

Source: Beth Stackpole, "Wash Me," *CIO Magazine,* Vol. 14, Issue 9, February 15, 2001, pp. 100–114.

[End Technology Application 5.1 box here]

[Start TECHNOLOGY INSIGHT 5.2 box here]

TECHNOLOGY INSIGHT 5.2

Business Intelligence Systems

Business Intelligence (BI) systems are Information Systems that assist managers with unstructured decisions by retrieving and analyzing data in order to identify, generate and interpret useful information. A BI system possesses interactive capabilities, aids in answering ad hoc queries, and provides data and modeling facilities, generally through the use of Online Analytical Processing (OLAP) tools, to support nonrecurring, relatively unstructured decision making. OLAP tools could be as simple as a spreadsheet add-on, or provide extended capabilities including what-if analysis, forecasting, allocations, statistical data mining, market basket analysis, business modeling, and real-time data filters.* The main components of a BI system are diagrammed in the accompanying figure. Notice that the data made available to the decision maker include both internal data from an entitywide database or a data warehouse, and data obtained from outside the organization, such as Dow Jones financial information.

[Insert UNF-p.149-1 here]

*Allocations of funds or other assets must be made to regulate the use of scarce or expensive resources. Statistical data mining employs sophisticated statistical techniques to search for patterns in large quantities of data. Market basket analysis examines a portfolio of products, and allows them to be studied as a collection instead of as individual goods. Real-time filters support the sorting of individual data records into groups as each is encountered.

[End TECHNOLOGY INSIGHT 5.2 box here]

[Start Technology Application 5.2 box here]

TECHNOLOGY APPLICATION 5.2

Group Support at PricewaterhouseCoopers

At the heart of PricewaterhouseCoopers TeamMate software is relational database technology that permits sorting and filtering of information by individual audit team members. The system captures, shares, and organizes information for the firm's auditors. In addition to the underlying database technology, TeamMate includes spreadsheet and word-processing programs, as well as software modules developed at PricewaterhouseCoopers (PwC).

At the start of an audit engagement, team members are set up with access rights to an intranet server that contains a master copy of the audit workpapers. These files include the audit programs—a listing of the work to be performed during the audit engagement. As each auditor completes portions of the audit program, he or she updates the shared set of audit workpapers, documenting the audit work performed, the conclusions reached, and any issues discovered. Once the workpapers are updated, the system automatically records electronic information related to when and by whom the workpapers were updated. Through the intranet server—*regardless of their location in the world*—all audit team members have virtually instant access to the updated versions of the audit workpapers on their laptops. These updated versions reflect changes made to the workpapers by *all members of the audit engagement team.* PwC reports that TeamMate has enhanced the *efficiency* and *effectiveness* of its audit engagements. Additionally, PwC believes that TeamMate dramatically improves technical proficiency and accelerates career development of new staff.

Source: *TeamMate98* (PricewaterhouseCoopers, www.pricewaterhousecoopers.com, June 1999).

[End Technology Application 5.2 box here]

[Start TECHNOLOGY INSIGHT 5.3 box here]

TECHNOLOGY INSIGHT 5.3

Expert Systems

An **expert system (ES)** is an Information System that emulates the problem-solving techniques of human experts. The components of an expert system are included in the figure that follows and are described as follows:

[Insert UNF-p.152-2 here]

- A *human expert* possesses relevant knowledge—including both facts and rules—accumulated through years of experience.
- The *knowledge engineer* is a person possessing both the skill to extract relevant knowledge from a human expert and the ability to capture this knowledge in the knowledge base.
- The *knowledge base* contains all the relevant expertise—often in the form of rules—that can be obtained from one or more human experts about a particular subject. This expertise is stored in the knowledge base in the form of decision rules-of-thumb *(heuristics)*, typically as if-then-else statements that are linked in a decision tree structure.
- The *knowledge acquisition facility* furnishes a computer interface in the form of dialogue and input screens to expedite creation and maintenance of the knowledge base. The human expert may use the knowledge acquisition facility, thus assuming the role of the knowledge engineer.
- The *inference engine* executes the line of reasoning by acting on the rules and facts stored in the knowledge base and the inputs from the system user. The inference engine may also have access to other data (described on the expert systems diagram as optional inputs) useful in arriving at a conclusion. For example, data related to the particular decision may be obtained from the *entitywide database* or a separate *data warehouse,* thus obviating the need for the user to enter such data.
- The ES's *user interface* provides a user-friendly interface for entering data and for asking and answering questions. It facilitates user input and contains the *explanation*

facility that traces progress through the reasoning process and provides the user, on request, a description of the logic supporting a decision.

How do we use an expert system? As we said before, we consult an expert system as we would any other expert, to diagnose the source of a problem, to determine how to solve a problem, or to make a decision. For example, in a typical help desk application, an ES might provide an automated troubleshooting guide for computers. In this case, an expert system would start by asking you questions to extract from you information about the problem that you are having with your computer. Expert systems can be used:

- *To perform complex analysis.* When the amount of data and the number of rules are more than the human expert can comprehend, an ES can perform the analysis and either recommend a course of action to a human user, or the ES can be designed to take the appropriate action without human intervention. For example, expert systems are used to monitor chemical production processes.
- *To distribute and preserve the expertise of an expert.* When only one (or only a few) person(s) know how to perform a certain task, an expert system can be "taught" to mimic the actions of the expert. Then the system can assist others in performing the action. For example, one of the "Big Three" U.S. automobile manufacturers developed an expert system to assist a mechanic in diagnosing problems in automobile engines. The knowledge base was extracted from a retiring expert in engine diagnosis. The computer troubleshooting system is another example of this type of expert system. In this case, the expertise of computer repair specialists is being preserved and distributed.
- *To teach.* As you use an expert system, the system's user interface and explanation

facility can help you—a nonexpert—learn the relevant facts and rules. For example, insurance reimbursement specialists can use an ES to learn the detailed rules for determining the amount of medical payments. The computer troubleshooting system can be used to teach personnel how to repair computers.

[End TECHNOLOGY INSIGHT 5.3 box here]

[Start Technology Application 5.3 box here]

TECHNOLOGY APPLICATION 5.3

Using Expert Systems Technology to Support Field Technicians

Picker International has had a long reputation as a quality support company for medical diagnostics systems. However, in the mid-90s, it faced a crisis in shrinking health-care product sales due to tightening expenditures under cost-containment pressures and regulatory questions. The bulk of the company's revenue was coming from field support, and the more information that could be provided to the field technicians, the greater the revenue and profitability forecast. Yet, the technicians headed out to the field with pagers, three-ring binders, schematic diagrams, parts catalogs, and related documentation.

Picker needed to find a way to improve efficiencies. In the current system, the technician was paged, phoned back for instructions, went to a job with a few clues as to the problem, fixed the equipment, and then called back in to report the work that had been completed, the labor hours expended, and the parts used. All of the information was subsequently entered into customer and service databases. The databases provided key information on worker productivity and systems reliability.

New systems were developed with the recognition that if problems could be diagnosed remotely before service calls, technicians would be better prepared to deal with the problems when they arrived. Additionally, access by the technicians to the histories in the databases on product reliability and past customer problems could improve the efficiency of problem diagnosis.

The solution included equipping each technician with a laptop and a new software package, Questor, an expert system for diagnostic support. Questor would both perform diagnostic testing on the equipment to scan the machine's memory for patterns leading to failures and at the same time automatically retrieve histories from the database as to product and customer service call patterns. Based on the retrieved information, the technician then answers a series of questions posed by Questor as it attempts to narrow down the problem possibilities.

The interaction between Questor, users, and the data stores provides identification of product weaknesses and subsequent improvements in design. In aggregate, the observations from multiple service calls develops a pattern of diagnostic tests and repair processes and procedures. These observations can be used to both improve design and to formulate improvements in service repair processes.

Source: Scott Wallace, "Experts in the Field," *Byte* (October 1994): 86–96.

[End Technology Application 5.3 box here]

[Start TECHNOLOGY INSIGHT 5.4 box here]

TECHNOLOGY INSIGHT 5.4

Neural Networks

Neural networks (NN) are computer-based systems that mimic the human brain's ability to recognize patterns or predict outcomes using less than complete information. For example, NN are used to recognize faces, voices, and handwritten characters. NN are also used to sort good apples from bad, to detect fraudulent users of credit cards, and to manage investment funds.

Given a volume of data, an expert system makes a decision by using the knowledge it has acquired from outside experts. Neural networks, on the other hand, derive their knowledge from the data. As an example, let's compare how an expert system and a neural network might predict whether a firm would go bankrupt. For the expert system, the knowledge base would include the rules that experts have used to predict bankruptcy. A rule might be: "If the current ratio is less than X and interest has not been paid on long-term debt, then bankruptcy is likely." The neural network, on the other hand, would be given data on firms that have gone bankrupt and firms that have not. (An expert must decide what data would be relevant.) The neural network "sifts" through the data and decides how to determine whether a firm will go bankrupt, thus developing its own knowledge base. This knowledge base includes an understanding of the patterns underlying the data and the logic necessary to reconstruct the patterns to solve future problems. There are four types of NN:

1. Prediction networks predict the value of an item given the value of other items and can, for example, forecast earnings and future stock prices.
2. Classification networks classify items as members of a specific group; for example, a firm that will go bankrupt or one that will not.
3. Data filtering networks filter imperfect data, such as those associated with language and writing, and decide what has been said or written.

4. Optimization networks find optimal solutions to complex problems. These networks deal with problems that have traditionally been solved with operations research tools.

Sources: Gene Bylinsky, "Computers that Learn by Doing," *Fortune* (September 6, 1993): 96–102; Kenneth O. Cogger, "A Primer on Neural Networks," *AI/ES* Update (Vol. 6, No. 2, 1997): 3–6; Harlan L. Etheridge and Richard C. Brooks, "Neural Networks: A New Technology," *The CPA Journal* (March 1994): 36–39, 52–55.

[End TECHNOLOGY INSIGHT 5.4 box here]

[Start Technology Application 5.4 box here]

TECHNOLOGY APPLICATION 5.4

Uses of Neural Networks

Here are some examples of neural networks (NN), showing how they operate and how useful they can be:

- At Signet Bank, neural networks read and automatically process student loan applications and canceled checks.
- Foster Ousley Conley uses a neural network-based system for residential real estate appraisal. The system performs better than humans because it can review data from hundreds of houses and analyze the data in many different ways.
- At Mellon Bank's Visa and MasterCard operations, NN outperform expert systems—and the experts themselves—in detecting credit card fraud. Since the neural network can learn by experience, it can find incidences of fraud *not anticipated by an expert.*

- The IRS in Taiwan is using a neural network to determine the likelihood of tax evasion and the necessity of further investigation.

In fact, neural networks have become so common that they are emerging as the tool of choice for fraud detection and order checking. Future applications will likely move increasingly toward more intelligent versions that will require even less user intervention.

Sources: "An Interview with Industry: Marge Sherauld, Vice President, Ward Systems Group, Inc." *AI/ES Update* (Vol. 6, No. 2, 1997): 2; Gene Bylinsky, "Computers that Learn by Doing," *Fortune* (September 6, 1993): 96–102; Kenneth O. Cogger, "A Primer on Neural Networks," *AI/ES Update* (Vol. 6, No. 2, 1997): 3–6; Harlan L. Etheridge and Richard C. Brooks, "Neural Networks: A New Technology," *The CPA Journal* (March 1994): 36–39, 52–55; Rebecca Chung-Fern Wu, "Integrating Neurocomputing and Auditing Expertise," *Managerial Auditing Journal* (Vol 9, Issue 3, 1994): 20–26.

[End Technology Application 5.4 box here]

[Start Technology Application 5.5 box here]

TECHNOLOGY APPLICATION 5.5

Use of Intelligent Agents in TurboTax

One of the most common areas for the use of intelligent agents is as software agents that help novice decision makers use specialized software packages. A prime example of such use is with tax return preparation software. The intelligent agents embedded in one of the more popular such packages, TurboTax, have three primary focus points: (1) support completing the entry of personal tax information, (2) use available information to identify additional possible tax deductions, and (3) identify potential red flags that may trigger an audit from the Internal Revenue Service (IRS).

Support for Information Entry: Two agents are used to support the information entry process. The first agent monitors information entered into the individual's tax return to control which questions are asked of the user. This helps avoid having the user answer lots of questions that are not relevant to the individual's particular return. Additionally, as the user answers questions and enters information, "frequently asked questions" are displayed on the margin along with explanations and answers. This saves the user time by anticipating questions the user may have.

Missing Tax Deductions: The agent for tax deductions monitors the individual's return and watches for patterns in the return that suggest legitimate tax deductions may not have been identified by the user. These patterns are based on historical information about tax returns and the relationships that have been identified between different revenue-generating activities and the expenses that are normally associated with them. When the user is finished entering information, the system then alerts the user to potential missing deductions.

Audit Flags: When the user is finished entering information into the tax return, the audit flag agent looks for patterns in the information that appear suspicious and/or may exceed normal tolerable levels, and identifies these areas to the user as possible areas that may trigger an audit by the IRS. The user can review the information flagged to ensure the reliability of the information.

Together, the intelligent agents embedded in the software help the user develop a more accurate and less risky return. The benefit of reduced frustration that comes from the helpful hints is likely to bring the customer back.

Source: *User's Guide TurboTax: Tax Year 1998* (Intuit Inc., Tucson, AZ, 1998).

[End Technology Application 5.5 box here]

[Start TECHNOLOGY INSIGHT 5.5 box here]

TECHNOLOGY INSIGHT 5.5

Peer-to-Peer Groupware

An alternative to groupware that relies on a server to store centralized data and programs is peer-to-peer computing, in which any computer can directly connect to any other computer over the World Wide Web. The popular music sharing software Napster was the first to exploit peer-to-peer networking (before it ran into legal trouble). Another popular application for peer-to-peer is instant messaging, which allows a direct network connection between any two or more computers to communicate instantaneously without going through an e-mail server.

Peer-to-peer can also be used for business applications such as groupware. One company, GrooveNetworks, has a test version of a peer-to-peer platform intended to support individual and small group interaction. In addition to individual communication and file sharing, there are several business applications that might be improved when built on this platform. The Groove Web site suggests that the product would fit within many business processes, including:

- Purchasing
- Inventory control
- Distribution

- Exchanges and auctions
- Channel and partner relationship management
- Customer care and support

For example, the computer of a firm needing to order a product could poll various vendors' systems and check inventory availability, select a vendor based on specified criteria (i.e., those with favored credit status, or inexpensive goods, or local access), and update internal records to indicate when the items are expected to arrive. Clearly, these systems need to be very reliable and highly secure to prevent malicious destruction or significant errors such as ordering more goods than are needed, or goods with less than desirable cost or quality.

Source: www.groove.net, April 2001.

[End TECHNOLOGY INSIGHT 5.5 box here]

[Start Technology Application 5.6 box here]

TECHNOLOGY APPLICATION 5.6

Enforcing Knowledge Management

An international consulting firm from Spain has succeeded in convincing its consultants that sharing their knowledge online is key to the company's survival. Cluster Competitiveness of Barcelona recently instituted a policy whereby all paper left on desks each evening was collected and destroyed. The policy underscored the company's belief that all consultants' work should be shared through their online knowledge management system. Within four months after paper was banned from the office, the collection process was no longer needed.

Because the company can't afford to hire highly experienced staff, or train bright new hires, it has set up this central repository of company knowledge so that even brand new hires get instant access to all of the company's files and intellectual capital. As a result, new hires can get to work quickly and productively.

The company is very pleased with the system and offsets its use with regular meetings at which war stories are traded and client relationships are analyzed. Staff members don't need elaborate offices, nor do they store large amounts of data on their own computers. Instead, they have access to everything they might need on the company's intranet, which is accessible any time and any place they might be working. The company is a model of the paperless office. The strategy must be working, as the company is growing and its clients are very satisfied with their products.

Source: Gary Abramson, "Operation Brain-Trap" *CIO Enterprise Magazine* (Vol. 13, Issue 4, November 15, 1999), p. 78–82.

[End Technology Application 5.6 box here]

Part III

Development of Information Systems

6 Systems Analysis

7 Systems Design and Implementation

[Insert UNF-p.167-1 here]

6

Systems Analysis

Oxford Health Plans, Inc. developed a new billing and claims processing system for its health maintenance organization intended to put the company on the IT cutting edge and secure its place in the leadership of its industry. It was not successful. The system was in development for more than 5 years, had 100 outside contractors, and cost more than $20 million per year to develop. When implemented, the system:

- Was three to four months behind in getting premium bills to customers.
- Left claims unpaid for six or more months. Medical providers were advanced $275 million against these claims.
- Could not handle the volume of transactions. For example, new member signup was to take 6 seconds but, instead, took 15 minutes.

These problems resulted in:

- Customers canceling their memberships, leaving customer rolls inflated by 30,000 and revenues overstated by $111 million.
- Unprocessed claims that led to higher-than-expected losses and refusal of some providers to service Oxford clients.
- Erroneous data being generated that caused Oxford to write off $94.1 million of uncorrectable accounts receivable leading to a loss in one quarter of $78.2 million ($0.99/share).

How did this disaster happen? Oxford did not have a clear definition of the project and was not prepared to manage it to successful completion. The high turnover of programmers led to a lack of development continuity. The work was poorly done and new systems inadequately tested.

Synopsis

Organizations exist in a dynamic environment. Driven by demands for IT services, competitive business pressures, and opportunities provided by availability of information technology, the *Information Services Function (ISF)* of the modern organization must adapt its services quickly and continuously. Examples of these demands include:

- Demand for increased customer service measured by flexibility, speed, quality, and 24-hour-a-day, seven-day-a-week (called

"24/7") availability.

- Demand for added functionality by users of an organization's IT infrastructure. For example, internal users need access to services away from the office and may want to employ new wireless technologies to do so.
- Implementation of *enterprise systems (ES)* to connect business processes and better manage the organization. These implementations often require reengineering of the business processes to match them with the processes in the ES.
- Change in processes and relationships along the *supply chain* to reduce costs and provide better customer service. These require changes to business processes, IT infrastructure, and IS processes.
- Use of the *Internet* and related technologies to collaborate with business partners in ways never before seen.

Thus, the ISF must align its strategy and objectives to the business' strategy and objectives and deliver new or modified quality IT solutions in a timely manner. This and the next chapter describe the processes (i.e., management practices, controls) typically employed to develop and modify these IT solutions.

LEARNING OBJECTIVES

- To name the systems development process and its major phases and steps

- To describe how Information Systems are planned, developed, and acquired or modified, so that those systems can be directed at achieving an organization's objectives
- To explain the importance of managing the systems development process to ensure attainment of development objectives
- To describe the nature and importance of your future involvement in systems development
- To name the goals, plans, tasks, tools, and results of the first two steps in systems development, the systems survey and systems analysis
- To explain the costs of developing, maintaining, and operating an Information System
- To list typical Information Systems benefits

Introduction

This chapter introduces the systems development process, which comprises four distinct phases: systems analysis, design, implementation, and operation. Because your involvement in the *systems development life cycle (SDLC)* typically will be that of a user or manager, discussions in this and the next chapter emphasize participating in, rather than conducting, systems development.

Our introduction to the systems development process begins with a definition of systems development and an assessment of how well organizations achieve their systems development objectives. Then we consider management processes (i.e., controls) that can advance the achievement of systems development objectives. Third, we discuss *business process engineering,* a phenomena that has been the source of many systems development initiatives. We conclude with a brief discussion of change management, a process to increase acceptance of new systems by an organization's personnel.

After this introduction, we examine the first phase in systems development: systems analysis. Organizations conduct the first step in systems analysis, the systems survey (often called a *feasibility study*) to decide what, if any, systems development efforts will be undertaken to solve an Information Systems problem. Organizations conduct the second step in the systems analysis phase, called structured systems analysis, to define the systems development problem and develop specifications for an Information System that will solve the problem.

Definition and Objectives of Systems Development

Organizations exist in a dynamic environment, and thus, they regularly experience changes in their

- Legal requirements, such as government reporting.
- Level and kinds of competition.
- Technologies, such as data entry devices, bar codes, and radio frequency identification (RFID) tags used to record and process

information.

- Lines of business or kinds of business activities.
- Management desire for better access to information and improved management reporting.

All of these challenges at varying times necessitate changes to organizations' Information Systems. These changes may either require the *creation* of new Information Systems or *significant modifications* to existing Information Systems. **Systems development** comprises the steps undertaken to create, modify, or maintain an organization's Information System. These steps, along with the project management concepts discussed below, guide the in-house development of Information Systems (i.e., *make*), as well as the acquisition of systems solutions (i.e., *buy*). A term often used synonymously with systems development is *systems development life cycle* or *SDLC.* The term **systems development life cycle (SDLC)** is used in several ways. It can mean:

Review Question

What is systems development?

1. A formal set of activities, or a *process,* used to develop and implement a new or modified Information System (referred to below as a *systems development methodology.*)
2. The documentation that specifies the systems development

process referred to as the *systems development standards manual.*

3. The progression of Information Systems through the systems development process, from birth through implementation to ongoing use.

Review Question

What is the difference between systems development and the systems development life cycle (SDLC)?

The "life cycle" idea comes from this last view and is the definition that we use in this text. Systems development is also an important—sometimes dominant—component of more comprehensive organizational change via *business process reengineering.* These terms as well as "systems life cycle" and "systems analysis and design" are also used to refer to the systems development process.

Review Question

What are the systems development objectives?

We propose the following *systems development objectives:*

- To develop information systems that satisfy an organization's informational, operational, and management requirements. Note that this objective relates to the *system* being developed.
- To develop information systems in an efficient and effective

manner.

Note that this objective relates more to the development *process* than to its outcome.

Review Question

What benefits are derived from using a systems development methodology?

Systems Development Methodology A **systems development methodology** is a formalized, standardized, documented set of activities used to manage a systems development project. It should be used when information systems are developed, acquired, or maintained. Exhibit 6.1 describes the characteristics of an SDLC. Following such a methodology helps ensure that development efforts are efficient and consistently leads to Information Systems that meet organizational needs.

[Insert Exhibit 6.1 here]

Systems Development Phases, Steps, Purposes, and Tasks Figure 6.1 (page 172) presents the systems development life cycle. The right side of the figure depicts the four *development phases:* systems analysis, systems design, systems implementation, and systems operation. The bubbles in Figure 6.1 identify the seven *development steps* undertaken to complete the four phases of development. Arrows flowing into each bubble represent the inputs needed to perform that step, whereas outward-flowing arrows represent the product of a step.

[Insert Figure 6.1 here]

Table 6.1 lists the key purposes and tasks associated with the seven development steps (bubbles) shown in Figure 6.1. You should take some time now to review both the table and the figure.

[Insert Table 6.1 here]

Review Question

What are the systems development phases, steps, purposes, and tasks?

In the past it often took a new system years to move through the initial steps (i.e., bubbles 1 through 5 in Figure 6.1) in the life cycle. Now business moves at "Internet speed" and must develop B2B (business-to-business) and other business infrastructure systems in 90 to 180 days. If they don't, they may be put out of business or absorbed by organizations that can.[1]

Systems development does not always proceed in the orderly, sequential course suggested by Figure 6.1. Some subset of steps may be repeated over and over until a satisfactory result is achieved. Or, we may undertake certain steps out of sequence. Finally, systems development may be outsourced to consultants or vendors, and personnel from within the organization will be part of the development team to serve as business process experts. The presentation in Chapters 6 and 7 assumes that systems development will be performed by an organization's own systems development personnel, proceeding as depicted in Figure 6.1. In Technology Insight 6.1 (page 174), we briefly describe some alternative approaches that may be used. The alternatives discussed there include who will develop the system and *how* the *SDLC* (Figure 6.1) might be altered. We also discuss alternative focuses for analysis and design—namely, *data, functions,* and *objects.*

[1] Peter G. W. Keen, "Six months—Or Else" *Computerworld* (April 10, 2000): 48.

[Insert TECHNOLOGY INSIGHT 6.1 box here]

Controlling the Systems Development Process

Would it surprise you to learn that many organizations are *not* successful at developing information systems? Unfortunately, this is true. Indeed, one report said one in four enterprise systems projects went over budget, 20 percent were terminated before completion, and 40 percent fail to achieve business objectives one year after completion.[2] Exhibit 6.2 (page 176)summarizes a few reasons why organizations fail to achieve their systems development objectives.

[2] Mitch Betts, "Why ERP Projects Cause Panic Attacks," *Computerworld* (September 24, 2001): 8.

[Insert Exhibit 6.2 here]

To overcome these and other problems, organizations must execute the systems development process efficiently and effectively. The key to achieving these objectives is to control the development process. Apparently, that is not an easy chore, or more organizations would be successful at it. We can understand the complexity of the systems development process by comparing it to a construction project. Assume you are in charge of the construction of an industrial park. What problems and questions might you encounter? First, you might want to know how much of the project is your responsibility. Are you to handle legal and financial matters? Who obtains the building permits? Are you to contact the tenants/buyers to determine special needs? The project's size and duration cause another set of problems. How will you coordinate the work of the carpenters, masons, electricians, and plumbers? Or, how will you see that a tenant's special needs are incorporated into the specifications and then into the actual construction?

Information Systems developers encounter similar problems. Given such problems, they have concluded that systems development must be carefully controlled and managed by following good project management principles and the organization's quality assurance framework embodied in its systems development life cycle methodology. These are described in the following subsections.

Project Management

A recent survey of IS audit and control professionals found the following project management items associated with failed projects:

- Underestimation of the time to complete the project
- Lack of monitoring by senior management
- Underestimation of necessary resources
- Underestimation of size and scope of the project
- Inadequate project control mechanism
- Changing systems specifications
- Inadequate planning.[3]

[3] Mark Keil and Joan Mann, "Results from a Survey of IS Audit and Control Professionals," *IS Audit & Control Journal* (Volume II, 1997): 66.

To manage projects well, organizations should adopt a framework for project management that includes the elements enumerated in Exhibit 6.3. The project work plan, including phases, work to be accomplished in each, times, and cost, are often documented using a project management tool such as Microsoft Project. Project management—particularly the planning process and establishing the project schedule—ultimately can determine the success of the project.

Review Question

What are the essential elements of good project management?

[Insert Exhibit 6.3 here]

Quality Assurance

Project management frameworks apply to any project. To ensure that Information Systems will meet the needs of customers, projects involving the creation or modification of Information Systems must include elements that specifically address the quality of the system being developed. **Quality assurance (QA)** addresses the prevention and detection of errors, especially defects in software that may occur during the system development process. By focusing on the procedures employed during the systems development process, QA activities are directed at preventing errors that may occur. QA activities are also directed at testing developed systems to eliminate defects—to ensure that they meet the users' requirements—before systems are implemented. Two prominent sources of guidance for QA are ISO 9000-3 and the Capability Maturity Model (CMM) developed by the Software Engineering Institute (SEI) at Carnegie Mellon University.

ISO 9000-3 **ISO 9000-3** is a set of standards developed by The International Organization for Standards (ISO), that describe what an organization must do to manage their software development processes. The assumption, as with all ISO standards, is that if the ISO 9000-3 standards are followed, the development process will produce a "quality" software "product." ISO defines a quality product as one that conforms to customer requirements. Notice that the ISO concepts of quality "products" and "processes" parallel our two systems development objectives. Exhibit 6.4 contains examples of the ISO 9000-3 standards. Review those examples and identify the elements that are common among *project management, a systems development methodology,* and the ISO standards.

[Insert Exhibit 6.4 here]

Capability Maturity Model The **Capability Maturity Model® for Software (SW-CMM)** is a model that helps organizations evaluate the effectiveness of their software development processes and identifies the key practices that are required to increase the maturity of those processes. Exhibit 6.5 describes the five SW-CMM maturity levels and the key principles and practices for each. Notice, for example, that project management is a key indicator that an organization has attained level 2. The Software Engineering Institute believes that predictability, effectiveness, and control of an organization's software processes improve as the organization moves up the five levels. However, moving from level 1 to level 2 may take an organization 2 years or more. Moving from level 2 to 3 may take another 2 years.

Review Question

What are the five maturity levels of the Capability Maturity Model (CMM)?

[Insert Exhibit 6.5 here]

A recent study found that achievement of a Level 3 SW-CMM maturity by an organization, along with the implementation of a structured systems development methodology, contributes to the quality and cost-effectiveness of the software development process. In fact, there was significant improvement on 11 of 14 measures after Level 3 was attained. Improvements included communication and teamwork, lower maintenance costs, and lower levels of system defects.[4]

[4] Kay M. Nelson, Martha M. Eining, and David Plumlee, "Potential Expansion of Assurance Services: An Examination of the Bluejay Organization," Unpublished manuscript, August 2000.

Involvement in Systems Development

Table 6.2 indicates the ways managers and other Information Systems users can become involved in systems development. You should keep these categories in mind because in this and the next chapter, your participation is discussed in terms of these categories.

Review Question

Describe the ways that a manager or system user might be involved in systems development.

[Insert Table 6.2 here]

Business Process Reengineering

So far we have introduced systems development, systems development objectives, and means for controlling the systems development process to ensure achievement of systems development objectives. Now we turn to discussion of an activity that has driven much of the systems development activities undertaken in organizations. Business process reengineering is an activity larger in scope than systems development, as it addresses all of the processes in the organization, including the information systems processes. Rapid developments in the capabilities and applications of IT, such as e-business, present organizations with increasingly difficult business opportunities/challenges. They are being asked—sometimes being forced in order to ensure their very survival—to abandon long-held business beliefs and assumptions and to rethink what they are attempting to accomplish and how they are trying to accomplish it. *Business process reengineering* has been likened to presenting an organization's management with a blank piece of paper and asking them to reinvent the organization from scratch. Why would management ever be motivated to engage in such an undertaking? In many cases, they have no alternative. Experiencing the harsh realities of an increasingly competitive environment, they recognize that their companies must make mega-changes in how they operate, or face extinction.

Business process reengineering (BPR) (or simply *reengineering*) is "the *fundamental* rethinking and *radical* redesign of business *processes* to achieve *dramatic* improvements in critical contemporary measures of performance, such as cost, quality, service, and speed."[5] The emphasis on four words in this definition focuses on those four key components of BPR.

[5] "Fortune Book Excerpt: The Promise of Reengineering," *Fortune* (May 3, 1993): 95.

1. *Fundamental* rethinking of business processes requires management to challenge the basic assumptions under which it operates and to ask such rudimentary questions as "Why do we do what we do?" and "Why do we do it the way we do it?" Without fundamental rethinking, technology often merely automates old ways of doing business. The result is that what was a lousy way of doing a job became simply a speeded-up, lousy way of doing the job.

2. *Radical* redesign relies on a fresh-start, clean-slate approach to examining an organization's business processes. This approach focuses on answers to the question, "If we were a brand-new business, how would we operate our company?" The goal is to reinvent what is done and how it is done rather than to "tinker"

with the present system by making marginal, incremental, superficial improvements to what's already being done. Achieving the goal requires forward-looking, creative thinkers who are unconstrained by what now exists.

3. Achieving *dramatic* improvements in performance measurements is related to the preceding two elements. The fundamental rethinking and radical redesign of business processes are aimed toward making quantum leaps in performance, however measured. We are not talking about improvement in quality, speed, and the like that is on the order of 10%. Improvement of that order of magnitude often can be accomplished with marginal, incremental changes to existing processes. Reengineering, on the other hand, has much loftier objectives. For example, the Ford Motor Company reengineered their procurement process and reduced the number of persons employed in the process by 75%.[6]

[6] Michael Hammer, "Reengineering Work: Don't Automate, Obliterate," *Harvard Business Review* (July–August 1990): 105–107.

4. Reengineering focuses on end-to-end business *processes* rather than on the individual activities that comprise the processes. BPR takes a holistic view of a business process as comprising a string of activities that cut across traditional departmental or

functional lines. BPR is concerned with the results of the process (i.e., with those activities that add value to the process).

Review Question

What are the key elements and principles of *business process reengineering (BPR)*?

As an example, let's look at the discrete activities that may be involved in completing a sale to a customer. These activities might include receiving and recording a customer's order, checking the customer's credit, verifying inventory availability, accepting the order, picking the goods in the warehouse, packing and shipping the goods, and preparing and sending the bill. Reengineering would change our emphasis by breaking down the walls among the separate functions and departments that might be performing these activities. Instead of order taking, picking, shipping, and so forth, we would examine the entire process of "order fulfillment" and would concentrate on those activities that add value for the customer. Instead of assigning responsibility for these activities to multiple individuals and organizational units, we might assign one individual to oversee them all. And, just as important, we might change measurement of performance from the number of orders processed by each individual to an assessment of customer service indicators such as delivering the right goods, in the proper quantities, in satisfactory condition, and at the agreed upon time and price.

Having reviewed the core elements of BPR, let's look at how these elements were applied in a real-world implementation. The late 1990s saw the rapid growth (and decline) of many Web-enabled e-business ventures. One of the more visible ones was Peapod, Inc., an online grocery superstore. "Peapod is America's largest Internet shopping and delivery service with about 100,000 customers. We have fulfilled over 1,000,000 orders and sold over 45,000,000 products to our customers in Chicago, IL; Boston, MA; Columbus, OH; San Francisco, CA; Long Island, NY; and Houston, Dallas, and Austin, TX."[7] Exhibit 6.6 (page 182)summarizes how the Peapod model for grocery delivery differs from that of a traditional grocery store. Notice, for example, the number of times the box of cereal is handled and moved in the two models.

[7] http://www.peapod.com/peaweb/pi/faq.html. July 18, 2001.

[Insert Exhibit 6.6 here]

Peapod's business model is built on the following propositions. First, Peapod uses a distribution model with two formats. In large metropolitan areas, Peapod uses a freestanding distribution center while in their smaller areas, they use fast-pick centers in the supermarkets owned by Ahold. The relationship with Ahold, the "bricks" element of their business model, combined with distribution centers used just for online orders, the "clicks" element of their business model, gives Peapod a lower cost of entry and stronger buying power, allowing Peapod to cut merchandise costs between 5 and 7 percent. The second element of Peapod's success is their process for picking, packing, and delivering customer orders. Orders pulled off the Web site go immediately into Peapod's routing system, customized software that uses maps and travel time to determine how many stops each vehicle can make. Meanwhile, a professionally trained Peapod Personal Shopper handpicks and packs the orders. Peapod makes use of zone and batch picking. Some employees pick perishables while others pick dry goods. If the customer orders produce, a Produce Specialist makes sure that the freshest produce available is chosen for the order, and the Quality Control Specialist ensures that the order is complete and that the groceries are expertly packed.

The Peapod inventory and delivery model was a *fundamental* rethinking and radical redesign of the traditional grocery store model. Peapod's business model is predicated on *dramatic* performance improvements for personnel and infrastructure. The Peapod model focuses on the end-to-end business *process,* getting the groceries to the customer and improving the customer's experience! For example, Peapod's prices are tied to the current off-line prices of their partnering retail stores, giving their customers the weekly advertised sale prices. Peapod's customers also get personalized and online coupons, the ability to create and save personal shopping lists, browse aisles, search for specific items, brands or flavors, and the ability to view nutrition labels. Finally, Peapod customers get a choice of delivery times and formats, minimal (and decreasing) time between ordering and delivery, and up-to-the minute information on order status. Peapod is a good example of a successfully reengineered business model.

When asked to identify the critical success factors for reengineering projects, a group of Chief Information Officers (CIOs) cited strong project management, a visible and involved executive sponsor, and a compelling case for change.[8] Organizational resistance to change, inadequate executive sponsorship and involvement, inadequate project management, and the lack of an effective change management program were described as significant barriers to change by this same group of CIOs. The following section describes methods that can overcome resistance to change.

[8] *Leading Trends in Information Services* (Kansas City, MO: Deloitte & Touche Consulting Group, 1996): 19.

Change Management

The modern business organization lives or dies by its ability to respond to change. It must embody a spirit of adaptation. However, most humans resist change. The introduction or modification of an Information System is one of the most far-reaching changes that an organization can undergo, especially when these changes are accompanied by, or driven by, business process changes. To reap the full benefits of a new system, management must find ways to overcome dysfunctional behaviors brought on by the implementation of a new Information System. Experience has shown that resistance to change can be the foremost obstacle facing successful system implementation.

People's concerns regarding IT and business process changes center on actual and perceived changes in work procedures and relationships, corporate culture, and organizational hierarchy that these changes bring. To address these fears, systems professionals and users must collaborate on the design and implementation of the new system. This collaboration must include the system itself and the process that will be followed during its development and installation. The change must be managed, but not directed. Rather, users must participate in the development and change processes.

Research and practice provide guidance to help us achieve successful change. A recent research study found that users who effectively participated in a systems change process were able to affect outcomes, and had a more positive attitude and a higher involvement with the new system. And, the system was more successful.[9] In practice, we find that successful, large IT change projects—especially those involving enterprise systems—must be driven by the business processes and managed by the business process owners. In these cases, IT assists with, but does not drive, the change process.

[9] James E. Hunton and Jesse D. Beeler, "Effects of User participation in Systems Development: A Longitudinal Field Experiment," *MIS Quarterly* (December 1997): 359–383.

Technological change is not welcomed if it comes as a surprise. Users at all levels must be brought into the process early in the SDLC to encourage suggestions and discussion about the change. Users involved from the start and given a say in redesigning their jobs tend to identify with the system. As problems arise, their attitude is more likely to be, "We have a problem," rather than, "The system makes too many mistakes."

In engineering a systems change, it is crucial to consider the human element. Resistance should be anticipated and its underlying causes addressed. User commitment can be enlisted by encouraging participation during development and by using achievement of business objectives, rather than IT change, to drive the process. Potential users must be sold on the benefits of a system and made to believe that they are capable of working with that system. A policy of coercion will lead to substandard performance.

Systems Survey

This section discusses the systems survey, the first step in the development of a system. The systems survey is conducted to investigate Information Systems problems and to decide on a course of action. One course of action will be to proceed with development. However, initial investigation may find that there is no problem and broader analysis is not warranted. We must be careful in reaching conclusions, because problems may be ill defined and not appropriately identified by users.

Triggering Systems Development

A *systems survey* is initiated when the organization's IT strategic plan prescribes the development or when a user requests the development or modification of a new system. In *planned* reviews, systems analysts may not be aware of any particular problems (other than those identified in preparing the strategic plan). In such cases, they conduct the systems survey to see whether information processing problems exist or if they can improve an Information System. Planned systems development determines whether:

- A system still satisfies users' information needs.
- New design ideas can be incorporated.
- Evolving environmental changes, such as competition, require system changes.
- New types of business by a firm require system changes.

Review Question

What events or conditions may cause a systems survey to be initiated?

The user *requests* systems development when a system no longer efficiently and effectively meets their goals. User-requested systems development may occur when:

- Government regulations require new or modified reports.
- Current reports do not meet decision-making needs.
- Erroneous system outputs occur.
- Escalating customer or vendor complaints are received.
- The information system causes delays that slow a business process.

Notice that many of those reasons are rooted in a desire to leverage new technology for competitive advantage.

The organization should have a formal process for selecting projects to ensure that they are consistent with the organizational goals and strategies identified in the strategic plan for IT. Potential projects should be prioritized and approved by the *IT steering committee* to ensure that:

- Efficient and effective use is made of existing IT resources.
- IT resources are directed at achieving organizational objectives.
- Information services are used consistently throughout the

organization.

Definition and Goals

The **systems survey**, often called a **feasibility study** or **preliminary feasibility study**, is a set of procedures conducted to determine the feasibility of a potential systems development project and to prepare a systems development plan for projects considered feasible. Refer to Figure 6.1 (page 172) to see the system survey's place in the SDLC (first), its inputs (request for systems development and miscellaneous environmental information), and its outputs (approved feasibility document).

Each step in the SDLC has goals that support the systems development objectives (to develop Information Systems that satisfy the organization's needs and to develop Information Systems efficiently and effectively). An organization conducts a systems survey to determine whether it is worthwhile to proceed with subsequent development steps. The *systems survey goals* are as follows:

- *Identify the nature and the extent of systems development* by determining for each reported problem the problem's existence (i.e., does a problem really exist?) and nature (i.e., what is causing the problem?).
- *Determine the scope of the problem.*

- *Propose a course of action that might solve the problem.*
- *Determine the feasibility of any proposed development.* Is there a *technically, economically,* and *operationally* feasible solution to the problem?
- *Devise a detailed plan for conducting the analysis step.* Determine who will conduct the analysis, who will head the project team, what tasks are required, and what the development timetable is.
- *Devise a summary plan for the entire development project.*

Review Question

What are the systems survey goals?

Gather Facts

The first task in the systems survey is to *gather* facts. In the systems survey, the analyst gathers facts to achieve the systems survey goals. That is, facts are gathered to determine the nature and scope of the reported problem, to perform the feasibility study, and to plan the development project.

The analyst tries to determine what the system does now (the "as is") and what we would like for it to do (the "to be"). To determine what the system is doing, we look at the system's documentation and examine the system's operation. To determine what the system should be doing, we obtain information from users and authoritative sources.

The extent of fact gathering must be consistent with cost and time constraints imposed on the systems survey. That is, the systems survey must be conducted as quickly and as inexpensively as possible, yet still accomplish its goals. If the project goes beyond the systems survey, additional, more detailed facts will be gathered during *structured systems analysis.*

Systems developers use a number of tools to gather facts. In Appendix 6A, we define and describe those fact-gathering tools typically used in systems development. Some of those tools may be used to gather facts during the systems survey.

Perform Preliminary Feasibility Study

Having completed the task of gathering and documenting facts, an analyst knows what the new system should do and what the present system or process actually does. The analyst undertakes the second systems survey task, the *preliminary feasibility study,* to determine whether we can solve the problem and whether we can do so at a reasonable cost. There are three aspects of feasibility:

- **Technical feasibility.** A problem has a technically feasible solution if it can be solved using available (already possessed or obtainable) hardware and software technology.
- **Operational feasibility.** A problem has an operationally feasible

solution if it can be solved given the organization's available (already possessed or obtainable) personnel and procedures. In assessing this aspect of feasibility, the analyst should consider behavioral reactions to the systems change. Projects that include reengineering of existing business processes may face strong resistance because personnel may envision shifts in power, changes in day-to-day activities, and layoffs. Timing and scheduling may also be factors. An organization may have the available resources but cannot or will not commit them to a particular project at this time. The organization may wish to scale down a project, take an alternative course of action, or break the project into smaller projects to better fit scheduling needs.

- **Economic feasibility.** Determining economic feasibility can be a bit more complex. A problem has an economically feasible solution if:
    - Costs for this project seem reasonable. For example, the benefits exceed the costs.
    - This project compares favorably to competing uses for the organization's resources.

Determining the costs and benefits for information systems is difficult at best. And, estimating project costs and benefits this early in the SDLC might seem premature. After all, we have done very little work on the development and know very little about the new system. But, management must decide *now* whether to proceed. Therefore, management must know the estimated costs and benefits of the development, no matter how roughly estimated.

Review Question

What are three aspects of feasibility? Explain each.

Devise the Project Plan

As described earlier in the chapter, project management is an important mechanism for controlling a systems development project. Control of a project becomes more important as the risks of failure increase. These risks, many of which are discovered during the feasibility study, include:[10]

[10] Our thanks to our colleague Janis L. Gogan, Bentley College, who adapted these ideas about project risk from Lynda M. Applegate, F. Warren McFarlan, and James L. McKenney, *Corporate Information Systems Management: Text and Cases,* 4th edition (Boston, MA: Richard D. Irwin Company, 1996): 624–639.

- Project size—both absolute and compared to other IT projects—as measured by staffing, costs, time, and number of organizational units affected. Projects that involve *reengineering* and/or the installation of an *enterprise system* are normally larger than those that do not.
- Degree of definition. Projects that are well defined in terms of

their outputs and the steps necessary to obtain those outputs are less risky than those that require user and developer judgment.

- Experience with technology. Risk increases as the organization's experience with the relevant technology decreases.
- Organizational readiness. This aspect of operational feasibility addresses the organization's experience with management of similar projects, as well as management and user preparation for and commitment to this project.

Although project management cannot address all of these risks, it is an important element in minimizing their impact.

If the preliminary feasibility evaluation indicates that further analysis of the problem is warranted, the analyst devises a *project plan.* A **project plan** is a statement of a project's scope, timetable, resources required to complete the project, and the project's costs. The systems survey's planning aspect is so important that the systems survey is often called "systems planning." The project plan includes a broad plan for the entire development, as well as a specific plan for structured systems analysis—the next development step.

We develop a project plan:

- *To provide a means to schedule the use of required resources.* What personnel and funds will be required and when?

- *To indicate major project milestones to monitor the project's progress.* Is the project on schedule? Has the project provided the required deliverables?
- *To forecast the project budget, which is used to authorize project continuation.* Given the project's progress to date, should additional funds be expended for this step? For the next step?
- *To furnish guidelines for making a go or no-go decision.* Are the costs and benefits as projected? Is the utilization of these resources (monetary and personnel) in the best interest of the organization at this time?
- *To offer a framework by which management can determine the reasonableness and completeness of the project's steps.* Is there a complete list of tasks, and are these tasks properly matched with the required skills? Are the proper information sources being investigated?

Review Question

Why develop a project plan?

We use a combination of diagrams, schedules, and other project management tools to develop and document the project plan.

Obtain Approvals

Prior to completing the systems survey, the analyst must obtain approvals (signoffs). As mentioned earlier, signoffs signify approval of both the development process and the system being developed. Obtaining systems survey approvals ensures that the feasibility document's contents are complete, reasonable, and satisfactory to the major development participants. Obtaining agreement on the document's contents is a key element in the development process because such agreement paves the way for cooperation as the project progresses.

Review Question

Why obtain signoffs on the feasibility document?

These approvals fall into two categories: approvals from users/participants and *management control point* approvals. User/participant approvals verify the accuracy of any interviews or observations and the accuracy, completeness, and reasonableness of the survey documentation and conclusions. Such approvals reduce resistance to the project and pave the way for accepting the effectiveness of the new system. The second type of signoff, called a **management control point**, occurs at a place in the systems development process requiring management approval of further development work (i.e., a go/no-go decision). Upper management control points occur at the end of each development phase (systems survey, analysis, etc.); IT management control points occur within phases; project management control points occur at the completion of individual work units. These ensure management commitment to the project and the resources required to bring the project to closure.

Structured Systems Analysis

As a result of decisions made in the *systems survey,* we know if and how to proceed with systems development. If we have decided to proceed, we perform the second step in systems development, structured systems analysis. We must perform the procedures in this step well to have any chance of achieving the first of our systems development objectives—to develop systems that meet user needs—because it is during systems analysis that we determine those needs. Without a well-understood and documented target (i.e., user requirements) we cannot hope to have a successful development process.

At one point or other in your professional career, you may be asked to take on both roles in this process. You will be a system user or business process owner articulating your needs or you will be a member of the development team that must determine and document those needs. Neither process is easy. The tools and techniques described in this chapter should help in the documentation of user requirements.

Management (or the *IT steering committee*) bases the decision about whether and how to proceed on information gathered in the systems survey and on other information. Management might decide to reduce the suggested analysis scope in order to reduce short-term development costs. Or management might cancel, postpone, or modify future systems work because a major modification is preferred to the maintenance approach being suggested (or vice versa).

In the case of reengineering and enterprise systems, management faces some challenging decisions. For example, an organization might decide early in the development process (e.g., during the *systems survey*) that the installation of an enterprise system would solve its Information Systems problems. To ensure a successful installation of an enterprise system, organizations must reengineer their business processes to make them compatible with the enterprise system. Management must decide how much analysis to undertake before and after purchasing the system and how much to change their business practices (versus attempting to change the enterprise system).

Figure 6.2 depicts the alternatives considered by one company, Boston Scientific Corporation, before its management decided to embark on a worldwide implementation of a leading enterprise system, SAP R/3. In addition to the alternative chosen—to standardize on SAP R/3 worldwide—Boston Scientific considered:

[Insert Figure 6.2 here]

- Interfaces: build interfaces among the many systems that existed at their worldwide affiliates.

- Standardize on one: implement at all of the worldwide affiliates the set of applications in use at one of those affiliates.
- Build it: build their own system by writing the necessary applications software.
- Best of breed: select the best system available for each application or business process.
- EBS (Enterprise Business Solution): Select an integrated software package (in their case, SAP R/3) to provide the processing functionality for all applications. Implement that package worldwide.

The development options in Figure 6.2 summarize the typical choices from which organizations may choose. In the systems survey we begin the get some sense of these alternatives and which one looks best at the time. In the analysis step of systems development, we must examine each alternative and gather enough information to make a choice to proceed with development along one of the alternative paths.

Structured systems analysis is a set of procedures conducted to generate the specifications for a new (or modified) Information System or subsystem. Refer to Figure 6.1 (page 172) to see systems analysis' place in the SDLC (second), its inputs (approved feasibility document and miscellaneous environmental information) and its outputs (physical requirements and logical specification).

Definition and Goals

Before we begin this section, let's define and clarify a few terms. First, **systems analysis** is the methodical investigation of a problem and the identification and ranking of alternative solutions to the problem. Systems analysis is often called *structured systems analysis* when certain "structured" tools and techniques, such as DFDs, are used in conducting the analysis. To simplify our discussions, we will refer to "structured" systems analysis as simply systems analysis.

Review Question

What are the differences among the systems survey, systems analysis, and the structured systems analysis steps in systems development?

The systems survey assists management in determining the existence of a problem and in choosing a course of action (i.e., to continue systems development or to cancel it). Systems analysis provides more information than was gathered in the systems survey. The additional information describes and explains the problem fully. Solutions are developed and evaluated so that management can decide whether to proceed with development and, if so, which potential solution should be developed.

To understand systems analysis, we'll return to the analogy

presented earlier in the chapter, in which we compared systems development to building an industrial park. Compare the architect's role for the industrial park to the analyst's role for systems development. In the preliminary stages of the industrial park project, the architect learns the general purpose of the industrial park (light manufacturing, warehousing, etc.). The architect also learns the approximate number of buildings and the size of each. From that information, the architect "sketches" a proposed park. From that sketch, the accompanying general specifications, and the estimated costs and estimated schedule, the developer decides whether or not to proceed with the proposed project at this time. This process is similar to that followed in the systems survey, with the systems analyst assuming the architect's role and the organization's management (or the IT steering committee) replacing the developer.

If the developer approves the continuation of the project, the architect must conduct a detailed study to determine each building's specific use, required room sizes, electrical and plumbing requirements, floor load weights, private versus public areas, number of personnel who will occupy the completed buildings, technical requirements, and so on. During this detailed study, the architect develops a functional model of the proposed project. The detailed study by the architect is similar to systems analysis, and the logical specification (one of the outputs of the analysis step) is the model for the new system.

Systems analysis goals are as follows:

- *Define the problem precisely.* In systems analysis, we want to know and understand the problem in enough detail to solve it.
- *Devise alternative designs (solutions).* There is always more than one way to solve a problem or to design a system, and we want to develop several solutions from which to choose.
- *Choose and justify one of these alternative design solutions.* One solution must be chosen, and the choice should be justified using cost/effectiveness analysis or some other criterion, such as political or legal considerations (e.g., government reporting requirements).
- *Develop logical specifications for the selected design.* These detailed specifications are used to design the new system.
- *Develop the physical requirements for the selected design.* For example, we want to define such requirements as data storage, functional layouts for computer inquiry screens and reports, and processing response times, which lead to equipment requirements.
- *Develop the budget for the next two systems development phases (systems design and systems implementation).* These budgets are critical in determining development costs and controlling later

development activities.

Review Question

What are the goals of structured systems analysis?

The logical specifications and physical requirements become the criteria by which the user will accept the new or modified system. The better we perform systems analysis, the more likely that the system will meet user requirements and be accepted, implemented, and used effectively. There are two issues here. First, as we see in Figure 6.3, the opportunity for errors is much higher in earlier phases of systems development. A typical early error is failure to define user requirements completely. Second, as we see in Figure 6.4, the later in the development process that an error or oversight is discovered, the more costly it is to fix. For example, if we fail to determine during analysis that the user needs a certain piece of data on an output screen, this data may not be easy to add to the database during the implementation phase.

[Insert Figure 6.3 here]

[Insert Figure 6.4 here]

It is especially imperative to perform a top-quality analysis when we are introducing an enterprise system. It is during the analysis step that we model the business processes and determine the process changes (i.e., reengineering) that will be required. Business process owners and system users must understand and accept these changes for successful implementation. Otherwise there may be strong resistance to the implementation that could lead to the failure of the new system. As mentioned earlier, business processes must be reengineered to fit the enterprise system's processes.

Determination of user requirements in the analysis step can be more difficult in an e-business implementation. In such an implementation we must determine user requirements inside *and outside* the organization. We must consider the functional needs of customers and business partners, as well any requirements for infrastructure to connect our internal systems to the outside users (e.g., customer, business partners).

Define Logical Specifications

The first step the analysis team performs on the road to defining the logical specification is to study and document the current physical system. The team wants to build on the information available in the approved feasibility document and understand completely the current system operations. The team answers such questions as these. Given the system's goals, what should the system be doing? Should the order entry system be supporting customer inquiries? What are the reasons the system is operating as it is? Why are there errors?

Review Question

Why do we study and document the current physical environment?

After the current system has been documented with a physical data flow diagram, the team derives the current logical equivalent while removing all the physical elements from the diagram to produce a current logical data flow diagram, a description of the current logical system.

Review Question

Why do we develop a current logical model of an Information System?

Working with the current logical system, the analysis team models the future logical system. Like the current logical DFD, the future logical DFD describes a system's logical features. However, unlike the current diagrams, the future diagram describes what a system *will do* rather than what it *presently does.* To model what the new system will do, the team adds new activities, remodels existing activities, and adds or changes control activities. For example, in developing the Information System for the reengineered processes at Peapod, the development team would have modeled *future* processes such as those that track the movement of groceries into and out of the distribution centers.

Review Question

Why do we develop alternative logical designs?

Design Alternative Physical Systems

We are now at the point to describe *how* the new system will operate. Working with the future logical system, an analysis team could devise several physical alternatives.

1. The first step in developing a future physical system is to decide which processes will be manual and which will be automated. For example at Peapod they must decide if the picking lists will be printed with the clerks recording the quantities picked by writing on the picking lists, or if the lists will be presented on the screen of a handheld computer with clerks recording quantities picked on the handheld's keyboard.
2. As a second step in developing an alternative physical design, the analyst must decide which processes will begin immediately upon occurrence of an event and which will only operate periodically (often with batches of transactions). For example, at Peapod, they must decide when they will record the movement and delivery of groceries. Will, for example, the deliveries be recorded in a batch at the end of the day or immediately recorded via handhelds as the groceries are delivered?

The final step in designing alternative physical systems is to complete specifications for the future physical system. Typically, specifications are written for each bubble in the future physical system. These specifications indicate how, where, and in what form inputs are processed; and how, where, and in what form outputs are produced. When specifying physical systems, we may choose from a host of alternatives typically dictated by alternative technologies and modes of processing.

Review Question

Why do we develop alternative physical designs?

Select the Best Alternative Physical System

The analysis team, working with the new system's users, must now recommend the implementation of one of the alternative physical systems. The ultimate selection involves two decisions. First, the analysis team must decide which alternative system to recommend to the users and management. Second, given the analysis team's recommendation, the firm's management, usually the IT steering committee, must decide whether to undertake further development. And, if further development is chosen, management must decide which alternative system should be developed.

This two-part decision process is often an iterative process. The analysis team may recommend one alternative, and the users may disagree, thus requiring that the team rework its proposed system. After agreeing on the proposed system, the user/analyst team's proposal is forwarded for approval by the IT steering committee.

This committee must decide whether the development effort justifies expenditure of the firm's cash. To reduce costs, for example, the IT steering committee may ask for revisions to the system, thus requiring yet another reworking of the proposed system.

To facilitate selecting a future physical system, the systems analysis team conducts a **cost/effectiveness study**, which provides quantitative and certain qualitative information concerning each of the alternatives. This information is used to decide which alternative best meets users' needs. In making this determination, the team asks two questions. First, "Which alternative accomplishes the users' goals for the least cost (or greatest benefit)?" This question is addressed by the **cost/benefit study** (or **cost/benefit analysis**). Second, "Which alternative best accomplishes the users' goals for the system being developed?" This is the **effectiveness study** (or **effectiveness analysis**).

Review Question

Why do we conduct a cost/benefit analysis?

Respondents to a recent survey of 63 companies with enterprise systems, such as SAP R/3 and PeopleSoft, reported an average negative value of $1.5 million when quantifiable costs and benefits were compared.[11] However, that does not mean that organizations should not implement enterprise systems. These systems often lead to better customer service, integration across organizational units, and improved decision making—intangible effectiveness benefits. These benefits show some of the difficulties present in performing effectiveness analysis. For example, we may know many of the direct costs, but we may not know the magnitude of indirect costs such as loss of productivity. Also, we may not be able to identify or quantify expected benefits. Finally, we may be asked to implement systems for which the costs exceed the benefits.

[11] Craig Stedman, "Survey: ERP Costs More than Measurable ROI," *Computerworld* (April 5, 1999): 6.

Review Question

Why do we conduct an effectiveness analysis?

Complete and Package the Systems Analysis Documentation

To complete the systems analysis, the project team must collect the products of the analysis and organize these products into the documentation required for subsequent development steps. Let's talk about how each piece is packaged.

The first analysis deliverable is the logical specification. This is used in systems selection to choose the appropriate software to be acquired from external sources. Or, if the software is developed in-house, it is used in structured systems design to design the software.

The second analysis deliverable is the physical requirements specification. These requirements are used in systems selection to acquire computer equipment for the new system. Table 6.3 summarizes typical physical requirements.

[Insert Table 6.3 here]

In addition to the physical requirements related to hardware, the physical requirements should include functional layouts of inquiry screens and reports. At this point, sample reports and screens are called functional layouts because they show the information elements that are needed without getting into all the details of the screen or report design.

Another deliverable, implicit at the conclusion of each systems development step, is the *budget and schedule* document.

- The *budget,* estimated during the cost/benefit analysis, specifies the expected costs to complete the systems development.
- *Schedules* control systems development efforts by setting limits on the time to be spent on development activities and by coordinating those activities.

The final step in completing and packaging the systems analysis documentation is to obtain approvals. As discussed earlier, signoffs may be obtained from users, information services, management, and internal audit. In addition, the controller may sign off to indicate that the cost/benefit analysis is reasonable.

Conclusions

This chapter has introduced you to some of the important management issues surrounding the development of new or revised Information Systems. It also describes how to conduct the first two steps in systems development, the systems survey and structured systems analysis. Let's expand on the implications of two issues that we raised.

As discussed in the next chapter, organizations continue to increase their reliance on outside resources to conduct their systems development projects and to operate their Information Systems. As this trend continues, the mix of IT-related skills that an organization must have in-house changes. For example, as an organization contracts out for the development of computer programs and communications networks, it needs to retain fewer of those technical skills in-house. At the same time, IT-savvy management team members must make decisions about these outsourcing arrangements and manage outsource contracts and relationships with the vendors.

Second, the implementation of very large systems, such as enterprise systems, makes project management more important and more difficult. These systems affect literally every unit and every person in an organization. If the organization is large and international, as many are, the project management problems are compounded. As a result, most major enterprise system vendors provide tools to help manage the implementation process.

Appendix 6A

Tools for Gathering and Analyzing Facts

This appendix describes tools that might be used to gather and analyze facts during systems development. Some of these tools could be used during the systems survey and some might also be used during systems analysis.

Literature Review

A common method for gathering initial information about an information system or the operations of a business process is the internal literature review. An **internal literature review** is the examination of documentation maintained within the organization, such as flowcharts, organization charts, data flow diagrams, and procedures manuals. Gathering information from documentation outside the organization (e.g., industry statistics) is an example of an **external literature review**.

Interviews

Interviews—in which information is gathered through direct contact, either face-to-face or via telephone—are widely used by analysts. Interviews provide an understanding of the system, the system's problems, and the users' requirements. The personal contact the interview offers is desirable because it can establish rapport with users, give them an understanding of the development effort, gain their support for the development effort, and involve them in the development process.

Although the interview is a good way to get information and generate ideas, it has some shortcomings. Interviews may obtain erroneous or partial information from a person unwilling or unable to cooperate or from one who is not sufficiently knowledgeable. Also, the interviewer may miss or misinterpret some information received during an interview. An interviewer can corroborate facts by conducting interviews with more than one person, by observation, by transaction review, or by study of databases and files.

Internal Presentation

When an analyst wishes to learn about the operation of a department, he or she might request that members of that department make an internal presentation. An internal presentation is a session at which members of the organization formally describe or display information to the analyst. In some situations, holding a presentation may be more efficient than conducting a number of interviews.

Observations

An analyst can also use **observations** to gather current information about how a system operates or to corroborate other information. Observation shows that systems often operate differently in practice than the business process owners (typically managers) believe that they do. Another related technique is a **walkthrough**, in which the analyst traces a business event as it is processed, observing and documenting what happens at each processing stage.

Database and Files Review

If the systems documentation gathered during the internal literature review is accurate, it gives us an understanding of the way a system is supposed to operate (the formal system). But, because this documentation often changes more slowly than the actual system, it is often out of date. Therefore, information from documentation must be supplemented by that gleaned from other techniques that tell how a system really operates currently (the informal system). An analyst can review an organization's database and paper files related to events processing; this is called a **database and files review**. Examples of items an analyst might review include a paper file of vendor invoices and inventory master data.

Questionnaires

Questionnaires—forms containing a standardized list of questions—structure the fact-gathering process and extend the geographic boundaries for that process. Questionnaires can also gather information when personal contact is either not necessary or not possible. For example, an analyst could e-mail a questionnaire to a firm's sales force to gather information about an order entry system being developed. Questionnaires can be administered to a population sample and, if the questionnaire is designed properly, the results can be analyzed statistically to generalize the findings to the entire population.

Review Question

Describe two situations in which you would use each of the following techniques: internal literature review, interview, internal presentation, observation, walkthrough, database and files review, and questionnaire.

REVIEW QUESTIONS

RQ6-1 What is systems development?

RQ6-2 What is the difference between systems development and the systems development life cycle (SDLC)?

RQ6-3 What are the systems development objectives?

RQ6-4 What benefits are derived from using a systems development methodology?

RQ6-5 What are the systems development phases, steps, purposes, and tasks?

RQ6-6 What are the essential elements of good project management?

RQ6-7 What are the five maturity levels of the Capability Maturity Model (CMM)?

RQ6-8 Describe the ways that a manager or system user might be involved in systems development.

RQ6-9 What are the key elements and principles of *business process reengineering (BPR)*?

RQ6-10 What events or conditions may cause a systems survey to be initiated?

RQ6-11 What are the systems survey goals?

RQ6-12 What are three aspects of feasibility? Explain each.

RQ6-13 Why develop a project plan?

RQ6-14 Why obtain signoffs on the feasibility document?

RQ6-15 What are the differences among the systems survey, systems analysis, and the structured systems analysis steps in systems development?

RQ6-16 What are the goals of structured systems analysis?

RQ6-17 Why do we study and document the current physical environment?

RQ6-18 Why do we develop a current logical model of an Information System?

RQ6-19 Why do we develop alternative logical designs?

RQ6-20 Why do we develop alternative physical designs?

RQ6-21 Why do we conduct a cost/benefit analysis?

RQ6-22 Why do we conduct an effectiveness analysis?

RQ6-23 **Appendix 6A:** Describe two situations in which you would use each of the following techniques: internal literature review, interview, internal presentation, observation, walkthrough, database and files review, and questionnaire.

DISCUSSION QUESTIONS

DQ6-1 Give five examples of why one Information System might experience more iterations of the SDLC than another Information System.

DQ6-2 Discuss several factors negatively or positively affecting the achievement of systems development objectives.

DQ6-3 "As long as we plan a systems development project and carry out the project in an orderly manner, we don't need a formal, documented systems development methodology." Do you agree? Why or why not?

DQ6-4 The chapter differentiates two different "triggers" for the systems development process: a planned, periodic review and a user-requested systems development. Compare and contrast those two triggers.

DQ6-5 Discuss specific examples of the importance of proceeding with systems development even when there is doubt as to the feasibility of the proposed development effort.

DQ6-6 "We don't have time to use a structured SDLC process. If we don't get this e-business application up next month, our competition will steal all our customers." Discuss.

DQ6-7 In doing a systems survey for the proposed automation of the cash disbursements system of XYZ Company, the analyst in charge reached the tentative conclusion that Larry Long, the popular cashier with more than 30 years of company service, will be displaced and perhaps asked to consider early retirement. Discuss how this scenario relates to the topic of "operational feasibility" presented in this chapter. Discuss the potential impact on the success of the new disbursements system.

DQ6-8 *Systems analysis* is defined in this chapter as the methodical investigation of a problem and the identification and ranking of alternative solutions to the problem. It seems that this definition also describes what occurred in the systems survey. How does the analysis phase of this chapter differ from the survey phase? Don't both phases involve "systems analysis," as defined in this chapter? Discuss fully.

DQ6-9 One of the goals of systems analysis is to choose and justify one of the alternative design solutions. Would it not be more effective, efficient, and practical for the systems analyst to pass along *all* alternative design solutions to top management (perhaps to the IT steering committee), together with arguments for and against each alternative, and let top management choose one of them?

DQ6-10 List the decisions that must be made prior to initiating structured systems analysis. Indicate how the systems survey contributed to the decisions.

DQ6-11 Identify the trade-offs of too broad an analysis scope versus too narrow an analysis scope.

DQ6-12 "We waste too much time studying and documenting the current physical environment." How would you respond to such a statement?

DQ6-13 "If a new Information System can't pay for itself, we won't develop it." How would you respond to such a statement?

DQ6-14 "If the results of the cost/benefit analysis do not agree with those of the effectiveness analysis, there is probably no difference among the alternatives." Do you agree with this thinking? Why or why not?

DQ6-15 **Appendix 6A:** "Questionnaires constrain the fact-gathering activity and stifle creativity." Discuss.

DQ6-16 **Appendix 6A:**

a. Speculate about how the use of questionnaires during the structured systems analysis stage would differ from their use during the systems survey.

b. Speculate about how the use of the interview to gather facts during the structured systems analysis stage would differ from its use during the systems survey.

DQ6-17 **Appendix 6A:** Discuss the relative advantages of the interview, the transaction review (walkthrough), the observation, the internal literature review, and the database and files review as they might apply to each of the following situations that might occur during the systems survey:

a. Gaining an initial understanding of the system under review.

b. Confirming the understanding obtained in part a.

c. Determining the nature and extent of reported system failure (e.g., in an Order-to-Cash process, numerous customer complaints, excessive bad debt losses, abnormally high sales returns, and unusual delinquency in shipping customer orders).

d. Assessing/evaluating (1) economic feasibility, (2) operational feasibility, and (3) technical feasibility.

DQ6-18 **Appendix 6A:** Refer to RQ6-23. In which situations is it debatable what is the most appropriate fact-gathering tool to use? In which situations is it *not* debatable? Explain your answer.

DQ6-19 "The more time that is invested in systems analysis, the better the system, the fewer the problems that will occur later in the system's life, and the less expensive the development process." Is this statement true? Why or why not?

DQ6-20 Refer to the story about Oxford Health Plans, Inc. at the beginning of the chapter (page 168). Describe how Oxford could have avoided or minimized the problems that they encountered by following the systems development procedures described in this chapter.

PROBLEMS

P6-1 The Sell-It-All Company is a wholesale distributor of office supplies. It sells pencils and pens, paper goods (including computer paper and forms), staplers, calendars, and any other items that you would expect to find in an office, excluding furniture and other major items such as computers. Sales have been growing at 5 percent per year during the last several years. Mr. Big, the Sell-It-All president, recently attended a national office supplies convention. In conversations during that convention, he discovered that sales for Sell-It-All's competitors have been growing at 15 percent per year. Arriving back home, he did a quick investigation and discovered the following:

- Sell-It-All's customer turnover is significantly higher than the industry average.
- Sell-It-All's vendor turnover is significantly lower than the industry average.
- The new market analysis system was supposed to be ready two years ago but has been delayed for more than one year in systems development.
- A staff position, reporting to the president, for a person to

prepare and analyze cash budgets was created two years ago but has never been filled.

Mr. Big has called on you to conduct a systems survey of this situation. You are to assume that a request for systems development has been prepared and approved.

Make and describe all assumptions that you believe are necessary to solve any of the following:

a. What are the specific goals of this systems survey?

b. Indicate specific quantifiable benefits and costs that should be examined in assessing the economic feasibility of any solutions that might be proposed. Explain how you would go about quantifying each benefit or cost.

c. Propose and explain three different scopes for the systems analysis. *HINT:* What subsystems *might* be involved in an analysis?

P6-2 a. Conduct research of current literature and databases to find a report of an enterprise system development project failure. Prepare a report or presentation (subject to your instructor's instructions) describing the failure. Include in your report the elements of feasibility and project risk that may have been miscalculated or mismanaged and led to the project failure.

b. Conduct research of current literature and databases to find a report of an e-business system development project failure. Prepare a report or presentation (subject to your instructor's instructions) describing the failure. Include in your report the elements of feasibility and project risk that may have been miscalculated or mismanaged and led to the project failure.

P6-3 David's Used Cars is a used car dealership owned and operated by David Steele. Steele has about 200 cars in stock and sells or buys an average of 10 cars per day. Steele buys cars that are trade-ins from new car dealers, repossessions from banks, and cars sold at auctions by municipal towing yards and insurance companies. Steele currently employs two full-time salespeople as well as five full-time mechanics who repair and prepare the cars for resale. Steele rarely accepts a car in trade as part of the payment for a car he is selling. Steele uses the following procedures relative to the purchase and sale of used cars.

Steele creates a folder for every car that he purchases. He accumulates information on a car in the folder. The folders are maintained in a filing cabinet alphabetically by car make and model. Each car and corresponding folder is assigned a five-digit sequence number for accurate identification on the lot and in advertisements. Each folder contains a preprinted master sheet. Initially, Steele enters the make, model, and year of the car, the purchase date, the name and address of the owner, the price paid, the odometer reading, the car lot parking space number, and the check number used to pay for the car. Steele and one of the mechanics then prepare a second form, a checklist of 25 descriptive criteria used to evaluate the car's condition. Each criterion is evaluated as poor, fair, good, or excellent. Steele then enters onto the master sheet the selling price he would want for the car if no repairs were made. He also makes out a price sticker and attaches it to the windshield of the car. If a repair is made, the mechanic fills out a repair description that contains a detail of the repairs, the cost, and the estimated retail value of the repairs based on a price list of industry averages for various standard repairs. Steele files this in the appropriate folder and enters the cost and retail values onto the master sheet. If the repair affects any of the evaluation criteria, he makes the appropriate adjustment to the affected criteria and to the price sticker on the car. When a car is sold, Steele enters the date, selling price, salesperson, and customer name and address onto the master sheet.

Steele approves all sales. All sales are for cash or cashier's check. Steele has a checking account used solely for car sales and purchase transactions. He uses another account for all other expenses. He transfers money to the second account from the sales and purchase account. After a car is sold, Steele places the corresponding folder in a drawer in his desk. Every Friday, he calculates the sales people's commissions based on the selling price recorded in the folder. He pays commissions for sales from the previous Friday to Thursday of the current week. He then files the folders by sequence number in the closed car file.

Steele's system is not without problems. Sometimes Steele forgets to change the prices on the car stickers to reflect repairs that have been made. This error frequently is not discovered until an agreement to sell a car to a customer has been reached. He occasionally files the current Friday's folders for cars sold this week in the closed car file, along with the folders for cars on which the sales commissions already have been paid. As a result, the salespeople do not receive their proper commission for the cars they sold in the most recent week. He also has found that some cars are on display on the lot for a long time before they are sold. However, Steele has not had the time to look at this problem closely enough to identify all such cars and to get them sold.

In spite of occasional help from his daughter, Steele still spends a lot of time on paperwork. This frustrates him because the information is still frequently inaccurate and processing the paperwork takes time away from managing the business and selling more cars. He believes that the inefficient use of his time is costing him money.

Steele has had no formal business education and has never used a computer. The thought of having to learn about computers scares him. However, he has read about how well computers can simplify manual clerical operations. He has also read that once a computer system has information stored in it, information can be used to generate all kinds of reports that would be useful for analyzing a business and improving cash flow. Steele has hired you to help determine what functions could be automated and how the information would have to be organized to perform those functions.

a. Identify two significant *operational* deficiencies and two significant *information system control* deficiencies. Next to each deficiency, suggest a potential solution. Present your answer in the following form:

Deficiency **Proposed Solution**

Operational:

1.

2.

Information system control:

3.

4.

Operational deficiencies would comprise process effectiveness, efficiency of resource use, and security of resources. Here, the process covers the acquisition, repair, and sale of used cars, as well as the payment of commissions. The resources are the inventory of cars, cash and checks, and the inventory file folders. **Information system control** deficiencies would undermine the goals of information validity, completeness, or accuracy of the records (e.g. folders) accompanying the operational process.

b. Suggest some *possible* effects that the installation of a computerized information system might have on (1) the organizational structure of David's Used Cars (job functions, realignment of duties, reporting responsibilities, etc.), and (2) the *behavior* of salespeople, mechanics, customers, or Steele himself.

P6-4 **Appendix 6A:** For each problem described, list and explain the documentation you would recommend for gathering and analyzing related facts. *Note:* It is *not* necessary to simulate the documentation. Confine your answer to a listing and brief explanation (one to two sentences) for each type of documentation that you recommend.

a. College admissions office is experiencing a decline in applications.

b. College admissions office is experiencing a decline in the percentage of students coming to the college after being accepted by the college.

c. College is experiencing an increase in the number of unpaid tuition bills.

d. Faculty member has noticed that fewer students are signing up for her classes.

P6-5 **Appendix 6A:** For each problem described, list and explain the documentation you would recommend for gathering and analyzing related facts. *Note:* It is *not* necessary to simulate the documentation. Confine your answer to a listing and brief explanation (one to two sentences) for each type of documentation that you recommend.

a. Insufficient parking at Enormous State University (ESU).

b. Overcrowding in dormitories/apartments/student center at ESU.

c. Inadequate computer support services for students and faculty at ESU.

d. Getting photocopying done in the Marketing department at ESU.

P6-6 Conduct research on ISO 9000-3 (see Exhibit 6.4 page 178) and the Capability Maturity Model (see Exhibit 6.5 page 179). Compare and contrast the requirements of those two standards with each other and with the procedures described in this chapter.

TABLES

[Start Table]

Table 6.1 Information Systems Development Phases, Purposes, and Tasks

Phase	**Purpose**	**Tasks**
Analysis (bubbles 1 and 2)*	Define project goals and scope. Develop specifications for the new or revised system's functions.	Study the problem and the users' requirements. Propose alternative problem solutions.
Design (bubbles 3 and 4)	Develop an appropriate system manifestation.	Describe desired features (e.g. screen layouts, business rules) in detail. Choose software and hardware. Write computer program specifications. Devise implementation plans, system tests, and training.
Implementation (bubble 5)	Prepare to begin using the new system.	Write, test, and debug the computer programs.
Operation (bubbles 6 and 7)	Use the new system.	Convert to new or revised system. Conduct post-implementation review. Perform systems maintenance.

*Refers to Figure 6.1.

[End Table]

[Start Table]

Table 6.2 Involvement in Systems Development

Category	**How Involved in Development**
Systems	As an employee of the organization—possessing some systems specialty, such as systems
Specialist	analyst—the manager undertakes many of the activities in a systems development project.
Consultant	Hired from outside the organization, the consultant

	manger may undertake many of the activities in a systems development project.
System	As an employee of the organization, a manager can become involved in systems development
User	as the user of the system and as the requester of the system changes. The manager might also join the development team.
Assurance	Internal and information technology (IT) auditors, independent auditors, and consultants may
Provider	be asked to review development projects to ensure that systems are developed efficiently and effectively and that the systems being developed will be reliable, have sufficient internal controls, and be auditable.

[End Table]

[Start Table]

Table 6.3 Physical Requirements Used in Systems Selection

Data requirements	**Operations requirements**	**Management requirements**
• Database size, growth, activity, access requirements, and update frequency • Event volume and expected growth, and sources (internal, external)	• Peripherals, such as printers, scanners, or PCs • Communications (LANs, Internet, security requirements) • Backup and security • Output distribution, uses, media, and formats	• Processing approaches (distributed, centralized) • Reliability (e.g., mean time between failure) • Response time requirements

[End Table]

BOXES

[Start TECHNOLOGY INSIGHT 6.1 box here]

TECHNOLOGY INSIGHT 6.1

Alternative Development Approaches

Gelinas 6-69

Alternatives to the SDLC. The *SDLC* described in this text epitomizes what is often called the **waterfall method** because the output of each step in the process becomes the input for the next step. This method is often seen as rigidly sequential and therefore works best for routine processes that are well understood and for which requirements can be completely specified in advance. For example, in Figure 6.1 the *logical specification* flows into SDLC steps 3.0 and 4.0. The assumption is that the user requirements for the new system that are embodied in this specification are completely and accurately specified at that point in the development process.

Rapid applications development (RAD) is a management approach to systems development that employs small teams of highly skilled developers using higher-order development tools, such as ICASE, PowerBuilder, or even Visual Basic, to develop the system iteratively. RAD uses the Joint Application Development (JAD) approach for requirements gathering and prototyping input/output screens, and in 90- to 120-days evolves the prototypes developed during JAD sessions into a running system during the construction phase of the RAD life cycle. This running system partially fulfills user requirements and in the next RAD cycle more user requirements are added to the system. Thus RAD is an iterative process that generates systems that are more effective in meeting user requirements and speeds the process of delivering running systems to the users. For medium-size business applications, the RAD process leads to a sixteen-fold productivity increase over traditional COBOL development and three-fold increase over 4GL developments environments.

An organization can avoid part of the development effort altogether by purchasing the software. Purchasing transfers to the vendor the risk of not completing the program on time and the risk that the program will not meet user needs. This common approach assumes that purchased software represents industry best practices and should meet most of the users' needs. For example, with *enterprise systems,* organizations purchase a system and then configure it to match the organization's business requirements. We discuss pros and cons of purchased software in the next chapter.

Alternative Approaches to Analysis and Design. In this text we use **functional decomposition,** a method that focuses on a system's functions, or processes, and utilizes top-down, hierarchical simplification to derive the new system's design. The DFDs that we use to analyze a system depict processes, or functions, and the flow of data between them. This approach produces models of systems emphasizing what the system must do; i.e., the activities that must be performed.

There are alternative approaches to analysis and design that focus on either data or objects as their primary building block. **Data-structured development** is based on the premise that the data make up the fundamental building blocks for a system. As described in Chapter 3, *data modeling* is an analysis of data conducted to develop a conceptual model of an organization's data. This conceptual model serves as the basis for the development of all systems subsequently developed by the organization. Because the data model represents the true nature of a system, it is less likely to change than are the applications using the data.

Object-oriented (OO) development regards the world as a set of objects that are related to one another and that communicate with one another. Systems developed using either function-oriented or data-oriented approaches consist of separate programs and data, while object-oriented systems consist of *objects* that contain both the data and the procedures, or methods, for manipulating the data. For example, to prepare a monthly sales report, a traditional program would include the actions that must be taken, such as accumulate the data, format the data, and print the report. An object-oriented program, on the other hand, would call for the object "monthly sales report." That object would include the data and procedures necessary to prepare the sales report. The monthly sales report object might itself contain an object designed to sort the data into the required sequence. Any object needing to sort data could use this sorting object. A big advantage of object-oriented programming is reusability. Programs can be built from prefabricated, pretested building blocks—such as the sorting object used by the sales report object—in a fraction of the time it would take to build them from scratch.

Unified Modeling Language™ (UML™) is a tool often associated with object-oriented development. According to the Object Management Group (OMG)[a], UML is used to specify, visualize, and document models of software systems, including non-object oriented applications. OMG reports that these models ensure that end user needs and program design requirements are met before program coding will make changes difficult and expensive. UML defines twelve types of diagrams to document an application's structure and behavior and to organize and manage application modules.

Another alternative approach to analysis and design is Extreme Programming. **Extreme Programming (XP)** is a deliberate and disciplined approach to software development[b] that emphasizes customer involvement and promotes teamwork. XP is characterized by communication among programmers and customers, simple design, early testing, and continuous integration of changes into the evolving system. Recall the current environment for information systems development. XP improves project success and developer productivity when used on risky projects with dynamic requirements, a large category of current development projects.

[a]http://www.omg.org/gettingstarted/what_is_uml.htm (September 24, 2002).

[b]http://www.extremeprogramming.org/ (September 24, 2002).

[End TECHNOLOGY INSIGHT 6.1 box here]

Gelinas 7-1

7

SYSTEMS DESIGN AND IMPLEMENTATION

Under Joe Hopper's leadership, Hopper Specialty Company had grown into the biggest distributor of industrial hardware in northwest New Mexico. To provide the systems infrastructure needed for future growth, Joe acquired an inventory management system from NCR. In addition to the NCR hardware and systems software, the system included the Warehouse Manager software from Taylor Management Systems. The system was supposed to track the thousands of items in the Hopper inventory, including prices and balances. However, had Joe thoroughly investigated and tested this system, he would have discovered that:

- Warehouse Manager had not worked anywhere on an NCR computer.
- When two terminals accessed the system at once, both terminals locked up.
- When the locked terminals went back online, information—including prices, item balances, and general ledger data—was altered.
- Sales at the counter were supposed to take fractions of a second. Actual response times were as high as several minutes.

How did Joe let this happen to his company? Joe needed to

conduct a more thorough investigation of the vendors and of existing installations of the proposed system. And, prior to implementation, the system should have been tested in an environment that resembled the one in which the system was to be asked to operate.

Synopsis

In this chapter, we complete our systems development study by discussing and illustrating the remaining phases of systems development, the systems design, implementation, and operation phases. As with Chapter 6, one goal is to highlight the technology that will help us achieve systems development objectives as we conduct systems selection and systems design. For example, we consider the software and hardware testing that may be necessary during the systems selection process. We need always to keep in mind that a major purpose for undertaking systems development is to leverage existing technology to provide competitive advantage to the organization. We also see the aspects of these systems development steps that are most affected by the implementation of enterprise systems and e-business systems.

Learning Objectives

- To name the goals, plans, tasks, and results of systems design, implementation, and operation
- To be able to evaluate the advantages and disadvantages of alternative sources for

computer software and computer hardware

- To describe the process of choosing computer software and hardware
- To explain the importance of implementation planning
- To name the interdependent tasks that must be accomplished during systems implementation
- To explain the importance of thoroughly testing the new or revised system prior to putting the system into operation
- To describe the dual functions of post-implementation review
- To explain the difficulties associated with systems maintenance

Introduction

Figure 7.1 (page 206) depicts the systems development life cycle, including the phases, steps, and inputs and outputs for each step. In Chapter 6, we began our study of the systems development process and described the first phase of systems development, the systems analysis phase. In this chapter we consider the remaining phases.

[Insert Figure 7.1 here]

The systems design phase includes two steps: systems selection (choosing software and hardware resources to implement new or revised systems) and structured systems design (detailed specification of new or revised software and the preparation of implementation plans). The systems implementation phase includes completing the design of the new or revised system and converting to that system. The systems operation phase includes two steps: the post-implementation review, during which we assess the adequacy of the new system to meet the users' requirements and the quality of the development process, and systems maintenance, which involves making minor system repairs and modifications.

Recall from earlier discussions that certain systems development tasks are comparable to tasks undertaken in the construction of an industrial park. In systems selection, choosing software and hardware resources is similar to choosing contractors for a construction project. Structured systems design, planning implementation, and designing software is similar to drafting blueprints and other construction-related plans.

Systems implementation (in which the computer programs are written, the design of databases, files, and documents is finalized, and the system is put into operation) is analogous to the process of actually constructing the industrial park. Post-implementation review, in which the organization checks to see that the system does what it was supposed to do, is similar to the building inspection that occurs soon after the industrial park is completed. Systems maintenance, in which system errors are corrected and enhancements are added to the system, is similar to undertaking plumbing or electrical repairs or minor building modifications, such as moving interior walls and relocating doors.

Systems Selection

As you can see in Figure 7.1, systems selection lies *between* structured systems analysis (bubble 2.0) and structured systems design (bubble number 4.0). Systems selection uses the new system's *functional requirements* (the logical specification) and *physical requirements* that were developed in the analysis phase to decide what resources will be used to implement the new system. Only after the resources are chosen does detailed design begin.

Review Question

What is systems selection?

Systems selection is a set of procedures performed to choose the computer software and hardware for an Information System. The *systems selection goals* are to:

- *Determine what computer software will implement the logical specification developed in structured systems analysis.* We must decide between in-house software development by Information Systems personnel, end-users, or contract programmers versus off-the-shelf rental or purchase. For instance, we should consider whether home grown systems can provide the level of integration and functionality that could be achieved through use of an enterprise system.

- *Determine what computer hardware will satisfy the physical requirements established in structured systems analysis.* We must evaluate and choose the architecture (e.g., client/server, LAN) and the type, manufacturer, and model of each piece of computer equipment.[1] In making our choice, we should also be aware of the implications for security and control of Information Systems. Additionally, to understand cost implications, consideration should be given in the decision to environmental controls (i.e., temperature, electrical, etc.).
- *Choose acquisition financing methods that are in the best interest of the organization.* We must decide whether it is better to purchase, rent, or lease the computer equipment. In addition, we must decide if our data center will be completely within our control or if we will use an applications service provider, or other outsourcing option.
- *Determine appropriate acquisition ancillaries.* We must establish contract terms, software site-licensing arrangements, computer maintenance terms, and software revision procedures and responsibilities.

[1] An organization's existing hardware might be used to implement a new Information System. In this case, the hardware phase of the study would verify that the existing hardware is adequate, given the physical requirements.

Review Question

What are systems selection goals?

Before we proceed, let's look at the sequence of activities presented in Figure 7.1 and in these goals. Historically, the logical specification and the physical requirements were developed in the systems analysis step *after* the business processes had been documented and accepted, or remodeled (e.g., business process reengineering). Then, a software package would be chosen (and modified, if necessary) or developed in house. This is the sequence depicted in Figure 7.1 and used in this text. As we said in Chapter 6, however, when we implement an enterprise system we change the sequence of activities. With enterprise system implementations we start by choosing the package and then retrofit business processes to match those required by the enterprise system. So, while we present the sequence of the *SDLC* as "typical," we ask you to be aware of the existence of practical variations in these activities.

Software and Hardware Acquisition Alternatives

Before proceeding to the intermediate steps in systems selection, let's spend time examining various software and hardware procurement options that an organization must consider. Computer software can be purchased, rented, leased, or developed in-house. Hardware can be acquired (rented, leased, or purchased) by an organization and managed by the organization's personnel.

Alternatively, the hardware can be owned and managed by external entities. Table 7.1 compares these external and internal sources for computer software and hardware.

[Insert Table 7.1 here]

A review of Table 7.1 should lead you to conclude that external sources usually provide more capacity and affect the organization's resources less, while internal sources can be matched more easily with the organization's needs. Organizations implementing e-business Web sites must balance the imperative to launch a site rapidly (i.e., purchase an off-the-shelf e-commerce suite) with their desire to tailor a site to their needs and present unique content and performance characteristics to distinguish their site from those operated by their competitors (i.e., develop their own proprietary site).

Review Question

What are reasons for developing software internally versus acquiring it from external sources?

Software Acquisition Alternatives

Internal Development Software can be developed internally, purchased or rented from a vendor, or, in some cases, leased from a third party. Table 7.1 lists criteria useful in making the develop-versus-buy decision. Within the organization, a systems development staff usually writes programs that are large and complex and involve a number of organizational units. Software development by users normally is appropriate when the program will be used by a small group or an individual, and must be tailored to that limited use. As more software becomes available, especially enterprise systems with many modules and add-on features, the option of in-house development has become increasingly rare.

External Acquisition Organizations not wishing to or unable to develop software in-house may purchase, rent, or lease a commercially available software package. Some organizations have rented software packages and used them to benchmark software being developed in-house. The rented software may also provide an interim solution while a system is developed in-house and might be retained on a long-term basis if it proves superior to the in-house solution.

Software can be acquired from computer manufacturers, software vendors, mail-order houses and retail stores (for personal computer software), as well as outsourcing firms, including service bureaus, systems integrators, and application service providers.

Review Question

What are the external sources of software?

In general, **outsourcing** is the assignment of an internal function to an outside vendor. An organization can outsource its accounting, payroll, legal, data processing, strategic planning, or manufacturing functions, and so on. Since 1989, when the Eastman Kodak Company signed an agreement with IBM whereby IBM would own and operate Kodak's data centers, outsourcing has increasingly been an option for organizations willing to have an outsider provide some or all of their Information Systems services. The Gartner Group asserts that "outsourcing has become a noncontroversial, mainstream approach to managing IT... and senior executives (IT and non-IT) endorse and promote its judicious use within multiple processes across their enterprise."[2] These projections show that, in addition to software, outsourcing is also a major alternative for the external acquisition of hardware and networks.

[2] "The Varied Industry Perspectives of Outsourcing," Gartner Group Advisory Note No. LE-18-0527, September 4, 2002.

A **service bureau** is a firm providing information processing services, including software and hardware, for a fee. The service bureau owns and manages the software and hardware, which is installed on the service bureau's property. Most of the services are on a fee-for-service basis, thus minimizing cost to the contracting organization. Many companies contract with service bureaus for payroll processing.

Systems integrators are consulting/systems development firms that develop and install systems under contract. EDS, Accenture, CAP Gemini, and other professional services firms are major players in systems integration. Advantages of systems integrators and consultants to develop systems include:

Review Question

What is a *systems integrator*?

- Consulting firms have broad experience and knowledge of specialty and leading edge technology, helpful if a project involves a substantial upgrade in technology beyond available in-house expertise.
- Consulting firms have experience and may specialize in organization change, helpful to organizations not accustomed to change.
- Quick action must be taken to catch up with aggressive competition. Consultant expertise is flexible and rapid, and usually readily available for required services.

There is evidence, however, that the use of systems integrators doesn't always work out. For example, one study looked at 16,000 IT projects and found that none of the projects that had heavy participation by big systems integrators was completed on time and within budget.[3] Technology Excerpt 7.1 proposes seven steps to preventing these disasters.

[3] Geoffrey James, "IT Fiascoes . . . and How to Avoid Them," *Datamation* (November 1997): 87.

[Insert Technology Excerpt 7.1 box here]

A rapidly developing segment of the outsourcing market is the *application service provider (ASP).* Technology Insight 7.1 discusses ASPs. ASPs are similar to service bureaus and other outsourcing options. The ASP, however, provides its services via an easy-to-use Web browser over public networks, rather than more expensive private lines. Several ASPs exist that specialize in providing *enterprise system* services to organizations. As the current generation of enterprise systems moves to Web-enabled clients that function through use of browser software, the usability of enterprise systems in an ASP environment should become less complex and make this model of delivery even more cost effective.

[Insert Technology Insight 7.1 box here]

The Gartner Group predicted that only 20 percent of the ASPs in existence at the end of 2000 would survive through the end of 2003.[4] Therefore, an organization should consider carefully the type of applications that it outsources. The outsourcing of critical applications should probably be kept in-house. They may be too important to hand over to another organization. Support applications such as human resources and accounting might be better outsourcing candidates.

[4] "Management Update: Application Service Provider Outlook for 2002," Gartner Group Research Note no. IGG-01092002-04, January 9, 2002.

Summary of Software Acquisition Alternatives An organization should consider the financial implications of the decision to develop (make) versus buy. Because software vendors can allocate software development costs across many products and across multiple copies of each product, the prices they charge to recover development costs are usually less than the organization would pay to develop the package in-house. Generally, software developed in-house for a mainframe computer can cost up to 10 times more than purchased software. And, annual maintenance of in-house software is typically 50 percent of the development cost, while annual maintenance for purchased software normally costs only 25 percent of the purchase price.

Review Question

What is an *application service provider (ASP)?*

To increase the potential market for a software package, vendors develop packages for a wide audience. This strategy leads to products that seldom possess characteristics exactly matching any particular organization's requirements. Organizations not satisfied with these generic packages can contract with a vendor to modify one of the vendor's existing software packages or develop a custom-tailored software package written specifically to meet the organization's unique requirements.

What is the bottom line from Table 7.1? When a *suitable* standard package exists, buy it rather than try to reinvent it in-house. Notice the emphasis on *suitable.* Other considerations must include the organization's internal resources (personnel, capital) and available vendor support. Enterprise systems, for example, are off-the-shelf packages that are highly configurable, but still require compromises to benefit from the off-the-shelf nature and cost savings.

Many external sources of software, such as ASPs, require little up-front implementation expense and provide the benefits of some of the best software solutions available. Even when providing enterprise systems services, ASPs tend to shorten implementation time for an organization drastically, albeit limiting the amount of tailoring that can be done to match a system with a business process. On the other hand, ASPs can provide business process reengineering specialists to help organizations implement best practices into their business processes and to match the processes with the enterprise system provided. In general with ASPs, implementation, operations, and maintenance requirements are minimal, freeing organization personnel time to focus on their mission.

Contracted, in-house development is a software development option that combines some advantages of both in-house development and software purchase. An organization hires contract (nonemployee) analysts and programmers to develop a system. Because the services of these persons end at the completion of the project, the contracting option provides short-term labor and expertise that the organization requires. Some organizations use contractors to train their personnel to work with new technologies. When benefits are figured in, the contractors cost about the same as employees. These contractors can be on-site or they can be outsourced from anyplace in the world. For example, outsourcing of systems development services is a $6.2 billion industry in India. Services provided include maintenance of existing (i.e., legacy) systems, e-business development, and integration of applications.[5]

[5] "Analysis of India: Today's Dominant Offshore Outsourcer," Gartner Group Research Note no. M-15-0304, January 16, 2002.

Hardware Acquisition Alternatives

Computer hardware can be purchased, rented, or leased from the manufacturer (vendor) or from a leasing company. Under these arrangements, hardware is acquired, installed in the organization's facilities, and operated by the organization's personnel. As noted in Table 7.1, possession and management by the organization is less flexible (because of fixed cost and limited capacity, for example) than is use of external sources, but it does permit the organization to control and tailor the system. An organization preferring not to own or manage its own computer facilities can use one of the outsourcing options described above, such as a *service bureau* or an *ASP*, to fulfill its hardware needs.

Review Question

What are reasons for using external and internal sources of hardware?

The Intermediate Steps in Systems Selection

There are three major tasks in the *systems selection* process: prepare requests for proposals, evaluate vender proposals, and complete configuration plan. We will now discuss each of those tasks.

Review Question

What is a request for proposal (RFP)?

Prepare Requests for Proposal

A **request for proposal (RFP)** is a document sent to vendors that invites submission of plans for providing hardware, software, and services. The organization may send an RFP to vendors from whom it has previously received proposals or with whom it has previously done business. The analysts assigned to conduct systems selection also might research vendor evaluations published in the computer press or in other computer-based or paper-based services. This research, an example of *external literature review,* is described in Technology Insight 7.2. Using the information contained in the *logical specification* and/or in the *physical requirements,* the analysts prepare the RFPs and send them to the chosen vendors. Exhibit 7.1 (page 214) lists typical contents of an RFP.

[Insert Exhibit 7.1 here]

[Insert Technology Insight 7.1 box here]

Review Question

What are the factors an organization must consider in structuring the RFP and deciding to whom the RFP will be sent?

The section on projected growth requirements is important relative to the RFP. The better an organization accurately projects the long-term requirements for a new system and obtains software and hardware that can satisfy that long-term demand, the longer it will be before the system needs to be revised and new software and hardware obtained. This principle may be less relevant to industries in which organizations need to apply rapidly evolving technology in order to remain competitive.

Review Question

What might be included in an RFP for software? In one for hardware?

Evaluate Vendor Proposals

Using vendor responses to the RFP, the logical specification, and the physical requirements, analysts must decide which, if any, proposal best meets the organization's needs. The process of evaluating the vendor proposals includes three steps:

1. Validate vendor proposals.
2. Consider other data and criteria.
3. Suggest resources.

Many organizations assign a team to evaluate the proposals. The team could consist of personnel with IT technical expertise, business process owners, system users, external consultants, lawyers, and accountants. The evaluation team completes these three steps to suggest the software, hardware, and services that best meet the organization's requirements.

Validate Vendor Proposals The first evaluation step is to **validate** the vendor proposal to assess whether the system (software or hardware) does what the organization requires by studying a proposed system's *specifications* and *performance. Specifications* are straightforward descriptions of the hardware and software—such as a software package's maximum table sizes or a printer's speed—that can be examined to determine whether the system has the ability to perform as required. *Performance* features can be determined only through testing, measurement, or evaluation and often include items such as user friendliness, vendor support,[6] quality of documentation, reliability, and ability of system to produce complete, accurate, and timely output.

[6] In a 1997 survey, financial and information technology executives rated superior vendor service as more important than the latest technology as a criterion for software selection. *Financial and Accounting Survey Results* (Deloitte & Touche LLP and Hyperion Software, 1997): 8.

Review Question

What is the difference between a specification and a performance measure?

One commonly used method for measuring system performance involves measuring the system's **throughput**, which is the quantity of work performed in a period of time. For instance, the number of invoices that a system processes in one hour is a measure of throughput. Other performance measures, such as ease of use, are more subjective and may be more difficult to determine. Technology Excerpt 7.2 (page 216) describes some performance factors to be considered when choosing an *ASP*.

[Insert Technology Excerpt 7.2 box here]

After eliminating those proposals that do not meet minimum requirements, the evaluation team tests[7] the remaining systems to determine the accuracy of the vendors' specifications and how well the equipment will work for the organization. Having determined what a system *is,* we test to determine what that system *can do.*

[7] Often, vendors will propose a system that does not actually exist *yet.* In such cases, we cannot test an actual system; our only option is to *simulate* the proposed system, as discussed later in this section.

An evaluation team can test a system by:

- Varying input (workload) parameters, such as quantity, timing, and type of input.
- Varying system characteristics (parameters), such as quantity and size of data storage devices.
- Varying the factors being measured, such as CPU cycle time (a system parameter) or execution time (a performance measure).
- Testing an actual workload, such as a weekly payroll, or testing a workload model that is representative of the workload.
- Testing the actual system or a model of the system.

The Internet has made it possible for vendors to demonstrate their software on their Web sites. For example, at mySAP.com (http://www.mySAP.com) you can see demonstrations of and "test drive" SAP's R/3 enterprise system. This site allows prospective buyers to evaluate the system's capabilities and to identify the modules that will best meet their needs. Other vendors providing similar services include Microsoft's Great Plains (http://www.greatplains.com), where you can test their enterprise system, and SBT (http://www.sbtcorp.com), where you can test their ACCPAC eTransact system.[8]

[8] Carlton Collins, "How to Select the Right Accounting Software" *Journal of Accountancy* (October 1999): 67.

Consider Other Data and Criteria Rather than estimate vendor and system performance internally, the evaluation team can interview users of the vendors' products and visit those sites to witness the system in action. Quite often, vendor presentations are made at the site of an existing user. **External interviews**—interviews conducted with personnel outside the organization—can provide valuable insights into vendor performance. Where appropriate, questionnaires can also be used to gather information from users. The following information might be collected from users:

- Were there delays in obtaining the software or hardware?
- Did the system have bugs?
- How responsive is the vendor to requests for service?
- Was the training the vendor provided adequate?

As mentioned in Technology Insight 7.2, there are several services that publish technical reviews, user surveys, and expert commentary on computer equipment, software, and a variety of related topics. The reviews and user surveys can be helpful when evaluating proposals.

A cost/benefit analysis is often used to determine the economic viability of the remaining vendor proposals. Quantifiable costs and benefits are summarized to determine whether vendor proposals can be justified economically. Ranking vendor proposals using the economic criteria is useful in the next step in systems selection, in which the evaluation team suggests which vendor proposal should be chosen. The identification and quantification of Information Systems costs and benefits, however, is a difficult process requiring as much art as science. Still, we must have some data with which to make a decision.

Suggest Resources At this point, the study team recommends one vendor proposal. Management then chooses the software and hardware resources. To recommend one vendor, the evaluation team compares the proposals that have not been eliminated. The evaluation team might list the relevant criteria and indicate the performance of each vendor on each criterion.

Complete Configuration Plan

To complete the *configuration plan*—the major output from the *systems selection* step in *SDLC*—the evaluation team must complete the software plan, complete the hardware plan, and obtain approvals. As with many of the steps in systems development, these processes are not necessarily sequential, but should be iterative.

The **software plan** documents how the logical specification will be implemented, using in-house development, vendor purchase or lease, ASP, or a combination of these. The **hardware plan** summarizes how the recommended vendor proposal will fulfill the physical requirements specified in structured systems analysis.

Once the configuration plan (i.e., the combined software and hardware plans) is completed, it must be approved by the Information Systems steering committee, IT management, internal auditor, the controller, legal counsel, and other appropriate management personnel. Once approved, the configuration plan is used in the next step in systems development: structured systems design.

Introduction to Structured Systems Design

Studies have shown that systems developed using structured systems design techniques are less costly over the life of the system because maintenance of the system is less expensive. Structured systems design also avoids design errors that further increase the cost of the system. Implementation planning, conducted during structured systems design and introduced in this section, increases the probability of a smooth transition to the new Information System.

Refer to Figure 7.1 (page 206) to see that structured systems design is the fourth major step in the development of an Information System. **Structured systems design** is a set of procedures performed to convert the logical specification into a design that can be implemented on the organization's computer system. Structured systems design is often called *detailed design* or *internal design.* Concurrent with specification of the system's design, plans are developed for testing and implementing the new system and for training personnel. Portions of the user manual are also developed at this time.

The *structured systems design goals* are as follows:

Review Question

What is structured systems design?

- *Convert the structured specification into a reliable, maintainable design.* This is similar to the process of converting a building model into a blueprint.
- *Develop a plan and budget that will ensure an orderly and controlled implementation of the new system.* Procedures must be devised to get the hardware in place, the programming completed, the training conducted, and the new system operating.
- *Develop an implementation test plan that ensures that the system is reliable, complete, and accurate.* A plan must be developed to test the system to ensure that it does what the user wants it to do.
- *Develop a user manual that facilitates efficient and effective use of the new system by operations and management personnel.*

Personnel must know how to use the new system effectively, and the information processing staff must know how to operate the system.

- *Develop a program that ensures that users and support personnel are adequately trained.*

Review Question

What are the structured systems design goals?

The Intermediate Steps in Structured Systems Design

The sequence of activities and the amount of effort expended for each activity in structured systems design differs depending on some of the decisions made earlier in the systems development process. For example, if the organization has chosen to install an enterprise system, the design steps will include reengineering of the business processes and specification of how the enterprise system will be configured to match those processes. If the organization has chosen to develop the software in-house, the structured systems design step includes design of the software that will be written during the implementation step.

Specify Modules

If the software is to be developed in-house, it is at this point in the development process that we must specify the software design (i.e., detailed, internal design). The modular design of the software is one of the features unique to *structured* systems development. The main tool of the structured design process is the **structure chart**, a graphic tool for depicting the partitioning of a system into modules, the hierarchy and organization of these modules, and the communication interfaces between the modules.[9]

[9] Meilir Page-Jones, *The Practical Guide to Structured Systems Design,* 2nd ed. (Englewood Cliffs, NJ: Prentice-Hall, 1988): 356.

The structure chart's overall appearance is similar to that of an organization chart. Each box on a structure chart is a **module**. These structure chart modules become computer program modules of 30 to 60 lines of computer program code (one-half to one page of code). During structured systems design, related activities are grouped together within a module. This grouping of activities leads to a more maintainable system because changes to one function of a system lead to changes in a minimum of modules.

Develop Implementation Plan and Budget

System designers possess valuable insights into how a system should be implemented. During the design phase, the project team documents these insights in an implementation plan. As the implementation plan evolves, the project team summarizes resources required to implement the new system into an implementation budget so that resources can be allocated and implementation tasks scheduled.

If the software is to be developed in-house, the structure chart, developed by the system designer, dictates which modules should be programmed and installed first, and this sequence becomes part of the plan. The systems designer uses the expected size and complexity of the computer programs to prepare a schedule and budget for the programmers required to write the program code.

Develop Implementation Test Plan

Each system module, *and any interactions between modules,* must be tested prior to implementation. Again, systems designers have valuable insights into how a system should be tested. As we saw in the discussion of structure charts, the inputs and outputs for each module (and module combination) are specified in the design phase so that the designers can specify test inputs and expected outputs and provide recommendations for the order in which the system's pieces should be tested. Examples of test control strategies are found in Technology Application 7.1 (page 220).

[Insert Technology Application 7.1 box here]

Develop User Manual

Because the designer knows how the system and each program will operate, how each input should be prepared, and how each output is used, preparation of the user manual can begin in the design phase. At this point in the SDLC, the manual is used to *begin* briefing and training users. The development of the user manual proceeds concurrently and interactively with many other design activities. For example, user procedures usually depend on computer system procedures, but some system functions may depend on user procedures. Development team members must also know about user procedures so that they can design tests of those procedures.

Develop Training Program

User training should begin before the system is implemented and therefore must be planned during the design phase. Deciding when to conduct training is tricky. While training must be conducted before implementation, it cannot be too much before or trainees may forget what they learned. Training materials, user manuals, and the system used for training must also be consistent with the system actually implemented.

Complete Systems Design Document

The *approved systems design document* has three main components: (1) the system design (structure charts and descriptions of logical processes); (2) the implementation, testing, and training plans; and (3) the user manual. The design project leader must assemble these components and obtain the required user approvals (to ensure the adequacy of the design and plans) and management approvals (to signify concurrence with the design, training, and implementation process). In addition, IS management furnishes a supervisory/technical approval of the adequacy of the software specifications. Auditors ensure adequacy of the controls and the design process (including implementation planning).

Introduction to Systems Implementation

At this point in the SDLC, we have completed the systems analysis phase (the *systems survey* and *structured systems analysis*). We have also completed the systems design phase by selecting hardware and software (*systems selection*) and by preparing the systems design and the implementation plan (*structured systems design*). It is time to install and begin to use our new or modified system.

Systems implementation is a set of procedures performed to complete the design (as necessary) contained in the *approved systems design document* and to test, install, and begin to use the new or revised Information System. Figure 7.1 (page 206) depicts systems implementation as the fifth major step in the development of an Information System.

Review Question

What is systems implementation?

The *systems implementation goals* are as follows:

- *Complete as necessary the design contained in the approved systems design document.* For example, the detailed contents of new or revised documents, computer screens, and database must be laid out and created.

- *Write, test, and document the programs and procedures required by the approved systems design document.*
- *Ensure, by completing the preparation of user manuals and other documentation and by training personnel, that the organization's personnel can operate the new system.*
- *Determine, by thoroughly testing the system with users, that the system satisfies the users' requirements.*
- *Ensure a correct conversion by planning, controlling, and conducting an orderly installation of the new system.*

Review Question

What are the systems implementation goals?

In this section we describe implementation approaches that can be taken to install the new or modified system. Figure 7.2 (page 222) depicts the three most common implementation approaches.

[Insert Figure 7.2 here]

Figure 7.2(a), the *parallel approach,* provides the most control of the three. In the **parallel approach**, both the old and new systems operate together for a time. During this period, time *x* to time *y* (which is usually one operating cycle, such as one month or one quarter), the outputs of the two systems are compared to determine whether the new system is operating comparably to the old. At time *y*, management makes a decision, based on the comparison of the two systems' outputs, whether to terminate the operation of the old system. The parallel approach provides more control because the old system is not abandoned until users are satisfied that the new system adequately replaces the old. Although this approach makes good intuitive sense, in practice it frequently alienates users who perceive parallel operations as doubling their workload.

Review Question

What are the three major approaches to implementing an Information System?

Figure 7.2(b), the **direct approach**, is often called the "Big Bang" approach and is the riskiest of the three approaches. At time *x* the old system is stopped and the new system cuts in with no validation that the new system operates comparably to the old. While we will see a little later that it need not be so, enterprise systems are often implemented using this approach. Sometimes, as you'll see in the Hershey story in Chapter 11, direct implementations can lead to disaster.

Figure 7.2(c), the modular approach, can combine parallel or direct approaches to tailor the implementation to the circumstances. With the **modular approach**, the new system is either implemented one subsystem at a time or is introduced into one organizational unit at a time. For example, a new Order-to-Cash system could be implemented by first changing the sales order preparation and customer inquiry portions, followed by implementing the link to the billing system, followed by the link to the inventory system. Figure 7.2(c) depicts the gradual implementation of a new system into three organizational units. A new payroll system is installed for the employees of plant 1 at time *x,* followed by plant 2 at time *y,* and finally by plant 3 at time z. Implementation at any plant could be direct or parallel. Modular implementation permits *pilot testing* of a system or system component and elimination of any problems discovered before full implementation.

Figure 7.3 depicts the modular schedule used at the Boston Scientific Corporation to implement SAP at all of its worldwide divisions and locations. As shown in this example, several installations were complete while two more were scheduled for the end of March. At Boston Scientific, several members of the project team were on location on each worldwide "go-live" date to provide assistance, ensure consistency of all implementations, and to learn and provide improvements for subsequent implementations.

[Insert Figure 7.3 here]

The Intermediate Steps in Systems Implementation

As with *structured systems design,* the sequence of activities and the amount of effort expended on each depends on some of the decisions made earlier in the development process. For example, if the organization has decided to install an enterprise system, software and hardware may have been purchased and installed at this point in the development process. Also, if the software has been acquired (vs. developed in-house), as with an enterprise system, the only programming likely required would be to connect the enterprise software to any remaining legacy systems (i.e., old systems being retained).

Complete the Design

During systems implementation, we need to *complete* the detailed design of the new or revised systems. This may sound a little confusing. Didn't we perform *structured systems design* in the previous development step? Yes, we did. But that design was related to the design of software that was to be developed. Now we must design input and output reports, documents, computer screens, database, manual processes, and certain computer processes, such as those needed to link new software to legacy systems.

Acquire Hardware and Software

At any time after the computer resources are chosen and indicated in the *approved configuration plan,* the software and hardware may be acquired, the site prepared, and the computer system installed.

Contract negotiation and site preparation are important parts of the computer acquisition process. Technical, legal, and financial expertise must be combined to negotiate and execute the contracts. Business process owners should review contracts to ensure that important user requirements, such as system availability and response times, are reflected. Detailed specifications protect both buyer and vendor. Technology Excerpt 7.3 provides some contract preparation guidelines.

[Insert Technology Excerpt 7.3 box here]

The site to receive the computer equipment must be prepared carefully. Sufficient electrical power and power protection, air conditioning, and security, as well as the computer room's physical structure and access to that room, must be planned for and provided. If contracts are well written and the site well prepared, installation of the computer hardware, software, and related equipment should be relatively straightforward. Contingency plans to allow for delays in site preparation or equipment delivery should be considered.

Write, Configure, Test, Debug, and Document Computer Software

The next task in systems implementation is to produce or configure the software, test and debug the software, and complete the software documentation. For internally developed systems, the programming step is important because the programming task in systems development consumes more resources and time than any other development task.

If we have purchased a software package, much of the programming step is replaced with procedures to configure the system for this application. During the implementation of an enterprise system, this process can be extensive as we configure the system to select, for example, the steps to be completed for each business process, the design of the screens to be displayed at each step of the process, and the data to be captured, stored, and output during the processes. This is the point at which we ensure matching business processes that we have reengineered within the organization to elements of the enterprise system. For example, we can configure the SAP system to create and record a customer invoice automatically upon shipment of the goods, or we can require that the billing process be triggered later.

Some programming may remain, however. To tie the new enterprise system modules to legacy systems, program code must be written—in ABAP for SAP and C+ + for J. D. Edwards, for example.

Select, Train, and Educate Personnel

The organization must choose personnel to use the new system and train them to perform their system-related duties. The system's users must be educated about the new system's purpose, function, and capabilities. Such training becomes even more important if jobs have been redesigned during *business process reengineering*. Training may come from a combination of schools run by software vendors, hardware vendors, vendors specializing in training, and programs conducted by the organization itself. Computer-assisted learning, such as interactive tutorials, might also be used. Online HELP and EXPLANATION facilities, along with well-designed screens and reports, can reduce the amount of up-front training necessary and provide ongoing guidance to system users.

Computer-based training (CBT) provides learning via computer directly to the trainee's computer screen. Training may be delivered over the Internet by vendors whose business it is to design, produce, and deliver such training. Enterprise system vendors, such as SAP and J. D. Edwards, have created extensive CBTs to help users learn the features of their systems. CBT can be much less expensive than lectures, and it also permits individualized instruction, which can take place when and where needed. The interactive nature of CBT can get and keep a trainee's attention. However, some employees, particularly middle and senior management, prefer more personal, traditional delivery methods.

Complete User Manual

A *user manual* should describe operating procedures for both manual and automated systems functions. The manual should cover user responsibilities, system inputs, computer system interfaces, manual files and databases, controls (including error detection and correction), distribution and use of system outputs, and manual and automated processing instructions. Good user manuals can improve system efficiency and effectiveness. If users know how to use a system properly and they employ it willingly, the system will be used more frequently, more correctly, and more productively.

The systems designer, the user, and the organization's technical writing and training staff should cooperate in preparing the user manual. Because the systems designer knows intimately what the system will do, he or she is well qualified to describe how to use the system. The user, who must study the manual to learn the system and then keep the manual as a reference for continued operation of the system, must make sure that the manual is relevant for the tasks to be performed and that it is complete, accurate, and clear.

The organization's training staff should be involved in preparing the manual because they must train users to operate the new system. The staff must learn the system themselves and develop separate training materials and/or use the user manual as the training vehicle. Therefore they are very interested in the user manual and should have input to its development.

Test System

Beyond testing program modules, the entire system is tested to determine that it meets requirements established by business process owners and users, and that it can be used and operated to the satisfaction of both users and system operators. Testing is carried out by systems developers, by developers and the users together, and finally by users. The more closely the test can simulate a production environment (e.g., people, machines, data, inputs), the more representative the test will be and the more conclusive the results.

Several types or levels of tests are usually completed before a system can be implemented. From the users' point of view, three of these tests are the most important. The **system test** verifies the new system against the original specifications. This test is conducted first by the development team and then by the users with the assistance of the team. The **acceptance test** is a *user*-directed test of the complete system in a test environment. The purpose is to determine, from the user's perspective, whether all components of the new system are satisfactory. The user tests the adequacy of the system, both manual and automated components; of the manuals and other documentation; and of the training the users received. Finally, the **operations test** or **environmental test** runs a subset of the system in the actual production environment. This final test determines whether new equipment and other factors in the environment—such as data entry areas, document and report deliveries, telephones, and electricity—are satisfactory.

As noted earlier, enterprise systems are often implemented using a direct (Big Bang) approach. Successful implementations often involve extensive testing. For example, before implementing SAP at Lucent Technologies, Inc., more than 70 business users tested the system for six months. At the Gillette Company, 150 workers ran test transactions for four months.[10]

[10] Craig Stedman, "ERP Requires Exhaustive Full-System Tests," *Computerworld* (November 8, 1999): 38.

Obtain Approvals

The *project completion report*—the systems implementation deliverable—is approved as follows:

- Users verify that the system, including the user manual, meets their requirements. Users also approve conversion and training plans to confirm that these plans are adequate.
- IT confirms that the system has been completed and that it works. IT also approves the training and conversion plans. Finally, IT performs a technical review of the system to determine that acceptable design and programming standards have been applied.
- Management reviews the systems performance objectives, cost, and projected benefits to ensure that implementation is consistent with the best interests of the organization.
- IT audit compares test results with the original system requirements and specifications to determine that the system has

been tested and will operate satisfactorily. IT audit is also interested in the adequacy of controls within the system and the controls identified for the conversion process.

Conduct Conversion

After all previous design steps have been completed and signed off, the organization carefully converts to the new system. Conversion includes converting data, converting processes (i.e., the programs), and completing documentation. Controls must be in place to ensure accurate, complete, and authorized conversion of data and programs.

As existing data are mapped into the new system, exception-reporting situations must be devised to ensure that data are converted accurately. Users must suggest control totals that can be used to test completeness and accuracy of data conversion. For example, the total number of inventory items, the total on-hand quantity for all inventory items, or a *hash total* (described in Chapter 9) of inventory item numbers might be used as totals.

Boston Scientific (see Figure 7.3, page 223) implemented SAP over the course of two years at each of its worldwide divisions and locations (i.e., *a modular approach*). But since SAP was implemented using the *direct approach* at each of those locations, the data conversion was tested at least *seven* times, until there were no errors! The company believes that this testing was the key to the successful implementations.[11]

Both manual and computer-based processes must be converted. Conversion to new computer programs must be undertaken using *program change controls* (described in Chapter 8) to ensure that only authorized, tested, and approved versions of programs are promoted to production status.

[11] Dave Ellard, Vice President, Global Systems, Boston Scientific, "Global Systems in 18 Months," a presentation made to the Advanced Accounting Information Systems classes at Bentley College, March 20, 2000.

The systems development project team now writes the *project completion report,* the final step in the implementation process. This report includes a summary of conversion activities and information with which to operate and maintain the new system.

Systems Operation

An organization should periodically examine the system in its production environment to determine whether the system is continuing to satisfy users' needs. If it is possible to make the system work better, its value to users will increase. There are three different types of periodic examination:

1. The *post-implementation review* is conducted to follow up a system's recent implementation. This review is analogous to a follow-up examination that a doctor might perform after an

operation.

2. *Systems maintenance,* performed in response to a specific request, is conducted if the system has a relatively minor deficiency. This examination is similar to one a doctor performs on sick people.
3. The periodic *systems survey* is undertaken whenever it is likely that the costs of the review will be less than the value of the improvements that the review will suggest. This reevaluation is like a periodic physical examination.

The Post-Implementation Review

The **post-implementation review** is an examination of a working information system, conducted soon after that system's implementation. The post-implementation review determines whether the user's requirements have been satisfied and whether the development effort was efficient and conducted in accordance with the organization's systems development standards. The post-implementation review should be brief and inexpensive. Examinations conducted in response to a specific deficiency, *systems maintenance*, are discussed in the next section.

Review Question

What is the post-implementation review?

Post-implementation review goals are as follows:

- Determine whether users are satisfied with the new system.
- Identify the degree of correspondence between system performance requirements and the system's achieved performance.
- Evaluate the quality of the new system's documentation, training programs, and data conversions.
- Review the performance of the new system and, if necessary, recommend improvements.
- Ascertain that the organization's project management framework and SDLC were followed during development.
- Perfect the cost/effectiveness analysis process by reviewing cost projections and benefit estimations and determining the degree to which these were achieved.
- Perfect project planning procedures by examining total project costs and the project team's ability to adhere to project cost estimates and schedules.
- Make any other recommendations that might improve the operation of the system or the development of other information systems.

Review Question

What are the post-implementation review goals?

Consultants, IT auditors, or systems analysts (other than those who developed the system) may conduct the post-implementation review. The post-implementation review is performed as soon as the system is operating at full capacity, which could be a month or a year after implementation. The review should examine a fully functioning system so as not to draw erroneous conclusions about system performance. The review should be conducted soon enough after implementation to be able to take advantage of any improvements that can be made to the system or to the systems development methods used.

Systems Maintenance

Systems maintenance is the modification (e.g., repair, correction, enhancement) of existing applications. Systems maintenance expenditures can account for 50 to 70 percent of the total cost of a system over its total life cycle. For example, 80 percent of the total cost of software is in maintenance.[12] Not all maintenance expense is necessarily bad; rather, the issue is the *relative* amount spent on systems maintenance. After all, applications must be adapted to a changing environment and improved over time.

[12] Carol Sliwa, "Web Site Upgrades: Build or Buy?" *Computerworld* (January 17, 2000): 16. "Sizing Up the SDLC," Gartner Group Research Note QA-05-9636, October 29, 1998.

Review Question

What is systems maintenance?

Organizations often adopt the following procedures and controls for their systems maintenance process:

- Because systems maintenance is like miniature systems development, it should include analysis, cost/benefit study, design, implementation, and approvals for each development step. In systems maintenance, certain SDLC procedures deserve more attention than others. For example, changes must be tested prior to implementation to determine that a change corrects the problem and does not cause other problems. Participants and signoffs should be the same as those required for systems development. For example, users should review system changes.
- By charging users for maintenance costs, an organization can reduce the submission of frivolous maintenance requests.
- By adopting a formal procedure for submitting change requests, batching these requests together for each application, and then prioritizing the batches, management can gain control of systems maintenance and reduce the expense and disruptions caused by maintenance.
- During systems maintenance, information should be gathered that provides feedback to improve the operation of the system and to improve the systems development process. For instance,

poor quality application documentation and inadequate user training can cause numerous systems maintenance requests. Correcting these deficiencies can preclude the need for similar maintenance requests in the future. Likewise, improvements in the systems development process can prevent deficiencies from occurring in other systems when they are being developed.

- Management should see that *program change controls* (see Chapter 8) are used to ensure that all modifications to computer programs are authorized, tested, and properly implemented.
- High-quality documentation must be created and maintained. Without current, accurate documentation, maintenance programmers cannot understand existing programs, and therefore cannot effectively or efficiently modify them.

Review Question

Why is the management and control of systems maintenance so important?

Conclusions

Systems selection is a process that is central to the success of systems development. Recall that the first objective of systems development is "to develop information systems that satisfy an organization's informational and operational needs." For this reason, one key to the success of systems development is to ensure that systems selection criteria are based on user requirements (i.e., the logical specifications and physical requirements) developed during the systems analysis phase of systems development.

Another key to systems development success is the full evaluation of available software and hardware resources. As the quantity of resources has grown, it has become more difficult to identify and evaluate all available resources. On the other hand, the Internet has made available to us large quantities of up-to-date, independent information to assist in the selection process. Indeed, as noted earlier in the chapter, we can see product demos or actually conduct tests at many vendor Web sites.

Finally, the success of systems development projects is found in the details. It may be such things as user manuals, training, and implementation schedules and plans that determine the success of the new or modified system.

There may be, however, another twist on the cause-and-effect relationship between successful completion of systems development steps and the achievement of the systems development objectives.[13] At the time we have implemented a system and conducted the post-implementation review, we might measure the development process as successful. That is, we have delivered a system that meets most of the user requirements, we have implemented the system on time and within budget, and there don't seem to be any bugs. These are all short-term measures.

[13] The ideas presented here are derived from Ed Yourdon, "Long-Term Thinking," *Computerworld* (October 16, 2000): 50.

It is not until we conduct systems maintenance that we discover that the system has some long-term faults. It may not be, for example, flexible, scalable, reliable, or maintainable. These faults are what drive up the life cycle cost of the system, that cause maintenance costs to be 50 to 70 percent of the long-term costs. The solution is to incorporate the long-term requirements (e.g., flexibility, maintainability) into the initial user requirements and to measure the success of the implementation over the long run, rather than at the time of implementation.

REVIEW QUESTIONS

RQ7-1 What is systems selection?

RQ7-2 What are systems selection goals?

RQ7-3 What are reasons for developing software internally versus acquiring it from external sources?

RQ7-4 What are the external sources of software?

RQ7-5 What is a *systems integrator*?

RQ7-6 What is an *application service provider (ASP)*?

RQ7-7 What are reasons for using external and internal sources of hardware?

RQ7-8 What is a request for proposal (RFP)?

RQ7-9 What are the factors an organization must consider in structuring the RFP and deciding to whom the RFP will be sent?

RQ7-10 What might be included in an RFP for software? In one for hardware?

RQ7-11 What is the difference between a specification and a performance measure?

RQ7-12 What is structured systems design?

RQ7-13 What are the structured systems design goals?

RQ7-14 What is systems implementation?

RQ7-15 What are the systems implementation goals?

RQ7-16 What are the three major approaches to implementing an Information System?

RQ7-17 What is the post-implementation review?

RQ7-18 What are the post-implementation review goals?

RQ7-19 What is systems maintenance?

RQ7-20 Why is the management and control of systems maintenance so important?

DISCUSSION QUESTIONS

DQ7-1 You are charged with recommending how to reengineer your company's SDLC so that the typical 9-month development process could be cut to 6 weeks. Describe your new process. Which steps take on more or less importance in your new approach?

DQ7-2 As discussed in the chapter, there are companies that specialize in providing "contract" analysis and programming services to clients for a fee. Discuss the relative advantages to the client of using contract services versus other available alternatives.

DQ7-3 "There are enough software packages on the market today to preclude any organization needing to write another application program." Do you agree? Why or why not?

DQ7-4 "An organization puts itself at a disadvantage by asking only one vendor (versus asking several vendors) for a proposal for software or hardware." Do you agree? Why or why not?

DQ7-5 "Nobody ever got fired for choosing IBM." Comment on this statement in light of the information in this chapter.

DQ7-6 "A vendor would not propose a system that would not meet an organization's needs. Therefore, 'validation' of vendor proposals is not really necessary." Do you agree? Why or why not?

DQ7-7 "Surveys of existing users of software and hardware, such as those published by Dataquest Market Intelligence and Datapro, are biased. Only those users who are very happy or very displeased with their software and/or equipment respond to such surveys." Do you agree? Why or why not?

DQ7-8 Compare and contrast the efficiency and effectiveness of an in-house data center; an arrangement with an *outsourcing* vendor to own and operate a data center for us; a *service bureau;* and an *application service provider (ASP).*

DQ7-9 Give examples, other than those used in this chapter, of situations in which each of the three implementation approaches is most appropriate. Explain why that implementation approach is most appropriate.

DQ7-10 Assume that you are the manager of an accounts receivable department. How might you be involved in system testing?

DQ7-11 Refer to the story about Hopper Specialty Company at the beginning of the chapter. Describe, using several examples, how Joe Hopper would have avoided or minimized the problems that he encountered by following the systems development procedures described in this chapter.

PROBLEMS

P7-1 Read the following article and answer the questions that follow: Milo Geyelin, "Doomsday Device: How an NCR System For Inventory Turned Into a Virtual Saboteur," *Wall Street Journal* (August 8, 1994): A1.

a. At the start of Hooper Specialty's inventory system conversion project, how would you characterize it in terms of size, degree of definition, technology familiarity, and organizational readiness? *Note:* See Chapter 6 for a description of these concepts. Your answer should include several risks for Hooper.

b. Given the risks that you identify in answering part a, as well as the control principles discussed in this text, what measures could Joe Hopper have taken to prevent, detect, or correct problems with the NCR inventory system?

c. Next, consider the situation from the point of view of NCR. What risk did they face? What measures could they have put in place to prevent, detect, and correct problems with the inventory software they acquired from Taylor Management Systems?

P7-2 Using the Web sites listed in Technology Insight 7.2 (page 213) as a starting point, answer the following questions:

a. Select sites (or parts of sites) that describe two similar software or hardware products. Write a summary that compares and contrasts the information provided about those products.

b. Select two sites that provide demos of a system. Write a report that compares and contrasts those demos in terms of the functionality and what you are able to learn about the system from the demo.

c. Select two sites that provide tests of a system. Write a report that compares and contrasts those tests in terms of the functionality and what you are able to learn about the system from the test.

P7-3 Obtain a computer operations "run manual" from an actual organization. Your college or university might be a source.

Prepare a report that summarizes the contents of the run manual. Comment on the apparent reason for including each major item in the manual. If you are unsure of the reason for including certain material, interview the computer operations manager to determine the reason.

P7-4 The Boston Edison Company provides electric service to the residents and businesses of Boston and several other eastern Massachusetts communities. This problem concerns the following *hypothetical* billing procedures for Boston Edison.

Field personnel take electric meter readings 10 days prior to the end of each customer's monthly billing cycle. These personnel key the meter readings into handheld units. In computer operations at the home office, the meter reading units are read by the computer, which also accesses the stored customer records and other necessary data. The quantity of kilowatts consumed and the amount due are computed, and the bill is printed (a sample bill is shown in Figure 7.4, page 234). Customers return the top half of their bills with their payments.

[Insert Figure 7.4 here]

Because of the steady growth in number of customers and the increased need for managerial information, Boston Edison's management has decided to upgrade its customer billing system. The new system will retain the present meter reading procedures, but the rest of the system will be modernized. The new system should also enable users to access customer records when desired and should provide improved information for decision making.

For each numbered item on the Boston Edison bill (Figure 7.4), indicate the immediate (versus ultimate) source of the item. For instance, the immediate source of the current meter reading would be the meter reading unit (i.e., event data), as opposed to the ultimate source, which is the meter itself. Some items may have more than one source. You have the following choices:

- C = customer records (a combination of customer and accounts receivable master data)
- CG = computer generated (such as a date or time supplied by the system)
- CC = computer calculated

- ED = event data
- CO = console operator (such as batch totals or a date to be used)

Arrange your answer as follows:

Item No.	Source
1.	C
2.	?
3.	CG
etc.	

P7-5 Assume that you are working with a payroll application that produces weekly paychecks, including paystubs. Listed below are 20 data elements that would appear on the paycheck/paystub. For each numbered item, indicate the immediate (versus ultimate) source of the item. For instance, the immediate source of the number of exemptions for an employee would be the employee master data, as opposed to the ultimate source, which is the W-4 form filed by the employee. Some items may have more than one source, as in the case of item 1. You have the following choices:

- E = employee master data
- T = time records (these are in machine-readable form and show, for each employee for each day, the time punched *in* in the morning, *out* at lunch, *in* after lunch, and *out* in the evening)

- H = table of hourly wage rates (i.e., wage rate "class" and hourly rate for each class)
- W = table of state and federal income tax withholding amounts plus FICA tax rate and annual "cutoff" amount for FICA wages
- CG = computer generated (such as a date or time of day supplied by the system)
- CC = computer calculated
- CO = console operator (such as batch totals or a date to be used)

Arrange your answer as follows:

Item No.	**Source**
1.	T, E
2.	?
etc.	

The items to be considered are as follows:

Number	**Description**
1.	Employee identification number
2.	Social security number
3.	Employee name
4.	Employee address
5.	Regular hours worked

Number	Description
6.	Overtime hours worked
7.	Pay rate classification
8.	Hourly pay rate
9.	Regular earnings
10.	Overtime earnings
11.	Total earnings

Number	**Description**
12.	Deduction for federal income tax
13.	Deduction for state income tax
14.	Deduction for FICA tax
15.	Union dues withheld (flat amount based on length of service)
16.	Net pay
17.	Check number (same number is also preprinted on each check form)
18.	Year-to-date amounts for items 11 through 14
19.	Pay period end date
20.	Date of check (employees are paid on Wednesday for the week ended the previous Friday)

P7-6 Shown in Figure 7.5 is a flowchart that depicts the computer logic for updating *sequential* inventory master data for either of two types of events: goods received or goods issued.

[Insert Figure 7.5 here]

Develop data to test the logic of the inventory update program. The test data should allow for all possible combinations of master data and event data records. **Note:** There can be more than one event for a particular part number; be sure to provide for this possibility.

P7-7 Read the scenario below and answer the following questions:

Fleet Shoe Company is having problems with its automated distribution system. The main warehouse is almost at a standstill and retailers are getting few if any Fleet shoes. Fleet had received recognition for its state-of-the-art warehouse system. However, just prior to switching over to this new system, Fleet scrapped the system's software and computer hardware and adopted a new architecture. During the development, there had been very high turnover of IT staff and Fleet had fired its lead systems integrator.

The new system was to automate the movement of goods in the warehouse and was to include tilting trays, conveyor belts, lifting equipment, and scanners. To operate properly, such systems require quite a bit of fine-tuning. The goal was to increase capacity, boost productivity, cut staff by 50 percent, and cut the time to get orders out the door to 24 hours. The software, not the hardware, seemed to be the problem. It was designed to run under UNIX, but Fleet decided to use fault-tolerant computers that run a proprietary (i.e., hardware specific) operating system. When the software vendor went out of business, they had not completed porting (i.e., transferring) their software to the proprietary operating system.

Fleet's choice to replace the original platform was a computer system that itself ran warehouse management software. It is this option that brought Fleet to it knees. The new system was slower than expected. To get shoes to retailers, Fleet shipped directly from overseas factories and warehouses. Comments from industry specialists and consultants pointed out the chaos that often results from instantaneous changeovers. Another speculated that Fleet did not place much importance on warehousing and rather concentrated on other aspects of its operations.

a. How would you characterize this project in terms of size, degree of definition, technology familiarity, and organizational readiness?

b. Describe specific risks or concerns that you have for this project. Clearly explain why each is a risk or concern and the specific actions that you would recommend to mitigate the risk or concern.

TABLES

[Start Table]

Table 7.1 Internal versus External Software and Hardware Sources

Internal	External
Software	
Can be developed to meet all user needs, but may take longer than would a purchase.	May be available more quickly, but we must pay for any modifications required to meet all user needs.
Two company assets are built: the software and the experience of the development team.	Purchased software may be an asset. But the software is probably similar to that owned by others. External expertise may be required to develop the software and to supplement and develop the internal staff expertise.
Initial costs are higher, but cost is difficult to assess because 80% of the cost of a system over its life is for maintenance.	Initial costs, being spread across many buyers, are lower, but we may have paid for features that are not required.
Outcome of the development process is uncertain. We don't know if the software will be delivered on time, within budget, and with required functionality.	We can test the software and examine documentation before purchase.
Ongoing support and maintenance must be provided in-house and staffing may not be adequate.	Purchased ongoing support and maintenance may be quite costly if we have modified the system and can't easily accept future releases.
Better option for software that may provide a competitive advantage.	Better option for straightforward, common applications.
Can control the development process.	Contract must specify performance requirements.
Can ensure compatibility with existing and future applications.	May require tailoring or development of bridging applications.
Can adapt software to changing needs.	Adaptations may not be forthcoming from the vendor and costly modifications may be required.
Hardware	
Can determine level of control, security, and privacy.	Level of control may vary and be difficult to attain, especially if many companies use the same hardware.
Management and staff must be in-house.	Management and staff are provided.

Capacity limited.	Additional capacity may be available.
Costs are mostly fixed.	Costs are mostly variable.
Tailored to our needs.	Tailoring varies.

[End Table]

BOXES

[Start Technology Excerpt 7.1 box here]

Technology Excerpt 7.1

Guidelines for Effective Use of Systems Integrators

Here are seven steps that may help prevent the disastrous situations associated with IT projects led by systems integrators (SI).

1. Before submitting a request for proposal, define the key project objectives and measures of success. If these can't be defined, don't proceed.
2. Review the SI's proposal to determine that they have conducted due diligence in developing their proposal and that the project sponsors—IT and business process owners—understand the proposed solution.
3. Break the project into chunks of six months and tie contract payments to specific milestones.
4. Ensure that the roles and responsibilities of the SI and sponsoring team members have been defined and that the qualifications of these team members have been determined.
5. At project kickoff, determine high-risk factors and contingency plans to deal with those factors.

6. The project sponsor must meet regularly with the project manager to determine that the project is progressing as planned.
7. Before completing the project, ensure the achievement of project objectives and milestones.

Source: Excerpted from Gopal K. Kapur, "Happier Projects," *Computerworld* (May 29, 2000): 48.

[End Technology Excerpt 7.1 box here]

[Start Technology Insight 7.1 box here]

TECHNOLOGY INSIGHT 7.1

Application Service Provider (ASP)

An **application service provider (ASP)** is an external organization that hosts, manages, and provides access to application software and hardware over the Internet to multiple customers. The fee is typically a rental based on usage, similar to the rental pricing model used by *service bureaus.* ASPs, like most external sources of software and hardware, relieve the organization of the burden of developing (or even buying) and installing software and hardware. Because ASPs are accessed over the Internet, a user needs only a Web browser and an inexpensive PC or Internet appliance to obtain the ASP service.

When using an ASP, a user obtains consistently updated software. The user does not need to install or update software on a client or a server and does not need to hire technical staff to operate the application. ASPs are a good choice for noncritical, niche applications such as human resources, employee travel and expense reporting, and disbursement, although some companies use them for their complete enterprise system solutions.

[End Technology Insight 7.1 box here]

[Start Technology Insight 7.2 box here]

TECHNOLOGY INSIGHT 7.2

Sources of Vendor Information

Analysts use a variety of paper-based, computer-based, and online services to identify and evaluate computer hardware, software, and vendors. The information contained in these services, especially that resulting from independent expert analysis of a vendor and its products or from user surveys, can provide valuable insight into the vendor's quality, financial condition, number of installed systems, and similar information. Some are reports such as those available from Gartner Group, Inc. (http://www.gartner.com). Gartner services include Dataquest Market Intelligence with research and advice in a number of areas including "Benchmarks," "Performance Measurement," software and hardware products, and "Vendor Selection." Another Gartner Service, Datapro, publishes reports in such categories as "Computer Systems and Software Library," "Communications Library," Managing Data Networks," "Computers and Peripherals," and "e-Business and Internet."

Magazines—both printed and online—also provide independent reviews of vendors, hardware, and software. For example ZDNet (http://www.zdnet.com) publishes reviews in their online magazine *eWEEK* and in magazines that are both printed and published online, such as *PC Magazine* and *Computer Shopper.*

In addition to these independent sources of information about software, hardware, and vendors, the Internet also provides a wealth of information directly from vendors. For example, a quick tour of the Web found sites for Symantec (network security, virus protection, etc. at smallbiz.symantec.com), IBM (http://www.ibm.com), Microsoft (http://www.microsoft.com), SAP (http://www.sap.com), J. D. Edwards (http://www.jdedwards.com), and Gateway (http://www.gateway.com). Through such sites, one could obtain news about upcoming products, lists of existing products, customer support, technical support, software purchases, and software fixes and upgrades.

[End Technology Insight 7.2 box here]

[Start Technology Excerpt 7.2 box here]

Technology Excerpt 7.2

Issues to Consider When Selecting an ASP

- Information obtained from present users about the ASP's technical and service capabilities.
- Level of systems availability. How is this measured? Do availability guarantees extend to services employed by the ASP (i.e., secondary ASPs)? What are the penalties for failure to meet targets?
- Provisions for security, data backup, and disaster recovery.
- Capabilities and certifications of technical support and operations personnel. What is the staffing at the hosting site? When are they there? Is technical support provided directly or by a third party?
- How much can the application be tailored?

- Software ease of use, reliability, and quality (particularly important when the system must be used with minimal training on a more occasional basis).
- What is covered by the cost?
- The ASP's partners, including their software and hardware vendors and ASPs from who they obtain services.

Sources: Excerpted from Gary Anthes, "Avoiding ASP Angst," *Computerworld* (October 16, 2000): 80–81; "Seven Issues to Consider When Using an ASP," Viking Software Solutions (http://www.vikingsoft.com), November 27, 2000.

[End Technology Excerpt 7.2 box here]

[Start Technology Application 7.1 box here]

TECHNOLOGY APPLICATION 7.1

Testing Practices

Case 1

Visa cannot afford any glitches or downtime in its charge processing software. Yet it must accommodate approximately 2,500 system changes monthly, resulting in yearly modifications to 2 million lines of code. The company recently spent three years upgrading its clearing process, which settles 50 to 100 million transactions nightly. The development team tested individual modules and systems, and then 50 quality assurance specialists in two groups conducted extensive testing of the software. The first group selected 600,000 transactions from their existing event data store to try out the new system. The second group recreated five days of processing, including 70 million daily transactions, to check the results against the old system. Member banks then conducted user testing. All told, more than 40% of the project budget was spent on testing efforts. Once the system began to be used, a command center helped users with problems and assisted business partners with adapting their own software to interface with the new Visa system.

Case 2

Until recently, test planning and execution was typically a manual procedure designed and executed by a group of quality assurance experts. Companies have only recently recognized the advantages of adopting automated software quality tools. Rapid e-business advances were the impetus for the growth of this software market. Companies realize that they cannot recover losses of business partner confidence once their online reputations have been damaged due to inaccurate Web processing or excessive downtime. Because development time for Web applications is far shorter than for traditional systems, companies need to focus on their testing efforts to ensure that module, system and user volume tests have been completed prior to installing the system on the Web. As an example, one dotcom, Guild.com Inc., typically encounters 10,000 visitors to its site daily. A popular advertisement might cause that number to increase by up to 600%. The site was especially stressed when it was named a top Internet art site by Time magazine, resulting in twenty times the traffic. It used this experience to justify the expense of testing tools, quality assurance staff, testing hardware, and testing consultants.

Sources: Gary H. Anthes, "Change Control," *Computerworld* (October 8, 2001); Billie Shea, "Software Testing Gets New Respect," *InformationWeek* (July 3, 2000).

[End Technology Application 7.1 box here]

[Start Technology Excerpt 7.3 box here]

Technology Excerpt 7.3

Guidelines for Preparing Contracts for Computing Resources

The following guidance regarding contracts for computer hardware, software, and computing services comes from experienced users of IT.

- Be cautious of a vendor contract that goes to great lengths to tell you what the vendor *won't* do.
- Be clear on what *is* being provided by the vendor, including measurable service levels, such as availability.
- Obtain vendor warranties for intellectual property infringements, third-party indemnification, and nonconforming services. Determine the remedies for failure to meet contracted obligations.
- For a consulting engagement, include the names of the people who will work on the project and set a maximum turnover rate.
- Include a detailed project plan that lists what will be delivered, when it will be delivered, and how it will perform.
- Tie payments to completion of project phases and acceptance of deliverables, such as software, hardware, documentation, and training.
- Obtain the services of a procurement professional to ensure consistency across contracts and to provide an independent viewpoint in contract negotiations.
- If you want to make changes to source code, or have a third-party make changes,

include this right in the contract.

Sources: Joe Auer, "Who Gets the Risk? And Who Ducks it?" *Computerworld* (June 26, 2000): 78; Kim S. Nash, "Users Say Consultants Play Role in IT Disasters," *Computerworld* (November 6, 2000): 20; Joe Auer, "Work Out Details Later? No! Now!" *Computerworld* (November 13, 2000): 90; Jaikumar Vijayan, "Court OKs Third-Party Software Maintenance," *Computer world* (June 26, 2000): 4.

[End Technology Excerpt 7.3 box here]

Part IV

INTERNAL CONTROL FOR BUSINESS PROCESSES AND INFORMATION SYSTEMS

[Insert UNF-p.239-1 here]

8

IT GOVERNANCE: THE MANAGEMENT AND CONTROL OF INFORMATION TECHNOLOGY AND INFORMATION INTEGRITY

At 8:46 A.M. on September 11, 2001, American Airlines Flight 11 crashed into the north tower of the World Trade Center (WTC) in New York City. A short time later, at 9:02 A.M., United Airlines Flight 175 crashed into the south tower of the World Trade Center. Two other flights were hijacked that day and crashed; American Airlines Flight 77 crashed into the Pentagon near Washington, DC, and United Airlines Flight 93 exploded in a field 80 miles southeast of Pittsburgh. By the end of the next day it was believed that over 6,000 lives had been lost (this number started at over 10,000 and was later revised to less than 3,000) and several buildings in or near the sixteen-acre WTC complex had collapsed or had been severally damaged. Those buildings included: WTC buildings One and Two (the north and south towers), WTC buildings Three through Six, 3 World Financial Center, The Millennium Hotel, and 1 Liberty Plaza. Incredible human suffering, as well as numerous acts of kindness and bravery, resulted from this tragedy. The day-to-day lives of individuals, governments, and businesses were also affected in many predictable and some unforeseen ways.

In the aftermath of this tragedy airlines did not fly for several days, Wall Street trading was suspended for the remainder of the week, and hundreds of businesses located in and around the WTC struggled to resume anything that might resemble normal operations. To do so, these businesses needed to replace infrastructure such as offices, phones, computers, and data. At the same time, they needed to locate their personnel and put them back to work using new facilities. Companies and individuals throughout the world were also affected. For example, supply chains that depended on the airlines were disrupted, as were organizations with operations, communications, or technology infrastructures that had been in or around the WTC. These recovery activities tested, under the most extreme circumstances, organizations' business continuity and contingency plans.

At almost the same time, events were unfolding in the fall of 2001 at Enron Corporation in Houston, Texas. These events, while not resulting in the same loss of lives and physical destruction as the events of September 11, would affect the lives of thousands and would have ramifications that would ripple throughout the world economy. Enron started the year 2001 as the seventh largest (in revenues) U.S. corporation, with a market value of $80 billion. During the course of the fall of 2001 it became known that Enron had overstated profits by $600 million over the previous four years. In November Enron issued revised financial statements to reflect correct numbers. On December 2, 2001, Enron declared bankruptcy, the largest U.S. bankruptcy claim in history.

Enron stockholders lost $80 billion in investments. Employees and retirees, whose 401(k) plans contained Enron stock, experienced disproportionate losses. Enron management, while encouraging the general public and Enron employees to purchase Enron stock, had divested themselves of hundreds of millions of dollars of the soon-to-be worthless stock. To inflate its earnings, Enron had engaged in business transactions with partnerships controlled by its own officers and had concealed the true nature of these partnerships.

In January of 2002 we learned more about the scope of this legal and ethical scandal. After the problems at Enron surfaced, documents were shredded at Enron and at the offices of Enron's auditors, Arthur Andersen. Enron V-P Sherron Watkins revealed a memo that she had sent to Enron CEO Kenneth Lay warning that accounting scandals might cause the downfall of Enron. As a result Enron became the target of Justice Department criminal probes, congressional and SEC investigations, and shareholder lawsuits.

Synopsis

Could a system of corporate governance, including internal control, have prevented the tragedies of September 11? Controls that might have prevented the hijackings and crashes are beyond the scope of this text. But, there are controls that would have prevented some of the resulting business losses. In many cases, existing controls, especially contingency plans, did assist in minimizing the impact on companies located at the WTC. There are also controls that could have prevented the accounting scandals at Enron. This chapter and Chapter 9 emphasize the importance of effectively controlling business processes to prevent such events or to minimize the losses that result from them. These chapters provide a solid foundation for later study of controls for specific business processes covered in Chapters 10 through 14.

Let's consider how this chapter addresses our three themes. First, consider how important controls are to organizations that are tightly integrated internally—such as with enterprise systems—or have multiple connections to its environment—such as when they conduct e-business. Management must be confident that each component of the organization performs as expected and interacts well with related components or chaos will prevail. Second, organizations engaged in e-business must have control processes in place to reduce the possibilities of fraud and other disruptive events and to ensure compliance with applicable laws and regulations. For example, when engaged in Internet-based commerce, an organization may need to comply with relevant privacy regulations. Or, they may need to replace the infrastructure—Web sites, communications, and so on—in the event of tragedy. Finally, recognize that the success of most organizations today is partly determined by their ability to employ their technology resources effectively. In the second half of this chapter we discuss the control process—the management practices—that can ensure that an organization's technology resources are directed at achieving the organization's objectives, and that those resources remain available after events such as those on September 11.

LEARNING OBJECTIVES

- To explain why business organizations need to achieve an adequate level of internal control
- To explain the importance of internal control to organizational and IT governance, and business ethics
- To enumerate IT resources and explain how difficult it is to control them
- To describe management fraud, computer fraud, and computer abuse

- To describe the major IT control processes organizations use to manage their IT resources
- To identify operations and information process control goals and categories of control plans

Why Do We Need Control?

This chapter explores the strategies used to control the *processes* of a business organization. Recall from Chapter 1 that business organizations are composed of three major components: the management process, the operations process, and the information process. This chapter concentrates on controlling the entire business process (i.e., the combined management, operations, and information processes).

It is management's responsibility to exercise control over the business process. The major reasons for exercising this control are (1) to provide reasonable assurance that the goals of each process are being achieved, (2) to mitigate the risk that the enterprise will be exposed to some type of harm, danger, or loss (including loss caused by *fraud*, natural disasters, and terrorist attacks, or other intentional and unintentional acts), and (3) to provide reasonable assurance that certain legal obligations, such as accurate financial reporting, are being met. The sections that follow address all of these reasons.

Review Question

What are the three primary reasons that management exercises control over business processes? Explain.

Corporate Governance

Picture yourself as the manager of customer sales and service at one of the insurance companies located in the World Trade Center. It is the afternoon of September 11. You are OK and have made your way across the Hudson River to New Jersey. Let's say that you have been able to contact your family and friends and they are all OK. Now you want to reestablish customer services for your company; to provide customers with information about their coverage and to process claims. To do so you need an office, phones, computers, internal and external data networks, customer data, and customer service personnel.

Without the control processes that ordinarily exist, could you accomplish your objective of providing timely customer service? Perhaps; perhaps not. While we can argue that process objectives might be achieved in the absence of control, the primary reason for control is to help *ensure* that process goals are achieved. For example, you might be able to buy the infrastructure necessary to resume operations. But, unless you had a *business continuity plan* in place, you might not be able to locate key customer service personnel and restore your customer data. Thus, you may have a low probability of resuming operations in a timely manner.

Now assume that you are an employee (probably a *former* employee) at Enron. You were well paid and your retirement was secured with Enron stock. Now, after the bankruptcy declaration and resulting layoffs, you have no job and no financial assets. How did this happen? How could it have been prevented? Why didn't Sherron Watkins' memo result in changes to the accounting practices at Enron? Did Enron management really believe that these accounting practices would accomplish long- and short-run Enron objectives? Why did Andersen employees shred documents? Again, internal control can provide the mechanisms to develop and achieve objectives.

The Committee of Sponsoring Organizations (COSO) of the Treadway Commission (National Commission on Fraudulent Financial Reporting) published a highly cited framework for internal control to help companies design effective control strategies. It says that "to effect control, there need to be predetermined objectives. *Without objectives, control has no meaning* (emphasis added)." The COSO report also states that control "involves influencing someone and/or something—such as an entity's personnel, a business unit or an entire enterprise—with the purpose of moving toward the objectives."[1] In support of this point, a survey of 300 executives working for major companies based in the United States reported that executives who believed that their companies had strong internal control systems also believed that their companies were more likely to be successful in achieving corporate objectives, that their company's return on equity had increased over the past three years, and that their company had been more profitable than its competitors.[2]

[1] *Internal Control—Integrated Framework—Framework Volume* (New York, NY: The Committee of Sponsoring Organizations of the Treadway Commission, 1992): 101.

[2] "The Coopers & Lybrand Survey of Internal Control in Corporate America: A Report on What Corporations Are and *Are Not* Doing to Manage Risks," Louis Harris and Associates, Inc., 1995: xiii–xiv.

Rather than express the purpose of control in terms of the good to be achieved, we can also state its purpose in terms of the bad to be avoided. For instance, in our WTC illustration, is there a *risk* of not being able to resume operations in the long run? Yes! Therefore, a second reason for controlling systems is to *lessen the risk* that unwanted outcomes will occur. We define **risk** as the possibility that an event or action will cause an organization to fail to meet its objectives (or goals). Organizations must identify and assess the risk that untoward events or actions will occur and then reduce the possibility that those events or actions will occur by designing and implementing systems of control.

Internal control has recently become more important because of the emphasis placed by shareholders on *corporate governance,* demands placed on boards of directors and executives to implement and demonstrate control over business processes. The events at Enron, and later WorldCom and others, will make this even more important. Enterprise systems help provide this control, because they can support global, comprehensive, and integrated information sharing. In a recent example, Boston Scientific uncovered fraudulent sales records in its Japan office soon after SAP, an enterprise system, was installed. The ability to track sales globally triggered a closer look at unusual sales return patterns in the Japanese operations. At least one high-ranking corporate officer resigned as a result of this $70 million loss.

Executives, in turn, must implement and demonstrate governance of IT operations. Indeed, technology often represents a major portion of an organization's costs. On the other hand, without that technology an organization could not perform important operational processes, make decisions, or survive. In both cases—corporate and IT governance—frameworks for control, such as those introduced here and expanded upon throughout this text, will be key elements in this governance process. The events of September 11 forced all organizations to look more carefully at the strategies they had in place to recover from terrorist attacks and other such events. The Enron debacle will drive additional changes in the controls over the financial reporting process.

Let's now examine a few of the added challenges that management must address when the organization is engaged in e-business. Organizations engaged in e-business must protect the privacy of any information that they may gather from their customers. They must install controls to provide assurance that their privacy-related practices comply with state and federal laws. Also, customers may choose to not do business with merchants that do not protect customer data consistent with their stated policies. The importance of privacy is illustrated by the rise of the Chief Privacy Officer, who is featured in Technology Excerpt 8.1.

[Insert Technology Excerpt 8.1 box here]

Fraud and Its Relationship to Control

Was the scandal at Enron the result of fraud, or poor—perhaps unethical—management practices? In this section, we discuss management fraud, computer fraud, and computer abuse. Let's begin by defining **fraud** as a deliberate act or untruth intended to obtain unfair or unlawful gain. Management's legal responsibility to prevent fraud and other irregularities is implied by laws such as the Foreign Corrupt Practices Act,[3] which states "a fundamental aspect of management's stewardship responsibility is to provide shareholders with reasonable assurance that the business is adequately controlled." Instances of fraud undermine management's ability to convince the various authorities that it is upholding its stewardship responsibility.

[3] See Foreign Corrupt Practices Act (FCPA) of 1977 (P.L. 95-213).

Why are Congress, the financial community, and others so impassioned about the subject of fraud? In some highly publicized business failures that caught people completely by surprise, financial statements showed businesses that were prospering. Tinkering with the financial statements, as at Enron, causes hardship or failure for many firms and individuals.

Let's examine some fraud-related problems that management must address when the organization is engaged in e-business. First, an organization that receives payment via credit card, where the credit card is not present during the transaction (e.g., sales via telephone or Web site), absorbs the loss if a transaction is fraudulent. To prevent this, the organization may install controls, such as antifraud software. Some banks will drop merchants who have unacceptably high fraud rates.

The proliferation of computers in business organizations has created expanded opportunities for criminal infiltration. Computers have been used to commit a wide variety of crimes, including fraud, larceny, and embezzlement. In general, these types of computer-related crimes have been referred to as *computer fraud, computer abuse,* or *computer crime*. Technology Insight 8.1 (page 246) describes some of the better-known techniques used to commit computer fraud or to damage computer resources.

[Insert Technology Insight 8.1 box here]

Be aware of two things: insiders commit the majority of computer crimes, and the methods listed in the summary are by no means exhaustive. For instance, two abuses not shown in Technology Insight 8.1 that typically are perpetrated by someone outside the organization are *computer hacking* and *computer viruses*. Technology Insight 8.2 (page 247) has a brief explanation of computer viruses. Both of these computer crimes, spreading viruses and hacking, are a major concern to organizations engaged in e-business because they affect the actual and perceived reliability and integrity of their electronic infrastructure.

[Insert Technology Insight 8.2 box here]

Here are three important facts to remember. First, those who have *authorized* access to the targeted computer perpetrate the majority of malicious acts. Second, it has been estimated that losses due to accidental, nonmalicious acts far exceed those caused by willful, intentional misdeeds. Third, the manipulation of events (i.e., adding, changing, or deleting of events) is one frequently employed method of committing computer fraud. The most cost-effective method for minimizing simple, innocent errors and omissions as well as acts of intentional computer crimes and fraud is to apply normal controls within existing systems conscientiously.

Review Question

What are the relationships between fraud, in general, and internal control? Between computer fraud, in particular, and internal control?

Review Question

What is a computer virus?

Defining Internal Control

In the preceding sections, we discussed the importance of an organization achieving an adequate level of internal control. But what do we mean by internal control? The COSO report mentioned earlier in the chapter emphasizes that internal control is a process.[4] A **process** is a series of actions or operations leading to a particular and usually desirable result. Results could be effective internal control, or a specified output for a particular market or customer. The idea of process is important to our understanding of internal control and business processes in modern organizations. Armed with this perspective, let's proceed to a working definition of internal control to use throughout the text.

[4] The COSO definition of internal control has become widely accepted and the basis for definitions of control adopted for other international control frameworks: *Internal control is a process—affected by an entity's board of directors, management, and other*

personnel—designed to provide reasonable assurance regarding the achievement of objectives in the following categories:

- *Effectiveness and efficiency of operations*
- *Reliability of financial reporting*
- *Compliance with applicable laws and regulations*

Internal Control—Integrated Framework—Framework Volume (New York, NY: The Committee of Sponsoring Organizations of the Treadway Commission, 1992): 9, 12 and 14. Our working definition of control, presented in the next section, classifies control *goals* into two broad groups only—those for the *operations process* and those for the *information process.* Our two groupings roughly parallel the first two COSO categories. In our control framework and control matrices in this and later chapters, we include COSO's third category—compliance with applicable laws, regulations, and contractual agreements—as one of the control goals of the *operations processes.*

A Working Definition of Internal Control

Internal control is a system of integrated elements—people, structure, processes, and procedures—acting together to provide reasonable assurance that an organization achieves its *business process* goals. The design and operation of the internal control system is the responsibility of top management and therefore should:

- Reflect management's careful assessment of risks.
- Be based on management's evaluation of costs versus benefits.
- Be built on management's strong sense of business ethics and personal integrity.

Before discussing two key elements of the definition, which we call *control goals* and *control plans*, let's pause to examine the underpinnings of the system—namely, its ethical foundation. As you read this section, consider the events that unfolded at Enron.

Ethical Considerations and the Control Environment

COSO places integrity and ethical values at the heart of what it calls the *control environment*. In arguing the importance of integrity and ethics, COSO makes the case that the best designed control systems are subject to failure caused by human error, faulty judgment, circumvention through collusion, and management override of the system. COSO goes on to state that:

> Ethical behavior and management integrity are a product of the "corporate culture." Corporate culture includes ethical and behavioral standards, how they are communicated and how they are reinforced in practice. Official policies specify what management wants to happen. Corporate culture determines what actually happens, and which rules are obeyed, bent or ignored.[5]

[5] *Internal Control—Integrated Framework—Framework Volume* (New York, NY: The Committee of Sponsoring Organizations of the Treadway Commission, 1992): 20.

Management is responsible for internal control and can respond to this requirement legalistically or by creating a "control environment." That is, management can follow the "letter of the law" (its form), or it can respond *substantively* to the need for control. The **control environment** reflects the organization's (primarily the board of directors' and management's) general awareness of and commitment to the importance of control throughout the organization. In other words, by setting the example and by addressing the need for control at the top of the organization, management can make an organization *control conscious.*

Review Question

Explain what is meant by the *control environment.* What elements might comprise the control environment?

For example, reward systems might consider ethical, legal, and social performance, as well as the bottom line. Strategies should be developed so as not to create conflicts between business performance and legal requirements. Management should consistently find it unacceptable for personnel to circumvent the organization's system of controls and, as importantly, *should impose stiff sanctions for such unacceptable behavior.* These actions are included in what some call the "tone at the top" of the organization. Some question whether the large campaign contributions made by Enron and its executives set the proper tone at the top of that organization.

A number of companies have articulated the ethical behavior expected of employees in a very tangible way by developing corporate *codes of conduct* that are periodically acknowledged (i.e., signed) by employees. The codes often address such matters as illegal or improper payments, conflicts of interest, insider trading, computer ethics, and software piracy.

Review Question

Explain how business ethics relates to internal control.

Business Process Control Goals and Control Plans

Our working definition of *internal control* describes it in the broad sense of both selecting the ends to be attained (*control goals*) and specifying the means to ensure that the goals are attained (*control plans*). Control also extends to the processes of reviewing a system periodically to ensure that the goals of the system are being achieved, and to taking remedial action (if necessary) to correct any deficiencies in the system (i.e., monitoring). Control is concerned with discovering courses of action that contribute to the general welfare of the business organization and with ensuring that the implementation of these actions produces the desired effects.

Review Question

What are the three generic control goals of the operations process and the five generic control goals of the related information process?

Control goals are business process objectives that an internal control system is designed to achieve. Table 8.1 (page 250) provides an overview of the *generic* control goals of the *operations process* and of the *information process.* To illustrate our discussion we use a cash receipts process, similar to the Causeway system depicted in Figure 2.13 (page 54).

[Insert Table 8.1 Here]

Control Goals of the Operations Process

The first control goal, ensure *effectiveness of operations*, strives to ensure that a given operations process (e.g., our cash receipts process) is fulfilling the purpose for which it was intended. Notice that we must itemize the specific *operations process goals*. These goals are specific to each organization and no uniform set of operations goals exists. In each of the business process chapters, we provide a representative listing of operations process goals.[6]

[6] As mentioned earlier in the chapter, we also include *compliance with applicable laws, regulations, and contractual agreements* (i.e., COSO's third category of entity objectives) as one of the goals of each operations process to which such laws, regulations,

or agreements might be appropriate. For instance, compliance with the Robinson/Patman Act is shown as a legitimate goal of the order entry/sales process in Chapter 10.

The next goal, *ensure efficient employment of resources*, can be evaluated in only a relative sense. For example, let's assume that one goal is to deposit all cash on the day received. To determine efficiency we would need to know the cost of the people and computer equipment required to accomplish this goal. If the cost is more than the benefits obtained (e.g., security of the cash, interest earned), the system might be considered *in*efficient. Likewise, if our system costs more to operate than a system in a similar organization, we would judge the system to be *in*efficient.

Let's now discuss the last operations process control goal in Table 8.1, to *ensure security of resources*. As noted in the table, resources take many forms, both physical and nonphysical. Information has become a key resource of most organizations. For example, the information about our customers (as stored in the accounts receivable master data) is very valuable for this company. An organization must protect all of its resources, both tangible and intangible.

Control Goals of the Information Process

A glance at Table 8.1 reveals that the first three control goals of the information process deal with entering event-related data into a system. Recall from Chapter 1 that data input includes *capturing* data (for example, completing a source document such as a sales order, or, in the case of a cash receipts system, writing the check number and amount on the RA). Data input also includes, if necessary, *converting* the data to *machine-readable form* (for example, keying in the remittance advices to add events to the cash receipts events data). Therefore, *events data* are the subjects of the *input* control goals shown in Table 8.1.

These three control goals trigger the following questions: "Did the event occur?" (input validity); "Is there a record of each event?" (input completeness); and "Is the record correct?" (input accuracy). Thinking about these control categories in this way may help you to identify controls that provide adequate coverage across all the categories.

To illustrate the importance of achieving the first goal, *ensure input validity*, assume that our accounts receivable clerk processes a batch of 50 cash receipts (including their payment stubs, or RAs). Further assume that two of the 50 RAs represent fictitious cash receipts (for example, a mailroom employee fabricates phony remittance advices for relatives who are customers). What is the effect of processing the 50 RAs including the 2 fictitious remittances? First, the cash receipts event data and the accounts receivable master data each have been corrupted by the addition of two bogus RAs. Second, if not detected and corrected, the pollution of these data will result in unreliable financial statements—overstated cash and understated accounts receivable—and other erroneous system outputs (e.g., cash receipts listings, customer monthly statements).

To discuss the second information process goal, *ensure input completeness*, let's return to the previous example and suppose that, while the 48 *valid* RAs are being key entered (we'll ignore the two fictitious receipts in this example), the accounts receivable clerk decides to get a cup of coffee. As the clerk walks past the batch of 48 RAs, 10 are blown to the floor and are not entered into the system. What is the effect of processing 38 RAs, rather than the original 48? First, the cash receipts transaction data will be incomplete; that is, it will fail to reflect the true number of remittance events. Second, the incompleteness of the data will cause the resulting financial statements and other reports to be unreliable (i.e., understated cash balance and overstated accounts receivable). In this example, the omission was unintentional. Likewise, fraudulent, intentional misstatements of organizational data can be accomplished by omitting some events.

When dealing with input completeness, we are concerned with the existence of documents or records representing an event or object, not the *correctness* or *accuracy* of the document or record.

Accuracy issues are addressed by the third information process goal, *ensure input accuracy*. This goal relates to the various data fields that usually constitute a record of an event, such as a source document. To achieve this goal, we must minimize discrepancies between data items entered into a system and the economic events or objects they represent. Mathematical mistakes and the inaccurate transcription of data from one document or medium to another may cause accuracy errors. Again, let's return to our example. Suppose that one of the *valid* RAs is from Acme Company, customer 159, in the amount of $125. The accounts receivable clerk mistakenly enters the customer number as 195, resulting in Ajax, Inc.'s account (rather than Acme's) being credited with the $125.

Missing data fields on a source document or computer screen represent another type of accuracy error. For example, the absence of a customer number on a remittance advice would result in "unapplied" cash receipts (that is, receipts that can't be credited to a particular customer). We consider this type of system malfunction to be an accuracy error rather than a completeness error, because the mere presence of the source document suggests that the event itself has been captured and that the input data are, by our definition, therefore complete.

Now let's examine the last two information process control goals shown in Table 8.1. These goals deal with updating *master data*. As we learned in Chapter 1, master data update is an information processing activity whose function is to incorporate new data into existing master data. We also learned that there are two types of updates that can be made to master data: information processing and data maintenance. In this textbook, we emphasize information processing; therefore, our analysis of the internal controls related to data updates is restricted to data updates from information processing.

In our cash receipts system, the goal of update completeness relates to crediting customer balances in the accounts receivable master data for *all* cash collections recorded in the cash receipts event data. The goal of *ensure update accuracy* relates to correctly crediting (e.g., correct customer, correct amount) customer balances in the accounts receivable master data.

Once valid data have been *completely* and *accurately* entered into a computer (i.e., added to event data such as our cash receipts event data), the data usually go through a series of processing steps. Several things can go wrong with the data once they have been entered into a computer for processing. Accordingly, the goals of update completeness and accuracy are aimed at minimizing processing errors. We should note, however, that if the events are processed using an *online real-time processing* system such as the one depicted in Figure 4.3 (page 114), the input and update will occur nearly simultaneously. This will minimize the possibility that the update will be incomplete or inaccurate.

Review Question

Explain the difference between the following pairs of control goals: (1) ensure effectiveness of operations and ensure efficient employment of resources; (2) ensure efficient employment of resources and ensure security of resources; (3) ensure input validity and ensure input accuracy; (4) ensure input completeness and ensure input accuracy; (5) ensure input completeness and ensure update completeness; and (6) ensure input accuracy and ensure update accuracy.

Control Plans

Control plans are information processing policies and procedures that assist in accomplishing control goals. Control plans can be classified in a number of different ways that help us to understand them. Figure 8.1 (page 254) shows one such classification scheme—a control hierarchy that relates control plans to the *control environment,* defined earlier. The fact that the control environment appears at the top of the hierarchy illustrates that the control environment comprises a multitude of factors that can either reinforce or mitigate the effectiveness of the pervasive and process control plans.

[Insert Figure 8.1 Here]

The second level in the Figure 8.1 control hierarchy consists of pervasive control plans. **Pervasive control plans** relate to a multitude of goals and processes. Like the control environment, they provide a climate or set of surrounding conditions in which the various business processes operate. They are broad in scope and apply equally to all business processes—hence, they *pervade* all systems. For example, preventing unauthorized access to the computer system would protect all of the specific business processes that run on the computer (such as sales and marketing, billing, "purchase-to-pay," business reporting, and so on). We discuss a major subset of these pervasive controls—IT processes (i.e., controls)—later in this chapter.

Process control plans are those controls particular to a specific process or subsystem, such as inventory or human resources, or to a particular mode of processing events, such as online or batch. Process control plans are the subject of the control framework introduced in Chapter 9.

Review Question

What is the difference between a process control plan, a pervasive control plan, and an IT control process?

Another useful and common way to classify controls is in relation to the timing of their occurrence. **Preventive control plans** stop problems from occurring. **Detective control plans** discover that problems have occurred. **Corrective control plans** rectify problems that have occurred. Let's use the WTC tragedy to illustrate. By operating two computer processing sites—one primary and one mirror site—companies located in the WTC could *prevent* the loss of their computer processing capabilities and the data and programs stored on the computers located in the WTC (i.e., duplicate copies would reside at the mirror site). Smoke and fire detectors could *detect* fires in the building that inevitably lead to the loss of processing capabilities. Other monitoring devices could *detect* the loss of phones, data communications, and processing capabilities. These devices, operating at an organization's facilities outside the WTC area, could have alerted company personnel to the loss of resources in the area of the WTC. Also, organizations can subscribe to services that will provide notification in the event of disaster. Finally, backup copies of programs and data could have been loaded onto computers at sites outside the WTC area to reinstate computer processing and related services. These are *corrective* controls because they replace data and services that were lost.

Introduction to Pervasive Controls

We begin our discussion of pervasive controls by introducing four broad IT control process domains and explain how IT control processes are directed at the control of IT resources and the attainment of the information qualities. Exhibit 8.1 defines IT resources that must be managed by the control processes. According to COBIT these IT resources must be managed to ensure that the organization has the information that it needs to achieve its objectives.[7] COBIT also describes the qualities that this information must exhibit in order for it to be of value to the organization. These qualities are defined in Exhibit 1.1 (page 17).

[Insert Exhibit 8.1 Here]

[7] *COBIT: Control Objectives for Information and Related Technology—Framework,* 3rd ed. (Rolling Meadows, IL: The Information Systems Audit and Control Foundation, 2000): 5.

Review Question

Name and describe the five IT resources.

We must determine how we can protect an organization's computer from misuse, intentional or inadvertent, from within and from outside the organization. Pervasive controls are directed at answering the following questions. How can we protect the computer room, the headquarters building, and the rooms and buildings in which other connected facilities are located? In the event of a disaster, will we be able to continue our operations? What policies and procedures can be established (and documented) to provide for efficient, effective, and authorized use of the computer? What measures can we take to help ensure that the personnel who operate and use the computer are competent and honest? An organization's **Information Systems function (ISF)** is the department that develops and operates an organization's Information System. The function (department) is composed of people, procedures, and equipment. This function is the object of many of the IT controls and its management, at the same time, is responsible for the implementation and operation of these processes.

Four Broad IT Control Process Domains

COBIT groups IT control processes into four broad domains: (1) planning and organization, (2) acquisition and implementation, (3) delivery and support, and (4) monitoring. Figure 8.2 (page 256) depicts the relationship among these four domains and lists the IT control processes within each domain. Notice that the monitoring domain provides feedback to the other three domains. In the remainder of this chapter we discuss these ten IT control processes.

[Insert Figure 8.2 Here]

Review Question

What are the four IT control process domains?

Before we move on to a discussion of the ten IT control processes, let's discuss the concept of a control process. A "control process" could easily be, and often is referred to as, a "management practice." This latter terminology emphasizes management's responsibility for control in the organization and the practices, or processes, which will bring about achievement of an organization's objectives. It is through a coordinated effort, across all IT resources and all organizational units, that the objectives of the organization are achieved.

Planning and Organization Domain

Within the planning and organization domain are processes to develop the strategy and tactics for an organization's information technology. The overriding goal of these processes is to identify ways that IT can best contribute to the achievement of the organization's objectives. Then, management must communicate that strategic vision to interested parties (within and outside the organization) and put in place the IT organization and technology infrastructure that enables that vision. These processes must identify and address external threats and internal and external requirements, and take advantage of opportunities for strategic implementation of emerging information technology.

IT Process 1: Establish Strategic Vision for Information Technology

To strike an optimal balance of IT opportunities and business requirements, management of the information systems function should adopt a process for developing a strategic plan for all of the organization's IT resources, and for converting that plan into short-term goals. The information systems strategic planning effort must ensure that the organization's strategic plan is supported and that IT is used to the best advantage of the organization. An organization wants to be sure that the ISF is prepared to anticipate the competition's actions and to take advantage of emerging IT. An organization must establish links between organizational and information systems strategic planning to ensure that strategies plotted in the organizational plan receive the IT support they need.

Elements of the strategic plan can help the organization achieve important *enterprise systems*, *e-business*, and *technology* objectives. For example, plans for any new lines of business, such as Internet ordering and payment, or changes in business processes, resulting from changes to an *enterprise system*, will require new data and new relationships among the data. These data elements and relationships must be incorporated into the organization's information architecture model. The plan must also include processes to review IT capabilities to ensure that there is adequate technology to perform the IS function and to take advantage of emerging technology. Finally, the plan must contain procedures that ensure compliance with laws and regulations, especially those related to e-business (e.g., privacy, transborder data flows).

Review Question

What is the purpose of the strategic IT plan?

IT Process 2: Develop Tactics to Plan, Communicate, And Manage Realization of the Strategic Mission

To ensure adequate funding for IT, controlled disbursement of financial resources, and effective and efficient utilization of IT resources, IT resources must be managed through use of information services capital and operating budgets, by justifying IT expenditures, and by monitoring costs (in light of risks).

To ensure the overall effectiveness of the ISF, IS management must establish a direction and related policies addressing such aspects as positive *control environment* throughout the organization, code of conduct/ethics, quality, and security. Then, these policies must be communicated (internally and externally) to obtain commitment and compliance. IS management's direction and policies must be consistent with the *control environment* established by the organization's senior management.

To ensure that projects are completed on time and within budget and that projects are undertaken in order of importance, management must establish a project management framework to ensure that project selection is in line with plans and that a project management methodology is applied to each project undertaken.

Management should establish a quality assurance (QA) plan and implement related activities, including reviews, audits, and inspections, to ensure the attainment of IT customer requirements. A systems development life cycle methodology (SDLC) is an essential component of the QA plan.

To ensure that IT services are delivered in an efficient and effective manner, there must be adequate internal and external IT staff, administrative policies and procedures for all functions (with specific attention to organizational placement, roles and responsibilities, and segregation of duties), and an IT steering committee to determine prioritization of resource use. We divide these controls into two groups: *organizational control plans* and *personnel control plans*.

Organizational Control Plans We will concentrate on two organizational control plans: *segregation of duties* and organizational control plans for *the information systems function*.

Segregation of duties control plan. The concept underlying segregation of duties is simple enough: Through the design of an appropriate organizational structure, no single employee should be in a position both to perpetrate and conceal frauds, errors, or other kinds of system failures. **Segregation of duties** consists of separating the four basic functions of event processing. The functions are:

- *Function 1:* authorizing events.
- *Function 2:* executing events.
- *Function 3:* recording events.
- *Function 4:* safeguarding resources resulting from consummating events.

Review Question

Segregation of duties consists of separating what four basic functions? Briefly define each function.

A brief scenario should illustrate this concept. John Singletary works in the general office of Small Company. He initiates a sales order and sends the picking ticket to the warehouse, resulting in inventory being shipped to his brother. When Sue Billings sends Singletary the customer invoice for the shipment, he records the sale as he would any sale. Sometime later, he writes his brother's account off as a bad debt. What is the result? Inventory was stolen and Singletary manipulated the information system to hide the theft. Had other employees been responsible for authorizing and recording the shipment or for the bad debt write-off, Singletary would have had a tougher time manipulating the system.

Table 8.2 illustrates segregation of duties in a typical system. Examine the top half of the table, which defines the four basic functions. The bottom half of the table extends the coverage of segregation of duties by illustrating the processing of a credit sales event.

[Insert Table 8.2 Here]

Now, let's examine Table 8.2 as a means of better understanding the control notion underlying segregation of duties. Ideal segregation of duties requires that different units (departments) of an organization carry out each of the four phases of event processing. In this way, there would need to be *collusion* between one or more persons (departments) in order to exploit the system and conceal the abuse. Whenever collusion is necessary to commit a fraud, there is a greater likelihood that the perpetrators will be deterred by the risks associated with pursuing a colluding partner and that they will be caught.

Controls to prevent *unauthorized* execution of events ensure that only *valid* events are recorded. Therefore, function 1—authorizing events—takes on particular significance in our segregation of duties model. Control plans for authorizing or approving events empower individuals or machines to initiate events and to approve actions taken subsequently in executing and recording events.

Authorization control plans often take the form of policy statements and are implemented by including necessary procedures and process controls within the information system that will process the events. For example, through proper design of the sales order form, an organization can see that credit is granted by including a block on the document that requires the credit manager's signature. Or, a computer-based system can be designed to approve events within some predetermined credit limits. **Digital signatures** on electronic documents also authenticate or authorize requests from external parties, as seen in Technology Excerpt 8.2 (page 260). These procedures receive management authorization when the system is approved during initial development, or when the system is changed.

[Insert Technology Excerpt 8.2 box here]

Organizational control plans for the information systems function. The information systems function normally acts in a service capacity for other operating units in the organization. In this capacity, it should be limited to carrying out function 3 of Table 8.2, recording events and posting event summaries. Approving and executing events along with safeguarding resources should be carried out by departments other than the ISF. This arrangement allows for effective implementation of segregation of duties. There are situations, however, where the functional divisions we mentioned can be violated. For instance, some ISFs do authorize and execute events; for example, the computer might be programmed to approve customer orders.

Within the ISF, we segregate duties to control unauthorized use of and/or changes to the computer and its stored data and programs. Segregation of duties within the ISF can be accomplished in a number of ways. One method of separating systems development and operations is to prevent programmers from operating the computer; thus reducing the possibilities of unauthorized data input or unauthorized modification of organizational data and programs. Passwords, assigned by an information security specialist, are critical to separating key functions between the ISF and operational units within the ISF.

Personnel Control Plans IT personnel resources must be managed to maximize their contributions to IT processes. Specific attention must be paid to recruitment, promotion, personnel qualifications, training, backup, performance evaluation, job change, and termination. As we discussed earlier in the chapter, an organization that does not have honest, competent employees will find it virtually impossible to implement other control plans.

The personnel control plans described in Table 8.3 help to protect an organization against certain types of risks. As you study each plan, think of the problems that the plan can prevent or the control goal that could be achieved by implementing the plan. Also, consider how much more important these plans are when we consider the impact that they have on systems personnel.

[Insert Table 8.3 Here]

Three plans in Table 8.3 require a little discussion. The control notion underlying *rotation of duties* and *forced vacation* is that if an employee is perpetrating some kind of irregularity, it will be detected by his/her substitute. Furthermore, if these plans are in place, they should act as a deterrent to the irregularity ever occurring in the first place (i.e., *a preventive control*). Beyond the control considerations involved, these two plans also help to mitigate the disruption that might be caused when an employee leaves the organization. When another person is familiar with the job duties of each position, no single employee is irreplaceable.

Review Question

What are personnel control plans? Define the plans.

Finally, rigorous application of *personnel termination policies* is particularly important in the ISF. Disgruntled employees working in the ISF have the opportunity to cause much damage in a short time. For example, computer operations personnel could erase large databases in a matter of minutes. For this reason, key employees who have access to important program and databases may be asked to leave the facility immediately, and in some cases, company security personnel may escort them from the premises.

Acquisition and Implementation

Within the acquisition and implementation domain are processes to identify, develop or acquire, implement IT solutions, and integrate them into the business processes. Once installed, procedures must also be in place to maintain and manage changes to existing systems. For example, if we do not correctly determine the requirements for a new information system *and* see that those requirements are satisfied by the new system, the new system could cause us to update the wrong data or perform calculations incorrectly. Or, we may not complete the development on time and within budget. Finally, should we fail to develop proper controls for the new system, we could experience inventory shortages, inaccurate record keeping, or financial loss.

IT Process 3: Identify Automated Solutions

To ensure the selection of the best approach to satisfying users' IT requirements, an organization's Systems Development Life Cycle (SDLC) must include procedures to define information requirements; formulate alternative courses of action; perform technological, economic, and operational feasibility studies; and assess risks. These solutions should be consistent with the strategic information technology plan and the technology infrastructure and information architecture contained therein.

IT Process 4: Develop and Acquire IT Solutions

Once IT solutions have been identified and approval to proceed has been received, development—and/or appropriate acquisition—of the application software, infrastructure, and procedures may begin. To ensure that applications will satisfy users' IT requirements, an organization's SDLC should include procedures to create design specifications for each new, or significantly modified, application, and to verify those specifications against the user requirements. Design specifications include those for inputs, outputs, processes, programs, and databases.

The SDLC should also include procedures to ensure that platforms (hardware and systems software) support the new or modified application. Further, there should be an assessment of the impact of new hardware and software on the performance of the overall system. Finally, procedures should be in place to ensure that hardware and systems software are installed, maintained, and changed so as to continue to support existing or revised business processes.

To ensure the ongoing, effective use of IT, the organization's SDLC should provide for the preparation and maintenance of service level requirements and application documentation. *Service level requirements* include such items as availability, reliability, performance, capacity for growth, levels of user support, disaster recovery, security, minimal system functionality, and service charges. These requirements become benchmarks for the ongoing operation of the system. As IT organizations become larger and more complex, especially those that must implement and operate *enterprise systems*, these service level requirements become important methods for communicating the expectations of the business units for IT services. Further, if the organization is engaged in *e-business* these service levels are benchmarks for service on a Web site or to and from business partners engaged in electronic commerce.

IT Process 5: Integrate IT Solutions into Operational Processes

To ensure that a new or significantly revised system is suitable, the organization's SDLC should provide for a planned, tested, controlled, and approved conversion to the new system. After installation, the SDLC should call for a review to determine that the new system has met users' needs in a cost-effective manner. When organizations implement *enterprise systems*, the successful integration of new information systems modules into existing, highly integrated, business processes becomes more difficult, and more important. The challenges are the result of the interdependence of the business processes and the complexity of these processes and their connections. Any failure in a new system can have catastrophic results.

IT Process 6: Manage Changes to Existing IT Systems

To ensure processing integrity between versions of systems and to ensure consistency of results from period to period, changes to the IT infrastructure (hardware, systems software, and applications) must be managed via change request, impact assessment, documentation, authorization, release and distribution policies, and procedures.

Program change controls provide assurance that all modifications to programs are authorized, and ensure that the changes are completed, tested, and properly implemented. Changes in documentation should mirror the changes made to the related programs. Figure 8.3 (page 264) depicts the stages through which programs should progress to ensure that only authorized and tested programs are placed in production, which means that the programs are in use by the organization in the conduct of business. Notice that separate organizational entities are responsible for each stage in the change process. These controls take on an even higher level of significance with *enterprise systems*. Should unauthorized or untested changes be made to such systems, the results can be disastrous. For example, let's say that a change is made to the inventory module of an enterprise system without testing to see the impact that change will have on the sales module used to enter customer orders. Since these two modules work together, and orders from customers for inventory cannot be processed without the inventory module, changes to either module must be carefully planned and executed.

[Insert Figure 8.3 Here]

Review Question

Name and describe the four IT control processes in the acquisition and implementation domain.

Delivery and Support

Within the delivery and support domain are processes to deliver required IT services, ensure security and continuity of services, set up support services, including training, and ensure integrity of application data. Failure of these processes can result in computing resources being lost or destroyed, becoming unavailable for use, or leading to unauthorized use of computing resources.

IT Process 7: Deliver Required IT Services

This process includes activities related to the delivery of the IT services that were planned by the IT processes in the planning and organization domain, and developed and implemented by the IT processes in the acquisition and implementation domain. Table 8.4 describes some of the key service-delivery activities.

[Insert Table 8.4 Here]

Review Question

Describe the four phases/storage locations through which a program under development should pass to ensure good program change control.

IT Process 8: Ensure Security and Continuous Service

The IS function must see that IT services continue to be provided at the levels expected by the users. To do so, they must provide a secure operating environment for IT and plan for increases in required capacity and potential losses of usable resources. To ensure that sufficient IT resources remain available, management should establish a process to monitor the capacity and performance of all IT resources. For example, the actual activity on an organization's Web site must be measured and additional capacity added as needed. To ensure that IT assets are not lost, altered, or used without authorization, management should establish a process to account for all IT components, including applications, technology, and facilities, and to prevent use of unauthorized assets. To ensure that IT resources remains available, processes should be in place to identify, track, and resolve in a timely manner problems and incidents that occur. Three important aspects of the IT processes designed to address these issues are discussed below: ensuring continuous service, restricting access to computing resources, and ensuring physical security.

Ensure Continuous Service To ensure that sufficient IT resources continue to be available for use in the event of a service disruption, management should establish a process, coordinated with the overall business continuity strategy, that includes disaster recovery/contingency planning for all IT resources and related business resources, both internal and external. These control plans are directed at potential calamitous losses of resources or disruptions of operations—for both the organization and its business partners. Catastrophic events, such as those experienced on September 11, 2001, have resulted in a heightened awareness of the importance of these controls. The types of *backup and recovery* covered in this section have been referred to in a variety of ways, including but not limited to: **disaster recovery planning, contingency planning, business interruption planning,** and **business continuity planning.** Regardless of the label, these controls must include a heavy dose of pre-loss *planning* that will reasonably ensure post-loss recovery.

Before we go further, let us note that contingency planning extends much beyond the mere backup and recovery of stored computer data, programs, and documentation. The planning involves procedures for backing up the physical computer facilities, computer, and other equipment (such as communications equipment—a vital resource in the event of a catastrophe), supplies, and personnel. Furthermore, planning reaches beyond the IS function to provide backup for these same resources residing in operational business units of the organization. Finally, the plan may extend beyond the organization for key resources provided by third parties. You might also note that the current thinking is that we plan contingencies for important *processes* rather than individual *resources*. So, we develop a contingency plan for our Internet presence, rather than for our Web servers, networks, and other related resources that enable that presence.

Numerous disaster backup and recovery strategies may be included in an organization's contingency plan. Some industries require instant recovery and must incur the cost of maintaining two or more sites. One such option is to run two processing sites, a primary and a **mirror site** that maintains copies of the primary site's programs and data. During normal processing activities, master data is updated at both the primary and mirror sites. Located miles away from the primary site, the mirror site can take over in seconds if the primary site goes down. Mirror sites are very popular with airline and e-business organizations because they need to keep their systems and Internet commerce sites online at all times. **Server clustering** can also be used to disperse processing load among servers so that if one server fails, another can take over.[8] These clustered servers are essentially mirror sites for each other.

[8] David Essex, "Data Resurrection," *Computerworld* (March 6, 2000): 76.

Here is one example of the importance of these contingency processes to e-business. In June 1999 the Web site for eBay, Inc., the online auctioneer, was unavailable for 22 hours. This downtime caused eBay to forego $3 to $5 million in fees and some erosion of customer loyalty. This failure spurred eBay to accelerate its plans for a better backup system.[9]

[9] George Anders, "eBay To Refund Millions in Listings Fees as Outage Halts Bis for About 22 Hours," *The Wall Street Journal* (June 4, 1999): B8.

For most companies, maintaining duplicate equipment is simply cost-prohibitive. Therefore, a good control strategy is to make arrangements with hardware vendors, service centers, or others for the standby use of compatible computer equipment. These arrangements are generally of two types—*hot sites* or *cold sites.*

A **hot site** is a fully equipped data center, often housed in bunker-like facilities, that can accommodate many businesses—sometimes up to 100 companies—and that is made available to client companies for a monthly subscriber's fee. Less costly, but obviously less responsive, is a **cold site**. It is a facility usually comprising air-conditioned space with a raised floor, telephone connections, and computer ports, into which a subscriber can move equipment. The disaster recovery contractor or the manufacturer provides the necessary equipment.

Review Question

What is the difference between a *hot site* and a *cold site*?

Ensuring continuous service in a centralized environment has become fairly straightforward. We know that we need to back up important databases, programs, and documentation, move those backups to recovery sites, and begin processing at that site. However, ISF environments are seldom that centralized; there are usually client-server applications and other distributed applications and connections. For example, a company may be doing business on the Internet and would need to include that application in their continuity plan. Technology Insight 8.3 describes several lessons about ensuring continuous service that were learned as a result of the events of September 11, 2001.

[Start Technology Insight 8.3 box here]

In the spring of 2000, several organizations, including Yahoo!, eBay, CNN.com, and Amazon.com, experienced a serious threat to their ability to ensure continuous service to their customers. The culprit was a relatively new phenomenon, the *distributed denial of service attack.* Technology Insight 8.4 (page 268) describes these attacks and the processes that might be put in place to detect and correct them to ensure that organizations achieve the level of service that they plan. The Yankee Group estimated that the overall cost of these attacks was $1.2 billion. For example, the Yahoo! site was unavailable for three hours, which cost Yahoo! $500,000. Amazon's site was down for an hour, resulting in a likely loss of $240,000.[10]

[10] Ann Harrison and Kathleen Ohlson, "Surviving Costly Web

Strikes," *Computerworld* (February 21, 2000): 6.

[Insert Technology Insight 8.4 box here]

Restrict Access to Computing Resources Can you believe that 90 percent of the respondents to a survey conducted by the Computer Security Institute (CSI) with the participation of the San Francisco Federal Bureau of Investigation's Computer Intrusion Squad reported security breaches in a recent 12-month period?[11] To ensure that organizational information is not subjected to unauthorized use, disclosure, modification, damage, or loss, management should implement logical and physical access controls to assure that access to computing resources—systems, data, and programs—is restricted to authorized users for authorized uses by implementing two types of plans:

1. Control plans that restrict physical access to computer facilities.
2. Control plans that restrict logical access to stored programs, data, and documentation.

[11] *Issues and Trends: 2000 CSI/FBI Computer Crime Survey* (San Francisco, CA: Computer Security Institute, 2000).

Review Question

What are the control plans for restricting access to computer facilities? What three "layers" of control do these plans represent? Explain each layer.

Figure 8.4 (page 269) shows the levels (or layers) of protection included in these two categories.

[Insert Figure 8.4 here]

Control plans for restricting physical access to computer facilities. Naturally, only authorized personnel should be allowed access to the computer facility. As shown in the top portion of Figure 8.4, control plans for restricting physical access to computer facilities encompass three layers of controls.

Review Question

What are the control plans for restricting access to stored programs, data, and documentation? Which of these plans apply to an online environment, and which plans apply to an offline environment? How does a security module work?

Control plans for restricting access to stored programs, data, and documentation. Control plans for restricting access to stored programs, data, and documentation entail a number of techniques aimed at controlling *online* and *offline* systems. In an online environment, access control software called the **security module** will ensure that only authorized users gain access to a system and report violation attempts. These steps are depicted in the lower portion of Figure 8.4.

The primary plans for restricting access in an offline environment involve the use of segregation of duties, restriction of access to computer facilities, program change controls, and library controls. The first three plans have been defined and discussed in previous sections. **Library controls** restrict access to data, programs, and documentation. Library controls are provided by a *librarian function*, a combination of people, procedures, and computer software. Librarian software can keep track of versions of event and master data and ensure that the correct versions of such data are used. The software can also permit appropriate access to development, testing, staging, and production versions of programs (see Figure 8.3 on page 264).

Ensure Physical Security To protect IT facilities against manmade and natural hazards, the organization must install and regularly review suitable environmental and physical controls. These plans reduce losses caused by a variety of physical, mechanical, and environmental events. Table 8.5 (page 270) summarizes some of the more common controls directed at these environmental hazards.

[Insert Table 8.5 Here]

Review Question

What kinds of damage are included in the category of environmental hazards? What control plans are designed to *prevent* such hazards from occurring?What control plans are designed to *limit losses* resulting from such hazards or to recover from such hazards?

The advanced state of today's hardware technology results in a high degree of equipment reliability. Even if a malfunction does occur, it is usually detected and corrected automatically. In addition to relying on the controls contained within the computer hardware, organizations should perform regular **preventive maintenance** (periodic cleaning, testing, and adjusting of computer equipment) to ensure its continued efficient and correct operation.

IT Process 9: Provide Support Services

To ensure that users make effective use of IT, management should identify the training needs of all personnel, internal and external, who make use of the organization's information services, and should see that timely training sessions are conducted. To use IT resources effectively, users often require advice and may require assistance to overcome problems. This assistance is generally delivered via a "help desk" function.

Monitoring

Within the monitoring domain is a process to assess IT services for quality and to ensure compliance with control requirements. Monitoring may be performed as a self-assessment activity within an organizational unit such as the ISF, by an entity's internal/IT audit group, or by an external organization such as a public accounting or IT consulting firm.

IT Process 10: Monitor Operations

To ensure the achievement of IT process objectives, management should establish a system for defining performance indicators (service levels), gathering performance data, and generating performance reports. Management should review these reports to measure progress toward identified goals. Independent audits or evaluations should be conducted on a regular basis to increase confidence that IT objectives are being achieved, that controls are in place, and to benefit from advice regarding best practices for IT.

Review Question

Why should an organization conduct monitoring activities?

The WebTrust Seal of Assurance discussed in Chapter 4 is one example of an independent review of IT processes that an organization might obtain. Another service, introduced by the AICPA and the Canadian Institute of Chartered Accountants in 1999, is SysTrust. In a SysTrust engagement, the CA or CPA tests a system to provide assurance that the system meets four criteria (see the qualities of information in Exhibit 1.1 on page 17): availability, security, integrity, and maintainability, while conducting business over the Web.

Similar services to Webtrust and Systrust are offered by many IT consulting and Internet security firms. Check your favorite Web sites to see if they host any "seals of approval" of their transaction security, privacy protection, or system reliability.

Conclusions

Three factors will likely cause managers to confront the issues addressed in this chapter much more directly than have their predecessors. First, the events of September 11, 2001, have changed the way we think about the protecting an organization's resources, especially its IT resources, and making them available for use. Second, as computer-based systems become more sophisticated, managers must continually question how such technological changes affect the system of internal controls. For example, some companies have already implemented paperless (totally electronic) Information Systems. Others employ electronic data interchange (EDI) technology, which we introduced in Chapter 4. The challenges to managers are to keep pace with the development of such systems, and to ensure that changes in any system are complemented by enhancements in the company's internal controls.

Third, the events associated with the downfall of companies such as Enron Corp. has heightened the concerns of an organization's stakeholders—stockholders, customers, employees, taxpayers, etc.—and has caused them to raise a number of *corporate (organizational) governance* issues. They are asking, for example, how well their board of directors governs its own performance and that of the organization's management. And, how do the board of directors and management implement and demonstrate that they have control over their business processes? The answers to these questions can be found only in a thorough and effective system of internal control.

REVIEW QUESTIONS

RQ8-1 What are the three primary reasons that management exercises control over business processes? Explain.

RQ8-2 What are the relationships between fraud, in general, and internal control? Between computer fraud, in particular, and internal control?

RQ8-3 What is a computer virus?

RQ8-4 Explain what is meant by the control environment. What elements might comprise the control environment?

RQ8-5 Explain how business ethics relates to internal control.

RQ8-6 a. What are the three generic control goals of the operations process and the five generic control goals of the related information process?

b. Explain the difference between the following pairs of control goals: (1) ensure effectiveness of operations and ensure efficient employment of resources; (2) ensure efficient employment of resources and ensure security of resources; (3) ensure input validity and ensure input accuracy; (4) ensure input completeness and ensure input accuracy; (5) ensure input completeness and ensure update completeness; and (6) ensure input accuracy and ensure update accuracy.

RQ8-7 a. What is the difference between a process control plan, a pervasive control plan, and an IT control process?

b. Name and describe the five IT resources.

c. What are the four IT control process domains?

RQ8-8 What is the purpose of the strategic IT plan?

RQ8-9 Segregation of duties consists of separating what four basic functions? Briefly define each function.

RQ8-10 What are personnel control plans? Define the plans.

RQ8-11 Name and describe the four IT control processes in the acquisition and implementation domain.

RQ8-12 Describe the four phases/storage locations through which a program under development should pass to ensure good program change control.

RQ8-13 What is the difference between a *hot site* and a *cold site?*

RQ8-14 What are the control plans for restricting access to computer facilities? What three "layers" of control do these plans represent? Explain each layer.

RQ8-15 a. What are the control plans for restricting access to stored programs, data, and documentation? Which of these plans apply to an online environment, and which plans apply to an offline environment?

b. How does a security module work?

RQ8-16 a. What kinds of damage are included in the category of environmental hazards?

b. What control plans are designed to *prevent* such hazards from occurring?

c. What control plans are designed to *limit losses* resulting from such hazards or to recover from such hazards?

RQ8-17 a. Why should an organization conduct monitoring activities?

b. Who might conduct monitoring activities?

DISCUSSION QUESTIONS

DQ8-1 Management is legally responsible for establishing and maintaining an adequate system of control. Discuss the implications of this obligation, and discuss how management discharges its responsibility.

DQ8-2 "If it weren't for the potential of computer abuse, the emphasis on controlling computer systems would decline significantly in importance." Do you agree? Why or why not?

DQ8-3 Provide five examples of potential conflict between the control goals of ensuring effectiveness of operations and of ensuring efficient employment of resources.

DQ8-4 "If we thoroughly check the background of every job candidate we want to hire, we'd never get to hire anyone in this tight job market! It just takes too long." Do you agree? Why or why not?

DQ8-5 Discuss the *efficiency* and *effectiveness* of the mass-transit system in a large city.

DQ8-6 What, if anything, is wrong with the following control hierarchy? Discuss fully.

Highest level of control	Pervasive control plans
	The control environment
	Process control plans
Lowest level of control	IT control processes

DQ8-7 "In small companies with few employees, it is virtually impossible to implement the *segregation of duties* control plan." Do you agree? Why or why not?

DQ8-8 "No matter how sophisticated a system of internal control is, its success ultimately requires that you place your trust in certain key personnel." Do you agree? Why or why not?

DQ8-9 Debate the following point. *"Business continuity planning is really an IT issue."*

DQ8-10 "Contracting for a standby *hot site* is too cost-prohibitive except in the rarest of circumstances. Therefore, the vast majority of companies should think in terms of providing for a *cold site* at most." Do you agree? Why or why not?

DQ8-11 "We use an ASP [Application Service Provider, see Technology Insight 7.1 (page 211)] to outsource all our systems processing. That's good enough to ensure segregation of duties because we don't even know who our systems staff is!" Do you agree? Why or why not?

DQ8-12 "The 'monitor operations' activity in IT process 10 must be performed by an independent function such as a CPA or a security firm." Do you agree? Why or why not?

DQ8-13 Your boss was heard to say, "If we implemented every control plan discussed in this chapter, we'd never get any work done around here." Do you agree? Why or why not?

PROBLEMS

P8-1 List 1 contains 12 terms from this chapter or from Chapter 1, and list 2 includes 10 definitions or explanations of terms. Match the definitions with the terms by placing a *capital* letter from list 1 on the blank line to the left of its corresponding definition in list 2. You should have two letters left over from list 1.

A. Process control plan
B. Control environment
G. Input accuracy
H. Input completeness

Gelinas 8-60

C.	Control goal	I.	Input validity
D.	Risk	J.	Pervasive control plan
E.	Data maintenance	K.	Preventive control plan
F.	Master data update	L.	Operations process goal

___ 1. The process of modifying master data to reflect the results of new events.

___ 2. A control designed to keep problems from occurring.

___ 3. A control goal of the information process that is directed at ensuring that fictitious or bogus events are not recorded.

___ 4. A goal of an operations process that signifies the very reason for which that system exists.

___ 5. The highest level in the control *hierarchy*; a control category that evidences management's commitment to the importance of control in the organization.

___ 6. The process of modifying *standing master data.*

___ 7. A type of control that is exercised within each business process as that system's events are processed.

___ 8. The probability that an adverse consequence could result from an organization's actions or inactions.

___ 9. The element that appears as a heading in each column of a *control matrix.*

___ 10. A control that addresses a multitude of goals across many business processes.

P8-2 Below is a list of eight generic control goals from the chapter, followed by eight descriptions of either system failures (i.e., control goals not met) or instances of successful control plans (i.e., plans that helped to achieve control goals).

List the numbers 1 through 8 on a solution sheet. Each number represents one of the described situations. Next to each number:

a. Place the *capital* letter of the control goal that *best* matches the situation described.

b. Provide a one- to two-sentence explanation of how the situation relates to the control goal you selected.

HINT: Some letters may be used more than once. Some letters may not apply at all.

Control Goals

A. Ensure effectiveness of operations.

B. Ensure efficient employment of resources.

C. Ensure security of resources.

D. Ensure input validity.

E. Ensure input completeness.

F. Ensure input accuracy.

G. Ensure update completeness.

H. Ensure update accuracy.

Situations

1. A company uses *prenumbered documents* for recording its sales invoices to customers. When the invoices for a particular day were entered, the system noted that invoice #12345 appeared twice. The second entry (i.e., the duplicate) of this same number was rejected by the system since it was unsupported by a shipment.

2. In entering the invoices mentioned in situation 1, the data for salesperson number and sales terms were missing from invoice #12349 and therefore were not keyed into the computer.

3. Instead of preparing deposit slips by hand, Causeway Company has them generated by the computer. The company does so in order to speed up the deposit of cash.

4. In the Causeway Company cash receipts system, one of the earliest processes is to endorse each customer's check with the legend, "for deposit only to Causeway Company."

5. XYZ Co. prepares customer sales orders on a multipart form, one copy of which is sent to its billing department where it is placed in a temporary file pending shipping notification. Each morning, a billing clerk reviews the file of open sales orders

and investigates with the shipping department any missing shipping notices for orders entered 48 hours or more earlier.

6. In situation 5, once a shipping notice is received in the billing department, the first step in preparing the invoice to the customer is to compare the unit prices shown on the sales order with a standard price list kept in the billing system.

7. Alamo Inc. posts its sales invoice event file against its accounts receivable master data each night. Before posting the new sales event data, the computer program first checks the old master data to make sure that it is the version from the preceding day.

8. MiniScribe Corporation recorded actual shipments of disk drives to their warehouse as sales. Those disks drives that had not been ordered by anyone were still the property of MiniScribe.

P8-3 In the first list below are 10 examples of the items described in the second list.

Match the two lists by placing the *capital* letter from the first list on the blank line preceding the description to which it best relates. You should have two letters left over from list 1.

A. Management philosophy and operating style.

B. Customer order received over the Internet.

C. Customer name and address.

D. The process of increasing customer balances for sales made.

E. Total monthly sales report.

F. Fire extinguishers.

G. Deleting an inactive customer's record from the accounts receivable master data.

H. Ensure input validity.

I. Ensure security of resources.

J. Software piracy.

___ 1. *Event data* in a computer system.

___ 2. A control goal of the *information process.*

___ 3. An element included in the *control environment.*

___ 4. An element of *standing data.*

___ 5. A control goal of the *operations process.*

___ 6. An instance of *data maintenance.*

___ 7. *Master data* in a computerized system.

___ 8. An illustration of a *master data update.*

P8-4 Investigate the internal controls in one of the following (ask your instructor which): a local business, your home, your school, or your place of employment. Report (in a manner prescribed by your instructor) on the controls that you found and the goals that they were designed to achieve.

P8-5 Two lists follow. The first is a list of 10 situations that have control implications, and the second is a list of 12 control plans from this chapter.

Control Situations

1. During a violent electrical storm, an employee was keying data at one of the computers in the order entry department. After about an hour of data entry, lightning caused a company-wide power failure. When power was restored, the employee had to rekey all the data from scratch.
2. The computer center at Otis Company was badly damaged during a thunderstorm. When they attempted to begin operations at their *hot site* they discovered that they could not read the tapes containing the backup copies of their data and programs. Apparently, the machines on which the tapes were made had not been operating correctly.
3. Your instructor made arrangements for your class to take a guided tour of the computer center at a large metropolitan bank. The father of one of your classmates had recently been fired as a teller at that bank. That classmate kept his visitor's badge and gave it to his father, who used it to access the computer center the next day. The father then erased several computer files.

4. The customer service representatives of We-Sell-Everything, a catalog sales company, have been complaining that the computer system response time is very slow. They find themselves apologizing to customers who are waiting on the phone for their order to be completed.

5. At Culpepper Company, most event processing is automated. When an inventory item reaches its reorder point, the computer automatically prints a purchase order for the predetermined economic order quantity (EOQ). Purchase orders of $500 or more require the signature of the purchasing manager; those under $500 are mailed to vendors without being signed. An applications programmer, who was in collusion with the vendor who supplied part 1234, altered the computer program and the inventory master data for that part. He reduced the EOQ and made certain program alterations, such that every time part 1234 reached its reorder point, two purchase orders were produced, each of which was under the $500 threshold.

6. The resume of an applicant for the job of CFO at OYnot Mills showed that the candidate had graduated, some 10 years earlier, magna cum laude from Large State University (LSU) with a major in finance. LSU's finance program was very well respected, and OYnot had hired several of its graduates over the years. In his second month on the job, the new CFO became

tongue-tied when the CEO asked him a technical question about their investment strategy. When later it was discovered that the CFO's degree from LSU was in mechanical engineering, he was dismissed.

7. June Plugger, the company cashier, was known throughout the company as a workaholic. After three years on the job, June suddenly suffered a gall-bladder attack and was incapacitated for several weeks. While she was ill, the treasurer temporarily assumed the cashier's duties and discovered that June had misappropriated several thousand dollars since she was hired.
8. A hacker accessed the Web site at Deuteronomy Inc. and changed some of the graphics to pornography. Outraged by these changes, some customers took their business elsewhere.
9. During a normal workday, Sydney looked through the trash behind Acme Company's offices and was able to find some computer reports containing user IDs and other sensitive information. He later used that information to gain access to Acme's enterprise system.
10. John, an employee at Smith & Company, successfully accessed the order entry system at Smith and entered some orders for goods to be shipped to his cousin at no cost.

Control Plans

Gelinas 8-68

A. Personnel termination policies

B. Biometric security systems

C. Personnel selection and hiring control plans

D. Rotation of duties and forced vacations

E. Program change controls

F. Mirror site

G. Service level agreement

H. Firewall

I. WebTrust audit

J. Visitor's log and employee badges

K. Preventive maintenance

L. Security module

Match the 10 situations from the first list with the items in the second list by creating a table similar to the following, and completing column 2, "Control Plan." In column 2, insert *one* letter to identify the control plan that would *best* prevent the system failure from occurring. You should have two letters left over.

Control	**Control**
situation	**plan**
1	—
2	—

3	—

P8-6 Listed here are 20 control plans discussed in the chapter. On the blank line to the left of each control plan, insert a P (preventive), D (detective), or C (corrective) to classify that control most accurately. If you think that more than one code could apply to a particular plan, insert all appropriate codes and briefly explain your answer:

Code **Control Plan**

___ 1. Biometric identification

___ 2. Program change controls

___ 3. Fire and water alarms

___ 4. Adequate fire and water insurance

___ 5. Install batteries to provide backup for temporary loss in power

___ 6. SysTrust examination

___ 7. Service level agreements

___ 8. Chief Privacy Officer

___ 9. Digital signatures

___ 10. Mirror site

___ 11. Rotation of duties and forced vacations

___ 12. Fidelity bonding

___ 13. Hot site

___ 14. Personnel termination policies

___ 15. Segregation of duties

___ 16. IT strategic plan

___ 17. Disaster recovery planning

___ 18. Restrict entry to the computer facility through the use of security guards, locks, badges, and identification cards

___ 19. Computer security module

___ 20. Computer library controls

P8-7 Two lists follow. The first is a list of 10 situations that have control implications, and the second is a list of 12 control plans from this chapter.

Situations

1. A computer programmer was fired for gross incompetence. During the 2-week notice period, the programmer destroyed the documentation for all programs that he had developed since being hired.

2. A fire destroyed part of the computer room and the adjacent library of computer disks. It took several months to reconstruct the data from manual source documents and other hardcopy records.

3. A competitor flooded the Oak Company Web server with false messages (i.e., a denial of service attack). The Web server, unable to handle all of this traffic, shut down for several hours until the messages could be cleared.

4. A junior high school computer hacker created a program to generate random telephone numbers and passwords. Over the Web, he used the random number program to "crack" the computer system of a major international corporation.

5. A computer room operator was not able to handle the simplest problems that arose during his shift. He had received all the training recommended for his position and had been counseled a number of time in an attempt to improve his performance.

6. During the nightly computer run to update bank customers' accounts for deposits and withdrawals for that day, an electrical storm caused a temporary power failure. The run had to be reprocessed from the beginning, resulting in certain other computer jobs not being completed on schedule.

7. A group of demonstrators broke into a public utility's computer center overnight and destroyed computer equipment worth several thousand dollars.

8. The computer users at the Barrington Company have experienced significant delays in receiving responses from the

computer. They thought that the computer should respond to inquiries in less than three seconds.

9. A disgruntled applications programmer planted a "logic bomb" in the computer program that produced weekly payroll checks. The bomb was triggered to "go off" if the programmer were ever terminated. When the programmer was fired for continued absenteeism, the next weekly payroll run destroyed all the company's payroll master data.

10. The computer systems at Coughlin Inc. were destroyed in a recent fire. It took Coughlin several days to get its IT functions operating again.

Control Plans

A. Off-site storage of backup computer programs and databases

B. Service level agreements

C. Personnel termination policies

D. Security guards

E. Program change controls

F. Selection and hiring control plans

G. Firewall

H. Batteries and backup generators

I. Help desk

J. Identification badges and visitor's log

K. Hot site

L. Security modules

Match the 10 situations from the first list with the items in the two other lists by making a table like that shown for Problem 1. In column 2, insert *one* letter to identify the control plan that would *best* prevent the system failure from occurring. You should have two letters left over.

P8-8 Assume that inventory records are kept in an enterprise system and that the options in the inventory system module are as follows:

1. Maintain inventory master data (i.e., add new products, change or delete old products in the inventory master data).
2. Record newly arrived shipments of inventory.
3. Record returns of incorrect or damaged inventory.
4. Select items to be reordered, the amount to reorder, and the vendor.
5. Print and record new orders.
6. Print inventory reports.

Further assume that personnel in the inventory department include the department manager and two clerks, R. Romeo and J. Juliet.

By placing a "Y" for yes or an "N" for no in the table below, show which users should (or should not) have access to each of the six accounts payable options. Make and state whatever assumptions you think are necessary. Explain in one or two paragraphs how your matrix design would optimize the segregation of duties control plan.

Option	Manager	Romeo	Juliet
1	—	—	—
2	—	—	—
3	—	—	—
4	—	—	—
5	—	—	—
6	—	—	—

P8-9 Conduct research on the events related to the Enron Corp. bankruptcy in December 2001. Prepare a report describing the controls that might have *prevented, detected,* or *corrected* the stakeholder losses associated with that bankruptcy.

P8-10 Conduct research on the events related to the disasters of September 11, 2001. Prepare a report describing the controls that might have *prevented, detected,* or *corrected* the losses suffered by companies in the World Trade Center.

BOXES

[Start Technology Excerpt 8.1 box here]

Technology Excerpt 8.1

Chief Privacy Officers

Ronald Hoffman, the privacy issues manager at Mutual of Omaha Insurance Co., is in the forefront of a new breed of executives who are working with CIOs to set corporate data-privacy policies. Hoffman is responsible for helping to establish privacy practices for Mutual of Omaha. His job has become a key part of the Omaha-based insurer's overall corporate strategy in response to new privacy regulations and an ongoing debate over whether the government should set more rules or allow companies to self-regulate themselves.

For Mutual of Omaha, it's a bottom-line issue. Creating data-privacy policies and then standing behind them is "something that is going to help build a trusting relationship with our customers that we hope will allow us to retain their business and acquire new business," said Hoffman.

Hoffman is currently working with Mutual of Omaha's information technology managers to document the way data flows through all of the company's systems in order to learn exactly what happens to the information and who has access to it.

"We really didn't have a good handle on information flows through the company," Hoffman said. But the documentation project now under way should lead to better risk management and security assessments in addition to helping the insurer develop its privacy policies, he added.

Corporate privacy officers work with a variety of corporate departments, including information systems, legal affairs, governmental affairs, and employee training. But the most important thing they need is buy-in from top management, said Tatiana Gau, vice president of integrity assurance at America Online Inc.

"There's no question in my mind that one of the most important roles of the Chief

Privacy Officer (CPO) is to ensure that the whole company is adhering to a privacy commitment," Gau said. At AOL, for example, the importance of data privacy has been "baked into all the lifecycles" of the company, she added.

Source: Extracted from "Chief Privacy Officers Emerge in Response to Data-privacy Concerns," by Patrick Thibodeau, *Computerworld*, September 14, 2000.

[End Technology Excerpt 8.1 box here]

[Start Technology Insight 8.1 box here]

TECHNOLOGY INSIGHT 8.1

Computer Abuse Technologies

Salami. Unauthorized instructions are inserted into a program to steal very small amounts. For example, a program is written to calculate daily interest on savings accounts. A dishonest programmer includes an instruction that if the amount of interest to be credited to the account is other than an even penny (for example, $2.7345)—the excess over the even amount (.0045) is to be credited to the programmer's account. While each credit to his account is minute, the total can accumulate very rapidly.

Trap Door (back door). During the development of a program, the programmer may insert a special code or password that enables him to bypass the security features of the program in order to simplify his work. These features are meant to be removed when the programmer's work is done, but sometimes they aren't. Someone who knows the code or password can still get into the program.

Logic Bomb. Similar to the trap door, unauthorized code is inserted into a program at a time when a programmer has legitimate access to the program. When activated, the code causes a disaster, such as shutting the system down or destroying data. The technique is usually tied to a specific future date or event, in which case it is a time bomb. For example, if the programmer's name no longer appears on the payroll records of the company, the bomb is activated and the disaster occurs.

Trojan Horse. Like a Logic Bomb, a Trojan Horse is a module of unauthorized instructions covertly placed in a program; a Trojan Horse, unlike the Logic Bomb, lets the program execute its intended function while also performing an unauthorized act. Some Trojan Horses are distributed by e-mail to steal passwords. This was an element of the ILOVEYOU virus of May 2000.

Worm. A program that replicates itself on disks, in memory, and across networks. It uses computing resources to the point of denying access to these resources to others, thus effectively shutting down the system. They also may delete files and be spread via e-mail. Many recent viruses have included these worm features.

Zombie. A program that secretly takes over another Internet-attached computer, then uses that computer to launch attacks that can't be traced to the zombie's creator. Zombies are elements of the denial-of-service attacks discussed in this chapter.

Sources: Esther C. Roditti, *Computer Contracts* (New York, NY: Matthew Bender & Co., Inc., 1998); Steve Alexander, "Viruses, Worms, Trojan Horses and Zombies," *Computerworld* (May 1, 2000): 74.

[End Technology Insight 8.1 box here]

[Start Technology Insight 8.2 box here]

TECHNOLOGY INSIGHT 8.2

Gelinas 8-78

Computer Viruses

A **computer virus** is a program that can attach itself to other programs (including macros within word processing documents), thereby "infecting" those programs and macros. Computer viruses may also be inserted into the boot sectors* of PCs. Viruses are activated when you run an infected program, open an infected document, or boot the computer from an infected disk. Computer viruses alter their "host" programs, destroy data, or render computer resources (e.g., disk drives, central processor, networks) unavailable for use. Unlike other malicious programs such as logic bombs and Trojan Horses, viruses differ in that they reproduce themselves in other programs.

Some viruses are fairly innocent—they might merely produce a message such as "GOTCHA" or play "The Blue Danube" through the computer's speakers. Other viruses can be more harmful. Some viruses delete programs and files; some even reformat the hard drive, thus wiping away all that is stored there. Finally, there are some viruses that will overload your network with "messages," making it impossible to send or receive e-mail or to connect to external sources, such as the Internet.

Many viruses first enter an organization through PCs; many have been introduced via electronic bulletin boards, shared software, and files attached to e-mail messages. This sharing allows viruses to become an epidemic like a biological virus. The real fear that causes information systems managers to lose sleep, of course, is that the virus will spread to the organization's networks (and networked computing resources) and destroy the organization's most sensitive data.

In May 2000, the "ILOVEYOU" virus quickly spread throughout the world, infecting a million computers. This virus was written in Visual Basic script (file extension .vbs) and came attached to an e-mail message. If the recipient launched the program, the virus deleted artwork files and altered music files. If the victim was using the Microsoft Outlook mail program, the virus mailed itself to everyone in the victim's e-mail address book. Thus, the "ILOVEYOU" virus would set a trap for many others who would think they were getting mail from a colleague. Finally, the virus contained a Trojan Horse that mailed victim passwords to an e-mail account in the Philippines.

How does one protect from a viral infection? If you are going to share files and disks with others, use virus protection software to scan all files and disks before the disks are used or the files are opened. This is, of course, especially true of files received as e-mail attachments. Don't open e-mail from people you don't know. Don't open e-mail with .xxx or .xbs extensions. Back up files regularly. Use an up-to-date anti-virus program to scan your hard disk regularly. E-mail servers could be set to block attachments written in Visual Basic script.

*The boot sector is the area of a hard or floppy disk containing the program that loads the operating system.

Sources: Ann Harrison, " 'Love Bug' Spotlights Misuse of VB Script," *Computerworld* (May 8, 2000): 1, 111; Ted Bridis, "Poisonous Messages Potential to Destroy Files Prompted Vast E-Mail Shutdown," *The Wall Street Journal*, (May 5, 2000): B1, B4; Stan Miastowski, "Virus Killers (Tips for Self-Protection)," *PC World* (March 1997): 180.

[End Technology Insight 8.2 box here]

[Start Technology Excerpt 8.2 box here]

Technology Excerpt 8.2

Gelinas 8-80

Digital Signatures

The passage of the Electronic Signatures in Global and National Commerce Act, nicknamed E-Sign, gives electronic signatures the same legal status as handwritten ones. This law translates into great opportunities for actually completing high-stakes transactions, agreements, and approvals on the Web. With digital signatures, the velocity of funds transfers increases, the cost of acquiring customers drops, and entire transaction processes, such as procurement, can be automated.

The biggest impact of digital signatures will come in financial services. Think of all the transactions that currently require physical signatures—mortgages, insurance policies, service contracts, and many business-to-business transactions. The cost of signing up a single customer can be significantly reduced because E-Sign enables these transactions to be completed online.

E-Sign will also have big payoffs for vertical online exchanges. For many transactions initiated through exchanges or marketplaces, the electronic interplay stops well short of completing the transaction.

Eventually, the trading partners step offline—and therefore off the exchange—to complete the paperwork and financing. E-Sign gets around this obstacle, and it also simplifies the process of third-party legal validation for deals involving more than one trading partner.

Digital signatures can be any form of electronic seal agreed to by the two parties. The most common approach relies on digital certificates and encryption. The encrypted signature can reside on a machine, be carried on smart cards, be authenticated via passwords or personal identification numbers, or even be a biometric authentication, such as a fingerprint or retinal pattern.

Legal status is one big step for digital signatures, but trust is the next. Trading partners need to have a great deal of trust in the technology, especially in purely electronic transactions in which the two sides haven't met or even spoken to one another. Technology needs to establish credibility, security, and trust.

Source: James K. Watson Jr. and Carol Choksy, "Digital Signatures Seal Web Deals," *Informationweek.com,* September 18, 2000: Rb26 and Rb28.

[End Technology Excerpt 8.2 box here]

[Start Technology Insight 8.3 box here]

TECHNOLOGY INSIGHT 8.3

Business and IT Continuity Lessons Learned as a Result of September 11, 2001

- Hot sites and cold sites were overwhelmed by the demands for their use by businesses located in and around the WTC. Contracts with these sites must now specify who gets priority for their use.
- Backup and recovery locations must not be located in proximity to the primary site. Some organizations stored their backup data within the WTC complex.
- There must be several post-disaster communication options, including multiple telephone carriers, cell phones, and e-mail. Some telephone and cell phone services were not available in the WTC area for months after the disaster.
- Employees calling *in* was much more effective than trying to call *out* to determine the

status and location of employees.

- Several organizations, especially those in financial services, realized that they needed their IT resources to be continuously available (i.e., *preventive*) rather than to be recovered after the disaster (i.e., *corrective*).
- Contingency plans must include alternative modes of transportation and should locate recovery sites near where employees live. For several days after 9/11, airlines did not fly, rental cars were hard to find, train and bus systems were severely taxed, and some roads, tunnels, and bridges were closed.
- Paperless offices are only an illusion and back-ups must be created for paper documents using *digital imaging* and other technologies. Organizations lost copies of paper documents and recordings of meetings and legal depositions.

[End Technology Insight 8.3 box here]

[Start Technology Insight 8.4 box here]

TECHNOLOGY INSIGHT 8.4

Denial Of Service Attacks

In a **denial of service attack,** a Web site is overwhelmed by an intentional onslaught of thousands of simultaneous messages, making it impossible for the attacked site to engage in its normal activities. A **distributed denial of service attack** uses many computers (called "zombies") that unwittingly cooperate in a *denial of service attack* by sending messages to the target Web sites. Unfortunately, the distributed version is more effective because the number of computers responding multiplies the number of attack messages. And, because each computer has its own IP address, it is more difficult to detect that an attack is taking place than it would be if all the messages were coming from one address.

Currently there are no easy *preventive* controls. To *detect* a denial of service attack, Web sites may employ *filters* to detect the multiple messages and block traffic from the sites sending them, and *switches* to move their legitimate traffic to servers and Internet Service Providers (ISPs) that are not under attack (i.e., *corrective action*). However, attackers can hide their identity by creating false IP addresses for *each* message, making many filtering defenses slow to respond or virtually ineffective. An organization might also carry insurance to reimburse them for any losses suffered from an attack (i.e., *corrective*).

[End Technology Insight 8.4 box here]

TABLES

[Start Table]

Table 8.1 Control Goals

Control goal	**Definitions**	**Discussion**
	Control goals of the operations process	
Ensure *effectiveness* of operations by achieving the following *operations process goals:* (itemize the specific goals for the process being analyzed)	**Effectiveness:** A measure of success in meeting one or more goals	Did we achieve our goal? If my goal was to get an A in the course, did I get an A?
	Operations process goals: Criteria used to judge the effectiveness of an operations process	If our goal is to deposit cash receipts on the day received, we are effective if cash receipts are deposited on the day received.
Ensure *efficient* employment of resources	**Efficiency:** A measure of the productivity of the resources applied to achieve a set of goals	What is the cost of the people, computers, and other resources needed to deposit all cash on the day received? Could it be accomplished at a lower cost?

Ensure *security* of resources. (specify the applicable operations process and information process resources)	**Security of resources:** Protecting an organization's resources from loss, destruction, disclosure, copying, sale, or other misuse	Are the physical (e.g., cash) and nonphysical (e.g., information) resources available when required? Are they put to unauthorized use?
	Control goals of the information process	
Ensure *input validity* (IV)	**Input validity:** A control goal that requires that input data be appropriately approved and represent actual economic events and objects	Are all of the cash receipts to be input into our computer supported by actual customer payments?
Ensure *input completeness* (IC)	**Input completeness:** A control goal that requires that every valid event or object be captured and entered into a system	Are all valid customer payments captured on a remittance advice (RA) and entered into our computer?
Ensure *input accuracy* (IA)	**Input accuracy:** A control goal that requires that events be correctly captured and entered into a system	Is the correct payment amount and customer number transcribed onto the RA? Is the correct payment amount and customer number keyed into our computer? Is the customer number missing from the RA?
Ensure *update completeness*	**Update completeness:** A control goal that requires that all events entered into a computer are reflected in their respective master data	Have all input cash receipts been recorded in our accounts receivable master data?
Ensure *update accuracy*	**Update accuracy:** A control goal that requires that data entered into a computer are reflected correctly in their respective master data	Are all input cash receipts correctly recorded in our accounts receivable master data?

[End Table]

[Start Table]

Table 8.2 Illustration of Segregation of Duties

Gelinas 8-85

Function 1	Function 2	Function 3	Function 4
Authorizing Events	**Executing Events**	**Recording Events**	**Safeguarding Resources Resulting from Consummating Events**
• Approve steps of event processing.	• Physically move resources.	• Record events in the appropriate data store(s).	• Physically protect resources.
	• Complete source documents.	• Post event summaries to the master data store.	• Maintain accountability of physical resources.
Example: Processing a credit sales event.			
Authorizing Events	**Physical Movement of Resources**	**Record Event Details**	**Physically Protect Resources**
• Approve customer credit.	• Pick inventory from bins.	• Update accounts receivable, sales, and inventory event data.	• Safeguard inventory while in storage at warehouse, while in transit to shipping department, and while preparing for shipment to customer.
• Approve picking inventory and sending inventory to shipping department.	• Move inventory from warehouse to shipping department.	**Post Event Summaries**	
• Approve shipping inventory to customer.	• Ship inventory to customer.	• Update general ledger and marketing master data.	
• Approve recording accounting entries.	**Complete Source Documents**		**Maintain Accountability**
	• Enter sales order.		• Examine and count inventory periodically, and compare physical total to recorded total.
	• Enter shipping document.		
	• Enter invoice.		

[End Table]

[Start Table]

Table 8.3 Personnel Control Plans

Control plans	**Discussion**
Selection and hiring	Job candidates should be carefully screened before being selected for a position
Retention	To retain employees, provide creative and challenging work opportunities and, when possible, offer open channels to management-level positions
Personnel development	Conduct performance reviews to: determine whether an employee is satisfying the requirements of a position as indicated by a job description, assess an employee's strengths and weaknesses, assist management in determining whether to make salary adjustments and whether to promote an employee, identify opportunities for training and for personal growth
Personnel management	• Project future managerial and technical skills of the staff, anticipate turnover, and develop a strategy for filling necessary positions
	• Lay out the responsibilities for each position on an organization chart
	• Identify the resources required by each staff member to perform their responsibilities
	• Prevent the organization's own personnel from committing acts of computer abuse, fraud, or theft of assets through:
	• **Rotation of duties**—require employees to alternate jobs or responsibilities periodically
	• **Forced vacations**—require that an employee take leave from the job and substitute another employee in his or her place
	• **Fidelity bond**—indemnifies a company in case it suffers losses from financial misbehavior by its employees; employees who have access to cash and other negotiable assets are usually bonded
	• **Personnel termination policies**—when an employee leaves an organization, collect keys and badges and change passwords

[End Table]

[Start Table]

Table 8.4 Delivering Required Services

Activity	**Discussion**
Define	To ensure that internal and third party IT services are effectively delivered,

	service level
service	requirements must be defined. Service levels are the organizational requirements for the
levels	minimum levels of the quantity and quality of IT services.
Manage	To ensure that IT services delivered by third parties continue to satisfy organizational
third-party	requirements, processes must be in place to identify, manage, and monitor outsourced IT
services	resources.
Manage IT	To ensure that important IT functions are performed regularly and in an orderly fashion,
operations	the information services function should establish and document standard procedures for IT operations.
Manage data	To ensure that data remain *complete, accurate,* and *valid,* management should establish a
	combination of process and general controls. *Process controls* relate directly to the data as it
	is being processed. *General controls* ensure data integrity once the data have been processed
	and include *production backup and recovery control plans* that address short-term disruptions to IT operations.
	Production backup and recovery starts with making a copy (i.e., a *backup*) of data files (or the database), programs, and documentation. The copies are then used for day-to-day operations, and the originals are stored in a safe place. Should any of the working copies be damaged or completely destroyed, the originals are retrieved (i.e., the *recovery*) from safekeeping.
Identify and	To ensure that IT resources are delivered in a cost-effective manner and that they are used
allocate	wisely, information services management should identify the costs of providing IT
costs	services and should allocate those costs to the users of those services.

[End Table]

[Start Table]

Table 8.5 Environmental Controls

Gelinas 8-88

Environmental hazard	**Controls**
Fire	Smoke detectors, fire alarms, fire extinguishers,
	fire-resistant construction materials, insurance
Water damage	Waterproof ceilings, walls, and floors, adequate drainage,
	water and moisture detection alarms, insurance
Dust, coffee,	Regular cleaning of rooms and equipment, dust-collecting
tea, soft drinks	rugs at entrances, separate dust-generating activities from
	computer, good housekeeping, prohibiting food and drinks
	within computing facilities
Energy increase,	Voltage regulators, backup batteries and generators,
decrease, loss	fiber optic networks

[End Table]

9

CONTROLLING INFORMATION SYSTEMS: PROCESS CONTROLS

It was 3:55 P.M. EST, just before the 4:00 P.M. closing of the New York Stock Exchange. A clerk on the trading floor of Salomon Brothers Inc. misread a program-trading order. Instead of entering the order correctly to sell $11 million worth of this particular stock, the clerk typed 11 million into the box on the screen that asked for the number of shares to be sold. Like most such firms, Salomon has direct computer links to the New York Stock Exchange (NYSE) that allow it to process security trades with lightning speed. When a second clerk failed to double-check the order as required by company policy, most of the trade as entered—amounting to $500 million, not $11 million—was sent to the NYSE's computer system. Although the firm's computer system did catch the error shortly after it was made and kept at least part of the trade from being executed, it was not before the error sent the stock market tumbling and caused near chaos at the Big Board.

Synopsis

This chapter presents a conceptual framework for the analysis of controls in business systems, describing process controls that may be found in any information process. As almost all business processes incorporate information technology, many of the controls you read about are automated and do not require human intervention. As more and more business is conducted over the Internet, organizations will be increasingly reliant on computerized controls to protect both their *operations processes* and *information processes*. These controls help *prevent* (or *detect* or *correct*) problems such as the one that occurred at Salomon Brothers.

You should notice that many of the controls described in this chapter provide assurance about the quality of the data entry process. Such controls take on increased importance with *enterprise systems* because they prevent erroneous data from entering the system and affecting the many tightly connected enterprise system processes that follow initial entry of the data. We want to have good controls, for example, over the entry of customer orders so that we correctly record data about the customer order, the shipment, the inventory balance, the customer's invoice, the general ledger entries for sales, accounts receivable, inventory, cost of goods sold, and the inventory replenishment process.

Good data entry controls are also important for those engaging in *e-business*. For example, if we are to receive customer orders electronically, our systems must have sufficient controls within them so that they accept only authorized, accurate order data. If we don't have these controls, we might make inaccurate shipments or shipments to those who have no intention of paying for the goods being shipped.

Gelinas 9-3

Learning Objectives

- To be able to prepare a control matrix
- To describe the generic process control plans introduced in this chapter
- To describe how these process controls accomplish control goals
- To describe why these generic process controls are important to organizations with enterprise systems and those that are engaged in e-business

Introduction

Having covered the control environment and IT control processes in Chapter 8, we are now ready to move to the third level of control plans appearing in the hierarchy shown in Figure 8.2 on page 256—process control plans (the first two were the control environment and pervasive control plans). We begin by defining the components of a control framework and introduce tools used to implement it. Then we apply the control framework to a few generic business processes. These generic processes include process controls that may be found in any information system. Later in the text, in Chapters 10 through 14, we examine process controls that might be found in particular business processes (e.g., order-to-cash, purchase-to-pay, and so forth).

Review Question

Explain the difference between the category of process control plans covered in this chapter and the process controls to be covered in

Chapters 10 through 14.

The Control Framework

In this section, we introduce a control framework specific to the control requirements of the operations process and the information process. We again use the Causeway Company cash receipts system, this time to illustrate the control framework.

The control framework provides a structure for analyzing the internal controls of business organizations. However, structure alone is of little practical value. To make the framework functional, you need to feel comfortable using the tools for implementing the framework. In Chapter 2, you saw one of the key tools—the systems flowchart. Now we use the other important tool—the control matrix.

Review Question

Describe the relationship between the *control matrix* and the *control framework.*

The Control Matrix

The **control matrix** is a tool used to analyze a systems flowchart (and related narrative) to determine the control plans appropriate to that process and to relate those plans to the processes control goals. It establishes criteria to be used in evaluating a particular process. We'll start by taking a look at the four essential elements of the matrix—*control goals, recommended control plans, cell entries,* and *explanations of the cell entries.* Then, we'll elaborate on the steps used to prepare the matrix.

Figure 9.1 presents a "bare-bones" outline of the control matrix, and Figure 9.2 (page 284) is the "annotated" flowchart produced as a by-product of completing the matrix. We explain how to annotate a flowchart later in this section. *The intent in Figure 9.1 is **not** to have you learn about the control goals and control plans for a cash receipts process. Those are covered in Chapter 11. Rather, we are trying to give you an overview of the four control matrix elements and how they relate to each other, and to walk you through, in a very basic way, the steps in preparing the matrix.* Please follow along in the figures as we describe how to prepare the control matrix.

[Insert Figure 9.1 here]

[Insert Figure 9.2 here]

Review Question

What are the four basic elements included in a control matrix?

Steps in Preparing the Control Matrix

Control goals represent the first element of the matrix. The goals are listed across the top row of the matrix; they should be familiar to you from discussions in Chapter 8. Indeed, in Figure 9.1, we have merely tailored the generic goals shown in Table 8.1 (see page 250) to Causeway's cash receipts system. The tailoring involves:

- Identifying *operations process* goals for a cash receipts process; we include only two examples here—namely,
    - Goal A—to accelerate cash flow by promptly depositing cash receipts.
    - Goal B—to ensure minimum cash balances are maintained in our depository bank.[1]

[1] Remember that one of the goals of any business process may be compliance with applicable laws, regulations, and *contractual agreements*. Depending on the particular process being analyzed, we tailor the matrix to identify the specific law, regulation, or agreement with which we desire to achieve compliance. In Causeway's case, we assume that its loan agreements with its bank require that it maintain certain minimum cash balances—known as compensating balances—on deposit.

(Other possible goals of a cash receipts process would be shown as goals C, D, and so forth, and would be included at the bottom of the matrix.)

- Listing the resources of interest in this process—namely, Causeway's physical asset, cash, and an information resource, the accounts receivable master data.
- Naming the information process inputs—namely, remittance advices representing cash receipts data.

- Identifying the master data being updated in this system—namely, the accounts receivable master data.

In determining what *operations process goals* are appropriate for the operations process under review, you may find it helpful to first ask yourself, "What undesirable events might occur?" For example, in deciding on Causeway's operations process goal of accelerating cash flow by promptly depositing cash receipts, we might have first speculated that there was a possibility that the mailroom could delay the processing of incoming payments, the cashier could hold endorsed checks for a time before taking them to the bank, and so forth. Noting these weak points can also be useful in deciding on recommended control plans, discussed next.

Recommended control plans, appropriate to the process being analyzed, represent the second element of the matrix. To illustrate, we list two representative plans for a cash receipts process such as Causeway's in the left column of Figure 9.1. Each of these plans (and others) will be explained in Chapter 11. Two other plans listed in Figure 9.1 are identified merely as plans 3 and 4.

In the body of the matrix, located at various intersections of goals and plans, are *cells*. Cells can have entries in them (P-1, P-2, M-1, M-2), or they can be left blank. Entries in cells represent the third element of the matrix. If a recommended control plan can help to achieve a control goal (i.e., there is a relationship between that plan and a particular goal), an entry—either a P or an M—should appear in that cell. A corresponding entry (e.g., P-1, M-2) is also made on the systems flowchart for purposes of cross-referencing. We refer to this technique as *annotating* a systems flowchart. The process of relating the plans listed in the matrix to the point where the plans can be located on the systems flowchart is illustrated in Figure 9.2, the annotated flowchart for Causeway. Take a few moments to trace the codes, P-1, P-2, M-1, and M-2, from Figure 9.1 to their locations in Figure 9.2. From the descriptions of plans P-1 and M-1 in Figure 9.1, do you agree with where we have put them in Figure 9.2? If not, check with your instructor.

Review Question

Describe the relationship between the *control matrix* and the *systems flowchart*. What does it mean to "annotate" the systems flowchart?

There are two types of entries that you can register in a cell. You can enter a "P," which indicates that a particular control plan is *present* in the flowchart. For example, in Figure 9.1, the entries "P-1" and "P-2" indicate that those plans are present in Causeway's system. A glance at the flowchart in Figure 9.2 shows the location of these plans. Alternatively, you can enter an "M," which signifies that a particular, recommended control plan is *missing* (for example, entries "M-1" and "M-2" indicate that those plans are not present in Causeway's system). Again, Figure 9.2 identifies the location of where these desirable, but missing, plans should be installed to control Causeway's cash receipts process more effectively.

Because the control plans listed in the first column of the matrix are all *recommended* plans, entering a "P" in a cell symbolizes a strength in the system. It depicts a control plan as contributing to the accomplishment of one or more control goals. For example, in Figure 9.1, the plan "Immediately endorse incoming checks" helps to ensure that the cash resource (customer checks) will not be misappropriated. We depict this relationship by entering a "P-1" in the cell where this plan intersects with the goal of ensuring security of resources. And as importantly, at the bottom of the matrix, we provide the fourth, and final, matrix element—the explanation of *how* this plan helps to achieve this particular goal. In this case, a restrictive endorsement on the check (i.e., "deposit only to the account of Causeway Company") prevents it from being diverted to any other purpose. Of the four matrix elements, many people have the most difficulty in providing these explanations. Yet this element is the most important part of the matrix because the whole purpose of the matrix is to relate plans to goals. Unless you can explain the association between plans and goals, there's a good possibility you may have guessed at the cell entry. Sometimes you'll guess right, but it's just as likely you'll guess wrong. Be prepared to defend your cell entries.

Review Question

How could the matrix be used to recommend changes in the system in order to improve control of that system?

Entering “M” in a cell symbolizes a weakness in the system. It tells us that a system does not incorporate a particular control plan that may be necessary to ensure the accomplishment of a related control goal. For example, in Figure 9.1, notice that the *recommended* plan, “Immediately separate checks and remittance advices,” is missing from Causeway’s system. The explanation of cell entries in Figure 9.1 goes on to explain what goals *would* be achieved if this plan were present.

Review Question

How would the matrix be useful in evaluating control *effectiveness*, control *efficiency*, and control *redundancy*? Include in your answer a definition of these three terms.

When your assessment leads you to the identification (and correction) of control weaknesses, you are fulfilling the fourth step of the control framework: recommending remedial changes to the system (if necessary) to correct deficiencies in the system.

In addition to telling you about the control strengths and weaknesses of a particular system, a completed matrix also facilitates evaluation from the perspectives of *control effectiveness* (are all the control goals achieved?), *control efficiency* (do individual control plans address multiple goals?), and *control redundancy* (are too many controls directed at the same goal?).

Exhibit 9.1 summarizes the steps we have just undertaken in preparing the illustrative control matrix in Figure 9.1. Combined with the preceding discussion and illustration, the steps should be self-explanatory. You should take a fair amount of time now to study each of the steps and to make sure that you have a reasonable understanding of them.

Review Question

What are the five steps involved in preparing a control matrix?

[Insert Exhibit 9.1 here]

Control Plans for Data Entry without Master Data

As mentioned before, perhaps the most error-prone—and inefficient—steps in an operations process or an information process are the steps during which data is entered into a system. While a lot has been done over the years to improve the accuracy and efficiency of the data entry process, problems still remain, especially when humans type data into a system. So, we begin our discussion of process controls by describing those controls that improve the data entry process. We divide our discussion of data entry controls into three parts: controls when master data is not available during data entry, controls when master data is available during data entry, and controls when the input data may be collected into batches.

As you study these controls, keep in mind improvements that have been made to address errors and inefficiencies of the data entry process. These improvements include:

- Automation of data entry. Documents may be scanned for data entry. Documents and labels may contain bar codes that are scanned. This automation reduces or eliminates manual keying.
- Business events, such as purchases, may be initiated in one (buying) organization and transmitted to another (selling) organization via the Internet or EDI. In this case, the receiving (selling) organization need not enter the data at all.
- Multiple steps in a business process may be tightly integrated, such as in an enterprise system. In these cases the number of data entry steps is greatly reduced. For example, there may be no need to enter a shipment (sale) into the billing system because the shipping system shares the same integrated database with the billing system where the data have already been entered.

System Description and Flowchart

Figure 9.3 shows the systems flowchart for a hypothetical system that we will use to describe our first set of controls. In our first pass through the system, please ignore the control annotations, P-1, P-2, and so forth. They have been included so that we will not have to repeat the flowchart later when we prepare the control matrix.

The processing starts in the first column of Figure 9.3 with the clerk typing in the input data. Usually, the data entry program would present the clerk with an input screen and then prompt the user to enter certain data into fields on that screen (e.g., *customer code, items numbers,* and so on).

Note that the first processing square in the data entry devices column "edits" the data before they are actually accepted by the system. The editing is done through various *programmed edit checks*; these are discussed later in this section. Having edited the input, the computer displays a message to the user indicating that the input either is acceptable or contains errors. If errors exist, the user may be able to correct them immediately. Once users have made any necessary corrections, they type in a code or click the mouse button to instruct the system to accept the input. That action triggers the computer to simultaneously:

- Record the input in machine-readable form—the event data disk.
- Inform the user that the input data have been accepted.

To verify that the event data were keyed correctly, the documents *could* be forwarded to a second clerk who would type the data again. This procedure, called *key verification*, was introduced in Chapter 2 and will be further explained below. Typically, key verification is applied only to important fields on low volume inputs.

Our flowchart stops at this point *without* depicting the update of any master data. Certainly our system could continue with such a process. We have not shown it here so that we can concentrate on the *input* controls.

Applying the Control Framework

In this section, we apply the control framework to the generic system described above. Figure 9.4 (page 290) presents a completed control matrix for the systems flowchart shown in Figure 9.3. Through the symbols P-1, P-2, . . . P-7, we have annotated the flowchart to show where specific control plans are implemented. We also have one control plan that we *assume* is missing (code M-1) because the narrative did not mention it specifically. The UC and UA columns in the matrix have been shaded to emphasize that they do not apply to this analysis because there is no update of any master data in Figure 9.3.

[Insert Figure 9.3 here]

As you recall from the previous section, step 2 in preparing a control matrix is to tailor the control goals across the top of the matrix to the particular business process under review. Because our model system does not show a specific system such as cash receipts, inventory, or the like, we cannot really perform the tailoring step. Therefore, in Figure 9.4 under the operations process section, we have shown only one operations process goal for illustrative purposes. We identify that goal as goal A: To ensure *timely* processing of (blank) event data (whatever those data happen to be). In the business process chapters (Chapters 10 through 14) you will see how to tailor the goals to the systems discussed in those chapters.

[Insert Figure 9.4 here]

The recommended control plans listed in the first column in Figure 9.4 are representative of those commonly associated with controlling the data entry process. The purpose of this presentation is to give you a sense of the multitude of control plans available for controlling such systems. The plans are *not* unique to a specific system such as sales, billing, cash receipts, and so forth. Rather, they apply to *any* data entry process. Therefore, when the technology of a system is appropriate, these controls are incorporated into the list of recommended control plans (step 3 in "Steps in Preparing a Control Matrix," Exhibit 9.1, page 287).

Let's take a general look at how several of the control plans work.[2] Then, in Exhibit 9.2 (page 293), we explain each of the cell entries in the control matrix. As you study the control plans, be sure to see where they are located on the systems flowchart.

[2] Many of the controls in this section are adapted from material

contained in the *Handbook of IT Auditing 2001 Edition,* (Chapters D2, D3, and D4 primarily), Copyright © 2000 by PricewaterhouseCoopers L.L.P.; published by Warren, Gorham & Lamont, Boston, MA.

[Insert Exhibit 9.2 here]

P-1: *Document design.* **Document design** is a control plan in which a source document is designed in such as way to make it easier to prepare initially and to input data from later. We designate this as a present plan because we assume that the organization has designed this document to facilitate the data preparation and data entry processes.

P-2: *Written approvals.* A **written approval** takes the form of a signature or initials on a document to indicate that a person has authorized the event.

P-3: *Preformatted screens.* **Preformatted screens** control the entry of data by defining the acceptable *format* of each data field. For example, the screen might require users to key in exactly nine alphabetic characters in one field and exactly five numerals in another field. To facilitate the data entry process, the cursor may automatically move to the next field on the screen. And the program may require that certain fields be completed, thus preventing the user from omitting any *mandatory* data sets. Finally, the system may automatically populate certain fields with data, such as the current date and default shipping methods, sales tax rates, and other terms of a business event. Automatic population reduces the number of keystrokes required, making data entry quicker and more efficient. With fewer keystrokes and by utilizing the default data, fewer keying mistakes are expected. To ensure that the system has not provided inappropriate defaults, the clerk must compare the data provided by the system with that on the input.

P-4: *Online prompting.* **Online prompting** asks the user for input or asks questions that the user must answer. For example, after entering all the input data for a particular customer sales order, you might be presented three options: (A)ccept the order, (E)dit the order, or (R)eject the order. By requiring you to stop and "accept" the order, online prompting is, in a sense, advising you to check your data entries before moving on. Many systems provide *context-sensitive help* whereby the user is automatically provided with, or can ask for, descriptions of data to be entered into each input field. Another way to provide choices for a field or to limit allowable choices is to restrict entry to the contents of a list that pops up. For example, a list of state abbreviations can be provided from which the user chooses the appropriate two-letter abbreviation.

P-5: *Programmed edit checks.* **Programmed edit checks** are edits automatically performed by data entry programs upon entry of the input data. Erroneous data may be highlighted on the terminal screen to allow the operator to take corrective action immediately. Programmed edits can highlight actual or potential input errors, and allows them to be corrected quickly and efficiently. The most common types of programmed edit checks are the following:

1. **Reasonableness checks.** Reasonableness checks, also known as **limit checks,** test whether the contents (e.g., values) of the data entered fall within predetermined limits. The limits may describe a standard range (e.g., customer numbers must be between 0001 and 5000, months must be 01 to 12), or maximum values (e.g., no normal hours worked greater than 40 and no overtime hours greater than 20).

2. **Document/record hash totals.** Document/record hash totals are a summary of any numeric data field within the input document or record, such as item numbers or quantities on a customer order. The totaling of these numbers typically serves no purpose other than as a control. Calculated before and then again after entry of the document or record, this total can be used to determine that the applicable fields were all entered and were entered correctly.

3. **Mathematical accuracy checks.** This edit compares calculations performed manually to those performed by the computer to determine if a document has been entered correctly. For this check, the user might enter the individual

items (e.g., quantity purchased, unit cost, tax, shipping cost) on a document, such as an invoice, and the total for that document. Then, the computer adds up the individual items and compares that total to the one input by the user. If they don't agree, something has likely been entered erroneously. Alternatively, the user can review the computer calculations and compare them to totals prepared before input.

4. **Check digit verification.** In many processes, an extra digit—a check digit—is included in the identification number of entities such as customers and vendors. More than likely you have a check digit as part of the ID on your ATM card. The check digit is calculated originally by applying a complicated and secret formula to an identification number; the check digit then is appended to the identification number. For instance, the digit 6 might be appended to the customer code 123 so that the entire ID becomes 1236. In this highly oversimplified example, the digit 6 was derived by adding together the digits 1, 2, and 3. Whenever the identification number is entered later by a data entry person, the computer program applies the mathematical formula to verify the check digit. In our illustration, if the ID were input as 1246, the entry would be rejected because the digits 1, 2, and 4 do not add up to 6. You are already saying to yourself, "But what about a transposition like 1326?" This entry

would be accepted because of the simple method of calculating the check digit. In practice, check digits are assigned by using much more sophisticated formulas than simple cross-addition; those formulas are designed to detect a variety of input errors, including transpositions.

Review Question

What are two common *programmed edit checks*? Describe each check.

P-6: *Interactive feedback checks.* An **interactive feedback check** is a control in which the data entry program informs the user that the input has been accepted and recorded. The program may flash a message on the screen telling a user that the input has been accepted for processing.

M-1: *Key verification.* With **key verification** documents are typed by one individual and retyped by a second individual. The data entry software compares the second entry to the first entry. If there are differences, it is assumed that one person misread or mistyped the data. Someone, perhaps a supervisor or the second clerk, would determine which typing was correct, the first or the second, and make corrections as appropriate.

P-7: *Procedures for rejected inputs.* **Procedures for rejected inputs** are designed to ensure that erroneous data—not accepted for processing—are corrected and resubmitted for processing. To make sure that the corrected input does not still contain errors, the corrected input data should undergo all routines through which the input was processed originally. A "suspense file" of rejected inputs is often retained (manually or by the computer) to ensure timely clearing of rejected items. To reduce the clutter in the simple flowcharts in this text, we often depict such routines with an annotation "Error routine not shown."

Explanation of control matrix cell entries. Armed with an understanding of the mechanics of certain control plans, let's now turn our attention to Exhibit 9.2—Explanation of Cell Entries for Control Matrix in Figure 9.4. See whether you agree with (and understand) the relationship between each plan and the goal(s) that it addresses. Remember that your ability to *explain* the relationships between plans and goals is more important than your memorization of the cell entries themselves.

Review Question

How does each control plan listed in the control matrix in Figure 9.4 (page 290) work?

Control Plans for Data Entry with Master Data

Our next set of input controls are those that may be applied when we have access to master data during the input process. The availability of such data can greatly enhance the control, and efficiencies, that be gained in the data entry process. For example, let's say that we are entering orders from our customers. If we have available to us data entry programs such as those depicted in Figure 9.3, we can check to see if the customer number is in the range of valid numbers (i.e., a *limit check*) or has been entered without error (e.g., *check digit verification*). But, these edits determine only that the customer number *might* be correct or incorrect. If we have available the actual customer master data, we can use the customer number to call up the stored customer master data and determine if the customer number has been entered correctly, if the customer exists, the customer's correct address, and so forth.

While access to master data may facilitate and control the data entry process, access to master data needs to be controlled. For example, when we allow customers or other users to communicate with us over the Web, we need to be extra cautious in protecting access to stored data. Technology Excerpt 9.1 provides some control guidelines to protect against unauthorized Internet-enabled access to stored data.

The next section describes some *additional* controls that become available when the master data is available during data entry.

[Insert Technology Excerpt 9.1 box here]

[Insert Top Ten box here]

System Description and Flowchart

Figure 9.5 (page 296)depicts another hypothetical system. As with Figure 9.3, we make some assumptions. First, we have event data entering the system from a *remote* location because communications with a data entry system may be from sites away from the computer center. For instance, an existing customer might enter an order through a Web site. Second, we show that the events are typed into the system without using a source document. Naturally, source documents could be used such as they were in Figure 9.3.

[Insert Figure 9.5 here]

Note that this system, unlike the one in Figure 9.3, validates input by reference to master data. Normally, if a user enters *valid data* such as a valid customer code, the system automatically retrieves certain *standing master data* such as the customer name and address. Having edited the input, the computer displays a message to the user indicating that the input either is acceptable or contains errors. If errors exist, the user may be able to correct them immediately. Once users have made any necessary corrections, they type in a code or click the mouse button to instruct the system to accept the input. As it did in Figure 9.3, that action triggers the computer to record simultaneously the input and inform the user that the input data has been accepted.

As with Figure 9.3, our flowchart stops at this point *without* depicting the update of any master data. Certainly our system could continue with such a process. We have not shown it here so that we can concentrate on the *input* controls.

Applying the Control Framework

In this section, we apply the control framework to the generic system described above. Figure 9.6 presents a completed control matrix for the systems flowchart shown in Figure 9.5.

[Insert Figure 9.6 here]

This matrix shows format and assumptions similar to those made in Figure 9.4. The recommended control plans listed in the first column in Figure 9.6 are representative of those commonly associated with controlling the data entry process when master data is available. Most of the control plans described with Figures 9.3 and 9.4 may also be applicable. But, for simplicity, we will not repeat them here.

In this section, we first see in general terms how several of the control plans work.[3] Then, Exhibit 9.3 (page 299) describes each of the cell entries in the control matrix. As you study the control plans, be sure to track where they are located on the systems flowchart.

[3] Ibid.

[Insert Exhibit 9.3 here]

P-1: *Enter data close to the originating source.* This is a strategy for capture and entry of event-related data close to the place (and probably time) that an event occurs. *Online transaction entry (OLTE), online real-time processing (OLRT),* and *online transaction processing (OLTP)* are all examples of this processing strategy. When this strategy is employed, databases are more current and subsequent events can occur in a more timely manner. Because data are not transported to a data entry location, there is less of a chance that inputs will be lost (*input completeness*). The input can be more accurate because the data entry person may be in a position to recognize and immediately correct input errors (*input accuracy*). Finally, some *efficiencies* can be gained by reducing the number of entities handling the event data.

P-2: *Digital signatures.* Whenever data are entered from remote locations via telecommunications channels like the Internet, there is the risk that the communication may have been sent by an unauthorized system user or may have been intercepted/modified in transit. To guard against such risks, many organizations employ **digital signatures** to *authenticate* the user's identity and to verify the integrity of the message being transmitted. To learn more about how digital signatures work, see Appendix 9A (pages 309 through 313), and Technology Application 9.1 (page 312).

P-3: *Populate inputs with master data.* Numeric, alphabetic, and other designators are usually assigned to entities such as customers, vendors, and employees. When we **populate inputs with master data**, the user merely enters an entity's identification code and the system retrieves certain data about that entity from existing master data. For example, the user might be prompted to enter the customer ID (code). Then, the system automatically provides information from the customer master data, such as the customer's name and address, preferred shipping method, and sales terms. Fewer keystrokes are required, making data entry quicker, more accurate, and more efficient. To ensure that system users have not made a mistake keying the code itself, they compare data provided by the system with that used for input. Finally, the entry cannot proceed without valid (authorized) master data that includes such items as terms and credit limits that were previously recorded via a *data maintenance* process.

P-4: *Compare input data with master data.* A data entry program can be designed to compare the input data to data that have been previously recorded. When we **compare input data with master data** we can determine the accuracy and validity of the input data. Here are just two types of comparisons that can be made:

1 **Input/master data dependency checks.** These edits test whether the contents of two or more data elements or fields on an event description bear the correct logical relationship. For example, input sales events can be tested to determine whether

the person entering the data is listed as an employee of that customer. If these two items don't match, there is some evidence that the customer number or the salesperson identification was input erroneously.

2 **Input/master data validity and accuracy checks.** These edits test whether master data supports the validity and accuracy of the input. For example, this edit might prevent the input of a shipment when there is no record of a corresponding customer order. If there is no match, we may have input some data incorrectly, or the shipment might simply be invalid. We might also compare elements *within* the input and master data. For example, we can compare the quantities to be shipped to the quantities ordered. Quantities that do not match may have been picked from the shelf or entered into the computer incorrectly.

Review Question

How does each control plan listed in the control matrix in Figure 9.6 (page 297) work?

Explanation of control matrix cell entries. Armed with an understanding of the mechanics of certain control plans, let's now turn our attention to Exhibit 9.3—Explanation of Cell Entries for Control Matrix in Figure 9.6. Notice how data entry by the customer affects these controls. See whether you understand the relationship between each plan and the goal(s) that it addresses. Remember that your ability to *explain* the relationships between plans and goals is most important.

Controls Plans for Data Entry with Batches

This section, as did the preceding two, presents a hypothetical system. This next flowchart, however, uses the example of a shipping and billing process to illustrate certain points. The distinguishing control-related feature in this system is that it processes event data in batches.

System Description and Flowchart

Figure 9.7 shows the systems flowchart for our hypothetical batch processing system. Again, please ignore the control annotations, P-1, P-2, and so forth, until we discuss them in the next subsection.

[Insert Figure 9.7 here]

Processing begins in the first column of the flowchart with picking tickets that have been received in the shipping department from the warehouse. Let's assume that accompanying these picking tickets are goods to be shipped to customers. Upon receipt of the picking tickets, a shipping department employee assembles them into groups or batches. Let's assume that the employee batches the documents in groups of 25 and takes batch totals.

The batch of documents is then scanned onto a disk. As the batch is recorded, the data entry program calculates one or more totals for the batch and displays those batch totals to the shipping clerk. The clerk determines if the displayed totals agree with the ones previously calculated. If they don't, error-correcting routines are performed. This process is repeated throughout the day as picking tickets are received in the shipping department.

Periodically, the file containing the shipment data is sent to the computer for processing by the shipment programs(s). This program records the sales event data and updates the accounts receivable master data to reflect a new sale. Invoices are printed and sent to the customer. Packing slips are printed and sent to the shipping department where they are matched with the picking ticket before the goods are sent to the customer. "Further processing" includes packing and shipping the goods.

One of the system outputs is usually an **exception and summary report**. This report reflects the events—either in detail, summary total, or both—that were accepted by the system, and those that were rejected by the system. Even though the keyed input was edited and validated, some data still could be rejected at the update stage of processing. In our system the totals on this report are compared to the input batch totals.

Review Question

In examining the systems flowchart in Figure 9.7, how would you discern from the symbols used (or perhaps the lack of certain other symbols) that the system (a) employs online data entry; (b) uses data communications technology; (c) processes events individually, rather than in groups of similar events; and (d) updates master data continuously?

Applying the Control Framework

In this section, we apply the control framework to the generic batch processing system described above. Figure 9.8 (page 302) presents a completed control matrix for the systems flowchart shown in Figure 9.7. Figure 9.7 has been annotated to show the location of recommended control plans that exist in the system (codes P-1, P2, . . . P-5). We also have some control plans that we *assume* are missing (codes M-1, M-2) because the narrative system description did not mention them specifically. In Figures 9.4 and 9.6, we could not complete certain parts of the top of the control matrix. However, for this example, we have assumed that we know the nature of the input (i.e., picking tickets), we know the resources that are to be protected (i.e., the inventory and the accounts receivable master data), and we know the data that are to be updated (i.e., the AR master data). Therefore, we have completed these elements in Figure 9.8.

[Insert Figure 9.8 here]

This section discusses each of the recommended control plans listed in the first column of the matrix, describing how the plans work.[4] Exhibit 9.4 explains the cell entries appearing in the control matrix. Be sure to trace each plan to the flowchart location where it is implemented (or could be implemented in the case of a missing plan).

[4] Ibid.

Before we start, let's explain what we mean by *batch controls*.[5] **Batch control plans** regulate information processing by calculating control totals at various points in a processing run and subsequently comparing these totals. When the various batch totals fail to agree, evidence exists that an event description(s) may have been lost (completeness problem), added (validity problem), or changed (accuracy problem). Once established, batch totals can be reconciled manually or the computer can reconcile them. In general, for batch control plans to be effective, they should ensure that:

[5] These batch controls apply to groups of documents. The *document/record hash totals* introduced earlier in the chapter apply to individual documents.

- *All* documents are batched; in other words, the batch totals should be established close to the time that the source documents are created or are received from external entities.
- *All* batches are submitted for processing; batch transmittals and batch logs are useful in protecting against the loss of entire batches.

- *All* batches are accepted by the computer; the user should be instrumental in performing this checking.
- *All* differences disclosed by reconciliations are investigated and corrected on a timely basis.

Batch control procedures must begin by grouping event data and then calculating a control total(s) for the group. For example, Figure 9.7 shows the shipping department employee preparing batch totals for the picking tickets documents to be scanned.

Several different types of batch control totals can be calculated, as discussed in the following paragraphs. You will note in the following discussion that certain types of batch totals are better than others in addressing the information process control goals of input validity, input completeness, and input accuracy.

Document/record counts are simple counts of the number of documents entered (e.g., 25 documents in a batch). This procedure represents the minimum level required to control input completeness. It is not sufficient if more than one event description can appear on a document. Also, because one document could be intentionally replaced with another, this control is not very effective for ensuring input *validity* and says nothing about input *accuracy*.

Item or line counts are counts of the number of items or lines of data entered, such as a count of the number of invoices being paid by all of the customer remittances. By reducing the possibility that line items or entire documents could be added to the batch or not be input, this control improves input *validity*, *completeness*, and *accuracy*. Remember, a missing event record is a *completeness* error and a data set missing from an event record is an *accuracy* error.

Dollar totals are a summation of the dollar value of items in the batch, such as the total dollar value of all remittance advices in a batch. By reducing the possibility that entire documents could be added to or lost from the batch or that dollar amounts were incorrectly input, this control improves input *validity*, *completeness*, and *accuracy*.

Hash totals are a summation of any numeric data existing for all documents in the batch, such as a total of customer numbers or invoice numbers in the case of remittance advices. Unlike dollar totals, hash totals normally serve no purpose other than control. Hash totals can be a powerful batch control because they can be used to determine if inputs have been altered, added, or deleted. These *batch* hash totals operate for a batch in a manner similar to the operation of *document/record hash totals* for individual inputs.

Review Question

Name and explain three different types of batch totals that could be calculated in a batch processing system.

Now we proceed with an explanation of the controls plans in Figures 9.7 and 9.8.

P-1: *Turnaround documents.* **Turnaround documents** are printed by the computer and are used to capture and input a *subsequent* event. Picking tickets, inventory count sheets, remittance advice stubs attached to customer invoices, and payroll time cards are all examples of turnaround documents. For example, we have seen picking tickets that are printed by computer, are used to pick the goods, and are sent to shipping. The bar code on the picking ticket is scanned to trigger recording of the shipment. When the bar code is scanned the items and quantities that *should* have been picked are displayed. If the items and quantities are correct, the shipping clerk need only click one key to record the shipment.

P-2: *Manual agreement of batch totals.* The manual agreement of batch totals control plan operates in the following manner:

- First, one or more of the batch totals are established manually (i.e., in the shipping department in Figure 9.7).
- As individual event descriptions are entered (or scanned), the data entry program accumulates independent batch totals.
- The computer produces reports (or displays) at the end of either the input process or update process, or both. The report (or display) includes the relevant control totals that must be

manually reconciled to the totals established prior to the particular process.

- The person who reconciles the batch total (see the shipping department employee in Figure 9.7) must determine why the totals do not agree and make corrections as necessary to ensure the integrity of the input data.

M-1: *Computer agreement of batch totals.* This control plan does not exist in Figure 9.7 and therefore is shown as a missing plan. Note in Figure 9.7 where we have placed the M-1 annotation. The computer agreement of batch totals plan is pictured in Figure 9.9 and works in the following manner:

[Insert Figure 9.9 here]

- First, one or more of the batch totals are established manually (i.e., in the user department in Figure 9.9).
- Then, the manually prepared total is entered into the computer and is recorded on the computer as batch control totals data.
- As individual event descriptions are entered, a computer program accumulates independent batch totals and compares these totals to the ones prepared manually and entered at the start of the processing.
- The computer then prepares a report, which usually contains details of each batch, together with an indication of whether the

totals agreed or disagreed. Batches that do not balance are normally rejected, and discrepancies are manually investigated. Such an analysis would be included in a report similar to the "Error and summary report" in Figures 9.7 and 9.9.

M-2: *Sequence checks*. Whenever documents are numbered sequentially—either assigned a number when the document is prepared or prepared using **prenumbered documents**—a sequence check can be applied to those documents. One of two kinds of sequence checks may be used—either a batch sequence check or a cumulative sequence check.

In a **batch sequence check**, the event data within a batch are checked as follows:

1. The range of serial numbers constituting the batch is entered.
2. Each individual, serially prenumbered event is entered.
3. The computer program sorts the event data into numerical order, checks the documents against the sequence number range, and reports missing, duplicate, and out-of-range event data.

Batch sequence checks work best when we can control the input process and the serial numbers of the input data. For example, this control would not work for entering customer orders that had a variety of numbers assigned by many customers.

A slight variation on the batch sequence check is the cumulative sequence check. The **cumulative sequence check** provides input control in those situations in which the serial numbers are assigned within the organization (e.g., sales order numbers issued by the sales order department) but later are not entered in perfect serial number sequence (i.e., picking tickets might contain broken sets of numbers). In this case, the matching of individual event data (picking ticket) numbers is made to a file that contains *all* document numbers (all sales order numbers). *Periodically,* reports of missing numbers are produced for manual follow-up.

Reconciling a checkbook is an example of a situation in which numbers (the check numbers) are issued in sequence. But when we receive a bank statement, the batch may not contain a complete sequence of checks. Our check register assists us in performing a cumulative sequence check to make sure that all checks are eventually accounted for.

P-3: *Agreement of run-to-run totals.* This is a variation of the agreement of batch totals controls. With this control, totals prepared before a computer process are compared, manually or by the computer, to totals prepared after the computer process. The controls after a process are often found on an *error and summary report.* When totals agree, we have evidence that the input *and* the update took place correctly. This control is especially useful when there are several intermediate steps between the beginning and the end of the process and we want to be assured of the integrity of each process.

P-4: *Tickler files.* A **tickler file** is a file that is reviewed on a regular basis for the purpose of taking action to clear items from that file. In Figure 9.7, we see a file of picking tickets representing items that should be shipped. Should these documents remain in this file for an extended period of time, we would fail to make the shipments or to make them in a timely manner. Tickler files may also be computer records representing events that need to be completed, such as open sales orders, open purchase orders, and so forth.

P-5: *One-for-one checking.* **One-for-one checking** is the detailed comparison of individual elements of two or more data sources to determine that they agree as appropriate. This control is often used to compare a source document to an output produced later in a process. Differences may indicate errors in input or update. If the output cannot be found for comparison, there is evidence of failure to input or process the event. While this procedure provides us details as to *what* is incorrect within a batch, *agreement of run-to-run* totals will tell us if there is *any* error *within* a batch. One-for-one checking is expensive and should be reserved for low-volume, high-value events.

Review Question

How does each control plan listed in the control matrix in Figure 9.8

(page 302) work?

Having examined what each of the recommended control plans means and how each operates, we can now look at how the plans meet the control goals. Exhibit 9.4 explains the relationship between each control plan and each control goal that it helps to achieve. As you study Exhibit 9.4, we again urge you to concentrate your energies on understanding these relationships.

[Insert Exhibit 9.4 here]

Conclusions

In this chapter, we began our study of process control plans, the third level in the control hierarchy (shown in Figure 8.2 on page 256). Our study of process control plans will continue in Chapters 10–14, where we will apply the control framework and explore controls that are unique to each business process.

Before we leave, let's address one more aspect of process controls. Many of these controls attempt to detect data that *may* be in error. For example, a reasonableness test may reject a price change that is beyond a normal limit. But, it may be that the price change has been authorized and correctly entered. As another example, perhaps a customer order is rejected because it does not pass the credit check. But, it might be that it is in the best interest of the company to permit the sale anyway. In these cases, we need to be able to *override* the control and permit the event to process. If our control system is to remain effective, these overrides must be used sparingly and require a *password* or key and signature be necessary to effect the override. Finally, a record of all overrides should be periodically reviewed to determine that the override authority is not being abused.

Appendix 9A

Data Encryption and Public-Key Cryptography

Data encryption is a process that employs mathematical algorithms and encryption "keys" to change data from plain text to a coded text form so that it is unintelligible and therefore useless to those who should not have access to it. Encryption is useful to preserve the data's privacy and confidentiality. For example, people are asking for and obtaining security of their Internet transmissions through cryptography. Technology Application 9.1 (at the end of this Appendix) describes three methods for conducting secure electronic commerce on the Internet using data encryption and public-key cryptography.

One of the earliest and most elementary uses of encryption dates back to the first century B.C. During the Gallic Wars, Julius Caesar encoded his messages by shifting the alphabet three letters forward so that an A became a D, an X became an A, and so on. For instance, if the message is NED IS A NERD—called *plaintext* in cryptography lingo—the *ciphertext* would appear as QHG LV D QHUG. The *Caesar cipher*—an example of a simple one-for-one letter substitution system—in effect used a *key* of 3 and an encrypting *algorithm* of addition. We see examples of this type of encryption in the cryptograms or cryptoquotes that are published in the puzzle pages of our daily newspapers.

With the use of more complex *algorithms* and encryption *keys*, coding a message can be made much more powerful than in the preceding example. Figure 9.10 contains an illustration of how the message NED IS A NERD could be made more difficult to decode. Keep in mind, however, that the figure also is a very basic, rudimentary example intended to convey the bare-bones mechanics of how encryption works. In practice, the algorithms and keys are much more sophisticated; so much so that good encryption schemes are virtually impossible to break.

[Insert Figure 9.10 here]

As shown in Figure 9.10, the crux of conventional encryption procedures is the *single key* used both by the sender to encrypt the message and by the receiver to decrypt it. A major drawback to such systems is that the key itself has to be transmitted by secure channels. If the key is not kept secret, the security of the entire system is compromised. *Public-key cryptography* helps to solve this problem by employing a *pair* of matched keys for each system user, one private (i.e., known only to the party who possesses it) and one public. The public key corresponds to—but is not the same as—the user's private key. As its name implies, the public key is assumed to be public knowledge and even could be published in a directory, in much the same way as a person's telephone number.

Figure 9.11 illustrates how public-key cryptography is used both to encrypt messages (part (a) of the figure) and to *authenticate* a message by appending a digital signature to it (part (b) of the figure). Please note that although we show both parts (a) and (b) being executed, in practice the parts are separable. That is, a message could be encrypted as shown in part (a) without having a *digital signature* added to it. Digital signatures enhance security by ensuring that the "signature" cannot be forged (i.e., that the message comes from an authorized source) and that the message has not been changed in any way in transmission.

[Insert Figure 9.11 here]

Note that Sally Sender and Ray Receiver each have a *pair* of keys. In part (a), Ray's *public* key is used to encrypt *all* messages sent to him. Privacy of the messages is ensured because only Ray's *private* key can decrypt the messages. The messages *cannot* be decoded using Ray's public key. Furthermore, the private decryption key never has to be transmitted; it is always in Ray's exclusive possession.

In part (b), Sally first uses a hashing function to translate the plaintext message into a binary number. Any message *other* than NED IS A NERD would not "hash" into the number, 11010010. By then using her *private* key to encrypt the binary number, Sally, in effect, has digitally "signed" the message. On the right side of part (b), Ray Receiver employs Sally's *public* key to decrypt her "signature." Since no public key except Sally's will work, Ray knows that the message comes from her. Note that *anyone* could use Sally's public key to decode her signature, but that is not important. The object is not to keep the signature secret or private but, rather, to *authenticate* that it was Sally—and *only* she—who "signed" the message.

To ensure the *integrity of the message* (received in part (a) of the figure), Ray

- runs the decrypted message, NED IS A NERD, through an encoding scheme called a hashing function—the same hashing function used by Sally—and
- compares the decoded digital signature (11010010) with the hashed output of the message *received* (11010010). If the two numbers don't agree, Ray knows that the message is not the same as the one Sally sent. For example, assume that Ted Tamperer was able to intercept Sally's encrypted message in part (a) and change it so that when Ray decoded it, he read NED IS A

NICE GUY. This message would *not* hash into the number 11010010; therefore, it would not match the decrypted digital signature from Sally.

Some experts predict that digital signatures will soon pave the way for a truly cashless society, talked about for years. The digital signatures will be used to create electronic cash, checks, and other forms of payment that can be used in electronic commerce (see Technology Application 9.1 on page 312 for examples). Others foresee digital signatures replacing handwritten ones on a multitude of business and legal documents, such as purchase orders, checks, court documents, and tax returns. The “E-sign”law, passed by Congress in June 2000, makes contracts “signed” by electronic methods legally valid in all 50 states. This law is accelerating the rate of growth of business-to-business (B2B) e-business by allowing companies to execute documents online immediately.[6] (Review Technology Excerpt 8.4 for more on E-sign and digital signatures.)

[6] Mitch Betts, “Digital Signatures Law to Speed Online B-to-B Deals,” *Computerworld* (June 26, 2000): 8.

[Insert Technology Application 9.1 box here]

For public-key cryptography to be effective, the *private* keys must be kept *private*. To do that we can employ a variety of techniques, some of which were introduced in Chapter 8. For example, the private key might be kept within a protected computer or device such as a *smartcard*, or *cryptographic box*. Access to the device, and to the private key, must then be protected with *passwords* or other *authentication* procedures. One such procedure involves the use of a thumbprint reader attached to the computer. With this device users must put their thumb onto the reader before the private key can be used to "sign" a message. The thumbprint reader is an example of the *biometric* devices introduced in Chapter 8.

Review Question

Distinguish among data encryption, public-key cryptography, and digital signatures.

REVIEW QUESTIONS

RQ9-1 Explain the difference between the category of process control plans covered in this chapter and the process controls to be covered in Chapters 10 through 14.

RQ9-2

a. Describe the relationship between the *control matrix* and the *control framework*.

b. What are the four basic elements included in a control matrix?

c. Describe the relationship between the *control matrix* and the *systems flowchart*. What does it mean to "annotate" the systems flowchart?

d. What are the five steps involved in preparing a control matrix?

RQ9-3 Explain how a manager would use the control matrix in performing step 4 of the control framework.

a. How could the matrix be used to recommend changes in the system in order to improve control of that system?

b. How would the matrix be useful in evaluating control *effectiveness*, control *efficiency*, and control *redundancy*? Include in your answer a definition of these three terms.

RQ9-4 What are two common *programmed edit checks*? Describe each check.

RQ9-5 How does each control plan listed in the control matrix in Figure 9.4 (page 290) work?

RQ9-6 How does each control plan listed in the control matrix in Figure 9.6 (page 297) work?

RQ9-7 In examining the systems flowchart in Figure 9.7 (page 301), how would you discern from the symbols used (or perhaps the lack of certain other symbols) that the system (a) employs online data entry; (b) uses data communications technology; (c) processes events individually, rather than in groups of similar events; and (d) updates master data continuously?

RQ9-8 Name and explain three different types of batch totals that could be calculated in a batch processing system.

RQ9-9 How does each control plan listed in the control matrix in Figure 9.8

(page 302) work?

RQ9-10 (Appendix 9A) Distinguish among data encryption, public-key cryptography, and digital signatures.

DISCUSSION QUESTIONS

DQ9-1 Discuss why the control matrix is custom-tailored for each process.

DQ9-2 Explain why input controls are so important for controlling an online system.

DQ9-3 Review the controls included in the Visa Top Ten and Best Practice Lists in Technology Excerpt 9.1 on page 294. Classify each item in the two lists according to the following categories:

a. Preventive, detective, or corrective controls.

b. Control environment, pervasive controls, or process controls.

DQ9-4 "The mere fact that event data appear on a prenumbered document is no proof of the validity of the event. Someone intent on defrauding a system, by introducing a fictitious event, probably would be clever enough to get access to the prenumbered documents or would replicate those documents so as to make the event appear genuine."

a. Assume for a moment that the comment is true. Present (and explain) a "statement of relationship" between the intended control plan of using prenumbered documents and the information process control goal of event "validity."

b. Do you agree with this comment? Why or why not?

DQ9-5 Describe a situation in your daily activities, working or not, where you have experienced or employed controls described in this chapter.

DQ9-6 When we record our exams into the spreadsheet used for our gradebook, we employ the following procedures:

a. For each exam, manually add up the grade for each exam and record on the front page.

b. Manually calculate the average grade for all of the exams.

c. Input the score for each part of each exam into the spreadsheet.

d. Compare the exam total on the front page of the exam to the total prepared by the computer.

e. After all the exams have been entered, compare the average grade calculated by the computer with that calculated manually.

Describe how this process employs controls introduced in this chapter.

DQ9-7 "My top management is demanding Web access to reports that would contain very sensitive data. They want to be able to call them up while they travel to get up-to-the-minute information about the company. Our auditors advise us not to make this data available over the Web because of security concerns. But if top management doesn't get what they want, I may lose my job! What can I do?" What would you advise this manager to do?

PROBLEMS

P9-1 You worked with the Causeway Company cash receipts system in Chapter 2. The narrative of that system and its systems flowchart are reproduced in Exhibit 9.5 and Figure 9.12, respectively.

[Insert Exhibit 9.5 here]

[Insert Figure 9.12 here]

Using Exhibit 9.5 and Figure 9.12, do the following:

a. Prepare a control matrix, including explanations of how each recommended existing control plan helps to accomplish—or would accomplish in the case of missing plans—each related control goal. Your choice of recommended control plans should come from Exhibits 9.2, 9.3, or 9.4 as appropriate. Be sure to tailor the matrix columns to conform to the specifics of the Causeway system. In doing so, assume the following two operations process goals only:

   - To deposit cash receipts on the same day received.
   - To ensure that customer balances in the accounts receivable master data reflect account activity on a timely basis.

b. Annotate the systems flowchart in Figure 9.12 to show the location of each control plan you listed in the control matrix.

P9-2 The following narrative describes the processing of customer mail orders at Phoenix Company.

Gelinas 9-50

Phoenix Company is a small manufacturing operation engaged in the selling of widgets. Customer mail orders are received in the sales order department, where sales order clerks open the orders and review them for accuracy. The clerks enter each order into the computer, where they are edited by comparing them to customer master data (stored on a disk). The computer displays the edited order on the clerk's screen. The clerk reviews and accepts the order. The order is then added to the sales event data (stored on a disk) and updates the sales order master data (also stored on a disk). As the order is recorded, it is printed on a printer in the warehouse (the picking ticket). A copy of the sales order is also printed in the sales order department and is sent to the customer (a customer acknowledgment).

(Complete only those requirements specified by your instructor)

a. Prepare a table of entities and activities.

b. Draw a context diagram.

c. Draw a physical data flow diagram (DFD).

d. Indicate on the table of entities and activities prepared for part a, the groupings, bubble numbers, and titles to be used in preparing a level 0 logical DFD.

e. Draw a level 0 logical DFD.

f. Draw a systems flowchart.

g. Prepare a control matrix, including explanations of how each recommended existing control plan helps to accomplish—or would accomplish in the case of missing plans—each related control goal. Your choice of recommended control plans should come from Exhibits 9.2, 9.3, or 9.4 as appropriate. Be sure to tailor the matrix columns to conform to the specifics of the Phoenix Company system. In doing so, assume the following two operations process goals only:

- To provide timely acknowledgment of customer orders.
- To provide timely shipment of goods to customers.

h. Annotate the systems flowchart prepared in requirement f to show the location of each control plan listed in the control matrix.

P9-3 The following is a list of 14 control plans from this chapter:

Control Plans

A. Populate inputs with master data

B. Online prompting

C. Interactive feedback checks

D. Programmed edit checks

E. Manual agreement of batch totals

F. Batch sequence check

G. Cumulative sequence check

H. Document design

I. Key verification

J. Written approvals

K. Procedures for rejected inputs

L. Compare input data with master data

M. Turnaround documents

N. Digital signatures

Listed below are 10 system failures that have control implications. On your solution sheet, list the numbers 1 through 10. Next to each number, insert the capital letter from the list above for the best control plan to *prevent* the system failure from occurring. (If you can't find a control that will prevent the failure, then choose a *detective* plan or, as a last resort, a *corrective* control plan.) A letter should be used only once, with four letters left over.

System Failures

1. At Datatech Inc., data entry clerks receive a variety of documents from many departments throughout the company. In some cases, unauthorized inputs are keyed and entered into the computer.

2. Data entry clerks at the Visitron Company use networked PCs

to enter data into the computer. Recently, a number of errors have been found in key numeric fields. The supervisor would like to implement a control to reduce the transcription errors being made by the clerks.

3. Purchase orders are prepared online by purchasing clerks. Recently, the purchasing manager discovered that many purchase orders are being sent to the wrong vendor, for the wrong items, and for quantities far greater than would normally be requested.

4. The tellers at Bucks Bank have been having difficulty reconciling their cash drawers. All customer events are entered online at a teller terminal. At the end of the shift, the computer prints a list of the events that have occurred during the shift. The tellers must then review the list to determine that their drawer contains checks, cash, and other documents to support each entry on the list.

5. At Helm Inc., clerks in the accounting offices of Helm's three divisions prepare prenumbered general ledger voucher documents. Once prepared, the vouchers are given to each office's data entry clerk, who keys them into an online terminal. Then, the computer records whatever general ledger adjustment was indicated by the voucher. The controller has found that several vouchers were never recorded, and some vouchers were

recorded twice.

6. At the Baltimore Company, clerks in the cash applications area of the accounts receivable office open mail containing checks from customers. They prepare a remittance advice (RA) containing the customer number, invoice numbers, amount owed, amount paid, and check number. Once prepared, the RAs are sent to a clerk who keys them into an online computer terminal. The accounts receivable manager has been complaining that the RA entry process is slow and error-prone.

7. Occasionally, the order entry system at Dorsam Inc. fails to record a customer order. After failing to receive an acknowledgment, the customer will call to inquire. Inevitably, the sales clerk will find the customer's order filed with other customer orders that had been entered into the computer. In each case, all indications are that the order had been entered.

8. The Stoughton Company enters shipping notices in batches. Upon entry, the computer performs certain edits to eliminate those notices that have errors. As a result, many actual shipments never get recorded.

9. A computer hacker gained access to the computer system of Big Bucks Bank and entered an event to transfer funds to his bank account in Switzerland.

10. Refer to the vignette at the beginning of the chapter. It describes a botched securities trade caused by a clerk's mistakenly entering the dollar amount of a trade into the box on the computer screen reserved for the number of shares to be sold, and then transmitting the incorrect trade to the stock exchange's computer.

P9-4 The following is a list of 12 controls from Chapter 9:

Controls

A. Turnaround documents

B. Tickler files

C. Public-key cryptography

D. One-for-one checking

E. Batch sequence check

F. Document/record counts

G. Written approvals

H. Hash totals (for a batch)

I. Limit checks

J. Procedures for rejected inputs

K. Digital signatures

L. Interactive feedback checks

Gelinas 9-56

Listed below are 10 definitions or descriptions. List the numbers 1 through 10 on your solution sheet. Next to each number, insert the capital letter from the list above for the term that *best* matches the definition. A letter should be used only once, with two letters left over.

Definitions or Descriptions

1. Ensures that transmitted messages can only be read by authorized receivers.

2. A control plan that cannot be implemented unless source documents are prenumbered.

3. In systems where accountable documents are not used, this control plan helps assure input completeness by informing the data entry person that events have been accepted by the computer system.

4. Used to determine that a message has not been altered and has actually been sent by the person claiming to have sent the message.

5. A *process control* plan that implements the *pervasive* control (see Chapter 8) of general or specific authorization.

6. Data related to open sales orders is periodically reviewed to ensure the timely shipment of goods.

7. Used to detect changes in batches of events to ensure the

validity, completeness, and accuracy of the batch.

8. Sales orders are compared to packing slips and the goods to determine that what was ordered is what is about to be shipped.

9. A system output becomes an input source in a *subsequent* event.

10. A type of programmed edit that is synonymous with a reasonableness test.

P9-5 The following is a description of seven control/technology descriptions and a list of seven control/technology names.

Control/Technology Descriptions	Control/Technology Names
A. When you type a customer code into the enterprise system the matching master data is called up to the screen.	1. Firewall
B. All enterprise systems can be programmed to consider a number of pieces of stored data and real-time calculations as business event data are being entered into the system.	2. Preformatted screens
C. Access to the company network from the Internet is through a server on which there are programs to monitor the traffic, coming and going.	3. Compare input data with master data, programmed edits, customer credit check
D. Workflow software within enterprise systems can be used to route business events to those who must work on the business event data, or approve the business event before it is finalized.	4. Populate inputs with master data
E. A standard practice at most firms is to develop profiles for each employee to grant them access to the appropriate computer resources.	5. Program change controls

F. To make changes to production programs, a copy of the program is moved successively through "development," "testing," and "staging," before the modified program is moved into production.	6. Approvals, such as POs
G. Enterprise system software can be configured to require that certain fields be completed on an input screen before being allowed to move on to the next screen.	7. Security module

Listed below are five potential risks or systems failures that can be addressed with a control or a technology from the lists above.

A. On the blank line to the left of each number (the "Description" column), insert the capital letter from the list above for the control/technology that *best* addresses the risk. A letter should be used only once, with two letters left over.

B. In the column titled "Explanation," provide an explanation of why you selected that control/technology description. You need to specifically describe how the control/technology addresses the risk.

C. In the right column (titled "Name") insert the number from the list above corresponding to the control/technology name for the answer provided in part A.

DESCRIPTION	POTENTIAL RISKS	EXPLANATION	NAME
	a. A computer		

Gelinas 9-59

	programmer altered the order entry programs so that the creditchecking routine was bypassed for one of the customers, a company owned by his uncle.		
	b. A hacker accessed the Web site at Dorothy's Gifts & Flowers and changed some of the graphics. Several customers, confused by the graphics, took their business elsewhere.		
	c. Roxy's Retailing maintains an extensive and valuable repository of information about its customers. Tricky Nick was fired from Roxy's and now works at a competing firm. Last night Nick dialed into the Roxy computer system and downloaded some valuable customer data to his own computer.		
	d. Cash application clerks at the Blanford Company have been posting payments to the incorrect customer accounts because the customer account numbers are		

	being keyed in incorrectly.		
	e. At Natick Company, customers who are four months late in making payments to their accounts are still able to have their orders accepted and goods shipped to them.		

BOXES

[Start Technology Excerpt 9.1 box here]

Technology Excerpt 9.1

Protecting Against Credit Card Fraud

Many people are reluctant to give their credit card number over the Web because they are afraid of credit card fraud. In one sense this fear is justified, because credit card fraud is estimated to be 12 times higher for online purchases than for offline merchants, according to a recent survey by the Gartner Group. However, in either case, the holder of the card is not responsible for the fraud. In the case of face-to-face transactions, the credit card companies usually absorb the bill, but online merchants are held responsible when stolen credit card numbers are used.

Visa is beginning to require its merchants to employ a series of online controls in order to better guard its cardholders' information. Merchants, gateways, and Internet service providers will be required to comply with Visa's broad online security program, or face fines, sales restrictions or loss of membership. The program, summarized in the list below, is taken from Visa's Web site.

[End Technology Excerpt 9.1 box here]

[Start Top Ten box here]

Top Ten List

At the most basic level, the program consists of a "Top Ten" list of requirements plus several "best practices" for protecting Visa cardholder information. The Top Ten requirements include the following:

1. Install and maintain a working network firewall to protect data accessible via the Internet.
2. Keep security patches up to date.
3. Encrypt stored data accessible from the Internet.
4. Encrypt data sent across networks.
5. Use and regularly update anti-virus software.
6. Restrict access to data by business' "need to know."
7. Assign unique IDs to each person with computer access to data.
8. Track access to data by unique ID.
9. Don't use vendor-supplied defaults for system passwords and other security parameters.
10. Regularly test security systems and processes.

In addition, Visa recommends the following three "best practices":

1. Screen employees with access to data to limit the "inside job."
2. Don't leave papers/diskettes/computers with data unsecured.
3. Destroy data when it's no longer needed for business reasons.

These top level principles apply to all entities participating in the Visa payment system that process or store cardholder information and have access to it through the Internet or mail-order/telephone-order.

Source: Maria Trombley, "Visa Issues 10 'Commandments' for Online Merchants," *Computerworld*, August 11, 2000. Reprinted with permission from Visa.

[End Top Ten box here]

[Start Technology Application 9.1 box here]

TECHNOLOGY APPLICATION 9.1

Using Data Encryption and Public-Key Cryptography for Electronic Commerce

Data encryption and public-key cryptography are being used to secure business transactions on the Internet. Below are three examples. The first two are in use, and the latter one was piloted until July 2001. The eCheck technology has been applied for online payments by firms such as Xign http://www.xign.com/) and Clareon (http://www.clareon.com). Only SSL is widely used.

Case 1: SSL

The secure sockets layer (SSL) protocol was developed by Netscape Communications Company (now owned by America Online) and uses public key cryptography to secure communications on the Internet. With SSL, a secure session is established during which messages transmitted between two parties are protected via encryption. For example, before a consumer transmits a credit card number to a merchant, the merchant's server establishes a secure session. The merchant decrypts the message, extracts the credit card number, and submits a charge to the consumer's credit card company (i.e., credit card issuing bank) to clear the transaction using traditional means. SSL protects the consumer from interception and unauthorized use of the purchase and credit card information while it is on the Internet (i.e., from the consumer's Web browser to the merchant's Web server). Normally, the merchant cannot authenticate the transmission to determine from whom the message originated and the consumer has only moderate assurance that they have sent their credit card number to a legitimate merchant.

Case 2: SET

The secure electronic transaction (SET) protocol was developed by MasterCard and Visa to secure credit card transactions on the Internet involving three parties: the consumer, the merchant, and one or more credit card issuing banks. With SET, the consumer separately encrypts the purchase message and the credit card number. The merchant decrypts the purchase message to proceed with the sale and submits a charge to the consumer's credit card company (i.e., credit card issuing bank) to clear the transaction using traditional means. However, unlike SSL, SET-based clearing will pass through the merchant and go directly to the consumer's credit card issuing bank. The consumer and the merchant sign their messages with certificates obtained from financial institutions that certify that the consumer holds the credit card in question and that the merchant has a credit card clearing relationship with the issuing bank. SET protects merchants and credit card issuing banks from unauthorized purchases, and consumers from credit card fraud.

Case 3: eCHECK

The electronic check (eCheck) is a payment mechanism developed by the Financial Services Technology Consortium (FSTC). Using public-key cryptography and digital signatures, trading partners and their banks can transmit secure messages and payment information. As with SET, eCheck certificates would be issued by banks certifying that the holder of the certificate has an account at that bank. And, payments would be processed automatically through the existing bank systems. Unlike SET, however, payments would be checks drawn on bank accounts. And, a feature beyond SSL and SET is that the eCheck protocol defines message formats, such as purchase orders, acknowledgments, and invoices, that can be processed automatically by trading parties. eCheck provides protections similar to those obtained with SET. That is, merchants and banks are protected from unauthorized use of checks, and the consumer is protected from check fraud.

Sources: For information about SSL, see, among other sites, the Netscape Web site at http://www.netscape.com/eng/ssl3/, March 18, 2002. For information about SET, see the MasterCard or SETCo (SET Secure Electronic Transaction LLC) Web sites at http://www.mastercardintl.com/newtechnology/set/ and http://www.setco.org/, March 18, 2002. For information about the FSTC electronic check project, see the eCheck Web site at http://echeck.commerce.net/ (March 18, 2002) or Ulric J. Gelinas, Jr. and Janis L. Gogan, "The FSTC Electronic Check Project," *American Institute of Certified Public Accountants Case Development Program*, 1996.

[End Technology Application 9.1 box here]

Part V

Core Business Processes

[Insert UNF-p.323-1 here]

10

The "Order-to-Cash" Process: Part I, Marketing and Sales (M/S)

Companies are putting their primary focus for new technology implementations on improved processes that foster strong customer relationships and systems that improve efficiency and effectiveness in dealing with customer problems. One method of improving customer service is to understand better how a company currently serves customers and then seek ways to improve those processes. Companies improve by ensuring the consistent application of successful processes, asking customers how they can be better served, and eliminating processes that fail to serve customers well.

The Internet provides both challenges and opportunities for improving customer relations. It is easy for a customer to comparison shop or switch to a glitzier vendor when all it takes is a few clicks of the mouse. One company that understands how the Internet can help retain happy customers by effectively marketing products is Ticketmaster Corp., which sells tickets for performances, sporting events, and travel packages over the Web.

This convenient method of electronically purchasing tickets to a Kid Rock concert or an Atlanta Braves baseball game also gives Ticketmaster a chance to cross-sell t-shirts, CDs, hotel bookings, and other related products to the same customers. And not only does Ticketmaster know more about customers who buy, it can collect information also about the unlucky people who don't succeed in purchasing tickets to a sold-out performance. The Web site can suggest other dates, performers, or venues that might appeal to these disappointed folks, or re-contact them when another show is scheduled in their area. "One of the realities about Springsteen is that 200,000 people want to buy tickets when we only have 20,000 seats," said Tom Stockham, Ticketmaster.com's president. "We used to know nothing about 180,000 of those people." Ticketmaster is careful to mine this data in ways that will not alienate their customer base by keeping close tabs on who has access to the data.

Surprisingly, these improvements in customer services are expensive. It costs 20% to 50% more to sell a ticket online than offline. Cross-selling and targeted marketing aid in offsetting these costs by increasing revenue from the same customer base.

Stockham anticipates future enhancements to the Ticketmaster.com marketing plan that will take advantage of the seamless integration of several technologies. He predicts that customers will soon be able to buy seats at a Los Angeles Lakers basketball game, and then pre-order hot dogs and beer online. Fifteen minutes after the tickets are scanned by a bar code reader at the gate, the refreshments will be delivered to the fans' seats. Now if they can only do something about the lines in the rest rooms![1]

[1] Fields, Robin, "Event Ticketers See Online Sales Setting the Stage for New Markets,.latimes.com/business/20000508/t000043365. html, May 8, 2000.

In order to compete effectively, companies must learn to collect, analyze, and feed back customer data. The integrated data within enterprise systems provides a clearer understanding of the current customer base and a company's operational processes. This knowledge can be used to improve internal processes, provide customers with better information about sales, and enable better levels of customer service.

Synopsis

In business process analysis and design, we must carefully consider the business process as a whole—including all the interrelated parts that work toward the common purpose of meeting business process requirements. We follow this model in examining each of the business processes that enable organizations to successfully achieve their organizational goals. Accordingly, Chapters 10 through 14 each explore aspects of business process design, including:

- Process definition and functions
- Organizational setting of the process
- E-business technology used to implement the process
- Enterprise system integration of related information processing activities
- Decision making supported by the process
- Logical process features
- Logical database design
- Physical process features
- Control analysis applied to the process (including an examination of process goals)

This chapter introduces the marketing and sales process, and lays out the important role of this function within an organization. Because the Order-to-Cash process is the first business process we will examine, we consider the above topics in this chapter's discussion of the Marketing and Sales (M/S) portion in some detail.

LEARNING OBJECTIVES

- To describe the business environment for the M/S process
- To analyze the effect of enterprise systems and other technologies commonly used in traditional implementations for the M/S process
- To analyze how the integration provided by enterprise systems and e-business add-ons can improve effectiveness and efficiency of the M/S process
- To describe the logical and physical characteristics of the M/S process and its support of management decision-making
- To describe and analyze controls typically associated with the M/S process

Introduction

Before we look at the details of the M/S process and how it functions, let's set the stage for our study by picturing again how this process relates to other processes in a company. Figure 10.1 depicts the business events that combine to form the Order-to-Cash process.

[Insert Figure 10.1 here]

You can see from Figure 10.1 that the M/S process triggers the revenue collection portion of the Order-to-Cash process and shares data with the purchasing and manufacturing processes (Chapters 12 and 13) but does not interact *directly* with the general ledger in the business reporting process (Chapter 14). When M/S prepares a sales order, it works with the inventory process so that the products can be sent to the customer. Later, when the goods are shipped, M/S informs the revenue collection process of the shipment so a bill can be sent. These interfaces are examined in detail later in this chapter.

The operational aspects of the M/S process are critical to the success—in fact, the very survival—of businesses today and in the future. Indeed, many organizations focus the bulk of their strategic Information Systems investment on supporting M/S process effectiveness. That is why later sections of the chapter discuss the vital topics of decision making, satisfying customer needs, and employing technology to gain competitive advantage.

Process Definition and Functions

The **marketing and sales (M/S) process** is an interacting structure of people, equipment, methods, and controls designed to achieve certain goals. The primary function of the M/S process is to support:

1. Repetitive work routines of the sales order department, the credit department, the warehouse, and the shipping department.[2]

[2] To focus our discussion, we have assumed that these departments are the primary ones related to the M/S process. For a given organization, however, the departments associated with the M/S process may differ.

2. Decision needs of those who manage various sales and marketing functions.

3. Information flows and recorded data in support of the

operations and management processes.

Let's examine each of these functions. First, the M/S process supports the repetitive work routines of the sales order, credit, and shipping departments by capturing and recording sales-related data. As but one example, a sales order form or screen often supports the repetitive work routines of the sales order department by capturing vital customer and order data, by facilitating the process of granting credit to customers, and by helping to ensure the timely shipment of goods to customers. To further illustrate this point, we can consider that a copy of the sales order (whether paper or electronic in physical existence) may serve as a communications medium to inform workers in the warehouse that certain goods need to be picked and transported to the shipping department.

Second, the M/S process supports the decision needs of various sales and marketing managers. Third, in addition to these managers, any number of people within a given organization may benefit from information flows generated by the M/S process. This information is critical to succeeding in a highly competitive economy.

Organizational Setting

In this section, we take both a horizontal and vertical view of how the M/S process fits into the organizational setting of a company. The horizontal perspective will enhance your appreciation of how the M/S process relates to the repetitive work routines of the sales order, credit, warehouse, and shipping departments. The vertical perspective will sharpen your understanding of how the M/S process relates to managerial decision making within the marketing function.

A Horizontal Perspective

Figure 10.2 and Table 10.1 present a horizontal view of the relationship between the M/S process and its organizational environment. The figure shows the various information flows generated or captured through the M/S process. The information flows are superimposed onto the organizational structures that house the departments. The figure also illustrates the multiple entities with which the M/S process interacts (customers, carriers, other business processes, and so forth).

[Insert Figure 10.2 here]

[Insert Table 10.1 here]

Figure 10.2 reveals nine information flows that function as vital communications links among the various operations departments. The information flows also connect those departments with the entities residing in the relevant environment of the M/S process. If the order itself were initiated over the Internet or other EDI-based system, many of the flows would be automated and require less human intervention.

For example, the first information flow apprises representatives in the sales order department of a customer request for goods. This information flow, the customer order, might take the physical form of a telephone call, a mailed document, or an electronic transmission. In turn, flow 5 informs workers in the shipping department of a pending sale; this communication facilitates the operational planning and related activities associated with the shipping function. This information flow, the sales order, might take the form of a copy of a paper copy of a sales order, or it might be electronically transmitted and observed on a computer screen in the shipping department.

Review Question

Which entities, shown as external to the M/S process, also are outside the "boundary" of the organization and which are not?

As noted earlier in the text, many of the information flows through an organization become automated when *enterprise systems* are in place. Having reviewed the information flows in Table 10.1 and Figure 10.2, you should take a few minutes now to read Technology Insight 10.1 (page 330), which discusses how the horizontal information flows in an enterprise system become automated and, therefore, more efficient in terms of supporting the M/S process.

[Insert Technology Insight 10.1 box here]

A Vertical Perspective

To understand the relationship between the M/S process and managerial decision making, you need to become familiar with the key players involved in the marketing function. Figure 10.3 (page 331) presents these players in the form of an organization chart.

[Insert Figure 10.3 here]

As the figure illustrates, sales-related data are captured in the sales order department and then flow upward (in a summarized format) to managers housed within the marketing organizational structure. Much of this information would be based traditionally on sales-related events and normally would be captured through the use of a sales order form or through entry of data directly into a computer database. As organizations become ever increasingly focused on customers, however, the information needed for decision making is less focused on executing and recording the sale and more on customer characteristics, needs, and preferences. The next section provides an overview of the relationship between management decision making and the M/S process, and how information technology facilitates these demands of decision makers.

Review Question

What key players would you expect to find in the marketing function's organization chart?

Managing the M/S Process: Satisfying Customer Needs

In recent years, the print media has been glutted with articles stressing that the most critical success factor for businesses entering the new millennium is their ability to know their customers better and, armed with that knowledge, to serve their customers better than their competition. With companies facing more and more global competition, a renewed emphasis on satisfying customer needs has emerged. To compete effectively, firms must improve the quality of their service to customers. A satisfied customer tends to remain a customer, and it's less costly to retain existing customers than to attract new ones. Technology Excerpt 10.1 illustrates how technology-enabled cross-selling can enhance the relationship between a firm and its customers.

[Insert Technology Excerpt 10.1 box here]

What does this situation mean for the M/S process? Most importantly, it has expanded the type and amount of data collected by the M/S process regarding customer populations. To respond to the increasing information demand, many organizations have developed a separate marketing Information System to assist decision making in the marketing function. Often, these are tightly coupled with the Information Systems supporting the M/S process. For example, a company using an enterprise system might have a *customer relationship management* system sharing the same underlying database (a topic we will explore in greater detail shortly). The focus of these new systems is generally on replacing mass marketing or segmented marketing strategies with approaches that use computing resources to zero in on increasingly smaller portions of the customer population, with the ultimate aim being to concentrate on the smallest component of that population—the individual consumer. Technology Insight 10.2 illustrates one way in which data generated over the Internet could be used to augment internal sales data.

[Insert Technology Insight 10.2 box here]

Decision Making and Kinds of Decisions

Now let's look at one brief example of decisions that marketing managers confront. Put yourself in the position of an advertising manager. A few representative questions for which you might need answers are:

- Where is sales volume concentrated?
- Who are our specific major customers, both present and potential?
- What types of advertising have the greatest influence on our major customers?

Could the Information System help you to obtain the answers? Certainly, if it captured and stored historical data related to sales events and additional data related to customers. For example, to answer the first question, you might find a sales report by region helpful, and a sales report by customer class could provide *some* answers to the second question.

Where might you find answers to questions like the third one? Census reports, market research questionnaires, and trade journals often are included in the broader marketing Information System. Research houses garner vast amounts of information from public records—drivers' licenses, automobile registrations, tax rolls, mortgage registrations, and the like—and sell that information to other companies. In certain industries, the mechanisms to collect data regarding customers, their buying habits, and other demographics have become quite sophisticated. Recent advances in database management systems and the underlying technologies are leading to a focus on the use of *data warehousing* and *data mining* techniques (as discussed in Chapter 4) to support marketing analysis. Let's take a closer look at some of the key technologies supporting these efforts.

Using Data Mining to Support Marketing

Data warehousing applications in organizations are usually viewed as focusing on either operational or analytical applications. Operational applications focus on providing decision makers the information they need to monitor and control their organization. Analytical applications, which include data mining, allow the use of sophisticated statistical and other analytical software to help develop insights about customers, processes, and markets.[3] Several analytical applications are discussed in Technology Application 10.1.

[Insert Technology Application 10.1 box here]

3 Shaku Atre, "Defining Your Warehouse Goals," *Computerworld* (January 30, 1998): 35.

Data warehouses can be a massive effort for a company. For instance, Wal-Mart's worldwide data warehouse is the largest in the world with over 16 terabytes of data in a single data warehouse.[4] For many companies, such integration of corporate-wide data is a taxing process that requires years of development. This complexity is raised another magnitude as companies increasingly try to use data warehousing tools in contemporary enterprise systems to merge data captured through processing with other types of data desired in a data warehouse.

4 "Pick the Right Strategy for Decision Support," *Computerworld* (February 20, 1998): 32.

Using this massive array of data from which customer buying habits, characteristics, and addresses can be analyzed and linked, marketing departments can undertake extensive studies. Researchers armed with *neural networks* (as discussed in Chapter 5), comprehensive statistical analysis packages, and graphical presentation software can rapidly begin to develop insights about relationships within the marketing information. Of course, as demonstrated in Technology Excerpt 10.2 (page 336), users of the data warehouse need to consider carefully what the outputs of such analyses really mean.

[Insert Technology Excerpt 10.2 box here]

Mastering Global Markets with E-Business

Recall that in Chapter 4 we studied various e-business systems in great detail. Here, we will explore how these e-business systems can be used to penetrate global markets and allow a company to easily process international orders without a physical presence. Two success stories are discussed in Technology Application 10.2.

[Insert Technology Application 10.2 box here]

In Chapter 4 we discussed one of the great challenges to EDI being the inconsistent document protocols used by different countries to complete electronic transactions. (Refer to the discussion in Chapter 4 and the example in Figure 4.7 on page 131.) Varying standards can be a barrier to penetrating new global markets. In recent years, software has emerged to facilitate the translation between these differing standards.

Review Question

What are some advantages of using EDI to support global sales activity?

While such products enable the efficient use of e-business in the global marketplace, the costs can still be formidable for small and medium-sized companies. This barrier is finally being overcome through Internet access that can be used to facilitate e-business in an inexpensive format.

A variety of software solutions are now available that take a company's business information transmitted over the Internet and convert it into EDI format. Likewise, when EDI information is transmitted to the company, the software translates the EDI format into an Internet transmission format that provides compatible business information for the organization's systems. Another alternative is to use XML to encode business data in a generally accepted Internet transaction standard. XML, as presented in chapter 4, is beginning to replace EDI standards in several industries, especially among Web-enabled large companies.

In EDI systems, the user receives orders and sends invoices via a Web-based interface. The electronic messages are processed by an intermediary that serves the role of both translator between Internet and EDI forms and provider of value-added network (VAN) services with EDI-enabled companies (as were discussed in Chapter 4). Recent estimates have placed the costs of processing a paper-based order at $50 as compared to $2.50 to process the order using EDI and $1.25 using an Internet-based solution.[5] Thus, companies using commerce-business may choose only to make purchases from vendors equipped to handle electronic orders.

[5] Julie Dunn and Lori Mitchell, "Internet-Based EDI Solutions: Make the Connection," *Info world* (April 6, 1998): 74–75.

Review Question

How does Internet-based EDI enhance sales opportunities with small and medium-sized companies?

Customer Relationship Management (CRM) Systems

Customer relationship management systems (CRM) are systems designed to collect all of the data related to customers, such as marketing, field service, and contact management data. Over the past few years, CRM has become the primary focus of information systems managers and CIOs responsible for prioritizing new systems acquisitions. CRM has also become the focus of enterprise system vendors who realize the need to tap into this growing market and to integrate CRM data with the other data already residing within the enterprise system's database.

The concept behind CRM is that better customer service means happier customers and greater sales—particularly repeat sales. Part of the concept is field-service support and contact management. Contact management facilitates the recording and storing of information related to each contact a salesperson has with a client and the context of the conversation or meeting. Additionally, each time the client makes contact regarding queries or service help, this information is also recorded as field service records. The result is that a salesperson can review all pertinent historical information before calling on a customer and be better prepared to provide that customer with targeted products and services. These systems also support the recording of information about the customer contact, such as spouse's name, children, hobbies, etc., that help a salesperson make quality contact with a customer.

At the same time, the software supports the organizing and retrieving of information on historical sales activities and promotions planning. This facilitates the matching of sales promotions with customers' buying trends. For example, the Ticketmaster vignette demonstrated how customer data can be used when competing over the Internet. This is a particularly crucial area for integration with any existing enterprise system as much of the information necessary to support sales analyses comes from data captured during the recording of sales event data in the enterprise system.

Review Question

How do customer relationship management (CRM) systems aid a salesperson in providing service to customers?

A third area prevalent in CRMs is support for customer service—

particularly for phone operators handling customer support call-in centers. For many organizations, phone operators who have not had previous contact with the customer handle the bulk of customer service activities. The CRM quickly provides the phone operator with information on the customer's history and usually links the operator with a database of solutions for various problems that a customer may have. These solutions may simply be warranty or contracts information, or at a more complex level, solutions to operations or maintenance problems on machinery or equipment. All of this information can be efficiently stored for quick retrieval by the system's user.

Logical Description of the M/S Process

Using data flow diagrams, this section provides a logical view of a typical M/S process. Although the narrative highlights certain key points in the diagrams, your study of Chapter 2 equipped you to glean much knowledge simply from a careful study of the diagrams themselves. The section ends with a description of data created or used by the M/S process.[6]

[6] As we have indicated in earlier chapters, whenever we show data being stored in separate data stores, you should recognize that such data stores represent a process's view of data that in reality may reside in an *entity-wide database.*

Logical Data Flow Diagrams

Our first view of the process is a general one. Figure 10.4 portrays the M/S process in the form of a *context diagram*. Recall that a context diagram defines our area of interest. Although it presents an abstract view of the process, it serves the purpose of delineating the domain of our study. In Figure 10.4, one input enters the process and seven outputs emerge. Also, notice the entities in the relevant environment with which the M/S process interacts. Some of these entities reside outside the organization (Customer and Carrier), whereas some are internal to the organization but external to the M/S process (payroll process and revenue collection process.)[7] These internal entities are covered in detail in subsequent chapters.

[7] The slash on the lower right corner of the Customer entity square indicates that there is another occurrence of this entity on the diagram.

Review Question

What are the three major processes? What are the subsidiary processes of each major process?

[Insert Figure 10.4 here]

Figure 10.5 presents a *level 0 diagram* of the M/S process. Observe that the inputs and outputs are identical to those presented in Figure 10.4. As you recall, this *balancing* of inputs and outputs is an important convention to observe when constructing a set of data flow diagrams. The single bubble in Figure 10.4 has been divided into three bubbles in Figure 10.5, one for each of the three major functions performed by the M/S process.[8] Additional data flows connecting the newly partitioned bubbles appear, as do the data stores used to store various sets of data.[9]

[8] To focus our discussion, we have assumed that the M/S process performs three major functions. A given M/S process, however, may perform more or fewer functions than we have chosen to illustrate here. Each of the three functions (process bubbles) shown in Figure 10.5 is decomposed (that is, "exploded") into lower-level diagrams in Appendix A.

[9] The line enclosing the right side of the Sales order master data store indicates that there is another occurrence of that data store on the diagram.

[Insert Figure 10.5 here]

The physical means used to disseminate the order may vary from using a paper sales order form to using computer screen images as illustrated in Figure 10.6 (page 342). Regardless of the physical form used, we generally expect the dissemination to include the following data flows:

[Insert Figure 10.6 here]

- A **picking ticket** authorizes the warehouse to "pick" the goods from the shelf and send them to shipping. The picking ticket identifies the goods to be picked and usually indicates the warehouse location.

- A **packing slip** is attached to the outside of a package and identifies the customer and the contents of the package.
- A **customer acknowledgment** is sent to the customer to notify him or her of the order's acceptance and the expected shipment date.
- A **sales order notification** is sent to the billing department to notify it of a pending shipment.
- The **bill of lading** represents a contract between the shipper and the carrier in which the carrier agrees to transport the goods to the shipper's customer.

The carrier's signature on the bill of lading, and/or the customer's signature on some other form of receipt, substantiates the shipment.

Review Question

What do the terms *picking ticket*, *packing slip*, *bill of lading, tickler file*, and *one-for-one checking* mean?

Logical Data Descriptions

Figure 10.5 shows that the M/S process employs the following seven data stores:

- Marketing data
- Customer master data
- Inventory master data
- Accounts receivable master data
- Sales order master data
- Completed picking ticket file
- Shipping notice file

With the exception of the inventory and accounts receivable master data, the other five data stores are "owned" by the M/S process, meaning that the M/S process has the responsibility for performing *data maintenance* and *master data updates* on these data stores. This section discusses the purpose and contents of each of these five data stores.

Earlier, we noted that the *marketing data* is the repository of a variety of sales-oriented data, some of which result from recording sales event data (i.e., processed sales orders) and some of which originate from activities that do not culminate in completed sales, such as customer requests for inventory not stocked and/or available. The marketing data also house information from the *marketing information system*. Typically, these data could include economic forecasts, census reports, responses to market research questionnaires, customer buying habits, customer demographics, and the like.

Customer master data include data that identify the particular characteristics of each customer, such as name, address, telephone number, and so forth. These data also contain various credit data. Although customer data may be altered directly, proper control techniques require that all such master data changes (i.e., *data maintenance*) be documented and approved, and that a report of all data changes be printed periodically.

Review Question

What data stores does the M/S process "own"?

As shown in the data flow diagrams, records in the **sales order master data** store are created on completion of a sales order. Each of the sales order master data records contains various data elements, typically those that appear on the sales order in Figure 10.6.

Like the sales order master data, the *completed picking ticket data* and the *shipping notice data* will parallel the contents of their related business documents. The bulk of the data elements on these two documents would be identical to those on the sales order. Recall that unlike the sales order itself, the completed picking ticket and the shipping notice would reflect the physical quantities *actually* picked and shipped. In addition, the shipping notice would include data concerning the shipment such as shipping date, carrier, bill of lading number, and the like. In practice all of this data could simply be added to the record of the sales order that is maintained in the database.

Review Question

What data stores are owned by *other* information processes that provide data to the M/S process? What data does the M/S process obtain from these stores?

Physical Description of the M/S Process

We have assumed a particular physical model to illustrate the M/S process. As you examine the process's physical features, notice a close resemblance between them and the logical design of the M/S process, as presented in Figures 10.4 and 10.5 and in Figures 10.10 through 10.12 in Appendix A. You should also relate the physical features to the technology discussion earlier in this chapter.

The M/S Process

Figure 10.7 (pages 344–345) presents a systems flowchart of the model. Take some time now to examine the flowchart. On this first pass, please ignore the control annotations, P-1, P-2, etc. Controls will be covered in later sections.

[Insert Figure 10.7 here]

Each field salesperson is provided with a laptop and a portable printer. The laptop is equipped with a modem that allows the salesperson to communicate with the centralized computer via 24-hour, toll-free, high-speed leased telephone lines.[10] With this type of direct access and the capabilities provided by order-taking software, a salesperson can perform a number of services for a customer, including the following:[11]

[10] Because the leased lines provide a relatively secure communication channel, the salespeople's transmissions are not *encrypted* nor are *digital signatures* (see Chapter 9) used.

[11] Note that salespeople may not have access to all the menu options. For example, they may not have access to certain *data maintenance* functions or reporting options.

- Checking availability of inventory
- Determining status of open orders
- Initiating sales
- Confirming orders immediately

To illustrate typical process features, let's assume that the salesperson invokes the option to process a sales order. The order might have been taken orally at the customer's office or by telephone at the salesperson's office. The first screen to appear generally contains information about the header section of the sales order form. Typically, the system *automatically* assigns sequential order numbers.

Review Question

Does Figure 10.7 (a) employ online data entry; (b) use data communications technology; (c) process event occurrences individually, or in batches; and (d) update data records continuously?

Then the system prompts the salesperson to enter the *customer code*. If the salesperson enters a customer code for which the system has no record, the system rejects the order, and recording of the event terminates. If the customer is new, the salesperson asks the customer to complete a credit application. The salesperson then forwards the application to the credit department. Next, a credit officer initiates a credit investigation, resulting in either credit approval (usually with a dollar ceiling) or credit denial. The third part of Figure 10.7 illustrates these procedures.

Assuming the salesperson enters a valid customer code, the system automatically retrieves certain *standing data*, such as customer name(s), address(es), and credit terms, from the customer data. Next, the salesperson enters the other data in the sales order header, guided by the cursor's moving to each new position in the *preformatted screen.*

After the user completes and accepts the header section, the PC displays the middle section of the sales order (i.e., sales order lines). The salesperson enters data for each item ordered, starting with the part number. The system automatically displays the description and price.

Finally, the salesperson enters the quantity ordered and the date the customer needs the goods. If the total amount of the current order, any open orders, and the outstanding receivable balance exceeds the customer's credit limit, the operator is warned of this fact, the order is suspended, and credit rejection procedures are initiated. If the total amount falls within the customer's credit range, processing continues. Should the balance shown on the inventory data be less than the quantity ordered, back order procedures commence.

Once the salesperson finishes entering the order data, the computer updates the sales order master data, the inventory master data, the shipment event data, and the sales commission data and produces an exception and summary report. A two-part customer acknowledgment prints on the salesperson's portable printer; the original is left with (or mailed to) the customer to confirm the order, and the duplicate is retained by the salesperson. Simultaneously, a three-part sales order and sales order (SO) bar code labels (BCLs)—containing the sales order header information—are printed and distributed. Note that the distribution of these documents is similar to that shown on the data flow diagrams presented earlier and in Appendix A.

The warehouse layout is optimized to facilitate order picking. Each item in the warehouse has a ticket attached to it that contains the product bar code as well as its printed identification code and product description. We call this a BCT—bar code ticket—in the flowchart. As the items are picked, the stub of each BCT is removed as that item is packaged in a shipping carton—several items are contained in each carton. One of the sales order bar code labels (BCL) is pasted to the outside of the carton, and the individual BCTs are temporarily stapled to the carton as well. When the entire order has been picked, warehouse personnel insert the picked quantities on the picking ticket, initial the ticket, and then move the goods and the completed picking ticket to the shipping department.

Shipping personnel compare the goods to the completed picking ticket and their copy of the packing slip. Then, they scan each carton's BCL and the individual product BCTs that comprise that carton. The scanning process automatically prints a two-part bill of lading and a shipping notification on a printer located in the shipping department and simultaneously updates the shipping notice data and sales order master data to reflect the shipment. The goods themselves plus the original of the bill of lading and the completed packing slip are given to the carrier for delivery, and the shipping notification is sent to the billing section of the accounts receivable department. The bill of lading duplicate, completed picking ticket, and product BCTs are filed in the shipping department.

Consider how the M/S process documented in Figure 10.7 might change in an enterprise system environment. After you have thought through the impact and the resulting changes to Figure 10.7, read

Technology Insight 10.3 (page 348),which provides an overview of how a fully implemented enterprise system impacts the M/S process discussed in this chapter.

[Insert Technology Insight 10.3 box here]

Other aspects of the process can also benefit from automation. For example, as mentioned in Chapter 5, *expert systems* are being used increasingly in practical business applications, including M/S processes. To illustrate, the American Express Company has developed an expert system called Authorizer's Assistant that helps the credit authorization staff to approve customer charges. The Authorizer's Assistant searches through 13 databases and makes recommendations to the person making the authorization decision. Authorizer's Assistant raises the user's productivity by 20 percent and reduces losses from overextension of credit. In addition to cost savings, this expert system application allows American Express to differentiate itself from its competition by offering individualized credit limits.

Management Reporting

In an online system that incorporates an inquiry processing capability, the need for regular preparation of printed management reports is reduced or eliminated. Instead, each manager can use a PC to access a marketing database or CRM system and retrieve relevant management information (see the third part of Figure 10.7). For example, a sales manager could access the marketing database at any time and assess the performance of particular salespeople.

Sales reports in many desired formats can be obtained on demand using a computer. For example, some of the report options could include sales analyses by part number, product group, customer, or salesperson as well as open order status, sorted and accumulated in a variety of ways. Figure 10.8 illustrates a sample sales analysis report generated in SAP. This report shows the five top selling items for a period.

[Insert Figure 10.8 here]

Application of the Control Framework

The methodology for studying process controls appeared in Chapter 9. In this section, we apply that control framework to the M/S process. Figure 10.9 presents a completed control matrix for the systems flowchart presented in Figure 10.7. The flowchart is annotated to show the location of the various process control plans.

[Insert Figure 10.9 here]

Control Goals

The control goals listed across the top of the matrix are no different from the generic goals presented in Chapter 9, except that they have been tailored to the specifics of the M/S process.

Two categories of control goals are presented in the matrix. The *operations process control* goals are:

- ***Effectiveness of operations.*** A through E in Figure 10.9 identify five representative operations process goals for the M/S process. Operations process goals support the purpose of the process. In the case of the M/S process, notice that for the most part the operations process goals address the issue of satisfying customers, a topic discussed earlier in the chapter. In addition, the control matrices in this text incorporate as one of the process goals the goal of complying with laws, regulations, and contractual agreements when applicable. For that reason, we include goal E for the M/S process—Comply with the fair pricing requirements of the Robinson-Patman Act of 1936. (Briefly stated, that act makes it illegal in industrial and wholesale markets for a seller to charge different prices to two competing buyers under identical circumstances unless the seller can justify the pricing differential based on differences in its cost to manufacture, sell, and deliver the goods.)
- ***Efficiency in employment of resources.*** These goals support the savings of time and money.
- ***Resource security.*** Note that in this column we have named two specific resources that are of concern to the M/S process. Control plans should be in place to prevent theft or unauthorized sale of merchandise inventory. Equally important are plans designed to

preclude unauthorized access to or copying, changing, selling, or destruction of the customer master data.

The *information process control goals* comprise the other category. These goals are divided into two sections—one section for sales order inputs and a second section for shipping notice inputs. To focus our discussion, we have not included other inputs (i.e., customer inquiries, credit applications, credit-limit changes, and management inquiries). The information process control goals are:

- ***Input validity (IV).*** A *valid* sales order is one from an existing customer—one contained in the customer master data—whose current order falls within authorized credit limits. Recall that to be added to the customer master data, a customer had to pass an initial credit investigation. By adding the customer to the customer master data, management has provided authorization to do business with that customer. Valid shipping notice events are those that are supported by both an approved sales order and an *actual* shipment of goods.
- ***Input completeness (IC) and input accuracy (IA) of sales orders or shipping notices.*** These goals ensure that all orders are entered and entered correctly.
- ***Update completeness (UC) and update accuracy (UA) of the sales order and inventory master data.***[12] We have seen earlier in the chapter that the sales order master data is updated twice—

once when a new sales order is created, and later to reflect the shipment of that order. The single inventory master data update occurs at the same time the new sales order is created.

[12] Again, to focus our discussion, we have limited our coverage of system updates to just the sales order and inventory master data.

Review Question

What five operations process goals does the matrix show?

Recommended Control Plans

Exhibit 10.1 (page 354) contains a discussion of each recommended control plan listed in the control matrix, including an explanation of how each plan meets the related control goals. As you study the control plans, be sure to see where they are located on the systems flowchart. Also, see whether you agree with (and understand) the relationship between each plan and the goal(s) that it addresses. Remember that your ability to *explain* the relationships between plans and goals is more important than your memorization of the cell entries themselves.

[Insert Exhibit 10.1 here]

Recall that process control plans include both those that are characteristic of a particular business process and those that relate to the technology used to implement the application. Therefore, Exhibit 10.1 is divided into two sections. Section A shows the process control plans that are unique to the M/S process. Section B reviews the technology-related control plans—introduced in Chapter 9—that apply to the particular M/S configuration in Figure 10.7. For simplicity, we have assumed that each of the plans in section B exists in our system (i.e., is a “P” plan), regardless of whether it was specifically mentioned in the narrative or not. One of the control plans described in Chapter 9—namely, *digital signatures*—is not used in this particular system because the salespeople communicate with the centralized data processing department over leased telephone lines.

You should recognize that the plans in section B (unlike those in section A) are not unique to an M/S process. Rather, they apply to *any* system implemented using this technology. However, when the technology of a system is appropriate, these controls are incorporated into the list of recommended control plans (step 3 in “Steps in Preparing a Control Matrix,” Exhibit 9.1, page 287).

We discussed each of the plans listed in section B in Chapter 9, including an explanation of how each plan helps to attain specific control goals. We will not repeat that discussion here except to point out, as necessary, how and where the plan is implemented in the M/S process pictured in Figure 10.7. If you cannot explain in your own words the relationship between the plans and goals, you should review the explanations in Chapter 9.

Review Question

How does each control plan listed in the control matrix in Figure 10.9 work?

Conclusions

The M/S process is critical to revenue generation for the organization and as such is often a priority process for new technology integration. We have demonstrated one such system in this chapter. You should be aware that organizations have differing levels of technology integration in their business processes. As these levels of technology change, the business processes are altered accordingly. As the business process evolves, so also must the specific internal control procedures necessary to maintain the security and integrity of the process. Keep this in mind as you explore the alternative levels of technology integration presented in Chapters 11 and 12. Think about how the control systems change and how the controls in the M/S process would similarly change given similar technology-drivers for the business process.

This chapter presented a Marketing and Sales process that relies on a knowledgeable salesperson for initiating orders. What's in store for the future? Well, consider an Internet storefront (as discussed in Chapter 4). Buyers can send **agents** over the Internet to browse through electronic catalogs or Internet portals to compare prices and product specifications; and can make purchases at any hour.

Consider that there are as many as 100 million people worldwide now using the Internet. In the United States alone, 10 million users have made at least one purchase over the Web. The much larger market supporting business-to-business orders is many times larger with an expected annual value of $7.29 trillion by 2004.[13] Many firms such as General Electric and Dell Computer generate large portions of their revenue from their e-businesses.

[13] "Gartner: Business-to-business e-commerce to hit $7.3 trillion by '04" *Computerworld Online* (January 27, 2000): A1, A6.

Appendix 10A

Lower Level DFDs

Figure 10.10 provides a lower-level DFD for bubble 1.0 of Figure 10.5, p. 341, Validate Sales Order.

[Insert Figure 10.10 here]

A customer order is the *trigger* that initiates process 1.1.[14] How does the M/S process validate a customer order? First, process 1.1 verifies the availability of requested inventory by consulting the inventory master data. If there is a sufficient level of inventory on hand to satisfy the request, the order is forwarded for further processing, as depicted by the data flow "Inventory available order." If a customer orders goods that are not in stock, process 1.1 runs a special back order routine. This routine determines the inventory requirement necessary to satisfy the order and then sends the back order request to the purchasing department. This activity is depicted by the "Back order" data flow, which is a specific type of *exception routine* (i.e., a specific type of reject stub). Once the goods have been received, the order would then be routinely processed. If the customer refuses to accept a back order, then the sales event terminates, and the order is rejected, as shown by the "Reject" data flow. Information from the order (e.g., in regards to sale region, customer demographics, and order characteristics that reflect buying habits) has potential value to marketing and would be beneficial if recorded with the marketing data.

[14] We use the term *trigger* to refer to any data flow or event that causes a process to begin.

Next, process 1.2 establishes the customer's existence and then approves credit. In some cases, another aspect of validating the order could be to ensure that we want to ship the ordered goods to *this* particular customer. For instance, we may reject an order because we don't want our goods to be marketed through a discount store outlet.

How does the process complete sales orders? First, process 1.3 receives accepted orders from process 1.2. It then completes the order by adding price information, which is ascertained from the inventory master data. Then, process 1.3 performs the following activities simultaneously:[15]

[15] We say *simultaneously* when there is no reason inherent in the logical process being performed to preclude simultaneous activities.

- Updates the inventory master data to reflect a reduced quantity on hand
- Notifies the general ledger that inventory has been reduced
- Updates the sales order master data to indicate that a completed sales order has been created
- Notifies the PtoP process of sales commissions that are applicable to salesperson's payroll account
- Disseminates the sales order.

Figure 10.11, a lower-level view of bubble 2.0 of Figure 10.5, describes activities that normally take place in a warehouse. Warehouse personnel receive a picking ticket, locate the goods, take the goods off the shelf (i.e., "pick" the goods), and match the goods with the picking ticket.

[Insert Figure 10.11 here]

The reject stub coming from bubble 2.1 indicates at least two situations that might occur at this point. First, the goods pulled from the shelf might not be those indicated on the picking ticket (i.e., goods have been placed in the wrong warehouse location). Second, sufficient goods may not exist to satisfy the quantity requested. The second situation may arise when goods have been misplaced or when the actual physical balance does not agree with the perpetual inventory balance indicated in the inventory data. These predicaments must be resolved and a back order routine may be initiated to order the missing goods for the customer.

In process 2.2, warehouse personnel write the quantities "picked" on the picking ticket and forward the picking ticket (along with the goods) to the shipping department.

Review Question

What three exception routines may occur when a customer order is processed?

Figure 10.12, a lower-level view of bubble 3.0 in Figure 10.5, describes activities that normally take place in a shipping department. The figure tells us that process 3.1 receives two data flows; namely, the packing slip from process 1.3 of Figure 10.10 and the completed picking ticket from process 2.2 of Figure 10.11. Process 3.1 matches the details of the data flows, looking for consistency between them. If the details agree, the completed picking ticket is filed, and the matched sales order is forwarded to process 3.2. If the details of the data flows do not agree, process 3.1 rejects the order and initiates procedures for resolving any discrepancies.

[Insert Figure 10.12 here]

Review Question

How is each lower-level DFD (Figures 10.10, 10.11, and 10.12) "balanced" with the level 0 diagram in Figure 10.5?

When process 3.2 receives a matched sales order from process 3.1, it produces and disseminates the shipping notice. The process also updates the shipping notice data and the sales order master data. We generally expect the shipping notice dissemination to include the following data flows: shipping's billing notification (to notify billing to begin the billing process), bill of lading, and completed packing slip.

Appendix 10B

Logical Database Design

In Chapter 3, we compared data as it would be stored in a file(s) with that same data when stored in a database, with emphasis on the relational database model (see Figures 3.7 and 3.8 on pages 79 and 83, respectively). In this section, we will depict the relational tables for the data we have just mentioned in the discussion of the:

- Customer master data
- Sales order master data
- Completed picking ticket file

- Shipping notice data

To do so, we are well advised to first redraw the E-R diagram appearing in Figure 3.9 on page 84. Figure 10.13 (page 362) is our new E-R diagram. It differs from Figure 3.9 in that the SALES event in Chapter 3 now has been divided into three events comprising the sale—namely, picking goods (STOCK PICKING event in Figure 10.13), shipping goods (SHIPMENT event), and billing the customer for the shipment (SALES INVOICE event). From Figure 10.13, we develop the relational tables appearing in Figure 10.14 (page 363).

[Insert Figure 10.13 here]

[Insert Figure 10.14 here]

Compare the CUSTOMERS relation in part (a) of Figure 10.14 with the discussion of the customer master data on page 342 and observe that the data elements (attributes) are essentially the same. Note that the relation allows for both a customer address and "ship to" address, each being subdivided into four attributes—street address, city, state, and ZIP code—to facilitate database inquiries using any of these attributes. Now compare part (b) of the figure—the SALES_ORDERS and SALES_ORDER *line item* INVENTORY relations, respectively—to the sales order screen in Figure 10.6 on page 342 and the discussion of the sales order master data on page 343. Here we see some marked differences. The two sales order tables contain far fewer data elements than the sales order document itself because many of the elements needed to complete the document are available from other relations. Recall that a major advantage of a database approach to data management is the elimination of redundant data items. Therefore, using the Cust_No from SALES_ORDERS, we can obtain the customer's name, address, ship to name, ship to address, and credit terms from the CUSTOMERS relation. Likewise, using Item_No from SALES_ORDER *line item* INVENTORY, we can obtain from the INVENTORY_ITEM relation the description of the goods and unit selling price. Finally, using the primary key from SALES_ORDER *line item* INVENTORY (i.e., the *combination* of SO_No/Item_No), we can determine the quantity picked/shipped from the INVENTORY *line item* STOCK_PICK relation in Figure 10.8 (page 350). Other items often found on the sales order form—quantity back ordered, extended price, and the components of the sales order trailerbe computed from other data and therefore need not be stored in any table.

Parts (c) (d) and (e) of Figure 10.14 need no particular comment, except to note once again that the four relations contain relatively few attributes because most of the data needed to complete a picking ticket or shipping notice document reside in other relations. For example, an actual picking ticket often takes the physical form of a duplicate copy of the sales order document. The primary item that differentiates the two documents is the warehouse location, which must appear on the picking ticket to facilitate the actual picking of the goods. Even in sophisticated enterprise systems, picking tickets can be paper based since the packers must move around a warehouse to find the ordered goods. Once the goods are picked, the picking ticket document could be completed by adding the quantity picked, date picked, and identification of the person who picked the items, attributes which appear in the two relations in part (c).[16]

[16] An assumption implicit in parts (c) and (e) of Figure 10.11 is one that was noted on the E-R diagram—namely, that all inventory line items that are picked are shipped as a single shipment. If the quantities shipped differed from those picked, we would need another relation in part (e) for INVENTORY *line item* SHIPMENTS.

REVIEW QUESTIONS

RQ10-1 Each of the following questions concerns Figure 10.2 (page 328) and Table 10.1 (page 329):

a. Which entities, shown as external to the M/S process, also are outside the "boundary" of the organization and which are not?

b. The revenue collection process is notified of the sale in flow 6 and the shipment in flow 9. Which of the two flows is the "trigger" for invoicing the customer?

RQ10-2 What key players would you expect to find in the marketing function's organization chart?

RQ10-3 What are some advantages of using EDI to support global sales activity?

RQ10-4 How does Internet-based EDI enhance sales opportunities with small and medium-sized companies?

RQ10-5 How do customer relationship management (CRM) systems aid a salesperson in providing service to customers?

RQ10-6 Each of the following questions concerns the logical description of the M/S process:

a. What are the three major processes? What are the subsidiary processes of each major process?

b. What data stores does the M/S process "own"?

c. What data stores are owned by *other* information processes that provide data to the M/S process? What data does the M/S process obtain from these stores?

d. What three exception routines may occur when a customer order is processed?

RQ10-7 What do the terms *picking ticket*, *packing slip*, *bill of lading*, *tickler file*, and *one-for-one checking* mean?

RQ10-8 Does Figure 10.7 (pages 344–346) (a) employ online data entry; (b) use data communications technology; (c) process event occurrences individually, or in batches; and (d) update data records continuously?

RQ10-9 Each of the following questions concerns the control matrix for the M/S process (Figure 10.9 on page 351) and its related annotated systems flowchart (Figure 10.7 on pages 344–346):

a. What five operations process goals does the matrix show?

b. In this process, what particular resources do we wish to secure?

c. What are the two kinds of data inputs in this system?

d. What constitutes a "valid" sales order? A valid shipping notice?

e. For what master data(s) do we want to ensure UC and UA?

RQ10-10 How does each control plan listed in the control matrix in Figure 10.9 (page 351) work?

RQ10-11 How is each lower-level DFD (Figures 10.10, 10.11, and 10.12 on pages 358–360) "balanced" with the level 0 diagram in Figure 10.5 (page 341)?

DISCUSSION QUESTIONS

DQ10-1 The chapter presented a brief example of how the M/S process might or might not support the decision-making needs of the advertising manager. For each of the other functional positions shown in the organization chart of Figure 10.3, speculate about the kinds of information needed to support decision making and indicate whether the typical M/S process would provide that information. Be specific.

DQ10-2 Explain how and where operations process goals would be shown in the goal columns of a control matrix prepared for the M/S process. At a minimum, include in your discussion the following topics from Chapter 9:

a. Differentiation between operations process control goals and information process control goals.

b. Distinction between process effectiveness and process efficiency, and between process effectiveness and security of resources.

DQ10-3 Discuss the nature and purpose of the completed picking ticket data store and the shipping notice data, both of which are shown in the logical DFDs and systems flowchart of this chapter. Among other points of discussion, identify each of these data stores as either "sales event" data or "master" data.

DQ10-4 "A control plan that helps to attain operational effectiveness by 'providing assurance of creditworthiness of customers' also helps to achieve the information process control goal of sales order input validity." Do you agree? Why or why not?

DQ10-5 Examine the systems flowchart in Figure 10.7 (pages 344–346). Discuss how this process implements the concept of segregation of duties, discussed in Chapter 8. Be specific as to which entity (or entities) performs each of the four processing functions mentioned in Chapter 8 (assuming that all four functions are illustrated by the process).

DQ10-6 Describe how a *business intelligence system* might be used by any of the managers depicted in Figure 10.2 (page 328)—A horizontal perspective of the M/S process—or in Figure 10.3 (page 331)—A vertical perspective of the M/S process.

PROBLEMS

Note: The first problems in this and several other application chapters ask you to perform activities that are based on processes of specific companies. The narrative descriptions of those processes (the cases) precede each chapter's problems. If your instructor assigns problems related to these cases, he or she will indicate which of them to study.

CASE STUDIES

Case A: Klassic Grocers, Inc.

Klassic Grocers is an online grocery service that provides home delivery of groceries purchased via the Internet. Klassic operates in the greater Tulsa area and provides delivery to precertified customers. In order to be certified, the customer must establish a credit or charge line and rent a refrigerated unit to store delivered goods at their residence should they not be home at the time of delivery.

The order process is triggered by the receipt of an order over the Internet from a customer. The system receives the order from a customer including the customer's name and ID number, and the list of items for purchase. The system accesses a customer database to ensure that the customer is in good standing and a refrigeration unit is in place at the residence. If the order is approved, it is automatically logged into the order database and an e-mail acknowledgement is sent to the customer. If it is rejected, the system sends the customer a message notifying him of the inability to process the order.

In the warehouse, a clerk downloads an outstanding order from the order database to a handheld computer. The downloaded order provides an electronic picking ticket for use in assembling the customer's order. The order is assembled, placed in a box, recorded via the handheld computer as completed by item, a bar code is printed on the handheld computer and affixed to the outside of the box, and placed on a conveyor belt to delivery services.

In delivery services, the delivery person uses another handheld computer device to read the barcode and access the sales order information from the order database. The items in the box for delivery are rechecked per the order and loaded for delivery to the customer. Confirmation of the order contents by the delivery person triggers the printing of delivery directions. Upon delivering the groceries to the customer, the delivery person once again reads the barcode with the handheld device, and presses the button for confirmation of delivery. The completion of the delivery is automatically recorded in the order database. The system at this time also updates the customer's master data for billing purposes.

Case B: Do-It-Right Company

The Do-It-Right Company is a wholesale distributor of office furniture. Customer orders are received in the mailroom, where clerks sort orders from the rest of the mail, group them into batches, prepare a transmittal sheet, and forward the orders and the transmittal sheet to the order entry department.

A clerk in order entry checks that the batch is complete, logs the batch into a batch control log, and begins to process the orders. The clerk keys the orders into the computer. Keying involves a two-step process in which the order entry clerk keys in the customer code. The customer data, stored on disk, are checked to see that the customer exists and has an acceptable credit record. If everything checks out, the clerk keys in the rest of the order.

The procedure results in the creation of an entry in the sales order event data store. At the end of the day, the data are processed against the customer data and the inventory data to create a picking ticket (sent to the warehouse), a sales order notification (sent to the shipping department), and a customer acknowledgment (sent to the mailroom for mailing to the customer). At this time, the sales order is also recorded in the sales order master data.

In the warehouse, the picking ticket is used to assemble the customers' orders. The completed orders (goods and attached picking ticket) are forwarded to the shipping department. The shipping clerk removes the sales order notification from a temporary file and compares the goods to the picking ticket and to the sales order notification. The clerk then keys the sales order number into the shipping department computer, which accesses the sales order master data and displays the order on the shipping clerk's screen. The shipping clerk keys in the items and quantities being shipped and, after the computer displays the shipment data, accepts the input. Once the shipment is accepted, the computer updates the sales order master data and creates a record for the shipments event data. The computer also prints a packing slip and bill of lading on a printer in the shipping department. These shipping documents and the goods are given to the carrier for shipment to the customer.

P10-1 For the company assigned by your instructor, complete the following requirements:

a. Prepare a table of entities and activities.

b. Draw a context diagram.

c. Draw a physical data flow diagram (DFD).

d. Prepare an annotated table of entities and activities. Indicate on this table the groupings, bubble numbers, and bubble titles to be used in preparing a level 0 logical DFD.

e. Draw a level 0 logical DFD.

P10-2 For the company assigned by your instructor, complete the following requirements:

a. Draw a systems flowchart.

b. Prepare a control matrix, including explanations of how each recommended existing control plan helps to accomplish—or would accomplish in the case of missing plans—each related control goal. Your choice of recommended control plans should come from section A of Exhibit 10.1 (pages 354–355) plus any technology-related control plans from Chapter 9 that are relevant to your company's process.

c. Annotate the flowchart prepared in part a to indicate the points where the control plans are being applied (codes P-1 . . . P-*n*) or the points where they could be applied but are not (codes M-1 . . . M-*n*).

P10-3 Study the narratives of specific companies assigned by your instructor. Also refer to operations process goals A through D for the M/S process in Figure 10.9 (page 352).

REQUIRED: In one paragraph for each of the four goals, compare and contrast the assigned case processes in terms of their ability to achieve the goals. Cite *specific* features that give a particular process a comparative advantage in terms of meeting a particular goal(s).

P10-4 The following capsule cases present short narratives of processes used by three actual companies whose names have been changed for the purpose of this problem. You will use the cases to practice the mechanics of drawing data flow diagrams.

Capsule Case 1: Bambino's Pizzeria

For its chain of fast food outlets, Bambino's Pizzeria has recently installed a system to speed up deliveries. In each of its stores, Bambino's has three or four PCs connected to incoming phone lines. When a customer calls in an order to have pizza delivered, an employee answers and Caller ID checks the phone number against a data store containing past phone orders. If the order is for a repeat customer, the system matches the number with the customer database and displays the customer record on the screen. (Customer records contain a variety of information, including whether the customer's dog bites.) For first-time customers, the employee verifies the caller's name and address, and creates a record in the customer database.

The order taker then types in the customer's pizza order. The system prints out a three-part order on a printer located in the kitchen. The original is used by the cook to prepare the order. When the order is ready, the cook marks the other two copies completed and gives them to the delivery driver to serve as delivery receipts for the driver and customer, respectively. At the same time that the order is printed, the order taker's computer displays a city locator grid that is used to help dispatch the drivers. From a copy of the display, a dispatch slip—showing the customer's street and connecting roads—is printed for the driver. The final system output generated at this time is a record of the order, which is the source for the event data written to the order system. The data will be used later to tally sales, calculate the driver's pay, and generate other reports. (Note: For this problem, assume that these activities are beyond the order-taking system's context.)

Capsule Case 2: Royal Casino

Waiters and waitresses at the Royal Casino's main dining room in Las Vegas use handheld, radio-frequency devices to take diners' orders and relay the orders to the kitchen. The data entry devices weigh just a few ounces and open like a wallet to reveal a keypad and a small screen. The devices are connected by radio signal to the dining room's computer. As diners place their orders, the device prompts the waiter through the order. For instance, if the customer asks for a sirloin steak, the system asks the waiter to choose a key corresponding to the desired degree of doneness (i.e., rare, medium rare, and so forth).

When the customer has completed ordering, the waiter hits a key to indicate that fact. The system prints or displays the incoming order for cooks in the kitchen. When the dining party has finished its meal, the waiter indicates this fact by pressing the appropriate key on the handheld device. The system communicates, over conventional wiring, with a point-of-sale (POS) computer at the cash register station, which prints out a guest check. At this time, the system also records the sales event data on the host computer.

Capsule Case 3: Pix for Pay

Background Information

Pix for Pay (PFP) is a company that offers pay-television movies and other cable television programming to subscribers for a fee. This case involves those subscribers who receive PFP's TV signal through a satellite dish. To restrict delivery of PFP broadcasts to paying subscribers only, the company scrambles its signal. A subscriber must have a descrambler box attached to the receiving dish and must pay a monthly subscription fee in order to receive a clear picture. Each descrambler box has its own unique ID number, so it will only respond to "on" signals meant for it. The descrambler boxes were designed by Spacecom, Inc., located in Los Angeles, California.

Gelinas 10-56

The Marketing and Sales Process

When a customer places an order for pay-TV service with a PFP-affiliated cable TV company, the cable company telephones that order to PFP's telemarketing center in Cincinnati, Ohio. There, a customer service representative enters the order, together with the customer's descrambler ID number, via a computer that is connected through a leased telephone line to PFP's system in New York City. The system updates the customer cable orders data and sends the descrambler code to a computer at Spacecom in Los Angeles, which then sends an encrypted activation message to PFP's uplink center in Buffalo, New York. The uplink center beams the activation message to a space satellite, and the message is echoed down to earth to the customer's satellite dish. The customer's descrambler box deciphers the encrypted message, which allows the customer to start receiving PFP's programming. From the time the customer places the order, the entire process takes less than a minute.

REQUIRED:

For the capsule case assigned by your instructor, complete the following requirements:

a. Prepare a table of entities and activities.

b. Draw a context diagram.

c. Draw a physical data flow diagram (DFD).

d. Prepare an annotated table of entities and activities. Indicate on this table the groupings, bubble numbers, and bubble titles to be used in preparing a level 0 logical DFD.

e. Draw a level 0 logical DFD.

f. Assume the data collected in this case are stored in a data warehouse. Describe the data and analysis that could be used to:

1) Help the advertising manager decide how best to reach new customers.

2) Guide the marketing intelligence manager in understanding which products appeal to which customers, in order to expand the product line to reach new customers.

3) Direct the sales promotion manager to design coupons or other promotions to bring in new customers and to retain repeat customers.

P10-5 The following is a list of 12 control plans from this chapter or from Chapters 8 and 9:

Control Plans

A. Enter data close to where customer order is prepared

B. Customer existence check

C. Independent shipping authorization

D. Completed picking ticket file

E. One-for-one checking of the goods, picking ticket, and packing slip

F. Preformatted screens

G. Interactive feedback check

H. Reasonableness check

I. Backup procedures (for data)

J. Program change controls

K. Librarian controls

L. Personnel termination controls

REQUIRED: Listed next are eight system failures that have control implications. List the numbers 1 through 8 on your solution sheet. Next to each number, insert one letter from the preceding list, identifying the control plan that would best prevent the system failure from occurring. Also, give a brief (one- to two-sentence) explanation of your choice.

A letter should be used only once, with four letters left over.

System Failures

1. A clerk logged on to the online sales system by entering the date of June 39, 20XX, instead of the correct date of June 29, 20XX. As a result, all sales orders entered that day were dated incorrectly.

2. The correct goods were delivered by the warehouse to the shipping department. However, a dishonest shipping clerk misappropriated some of the goods and short-shipped the customer. When the customer complained, the dishonest clerk claimed that the goods must have never been received from the warehouse. Because there was no way to prove otherwise, the company had to provide the additional goods to the customer.

3. A former employee of the order entry department gained access to the department after hours and logged on at one of the computers. He entered an order for a legitimate customer but instructed the system to ship the goods to his home address. Consequently, several thousand dollars worth of inventory was shipped to him. When the misappropriation was discovered, he had long since left the company and had changed addresses.

4. Century Inc.'s field salespeople record customer orders on prenumbered order forms and then forward the forms to central headquarters in Milwaukee for processing. Fred Friendly, one of Century's top salespeople, had a very good week; he mailed 40 customer orders to headquarters on Friday afternoon. Unfortunately, they were misplaced in the mail and did not reach Milwaukee until two weeks later. Needless to say, those 40 customers were more than a little displeased at the delay in their orders being filled.

5. Ajax Corporation recently converted to a new online sales system. Clerks key in order data at one of several computers. In the first week of operations, every sales order produced by the system was missing the data for the "ship to" address.

6. At XYZ Co., the finished goods warehouse delivers goods to the shipping department, accompanied by the picking ticket. After checking the goods against the picking ticket, the shipping employee signs the picking ticket and gives it to the warehouse employee. Then the shipping department prepares a three-part shipping notice, one copy of which serves as the packing slip. A recent audit discovered that a dishonest warehouse employee had been forging picking ticket documents, allowing her to have goods shipped to an accomplice.

7. The job of a systems programmer included doing maintenance programming for the marketing and sales system. He altered the programs so that the credit-checking routine was bypassed for one of the customers, a company owned by his uncle. The uncle obtained several thousand dollars of merchandise before his firm went bankrupt.

8. To encourage new business, Carefree Industries adopted a policy of shipping up to $1,000 of orders to new customers during the period in which the customer's credit was being

investigated. A recently terminated order entry manager at Carefree, aware of the policy, placed several bogus telephone orders, disguised each time as a first-time customer. She absconded with over $10,000 of merchandise that was shipped to her.

P10-6 The following is a list of 9 control plans from this chapter or from Chapter 8:

Control Plans

A. Customer credit check

B. Packing slip tickler file in shipping department

C. One-for-one checking of customer order and sales order

D. Populate inputs with master data

E. Online prompting

F. Preformatted screens

G. Programmed edit checks

H. Application documentation

I. Segregation of duties

REQUIRED: Listed next are nine statements describing either the achievement of a control goal (i.e., a system success) or a system deficiency. List the numbers 1 through 9 on your solution sheet. Next to each number, insert *one* letter from the preceding list, identifying the *best* control plan to achieve the desired goal or to address the system deficiency described. A letter should be used only once.

Control Goals or System Deficiencies

1. Helps to ensure the operations process goal of timely shipment of goods to customers.
2. Results in the efficient employment of resources; when the order entry clerk keys in the customer number, the system supplies the customer name, billing address, and other standing data about the customer.
3. Meets both the operations process goal that sales are made only to credit-worthy customers and the information process control goal of sales order input validity.
4. Helps to achieve the information process control goal of input accuracy by ensuring that dates are entered as MM/DD/YYYY.
5. Helps to achieve the information process control goal of input accuracy by providing interactive dialogue with the data entry person.
6. Results in the efficient employment of resources by providing detailed instructions to computer operations personnel for running production jobs.
7. Addresses the information process control goals of both input

accuracy and input completeness.

8. Could have prevented the clerk from entering 10 boxes of an item when a customer ordered 10 each of an item.

P10-7 (Appendix A) Use the data flow diagrams in Figures 10.5 (page 341), 10.10 (page 358), 10.11 (page 359), and 10.12 (page 360)to solve this problem.

REQUIRED: Prepare a 4-column table that summarizes the M/S system's processes, inputs, and outputs. In the first column, list the three processes shown in the level 0 diagram (Figure 10.5). In the second column, list the subsidiary functions shown in the three lower-level diagrams (Figures 10.10, 10.11, and 10.12). For *each* subsidiary process listed in column 2, list the data flow names or the data stores that are inputs to that process (column 3) or outputs of that process (column 4). (See **NOTE.**) The following table has been started for you to indicate the format for your solution.

NOTE: To simplify the solution, do *not* show any reject stubs in column 4.

SOLUTION FORMAT

Summary of the M/S processes, subsidiary functions, inputs, outputs and data stores

Process	Subsidiary Functions	Inputs	Outputs
1.0 Validate sales order	1.1 Verify inventory availability	Customer order inventory master data	Marketing data Inventory available Inventory—available order and back order
	1.2 Check	. . . Continue solution . . .	. . . Continue solution. . .

TABLES

[Start Table]

Table 10.1 Description of Horizontal Information Flows *

Flow No.	Description
1	Customer places order.
2	Sales order department requires credit approval from credit department.
3	Credit department informs sales order department of disposition of credit request.
4	Sales order department acknowledges customer order.
5	Sales order department notifies shipping department of sales order.
6	Sales order department notifies warehouse, revenue collection process, payroll process, and general ledger process of sales order.
7	Warehouse sends completed picking ticket to shipping.
8	Shipping department informs sales order department of shipment.
9	Shipping department informs carrier and revenue collection process of shipment.

*Many of these steps may be automated. See Technology Insight 10.1 for a description of these steps in an enterprise system implementation.

[End Table]

BOXES

[Start Technology Insight 10.1 box here]

TECHNOLOGY INSIGHT 10.1

Enterprise System Support for Horizontal Information Flows

The information flows presented in Figure 10.2 (page 328) are very similar to what we would expect when an organization uses an enterprise system. However, many of the tasks outlined could occur quite differently because of the messaging capabilities embedded in contemporary enterprise systems. Let us take another look at each of the information flows in Figure 10.2.

1. The customer places the order (While this could be done electronically over the Internet, we will assume for now it is placed as in the system discussed in this chapter.)
2. Because the sales order department requires credit approval from the credit department, the approval process is automatically incorporated into the routing set-up within the enterprise system. Hence, once the sales order department releases the order to credit approval, the document is automatically routed electronically to the credit department and queued for their approval.
3. The credit department's approval requires a few simple data entry steps and the approval is automatically routed electronically back to the sales order department by the enterprise system. [This step assumes that the order requires a manual credit approval. If the credit-approval rules can be programmed (or configured) into the system, the entire credit approval would be performed by the enterprise system.]
4. The sales order department's response to the customer is also automatically triggered by the enterprise system in most implementations. This response may be

electronic or may still be paper-based as in traditional systems.

5. The routing to the shipping department is very likely triggered by the enterprise system simultaneously with customer notification and likely not to require any additional entry by the sales order department beyond that entered to trigger information flow #4.
6. Similarly, routings to the warehouse, payroll, revenue collection, and general ledger are also more than likely triggered by the same action as that in flows #4 and #5.
7. Once the warehouse has completed picking the order, the information is entered into the system to reflect that the goods have been picked and are ready for shipment. Should the sales order department receive any inquiries from the customer, it can tell the customer that the goods have been picked and await shipment.
8. Once the shipping department releases the shipment, the information is entered into the enterprise system at the shipping location to record the order as shipped. Should the sales order department receive any inquiries from the customer, it can tell the customer that the goods have been shipped.
9. Similarly, the carrier and the billing personnel may inquire about the status of the order.

As demonstrated in this overlay to the M/S process, an enterprise system may not change many of the workings of the business process but, rather, removes much of the wasteful time and paper shuffling that takes place in traditional systems, incorporating electronic messaging systems that speed notifications. Also, the use of automated triggers ensures that various steps in the process will not be omitted, as the system requires each process activity to be completed before triggering the next process activity.

[End Technology Insight 10.1 box here]

[Start Technology Excerpt 10.1 box here]

Technology Excerpt 10.1

Customer-Centric Application

Petroleum giant BP Amoco PLC will spend $200 million over the next two years to outfit 28,000 gas stations worldwide with Internet-ready gas pumps customers can use to check directions, book a hotel room, or even order a ham sandwich while they fill their tanks. The technology overhaul will allow drivers to pay online for gas and snacks before or during a visit to a BP Amoco gas station. The Internet-ready pumps will have touch screens customers can use to select made-to-order sandwiches or pastries online. Once customers have finished filling their tanks, their orders will be ready inside the store.

Source: Julia King, "BP Amoco to Launch Net-Ready Gas Pumps," *Computerworld* (July 31, 2000), p. 6.

[End Technology Excerpt 10.1 box here]

[Start Technology Insight 10.2 box here]

TECHNOLOGY INSIGHT 10.2

Cookies

The controversial "cookie" is a segment of code that gets written to your hard drive when visiting most Web sites. Cookies can save the Web visitor time by recording parameters and data that do not need to be typed in on repeat visits. This same data can be analyzed by Web site owners to get a better understanding of the makeup and usage patterns of their site visitors. Site owners store the data in codes to be able to recognize repeat users and monitor how the site is used over time. Sample cookie data for a site that reviews restaurants is shown below. As you can see, many of the codes contained in the file are meaningless to the recipient. They are used to assist the site in personalizing the view of the pages when the user revisits them. Many Internet users who value their privacy prefer that Web site owners be preempted from reading their cookie file because of their potential for containing personal information. Internet users may choose to not accept cookies, delete unwanted cookies, or refrain from using Web sites that produce them. However, they do save time for repeat users of Web sites, and can help site owners decide how to improve their offerings. If you are concerned about how your cookies are used, consult the privacy statement on a site's home page.

CFID

6107643

www.restaurantrow.com/

0

3546759168

32088942

3700504960

29389240

*

CFTOKEN

96533504

www.restaurantrow.com/

0

3546759168

32088942

3700504960

29389240

*

VISITOR

DF133C94%2DDD60%2D11D4%2DBBC6009027BBABDF

www.restaurantrow.com/

0

3546759168

32088942

3700504960

29389240

*

[End Technology Insight 10.2 box here]

[Start Technology Application 10.1 box here]

TECHNOLOGY APPLICATION 10.1

Applications of Data Mining

Case 1

National Australia Bank recently implemented data mining tools from the SAS Institute to aid particularly in the area of predictive marketing. The tools are used to extract and analyze data in the bank's Oracle database. Specific applications currently focus on assessing how competitors' initiatives are affecting the bank's bottom line. The data mining tools are used to generate market analysis models from historical data recorded in event-level form. The addition of data mining tools is one more step in a strategic set of initiatives focusing on the development of a comprehensive data warehouse. National Australia Bank considers the data warehousing initiatives to be crucial to maintaining an edge in the increasingly competitive financial services marketplace.

Case 2

National Data Corporation/Health Information Services (NDC/HIS) has found a way to leverage its extensive database of pharmaceutical firm data into a new market of information services through the use of data mining tools. A long-time supplier of information to the pharmaceutical industry, NDC/HIS recently released a new subscription service, Intellect Q&A, that provides in-depth information that subscribers can mine for key data. One happy client is Lowe McAdams Health Care, a Manhattan advertising agency. It recently won a $20 million contract with a client after mining through NDC/HIS data and developing detailed financial information on the client that the client's own internal reporting systems had yet to compile. The client was so impressed by Lowe's depth of knowledge that they signed the contract. NDC/HIS was also thrilled as it created an excellent example for demonstration in selling access to their data warehouse to other potential clients.

Case 3

FAI Insurance group also recently implemented a large data warehouse. Insurance companies are broadly recognized to be heavily reliant on demographic data that support assessment of insurance risk. FAI Insurance decided to use its data warehouse to reassess the relationship between historical risk from insurance policies and the pricing structure used by its underwriters. The data analysis capabilities should allow FAI to better serve its customers by more accurately assessing the insurance risk associated with a customer request. Developers of the data warehouse note that the models that can be built through data mining are much larger than those the company could previously develop. Through the use of *neural networks* and linear statistics, the analysts comb the data for trends and relationships. Out of 25 users currently on the research system linked to the data warehouse, 12 researchers work almost full-time on mining the data in the system. The strong relationship between the information technology group and the researchers has resulted in what FAI believes to be the most effective data-mining and data-warehousing approach in the industry.

Sources: Iain Ferguson, "Data Mining Lifts Competitive Edge," *Computerworld* (February 6, 1998): 18; Linda Wilson, "Data Mining Strikes Gold," *Computerworld* (August 8, 1997): 34; Merri Mack, "Data Quality and Analysis are FAI's Secret

Weapons," *Computerworld* (April 4, 1997): 24.

[End Technology Application 10.1 box here]

[Start Technology Excerpt 10.2 box here]

Technology Excerpt 10.2

The Surprising Discoveries in Data Mining

All This Mining Can Be a Dirty Business by Shaku Atre

FRAMINGHAM, MASSACHUSETTS—First, they told us to go work in a data warehouse, forklifting loads of data and doing lots of heavy lifting. We were told to establish total control over the company's data inventory so end users could order any combination of items at any time. Before long, we were in the big boss's office, requesting the kind of hardware and staffing used at NASA to calculate interplanetary space shots.

And we wondered whether we would need a UN peacekeeping team to help departments agree on what the terms "sale" and "customer" meant, so we could model the enterprise. When the boss said we might be happier in outer space and put us on a stricter allowance, we looked into data marts. That was a way in which each user department could create a decision-support solution that would stand alone as a beautiful, tropical island of information.

Now they're sending us to the mines. The data mines. We're supposed to dig out diamonds of information. A diamond mine is the kind of place where—in a prison movie—they send lifers.

Couldn't we just strip-mine for coal and avoid a bowels-of-the-earth excavation?

If the metaphor holds true, we're in for some very dirty business, laboured breathing and low pay, in an effort to harvest baubles. In a famous data mining example, a large retailer discovered that beer and nappies often wind up in the same shopping cart at convenience stores on Friday nights.

The analysts theorise that Mum sends Dad out for nappies, and he picks up a six-pack while he's at the store. But the analysts aren't positive. Maybe Mum is going out for a six-pack, and the baby starts to cry. That's where the results of data mining can get tricky. Armed with the market-basket correlation of beer and nappies, what action do we take? The experts say we can stock beer and nappies side by side. Or place those items at opposite ends of the store, so Dad or Mum will have maximum exposure to the temptation of impulse shopping when travelling between beer and nappies.

But why stop there? We can stock nappies in the refrigeration unit and put warm beer next to the baby formula. We can put them in the same package. If Dad or Mum pays by credit card, we know where they live, and we can manipulate the information. For starters, we can mail them discount coupons. Then, we can sell their information so that bags full of catalogues and special offers clog their mailbox, and telemarketers ruin their dinner hour. From there, the sky's the limit.

As a technologist, I recognise that data mining offers great value to businesses. It can improve efficiency and increase precision in supplying what customers want.

But as a person on the receiving end of data mining's insights, I feel a growing dread as marketers and others sharpen their aim in trying to influence and manipulate me. Who wants to shop in a store that runs you around like a rat between special offers? Who wants to order some clothes by telephone and, as a result, come to the attention of hundreds of companies that want to sell you something or change your behaviour? Who wants to be denied credit, a job or insurance—because you fall inadvertently into a pattern found by a computer? In short, who wants to feel that whatever move you make is captured and engenders the attempts to influence your next move?

Source: Shaku Atre, "All This Mining Can Be a Dirty Business," *Computerworld* (August 22, 1997): 24. Reprinted with permission.

Note: For our American readers, we should probably note that a nappie is more commonly referred to as a diaper in the United States.

[End Technology Excerpt 10.2 box here]

[Start Technology Application 10.2 box here]

TECHNOLOGY APPLICATION 10.2

E-Business in Global Markets

Case 1

Queensland Rail in Brisbane, Australia, has recently entered the EDI marketplace in order to streamline the scheduling process for shipments. In the past, the railroad had great difficulty identifying incoming shipments before they arrived. Thus, they were ill-prepared to handle the shipments quickly, and unable in many cases to make arrangements with connecting shippers (for handling nonrail segments of the delivery process) for timely pickup. With the new EDI system operating exclusively over the Internet, customers make "electronic wagon consignment bookings" that are automatically communicated to the railway and other third parties—including the connecting shippers. The bookings are sent as e-mail attachments or through file transfer protocol (FTP) in EDI format. All paper-based scheduling is cut out, making freight information much more timely. Most importantly, the railway station staff know what is coming before it arrives and can plan accordingly.

Case 2

Lite-On Technology Corp. in Taiwan has been forced to adapt very quickly to the demand for EDI communication by global business partners such as IBM and Compaq Computer. Concurrent with the move to EDI, cycle time to process sales orders has shrunk from a month to two days or less. In the case of CD-ROM drives, customers demand shipping just four hours after orders are placed. This scenario is not atypical for Asian manufacturers in a host of different business lines. In order to cope, many Asian companies are reacting much like Lite-On has by developing factories in other countries, such as the United States. All of the manufacturing operations are linked with the home office. As orders are received in the Taiwan offices, the information is electronically redistributed to the closest manufacturing facility having the capacity to complete the order in a timely fashion. Much of the communication is handled via Internet transmissions. The demands of electronic commerce and speed of delivery have outpaced the importance of lower labor costs in the region.

Sources: Mandy Bryan, "Old Rail Steams Ahead to E-freight," *Computerworld* (April 3, 1998): 36; Jonathan Moore, "Racing to Get Asia Globally Wired," *Business Week* (April 20, 1998).

[End Technology Application 10.2 box here]

[Start Technology Insight 10.3 box here]

TECHNOLOGY INSIGHT 10.3

Enterprise Systems Support for the M/S Process

The main effect of the introduction of an enterprise system into the M/S process depicted in Figure 10.7 is the integration of the processing programs and the various data stores into a single unified processing system with a single underlying database. In terms of the diagrams, the primary impact is therefore on the activities depicted within the "centralized data processing department." These changes are demonstrated in the diagram on page 349. You should note while studying this diagram, that while the systems flowchart has significantly simplified, the consolidation of all of the processes and databases shown in Figure 10.7 to the single process and database in the figure shown here suggests the complexity involved in the implementation of an enterprise system. Careful design is required.

[Insert UNF-p. 349-2 here]

[End Technology Insight 10.3 box here]

11

The "Order-to-Cash" Process: Part II, Revenue Collection (RC)

Will Hershey ever be able to recoup the market share lost in the debacle of Halloween 1999? During the late summer, Hershey made the decision to implement their SAP enterprise system using the "Big Bang" approach. In enterprise system terminology, Big Bang is the immediate cut-off of the old Information System with a complete implementation of the new enterprise system. When Hershey made the conversion to the SAP system, they were unable to match orders with production and delivery systems. Additionally, information did not flow through properly to billing systems, causing billing errors, delayed collections, and erosion of customer goodwill. Ultimately, Hershey was unable to fulfill customers' orders for Halloween candy and seasonally adjusted sales dipped an estimated 5%–7%. Many analysts believe that Hershey will never regain lost market share of 3%–5%. This is but one of many cases of such failures and highlights the importance to organizations of having well-integrated systems for the M/S and RC processes. Failure to integrate data between the two processes may leave a company suffering from the "trick" rather than enjoying the "treat."

Synopsis

This chapter covers the revenue collection (RC) process. In enterprise system terms, the marketing and sales (M/S) and RC processes jointly fulfill what is commonly known as the "Order to Cash" process you saw in Figure 10.1 on page 326. The RC process is triggered by the M/S activities covered in Chapter 10. In fact, many firms do not distinguish between the two processes as clearly as we have in this book.

This chapter first defines the RC process and describes its functions. Over and above event recording aspects of the process, we examine RC's importance in meeting customer needs and show how companies have used the RC process to gain competitive advantage. We explore technologies that have been used to leverage the process and to compete in an environment increasingly driven by enterprise systems and e-business. Based on this business environment, we consider the imprint of the RC process on the organization, again taking both a horizontal and vertical perspective. We follow this with discussion of both the logical and physical aspects of a typical process implementation. As in Chapter 10, control issues are dispersed throughout the chapter and are summarized by application of the control framework of Chapter 9.

Learning Objectives

- To describe the business environment for the revenue collection (RC) process
- To analyze the effect of enterprise systems and other technologies on the RC process

Gelinas 11-3

- To describe the RC process logic, physical characteristics, and support of management decision making
- To describe and analyze controls typically associated with the RC process

Introduction

The M/S process performs the critical tasks of (1) processing customer orders and (2) shipping goods to customers. The RC process completes the Order-to-Cash business process by accomplishing three separate yet related activities: (1) billing customers, (2) managing customer accounts, and (3) securing payment for goods sold or services rendered.

The **revenue collection (RC) process** is an interacting structure of people, equipment, methods, and controls designed to:

1. Support the repetitive work routines of the credit department, the cashier, and the accounts receivable department[1]

[1] To focus our discussion, we have assumed that these departments are the primary ones related to the RC process. For a given organization, however, the departments associated with the RC process may differ.

2. Support the problem-solving processes of financial managers
3. Assist in the preparation of internal and external reports
4. Create information flows and recorded data in support of the operations and management processes

Review Question

What is the revenue collection (RC) process?

First, the RC process supports the repetitive work routines by capturing, recording, and communicating data resulting from the tasks of billing customers, managing customer accounts, and collecting amounts due from customers. Next, the RC process supports the problem-solving processes involved in managing the revenue stream of the company. As but one example, the credit manager, reporting to the treasurer, might use an accounts receivable aging report such as the one in Figure 11.1 to make decisions about extending further credit to customers, pressing customers for payment, or writing off worthless accounts. Third, the RC process assists in the preparation of internal and external reports, such as those demanded by investors and bankers. Finally, the information process creates information flows and stored data to support the operations processes and decision-making requirements associated with the process.

[Insert Figure 11.1 here]

Review Question

What primary functions does the RC process perform? Explain each function.

The RC process occupies a position of critical importance to an organization. For example, an organization needs a rapid billing process, followed by close monitoring of receivables, and a quick cash collections process to convert sales into cash in a timely manner. Keeping receivables at a minimum should be a major objective of an RC process. While we tend to associate the RC process with mundane recordkeeping activities, the process also can be used to improve customer relations and competitive advantage. First, let's take a look at the organizational aspects of the RC process.

Organizational Setting

Figure 11.2 (page 376) presents a horizontal view of the relationship between the RC process and its organizational environment. Like its counterpart in Chapter 10, it shows typical information flows handled by the RC process. The flows provide an important communications medium among departments and between departments and entities in their relevant environment. The object here is simply to have you identify the major information flows of the RC process. Technology Insight 11.1 (page 377) discusses how horizontal information flows in an enterprise system become automated and therefore more efficient in terms of supporting the RC process.

Review Question

How does the RC process relate to its organizational setting?

[Insert Figure 11.2 here]

[Insert Table 11.1 here]

[Insert Technology Insight 11.1 box here]

Next, we introduce the key "players" shown within the "Finance" entity of Figure 11.2 (i.e., those boxes appearing in the right-most triangle of that figure). As illustrated by the figure, the major organizational subdivision within the finance area is between the treasury and controllership functions. Most organizations divorce the operational responsibility for the security and management of funds (treasury) from the recording of events (controllership). In other words, the treasurer directs how the company's money is invested or borrowed (i.e., an external focus), and the controller tracks where sales and other income comes from and how it is spent (i.e., an internal focus). The pervasive control plans (see Chapter 8) of *segregation of duties* and *physical security of resources* motivate this division between the treasury and the controllership functions.

Within the treasury function, the activities having the greatest effect on the RC process relate to the credit manager and the cashier. First, note that the credit manager is housed within the finance area rather than within marketing. This separation of the credit and sales functions is typical. If the credit function were part of marketing, credit might be extended to high-risk customers simply to achieve an optimistic sales target.

It is important also to separate the credit function (event *authorization*) from the *recordkeeping* functions of the controller's area. Within the controller's area, the major activities involved with the RC process are those of the accounts receivable department. This functional area is primarily involved in recordkeeping activities.

Managing the RC Process: Leveraging Cash Resources

It seems a simple concept—to increase net income without increasing the amount of sales you must reduce costs. The RC process provides several opportunities to cut costs through emerging technologies and improved management processes. We discuss three frequently used methods in this section: (1) customer self-service systems, (2) digital image processing systems, and (3) cash receipts management.

CRM: Customer Self-Service Systems

In Chapter 10 we saw customer relationship management (CRM) systems and how they can be used to improve customer management and service during the M/S process. We extend that discussion here by looking at another common feature of CRM systems—*customer self-service systems.* A **customer self-service system** is an Information Systems extension that allows a customer to complete an inquiry or perform a task within an organization's business process without the aid of the organization's employees.

Banks were probably the first industry to implement such systems on a broad base with the introduction of automated teller machines (ATMs). ATMs allow a customer to withdraw cash, make deposits, transfer funds between accounts, and so forth, without the help of a teller. Another place where similar added convenience has become widespread is the so-called "pay-at-the-pump" system for purchasing gasoline. In many cases, a human worker is not even required on-site, as a set of gasoline pumps are provided on location and purchases are made with either credit or debit cards. Telephone systems through which the customer selects options and enters account information with number keys are a common self-service application.

Internet systems that provide access to customers are now the norm in many industries. While these systems tend to take customers about as much time to use as telephone-based systems, studies show that consumers prefer Internet-based systems to the much-maligned phone-based systems. Internet-based systems also bring much more capability to systems. For instance, delivery companies (i.e., FedEx, UPS, etc.) now allow users to connect through the Internet and identify where their package is currently located, and if delivered, who signed for it.

A major benefit of these systems arises from the interconnection of customer self-service systems with enterprise systems. In some companies, customers can now check on their orders as they progress through the manufacturing process or even check on inventory availability before placing orders. Some of the more advanced systems also let customers check production planning for future manufacturing to determine if goods will be available at the time they will be needed.

Why are companies so interested in customer-self service systems and willing even to allow access to information in their internal systems? Quite simply, the payback on such systems is huge because of the reduced number of people needed to staff customer call centers. Reduction of staffing needs for call centers counterbalances the high human turnover in such centers, a result of boredom associated with the job.

Review Question

Why are customer self-service systems generally helpful in cutting customer service costs?

Digital Image Processing Systems

Many of the capabilities of digital image processing systems were explored in Chapter 4. Here, we take a brief look at the use of digital image processing systems in the RC process. Because of the amount of paper documents that traditionally flowed through the RC process, the ability to quickly scan, store, add information to, and retrieve documents on an as-needed basis can significantly reduce both labor costs for filing and the physical storage space and structures necessary for storing paper-based files.

Here is how digital image processing systems typically work. Given the abundance of digital image documents that rapidly stack up in a large payment processing center, these documents need to be organized and filed away (much like their paper counterparts). Electronic folders are created to store and organize related documents. The folders are retrievable via their electronic tabs. As a result, the image storage and retrieval processes logically parallel the same processes used in traditional paper systems, without the headache of storing the mounds of paper and having to deliver requested documents by hand across the building or even across the world. Likewise, if a customer contacts a customer service representative, the representative can quickly retrieve the digital image of each customer statement and provide the customer a timely response—avoiding wasted time with retrieving paper documents and possible call-backs to the customer. Specific examples from practice are discussed in Technology Application 11.1 (page 380). We will take another look at the use of digital image processing during the controls discussion later in this chapter.

[Insert Technology Application 11.1 box here]

Managing Cash Receipts

Gelinas 11-11

The advent of electronic banking has made companies acutely aware of the critical importance of sound *cash management* for improving earnings performance. The name of the cash management game is to free up funds so that they either can be invested to earn interest or used to reduce debt, thus saving interest charges. Of course, before cash can be invested or used for debt reduction by the treasurer, it first must be received and deposited. The overall management objective, therefore, is to shorten as much as possible the time from the beginning of the selling process to the ultimate collection of funds.

In the billing function, the goal is to get invoices to customers as quickly as possible, with the hope of reducing the time it takes to obtain payments. Having the RC process produce invoices *automatically* helps ensure that invoices are sent to customers shortly after the goods have been shipped.

At the other end of the process, the treasurer is concerned with potential delays in collecting/depositing customer cash receipts and having those receipts clear the banking system. The term **float,** when applied to cash receipts, is the time between the customer's making payment and the availability of the funds for company use. Float is a real cost to a firm. Enhanced processing of checks, charge cards, and debit cards can reduce or eliminate float associated with cash receipts.

Review Question

What is a lockbox? Why is a lockbox used?

Technology Insight 11.2 (page 381)discusses four other Internet-enabled mechanisms that organizations have used to shorten the float, improve e-business practices, or achieve other economies. As e-business opportunities increase, these e-payment mechanisms will become the norm in the cash receipts process.

Review Question

Describe several ways that companies have used IT to reduce the float connected with cash receipts.

[Insert Technology Insight 11.2 box here]

Logical Process Description

The principal activities of the Revenue Collection process are to bill customers, collect and deposit cash received from those customers, record the invoices and cash collections, and inform the general ledger system to make entries for sales and cash receipts. In addition to the billing and cash receipts functions, the RC process *manages customer accounts.* Activities normally included in this process are sales returns and allowances, account write-offs, and sending periodic statements to customers. This section shows and explains the key *event data* and *master data* used by the process.

Logical Data Flow Diagrams

As you learned in Chapter 2 and saw applied in Chapter 10, our first view of the process is a general one, shown in the form of a *context diagram.* For the RC process, that view appears in Figure 11.3. Note the external entities with which this process interacts and the data flows running to and from those entities.

[Insert Figure 11.3 here]

Now let's explode Figure 11.3 into the level 0 diagram reflected in Figure 11.4. In this expanded view of the process, we see that the single bubble in Figure 11.3 has become three process bubbles. We also see the event and master data for this process. At this point, review Figure 11.4 and compare it to Figure 11.3 to confirm that the two figures are "in balance" with each other. Each of the three process bubbles shown in the level 0 diagram are decomposed into their lower-level diagrams in Appendix A.

[Insert Figure 11.4 here]

In the section "Logical Data Descriptions" that follows later in the chapter, we define or explain the *accounts receivable master data, sales event data,* and *invoice data.* Before proceeding, let's take a brief look at the information content of an invoice. Figure 11.5 (page 384) is an example of a sales order inquiry of invoice items.

[Insert Figure 11.5 here]

The **invoice** is a business document used by a vendor to notify the customer of an obligation to pay the seller for the merchandise ordered and shipped. Notice that the information at the top of the screen represents that part that would be printed to an invoice to identify the unique order placed and associated with a specific customer. The body of the screen captures the item or items ordered by the customer and the related pricing information. When the invoice is printed, it may often include the payment details.

Logical Data Descriptions

Seven data stores appear in Figure 11.4, the level 0 diagram, five of which are related to event occurrences. Of the two *master data stores,* the *customer master* was defined in Chapter 10.

Accounts receivable master data contain all unpaid invoices issued by an organization and awaiting payment. As the invoice is created, a record of the receivable is entered in the master data. Subsequently, the records are updated—i.e., the receivable balance is reduced—at the time that the customer makes the payment. The records also could be updated to reflect sales returns and allowances, bad debt write-offs, or other adjustments.

The accounts receivable master data provide information useful in minimizing outstanding customer balances and in prompting customers to pay in a timely manner.

Now let’s look at the event data maintained in the RC process.

First, the process records an entry for the sales data after it has validated the shipment and as it produces an invoice. In the previous section, we showed you a specimen invoice (see Figure 11.5). The logical data definition for **sales event data** would essentially comprise one or more records of invoices. However, each data record would not contain all of the details reflected on the invoice itself. For example, item numbers, descriptions, quantities ordered, quantities shipped, and quantities back ordered typically are not recorded in the sales event data. Rather, these details would be found in the *invoice data.*

Review Question

What are the sales data and accounts receivable data stores?

Accounts receivable adjustments data are created as sales returns, bad debt write-offs, estimated doubtful accounts, or similar adjustments are processed as part of managing customer accounts. As in any event data, records in this data store are typically keyed by date.

Cash receipts data, created when customer payments are recorded, contain details of each payment as reflected on the *remittance advice* accompanying a payment. A **remittance advice (RA)** is a business document used by the payer to notify the payee of the items being paid. The RA can take various forms. For instance, it may be a copy of the invoice, a detachable RA delivered as part of a statement periodically sent to the customer (often a "stub" attached to the statement, a *turnaround document*), or a stub attached to the payer's check. In any case, RC uses the RA to initiate the recording of a cash receipt. Finally, as its name suggests, the *remittance advice file* contains copies of the remittance advices themselves.

Types of Billing Systems

In general, there are two kinds of billing systems. A **postbilling system** prepares invoices after goods have been shipped and the sales order notification has been matched to shipping's billing notification. The data flow diagrams in this section and in Chapter 10 assume a postbilling system.

A **prebilling system** prepares invoices immediately on acceptance of a customer order—that is, after inventory and credit checks have been accomplished. Prebilling systems often occur in situations where there is little or no delay between receipt of the customer's order and its shipment. For instance, prebilling systems are not uncommon in catalog sales operations such as that of L.L. Bean. In such systems, there is no separate sales order document; copies of the invoice serve as the picking ticket, packing slip, and other functions required by the M/S process.[2] In other words, the customer is billed (and the inventory, accounts receivable, and general ledger master data are updated) at the time the customer order is entered. However, the customer copy of the invoice is not released until shipment has been made. For this type of system to operate efficiently, the inventory control system must be very reliable. If an order is accepted and an item then turns out to be unavailable, all financial records have to be adjusted.

[2] By eliminating one source document (the sales order) and a separate data transcription step (from shipping documents to the customer invoice), prebilling helps to ensure certain control goals. For that reason, we include prebilling procedures as a control plan for the billing process in a later chapter section.

Review Question

What is the difference between a postbilling system and a prebilling system?

Physical Process Description of the Billing Function

Figure 11.6 presents a process for billing events. From Chapter 10, you have an understanding of the order entry and shipping functions leading up to billing. Review the flowchart for general ideas.

[Insert Figure 11.6]

The Billing Process

At the time the sales order documents were prepared in the order entry department, copy 1 was sent to the billing department (the annotation to the left of the sales order data indicates that these "sales order notifications" are held pending receipt of the shipping notices). At the end of each day, billing receives (from the shipping department) batches of bills of lading (copy 1), accompanied by shipping notices (sales order copy 2).

In the billing department, a clerk compares the details of these documents. Data that fail to pass the document-matching control are removed from the batch; these data are handled by a separate exception routine. Corrected data will be submitted to the computer during a subsequent processing cycle.

If there is agreement among the data items, the billing clerk prepares batch totals, logs each batch, and sends the batches to data control. Data control logs the batches and forwards them to data preparation. Data preparation clerks records the shipping notices to the sales event database. A second clerk reenters the inputs. After reconciliation of any differences between the manually calculated batch totals and the batch totals calculated by the program, the sales data are forwarded to computer operations. This concludes the recording process.

The first step of the update process is to sort and merge sales data in order to prepare the data for sequential processing against the accounts receivable master data. A maintenance run brings the master data up to date and prints one or more reports. Any errors discovered during the process run are recorded with the error suspense data along with a record of each sales order (i.e., shipping notice) number processed during the run.

Output invoices are sent back to data control to be logged out and then are sent to the billing department. Once the invoices have been received by the billing department, a clerk logs the batch back in and matches the invoices with the sales orders and bills of lading. If the documents match, the original invoice is sent to the customer, and the copy is filed with the sales order and bill of lading.

Once you have had the opportunity to study the billing process documented in Figure 11.6, stop and consider how this might change in an enterprise system environment. After you have thought through the impact and the resulting changes to Figure 11.6, read Technology Insight 11.3, which provides an overview of how a fully implemented enterprise system impacts the billing process discussed in this chapter.

[Insert Technology Insight 11.3 box here]

Selected Process Outputs

A variety of outputs (records, documents, statements, and reports) are generated in this process. The key document/record produced by the process depicted in Figure 11.6 is the sales invoice. (Invoice records are depicted in Figure 11.5 on page 384.) The computer numbers these documents/records sequentially.

Another important document, the *customer monthly statement,* is prepared at the end of each month from data appearing in each customer's accounts receivable master data record. Sending periodic customer statements is part of the function of *managing customer accounts.* Other analyses and reports can be prepared as needed. For example, if an accounts receivable aging report were desired, the relevant account data would be extracted from the accounts receivable master data. (Figure 11.1, page 375, illustrates a typical accounts receivable aging report.)

[Insert Figure 11.7 here]

Application of the Control Framework for the Billing Function

This section applies the control framework to the billing function. Figure 11.7 presents a completed *control matrix* for the systems flowchart depicted in Figure 11.6. Figure 11.6 is annotated to show the location of the control plans keyed to the control matrix.

Control Goals

The control goals listed across the top of the matrix are derived from the framework presented in Chapter 9. Effectiveness of operations shows only two representative *operations process* goals. Obviously, in actual billing processes, other operations process goals are possible. As mentioned in Chapter 9 and reinforced in Chapter 10, the resource security column should identify only the assets that are *directly* at risk. For that reason, cash is not listed because it is only indirectly affected by the validity of the billings. The resource of interest here is the accounts receivable master data. Controls should prevent unauthorized access, copying, changing, selling, or destruction of the accounts receivable master data.

To focus our discussion, we limit our coverage of process inputs to just the shipping notice. Note, however, that other process inputs could be included in the matrix. From the point of view of the billing process, valid bills are those that are properly authorized and reflect actual credit sales. For example, a bill should be supported by a proper shipping notification and should be billed at authorized prices, terms, freight, and discounts.

Recommended Control Plans

Each of the recommended control plans listed in the first column of the control matrix is discussed in Exhibit 11.1 (page 392). This exhibit is divided into two sections:

[Insert Exhibit 11.1 here]

- A. Billing process control plans that are unique to the billing process.
- B. Controls for the processing technology in place or that apply to any business process. Your study of Chapter 9 supplies understanding of how these plans relate to specific control goals. In other words, you should be able to explain the cell entries in

Figure 11.7 for these four control plans. If you cannot do so readily, review Chapter 9.

As usual, you will find that some of the recommended control plans are present in the process and others are missing. As you study the control plans, be sure to notice where they are located on the systems flowchart.

Review Question

What controls are associated with the billing function? Explain each control.

Physical Process Description of the Cash Receipts Function

As discussed earlier, the procedures employed in collecting cash vary widely. For example, some companies ask customers to mail checks along with remittance advices to the company, others ask customers to send payments to a designated bank lockbox, while in e-business environments some form of electronic funds transfer is generally used.

Figure 11.8 (page 396) depicts a process in which customer payments arrive by mail. The source documents include checks and remittance advices.

[Insert Figure 11.8 here]

Each day, the process begins with mailroom clerks opening the mail. Immediately, the clerks endorse all checks. They assemble enclosed statements (remittance advices that come in the form of billing statement detachments from the customer invoice—i.e., *turnaround documents*) in batches and prepare batch totals for control purposes. The receipts data—batch total and remittance details from the customer billing statements—are then entered into the computer system via a scanning process and use of *optical character recognition* technology in the mailroom. The computer edits the data as they are entered and computes batch totals. Once the data are verified, details are written to the *cash receipts event data.* The batched statements are sent to the accounts receivable department for filing, and the checks are transferred to the cashier.

For most processes of the type illustrated in Figure 11.8, input requirements are minimal. As indicated, the editing process verifies the correctness of the entered data, including customer number and so forth. By accessing open invoice data that reside within the accounts receivable master data, the process also verifies that any cash discounts taken by the customer are legitimate (i.e., they have been *authorized*). To check the dollar amount of each invoice remitted, the system calculates the balance due by adding the cash payment to the cash discount taken (if any); it then compares the computed balance-due total to the balance-due total scanned in by the mailroom clerk.

Once the data have passed all the control checks, the accounts receivable master data are updated. Also, the computer generates various cash reports and prepares the deposit slip. The deposit slip is transferred to the cashier. The cashier compares the checks and the deposit slip; if they agree, all documents are sent to the bank.

Once you have had the opportunity to study the cash receipts process documented in Figure 11.8, consider how this process might change in an enterprise system environment. After you have thought through the impact and the resulting changes to Figure 11.8, read Technology Insight 11.4, which provides an overview of how a fully implemented enterprise system affects the cash receipts process discussed in this chapter.

[Insert Technology Insight 11.4 box here]

Application of the Control Framework for the Cash Receipts Function

The control framework is applied to the cash receipts function in this section. Figure 11.9 presents a completed *control matrix* for the annotated systems flowchart depicted in Figure 11.8.

Control Goals

By now, you are familiar with the control goals listed in the column headings of the matrix. We will discuss only two of those goals. First, as you learned in Chapter 7, the COSO study and report on internal control recommends three categories of control goals, the third being compliance with applicable laws, regulations, and contractual agreements. Also, recall that we elect not to show the "compliance" goal as a separate category but to include it under the system goals for the operations system. As we did with Causeway's cash receipts process in Chapter 9, we assume that the company whose process appears in Figure 11.8 has loan agreements with its bank that require it to maintain certain minimum cash balances on deposit. For that reason, operations process goal C—"To comply with minimum balance agreements with our bank"—appears in Figure 11.9.

[Insert Figure 11.9 here]

Our second comment concerns the input validity (IV) control goal. We define *valid* remittance advices as those that represent funds *actually received* and for which cash discounts have been *authorized and approved.*

Review Question

What controls are associated with the cash receipts function? Explain each control.

Recommended Control Plans

Each of the recommended control plans listed in the matrix is discussed in Exhibit 11.2 (page 400). We have intentionally limited the number of plans to avoid redundancy. As you study the recommended control plans, be sure to check where they are located on the systems flowchart. Note that Exhibit 11.2 is divided into two sections: (A) Cash receipts process control plans that are unique to the cash receipts function, and (B) other control plans.

[Insert Exhibit 11.2 here]

Conclusions

With the conclusion of this chapter, we complete the discussion of the order-to-sales process, as depicted in Figure 10.1 (page 326). In later chapters, we discuss the interaction of M/S and RC with the other key business processes in an organization.

This chapter presented a number of ways that technology can affect the operations of RC. For example, technology was discussed as a means of solving certain problems regarding cash flow. What's in the future? We are rapidly moving toward a checkless society. Even cash is becoming less of an accepted medium for payment. Your challenge will be to keep abreast of the ways businesses are affected by the transition from checks and cash to electronic transfers of money.

Appendix 11A

Lower-Level DFDs

Figure 11.10 decomposes bubble 1.0 of Figure 11.4 (page 383). Most of Figure 11.10 should be self-explanatory. As you saw in Chapter 10, when the M/S process produces a *sales order,* it notifies the RC process to that effect. These notifications are filed temporarily,[3] until such time that M/S informs RC that the goods have been shipped. When *triggered* by the data flow "Shipping's billing notification," process 1.1 validates the sale by removing the sales order notification from the temporary file and comparing its details to those shown on shipping's billing notification. If discrepancies appear, the request is rejected, as shown by the reject stub coming from bubble 1.1. Rejected requests later would be processed through a separate *exception routine.*

[3] Please recognize that, *physically,* this temporary data could take the form of an open sales order (i.e., an order not yet shipped) in a *sales order master data store* or SALES_ORDERS relational table, both of which you saw in Chapter 10.

[Insert Figure 11.10 here]

If the data flows match, process 1.1 sends a validated shipping notification to process 1.2. Process 1.2 then performs the following actions simultaneously:

- Obtains from the customer master certain standing data needed to produce the invoice.
- Creates the invoice and sends it to the customer.
- Updates the accounts receivable master data.
- Adds an invoice to the sales event data.

- Files a copy of the invoice in the invoice file.
- Notifies the general ledger that a sale has occurred (GL invoice update).

Now let's take a closer look at process 2.0 in Figure 11.4. Figure 11.11 is the lower-level diagram of that process.

[Insert Figure 11.11 here]

As mentioned earlier, managing customer accounts involves an array of activities that typically occur between customer billing and later cash collection. Three of those activities are reflected in Figure 11.11: (1) sending periodic statements of account to customers, (2) accounting for sales returns and allowances or other accounts receivable adjustments, and (3) accounting for bad debts. The tasks required to maintain customer accounts can be resource intensive for an organization.

Now let's examine briefly the processes that are diagrammed in Figure 11.11. In general, adjustments will always be necessary to account for sales returns, allowances for defective products or partial shipments, reversals of mispostings and other errors, estimates of uncollectible accounts, and bad debt write-offs. In Figure 11.11, processes 2.1 through 2.3 relate to sales returns adjustments. Process 2.5, "Prepare bad debts journal entry," is triggered by a *temporal* event; namely, the periodic review of aging details obtained from the accounts receivable master data. One of two types of adjustments might result from this review:

- The recurring adjusting entry for *estimated* bad debts
- The periodic write-off of “definitely worthless” customer accounts

Note that, regardless of type, adjustments are recorded in the event data, updated to customer balances in the accounts receivable master data, and summarized and posted to the general ledger master data by the general ledger system.

Like process 2.5, bubble 2.4, “Prepare customer statements,” is also triggered by a temporal event. In other words, it recurs at specified intervals, quite often on a monthly basis in practice. Details of unpaid invoices are extracted from the accounts receivable master data and are summarized in a statement of account that is mailed to customers. The statement both confirms with the customer the balance still owing and reminds the customer that payment is due. Therefore, it serves both operating and control purposes.

Figure 11.12, a lower-level diagram of process 3.0 “Receive payment” in Figure 11.4, completes our analysis of the events comprising the RC process. In this diagram, we see our earlier activities culminate in the collection of cash from customers. The check and remittance advice trigger the *Receive payment process.*

[Insert Figure 11.12 here]

On receipt of the check and remittance advice from a customer, process 3.1 first validates the remittance by comparing the check to the RA. Mismatches are rejected for later processing. If the check and RA agree, the validated remittance is sent to process 3.2, which endorses the check and separates the check from the RA. Process 3.3 accumulates a number of endorsed checks, prepares and sends a bank deposit to the bank, records the collection with the *cash receipts data,* and notifies the general ledger system of the amount of the cash deposited.

While process 3.3 is preparing the deposit, process 3.4 uses the RA to update the *accounts receivable master data* to reflect the customer's payment and then files the RA in the remittance advice file.

Appendix 11B

Logical Database Design

As we did in Chapter 10, we now look at how RC data would be structured in a *database.* To keep the discussion simple, we will look only at two basic economic events as they relate to this process—sales invoicing and cash receipts. We will not cover adjustments resulting from sales returns, bad debt write-offs, and estimated doubtful accounts. First, in Figure 11.13, let's look at an E-R diagram of the invoicing and cash receipts events.

[Insert Figure 11.13 here]

The SHIPMENT, CUSTOMER, and SALES INVOICE entities should look familiar from the E-R diagram in Chapter 10 (see Figure 10.13 on page 362). To those three, we have added a CASH RECEIPT entity. In this section, we will examine the relationships among SALES INVOICE, CUSTOMER, and CASH RECEIPT entities. Let's next translate the E-R diagram into relational tables.

Figure 11.14, parts (a) and (b), reproduces selected relations from Figure 10.14 (see page 363) in order to emphasize the connections (linkages) among relations. These selected relations also remind us that before invoicing a customer, we first have accepted a customer's sales order, picked the goods, and shipped the goods to the customer. Part (c) shows the *new* relations depicted in the E-R diagram in Figure 11.13. To simplify the tables, we have assumed that each inventory line item picked and shipped is billed at a single unit sales price from the INVENTORY_ITEM table. Further, SALES_INVOICES (part b) ignores freight, sales taxes, or other items that might be billed to a customer. By using the SALES_INVOICES relation in part (b) and extracting other data, as needed, from other relations, consider how you would prepare the invoice *record* shown earlier in the chapter (see Figure 11.5, page 384).

[Insert Figure 11.14 here]

The CASH_RECEIPTS and CASH_RECEIPT *pays for* SALES_INVOICE tables in part (c) substitute for the cash receipts data and remittance advice data discussed in the preceding section. For simplicity, we ignore customer cash discounts in the tables shown. First, note that Cust_No in CASH_RECEIPTS allows us to associate cash receipts with particular customers for the purpose of monitoring customer accounts and assessing any needed bad debt adjustments. In addition, Invoice_No in CASH_RECEIPT *pays for* SALES INVOICE can be used to apply collections against specific open invoices. Finally, the linkages among CASH_RECEIPTS, CASH_RECEIPT *pays for* SALES_INVOICE, SALES_INVOICES, and CUSTOMERS can be used to determine customer accounts receivable balances at any moment in time.

REVIEW QUESTIONS

RQ11-1 What is the revenue collection (RC) process?

RQ11-2 What primary functions does the RC process perform? Explain each function.

RQ11-3 How does the RC process relate to its organizational setting?

RQ11-4 Why are customer self-service systems generally helpful in cutting customer service costs?

RQ11-5 What is a lockbox? Why is a lockbox used?

RQ11-6 Describe several ways that companies have used IT to reduce the float connected with cash receipts.

RQ11-7 What are the sales data and accounts receivable data stores?

RQ11-8 What is the difference between a postbilling system and a prebilling system?

RQ11-9 What controls are associated with the billing function? Explain each control.

RQ11-10 What controls are associated with the cash receipts function? Explain each control.

DISCUSSION QUESTIONS

DQ11-1 Identify several examples of possible goal conflicts among the various managers and supervisors depicted in Figure 11.2 (page 376).

DQ11-2 Based on the definition of *float* presented in the chapter, discuss several possibilities for improving the cash float for your company.

DQ11-3 (Appendix A) Using Figure 11.11 (page 404), list the kinds of data that might be running along the data flow that comes from the accounts receivable master data to bubble 2.1. Be specific, and be prepared to defend your answer by discussing the use(s) to which *each* of those data elements could be put.

DQ11-4 Discuss the information content of Figure 11.1 (page 375). How might this report be used by the sales manager, the credit manager or by the accounts receivable manager? If you were one of these managers, what other reports concerning accounts receivable might you find useful, and how would you use them? Be specific.

DQ11-5 Consult the systems flowcharts of Figures 11.6 (page 387) and 11.8 (page 396). Discuss how *each* of these processes implements the concept of segregation of duties discussed in Chapter 8. For each of the two processes, be specific as to which entity (or entities) performs each of the four data processing functions mentioned in Chapter 8 (assuming that all four functions are illustrated by the process).

DQ11-6 a. Discuss the conditions under which each of the following billing systems would be most appropriate: (1) prebilling system and (2) postbilling system.

b. Discuss the relative advantages of each of the billing systems mentioned in part a, from the standpoint of *both* the selling company and the customer.

PROBLEMS

NOTE: As mentioned in Chapter 10, the first couple of problems in the application chapters are based on the processes of specific companies. Therefore, the problem material starts with case narratives of those processes.

CASE STUDIES

Case A: Midwest Insurance Co.

Background Information

Midwest Insurance Co. is a major property/casualty underwriter based in St. Louis. It uses more than 3,000 independent insurance agents to market its products and collect premiums. In the past, agents typically have remitted the premiums to Midwest at a predetermined time each month by mailing the checks to a lockbox site or to a regional office of the insurance company. This method of cash collections has been slow, and accounting for the agents' payments has been fraught with problems. Therefore, Midwest sought the help of Nationwide Bank (NB) in developing a more automated collection process. NB responded by developing an ACH-based "Customer-Initiated Payment Service (CIPS)" that allows the independent agents to pay Midwest with ACH debits initiated via a toll-free phone call or over the Internet. The next section describes how the CIPS process works; for simplicity, the description is limited to telephone-initiated payments.

Operation of the CIPS Process

By 8:15 p.m. EST on the 14th of each month, an agent calls the toll-free number and gives the bank operator the following information:

- The company number—Midwest's four-digit designator
- The unit number—the agent's eight-digit unique identifier

- The payment amount
- The agent's PIN
- The effective date of the payment—a day (within the next 30 days) on which the payment is to be made

The bank operator keys the information to a payment database. Alternatively, the same information could be keyed in via the bank's Web site. A preprocessing program checks to make sure all fields were filled in. Later in the evening, the bank uses the payment data to create a new file of transactions formatted to ACH standards. On each effective payment date, the ACH payment data is used to update the bank accounts of the agents and Midwest's ACH concentration account at NB. Funds are then transferred from this ACH concentration account to Midwest's primary concentration bank in New York City so they are available for investment on the transaction's effective date.

The evening of the payment date, NB also transmits a data file of the settled payments to Midwest's data center in Delaware. The data center uses the payments data to update its agents' accounts receivable database and to post the payments to the general ledger. The following morning, the database is used to generate several reports, which can be viewed online or printed, depending on the option chosen by the users (i.e, by managers who access the database from Midwest's St. Louis office).

Case B: Panhandle Department Stores (I)

Panhandle Department Stores operates at 30 locations in Texas and Oklahoma. The company's headquarters are in Oklahoma City. The company accepts cash, national credit cards (VISA and MasterCard), and its own Panhandle charge card (PCC). Procedures for cash receipts are standard at each location. PCC billing and the treasury function are located at headquarters.

Customers present their purchases at a central checkout location at each store. Point-of-sale registers provide immediate updates to quantities on hand in the inventory master data, compile detailed data on sales, and accumulate "proof figures" used in cashing out the drawer at the end of each shift. Each store's registers are tied to the central computer system in Oklahoma City.

Throughout the shift, clerks process the several forms of sales. At the end of the shift, the next clerk resets the proof totals. The front manager takes a hard copy of the proof totals for the shift completed and the drawer of the clerk whose shift was completed to the cashier, for "proving." The cashier reconciles the drawer to the totals, prepares a two-part "cash out report" for each clerk on the shift, and updates the "over and short summary" maintained for each clerk. After the work for each shift is complete, these reports are sent to the front manager for review. Meanwhile, the clerk for the next shift has installed his own cash drawer and has begun processing sales.

Store deposits are made whenever the cash-on-hand balance reaches $25,000 and at the end of the day. For each deposit, the system prints out a deposit slip; a designated employee makes the trip to the local bank. The employee brings back a receipted deposit slip. Daily, the cashier prepares the national credit card (NCC) settlement sheets in duplicate for each credit company. One copy of the settlement sheet and the supporting charge sales slips are submitted to the appropriate charge company for payment. The PCC slips, a copy of the NCC settlement sheet, a copy of the cash out report, and the day's deposit slips are sent to Oklahoma City at 5:00 p.m. by courier mail.

In the cash receipts department at Oklahoma City, a sales report is obtained from the process at the end of each day. That report is reconciled to the cash out report and the deposit slips. The PCC slips are reconciled to that line on the cash out report. The PCC slips are then sent to data processing, where data preparation clerks enter the charges into a batch file on the computer. At 9:00 p.m. the batch is used to update the accounts receivable master data.

Case C: Panhandle Department Stores (II)

Before starting this case, review the facts in Case B.

Reimbursements from the national credit cards are deposited directly in the company's main Oklahoma City bank, and the bank notifies Panhandle of these receipts. The cash receipts department reconciles these receipts to the NCC settlement sheets that previously had been submitted to the card companies (the settlement sheets had been filed by date until this time). All receipts from the company's proprietary cards (PCCs) are received in Oklahoma City. The company uses a turnaround document, so it receives a check and a portion of the monthly charge card statement (on which the customer has filled in the amount remitted). The cash receipts clerk examines the check against the amount written on the document and, in a space reserved, enters the amount received on the document so that it can be computer scanned.

Checks and turnaround documents are batched. The documents are sent to data processing. The checks are deposited, and the deposit slip is photocopied. Copies of the batch totals and the deposit slips are filed separately by date. A copy of the deposit slip is sent to the treasurer's office.

The turnaround documents are then scanned. Each evening at 10:00 p.m., customers' accounts are updated with scanned data, and a cash receipts listing is produced and sent to cash receipts each morning, where it is checked against and filed with the related batch totals. A copy of the cash receipts listing is sent to the treasurer's office.

P11-1 For the company assigned by your instructor,[4] complete the following requirements:

[4] If the assigned case is an extension of an earlier case, limit your solution to the narrative contained in the assigned case.

a. Prepare a table of entities and activities.

b. Draw a context diagram.

c. Draw a physical data flow diagram (DFD).

d. Prepare an annotated table of entities and activities. Indicate on this table the groupings, bubble numbers, and bubble titles to be used in preparing a level 0 logical DFD.

e. Draw a level 0 logical DFD.

P11-2 For the company assigned by your instructor,[4] complete the following requirements:

a. Draw a systems flowchart.

b. Prepare a control matrix, including explanations of how each recommended existing control plan helps to accomplish—or would accomplish in the case of missing plans—each related control goal. Your choice of recommended control plans should come from section A of Exhibit 11.1 (pages 392–394) or Exhibit 11.2 (page 400)plus any technology-related control plans from Chapter 9 that are germane to your company's process.

c. Annotate the flowchart prepared in part a to indicate the points where the control plans are being applied (codes P-1 . . . P-*n*) or the points where they could be applied but are not (codes M-1 . . . M-*n*).

P11-3 Study the narratives of the case indicated by your instructor. Also refer to the two operations process goals for the billing function in Figure 11.7 (pages 391–392), and operations process goals A and B for the cash receipts function in Figure 11.9 (page 399).

In one paragraph for each of the four goals, compare and contrast the assigned case processes in terms of their ability to achieve the goals. Cite specific features that give a particular process a comparative advantage in terms of meeting a particular goal. Also, be specific in identifying the query or reporting opportunities in the assigned cases.

P11-4 Assume the data collected in this case are stored in a data warehouse. Describe the data and reports that could be used to help:

a. The treasurer decide how to invest the company's money.

b. The controller determine if the company will have enough cash on hand.

c. The credit manager determine when to increase credit lines or cut off credit to existing customers.

P11-5 The following capsule cases present short narratives of processes used by three actual organizations whose names have been changed for the purpose of this problem. You will use the cases to practice the mechanics of drawing data flow diagrams.

Capsule Case 1: Cumberland County Registry of Motor Vehicles

The Registry of Motor Vehicles (RMV) in Cumberland County, Kansas, has recently simplified its license renewal process by automating the test-taking and fee-collection steps in the process. RMV notifies drivers when their licenses are about to expire. Drivers who renew their licenses in person at the RMV work with a computer that looks and functions like an ATM machine. The process is described in the following paragraphs.

After keying in his or her current driver's license number, the applicant is presented with a touch-screen display that pulls up test questions stored within the computer. Short video clips of typical traffic situations are shown, and questions are asked about each clip. The applicant responds to the questions by selecting from options presented on the screen.

The terminal scores the test, allows users to change address or other personal information appearing on the screen, and "collects" the renewal fee. The user "pays" the fee by inserting his or her VISA or MasterCard into a designated slot on the computer.

The computer then prints a scored answer sheet, which the applicant takes to a registry clerk. The clerk completes the process by administering a vision test, taking a picture of the applicant, and issuing a license.

Capsule Case 2: Down Under Airlines

Background Information

Down Under Airlines (DUA) processes over 400 million tickets a year. The process of issuing the tickets is highly automated; a record of each ticket sold is stored in DUA's database. But when passengers turn in tickets, gate agents stuff the flight coupons into envelopes and ship them to DUA's Denver headquarters. Because of discrepancies between the original records housed in the ticket database and actual ticket use as reflected by the flight coupons (see the following NOTE), DUA, like other airlines, has to match every coupon against every ticket in the database in order to accurately account for passenger revenues. With the volume of tickets involved, manual matching is a daunting task. Image processing to the rescue!

(*Note:* For example, passengers might use a ticket from one airline to fly with another, or they might use only the A-B leg of an A-B-C flight, and so forth.)

Description of the New Image Processing System

DUA's new system, designed by one of the Big Four professional service firms, functions as follows:

When a ticket is sold to a passenger by a travel agent or by one of DUA's own 30,000 ticket agents, the seller enters a record of the ticket into DUA's database, just as in the past. However, when flight coupons are received in Denver, they are now read by an image scanner that captures the images and stores them in an optical storage and retrieval library called Big File.

The ticket number appearing on the flight coupon is also scanned by an optical character recognition (OCR) system. The ticket numbers—an index to the ticket images themselves—are stored in a relational database, which is used to track the location of each ticket image in Big File.

Operators use a network of workstations to access ticket images. Special audit software matches each ticket image in Big File with ticket records in the mainframe database. If the image and record do not match (for instance, a three-leg ticket sold but only two legs used), the ticket number is included in the audit data. If the image and record do match, the ticket record is written to the passenger revenue data.

Capsule Case 3: Rosebud Supermarkets

Background Information

Rosebud Supermarkets Inc. operates a chain of grocery stores in Vermont. Rosebud accepts credit cards and debit cards at the point of sale (POS). To offer this service to customers, Rosebud has placed a pinstripe terminal within the reach of the customer at each checkout counter. The terminal, which is attached to the transport belt area that moves the groceries past the cashier, interfaces with the POS cash register. For customers who want to pay for their orders using a means *other* than with cash, the system works as described below.

Partial Description of Rosebud's Checkout Process

(*Note:* Exception routines are among the features not described.)

When a customer presents his or her order at the checkout station, the cashier uses a POS scanner at the end of the belt area to ring up the customer's order in the cash register and to produce a register tape for the customer. After the groceries have been scanned, the cashier obtains the POS register total for the groceries purchased. Then, the customer hits the "enter" key in the pinstripe terminal. A screen display appears that shows the purchase total and asks the customer what type of payment option is desired. The customer selects from three options—credit card, direct debit (through local participating banks), or check authorization—by pressing a key opposite that option.

In the case of credit, the customer runs the credit card through the terminal's magnetic stripe reader. The request for credit authorization is then transmitted to the appropriate credit card company. The credit card company sends back a credit authorization number for the purchased amount.

For the debit option, the customer runs a bank debit card through the card reader and then enters his PIN. As in the case of credit purchases, the data are transmitted to the appropriate bank. The bank responds by transmitting back an approval message.

For check authorization, Rosebud uses scannable courtesy cards. The courtesy card number and grocery total are transmitted to Rosebud's internal check authorization system. The authorization system looks up the customer in its courtesy card data and notifies the cashier whether or not the check should be accepted.

For the capsule case assigned by your instructor, complete the following requirements:

a. Prepare a table of entities and activities.

b. Draw a context diagram.

c. Draw a physical data flow diagram (DFD).

d. Prepare an annotated table of entities and activities. Indicate on this table the groupings, bubble numbers, and bubble titles to be used in preparing a level 0 logical DFD.

e. Draw a level 0 logical DFD.

P11-6 Airlines have issued paperless tickets for several years now. Recently, they have begun experimenting with allowing travelers to print their own tickets using special bar coding technology located at commercial customer locations. The bar-code ticket system can be used to communicate with business customers' accounting systems and other internal databases to speed up the billing process. These tickets would be scanned at the airport in the same way as paper tickets or airport generated boarding cards, when the passenger boards the plane.

a. Describe the advantages to the airline of this process. Compare it to both travel-agent-issued paper tickets and to paperless tickets.

b. Describe the advantages to the customer of this process.

c. Review Capsule Case 2 on Down Under Airlines. How would this change affect the process you diagrammed for Down Under Airlines? Make a copy of your diagrams, and show the changes you envision.

P11-7 The following is a list of 13 control plans from this chapter or from Chapter 9.

Control Plans

A. Independent billing authorization

B. Sales order tickler file in billing

C. One-for-one checking of sales order and invoice

D. Programmed edits of shipping notification

E. Interactive feedback check

F. Computer agreement of batch totals

G. Cumulative sequence check

H. Document design

I. Prenumbered documents

J. Procedures for rejected inputs

K. Turnaround documents

L. One-for-one checking of deposit slip and checks

M. Deposit slip file

Listed next are 10 statements describing either the achievement of a control goal (i.e., a system success) or a system deficiency (i.e., a system failure). List the numbers 1 through 10 on your solution sheet. Next to each item, insert *one* letter from the preceding list indicating the *best* control to achieve the desired goal or to address the system deficiency described. A letter should be used only once, with three letters left over.

Control Goals or System Deficiencies

1. Helps to ensure the validity of shipping notifications.
2. Provides a detective control to help ensure the accuracy of billing inputs.
3. Provides a preventive control to help ensure the accuracy of billing inputs.

4. Helps to ensure input validity by preventing duplicate document numbers from entering the system.

5. Helps to identify duplicate, missing, and out-of-range numbers by comparing input numbers to a previously stored number range.

6. Precludes a field salesperson from omitting the sales terms from the sales order, thus avoiding having the order rejected by the computer data entry personnel.

7. Helps to ensure the Information System control goal of input completeness in a periodic/batch environment.

8. Helps to ensure that all shipments are billed in a timely manner.

9. Meets the operations system control goal of efficiency of resource use by reducing the number of data elements to be key entered from source documents.

10. Provides an "audit trail" of deposits.

P11-8 The following is a list of 15 control plans from this chapter or from Chapters 9 and 10.

Control Plans

A. Sales order tickler file in billing

B. One-for-one checking of sales order and shipping notice by shipping department personnel

C. Confirming customer balances regularly

D. Entering shipping notice close to location where order is shipped

E. Checking for authorized prices, terms, freight, and discounts

F. Hash totals (e.g., of customer ID numbers)

G. Computer agreement of batch totals

H. Manual agreement of batch totals

I. Batch sequence check

J. Key verification

K. Written approvals

L. Immediately endorsing incoming checks

M. One-for-one checking of checks and remittance advices

N. Immediately separating checks and remittance advices

O. Reconciling bank account regularly

Listed below are 10 system failures that have control implications. List the numbers 1 through 10 on your solution sheet. Next to each number, insert *one* letter from the preceding list corresponding to the control plan that would *best* prevent the system failure from occurring. Also, give a brief (one- to two-sentence) explanation of your choice. A letter should be used only once, with five letters left over.

Gelinas 11-51

System Failures

1. Once goods are delivered to the common carrier, the shipping system at Goodtimes Video Corp. prepares a three-part shipping notice. Copy 2 of the notice is sent to billing to initiate the billing process. Many shipping notices have either been lost in transit or have been delayed in reaching the billing section.

2. A dishonest order entry clerk bypasses the credit-checking procedures every time a customer order is received from his brother-in-law's firm. The clerk releases sales order copies to the warehouse and to the shipping department without submitting the orders to the credit department.

3. Because the mailroom clerks at Laxx Company do not take batch totals of incoming customer checks, the cashier has misappropriated several thousand dollars over the years by depositing company checks to his personal bank account.

4. Potpourri Merchandising Mart uses periodic processing for entering sales invoice inputs and updating customer accounts. Although it uses certain batch total procedures, Potpourri has experienced a number of instances of recording sales invoices to incorrect customer accounts.

5. The billing department at Gerrymander Corp. employs batch processing and uses prenumbered invoice documents.

Nevertheless, a number of duplicate invoice numbers has been processed, resulting in numerous customer complaints.

6. Because Abraham Co. had been privately owned for years, it had never undergone an independent audit. When Abraham finally went public, the Securities and Exchange Commission required an audit of its financial statements. As part of its audit, the independent CPA firm found a large discrepancy between the accounts receivable general ledger balance and the underlying details of individual customer balances.

7. At Jonquil, Inc., billing sends shipping notices to the data entry group in data processing, where they are keyed into the computer. During the last month, an inexperienced data entry clerk made several errors in keying the shipping notices. The errors were discovered by the internal auditors as part of their routine examination of the data processing department.

8. Sales at Defrod Corporation have declined considerably over those of the preceding year. In an effort to improve the financial statements, the vice-president

of finance obtained a supply of blank shipping notices on which she fabricated 100 fictitious shipments. She submitted the fictitious documents to the billing department.

9. The mailroom at Whipoorwill Co. forwards checks and

remittance advices to the accounts receivable department. A clerk checks the remittance advices against open invoices, as reflected in the accounts receivable master data. It is not uncommon for the clerk to note discrepancies, in which case the customer is contacted in an effort to reconcile the differences. Once all the discrepancies have been investigated and cleared, the accounts receivable clerk releases the checks to the cashier for deposit.

10. Clerks in the billing department at Abacus Enterprises, Inc., prepare sales invoices from a copy of the packing slip received from the shipping department. Recently, the company has experienced a rash of customer complaints that the customers have been billed for freight charges, despite the fact that they were promised free shipping.

P11-9 a. Redraw the appropriate part of Figure 11.4 (page 383), assuming a lockbox system is used. Also, prepare a lower-level data flow diagram for the cash receipts function, using the same assumption.

b. Redraw the appropriate part of Figure 11.4 assuming that, in addition to cash collections from charge customers, the organization also has cash sales and receives cash from the sale of equity securities. Prepare a brief, one- to two-sentence defense for each of the changes made.

Do *not* draw an entirely new Figure 11.4 for either part (a) or part (b). You might want to photocopy the figure from the chapter and then draw your additions and changes on the photocopy.

TABLES

[Start Table]

Table 11.1 Description of Horizontal Information Flows*

Flow No.	Description
1	Shipping department informs the accounts receivable department (billing section) of shipment.
2	Accounts receivable department (billing) sends invoice to customer.
3	Accounts receivable department (billing) informs general ledger that invoice was sent to customer.
4	Customer, by defaulting on amount due, informs credit department of nonpayment.
5	Credit department recommends write-off and informs accounts receivable department.
6	Credit department, by changing credit limits, informs sales order department to terminate credit sales to customer.
7	Accounts receivable department informs general ledger system of write-off.
8	Customer makes payment on account.
9	Cashier informs accounts receivable department (cash applications section) of payment.
10	Cashier informs general ledger of payment.

*Many of these steps may be automated. See Technology Insights 11.1 and 11.3 for descriptions of these steps in an enterprise system implementation.

[End Table]

BOXES

[Start Technology Insight 11.1 box here]

TECHNOLOGY INSIGHT 11.1

Enterprise System Support for Horizontal Information Flows

The information flows presented in Figure 11.2 are very similar to what we would expect if the organization were using an enterprise system. However, many of the tasks outlined would occur quite differently because of the messaging capabilities embedded in contemporary enterprise systems. Let's take a look at each of the information flows in Figure 11.2.

1. The flow of information from the shipping department to the accounts receivable department (billing section) is an automatic trigger from the enterprise system. As soon as the shipping department enters the shipment into the enterprise system, a message is sent to the billing module in preparation for step 2. If necessary, a message of the update could also be routed to the accounts receivable department.
2. As a regularly scheduled event, the billing department uses the enterprise system to generate an invoice and transmit the invoice to the customer either by mail or electronically.
3. The generation of the invoice (step #2) automatically updates the accounts receivable balances in the general ledger portion of the enterprise system.
4. Periodic reports are generated based on lack of customer payment and trigger a credit hold on the account. A message is also automatically routed to the credit department to review the account.
5. As a regularly scheduled event, the credit department reviews accounts and determines when accounts should be written off. A message is routed to the

accounts receivable department authorizing a write-down, and accounts receivable confirms.

6. As a regularly scheduled event, the credit department reviews and revises credit for customers and changes are automatically made to the credit data accessible by the sales order department.
7. Authorization of write-down in flow #5 by the accounts receivable module automatically updates general ledger balances.
8. Customer payment is received either by mail or electronically.
9. Cashier records payment into the enterprise system and the accounts receivable balances are updated. Accounts receivable instantly has updated information.
10. Recording of payment by cashier (step #9) automatically updates general ledger balances.

As is apparent, much of the processing of information flows becomes simply automatic updating of relevant data stores. These automatic updates occur because of the integrated nature of the enterprise system and its underlying database. If the information needs to draw the attention of another person, automatic messaging systems can automate the notification process as well.

[End Technology Insight 11.1 box here]

[Start Technology Application 11.1 box here]

TECHNOLOGY APPLICATION 11.1

Uses of Digital Processing Systems in RC Processes

Gelinas 11-57

Case 1

At Macquarie Bank, copies of all customer documentation including billing statements, customer-generated correspondence, and computer summary data are scanned and sorted by computer. With the document management system, service representatives can recall on-screen copies of documents while speaking with the customer, and can print a copy with the touch of a button for mailing or faxing to the customer. Additionally, documents are much easier to find, as they can be cross-indexed by customer account, invoice number, date of occurrence, customer name, or other ways.

Case 2

Another approach to digital image processing is to render the source form of a bill as a digital image and to transmit that image to the customer. The utilities industry is one of many industries attempting to make billing processes all digital. Killen & Associates, Inc., estimates that utility companies would save $1.2 billion annually by going to electronic billing and requiring electronic payment. However, Southern California Edison, the first utility company experimenting with electronic billing, has not seen any such savings to date during its pilot implementation. Electronic payment has not been mandatory for customers, and the savings will not come until consumer interest in electronic billing and payment rises. Still, Southern California Edison continues to support the project with the belief that savings will come in the future.

Sources: "Bank Optimizes Customer Service with Document Management," *Computerworld* (September 26, 1997): 56; Lauren Gibbons Paul, "E-billing: The Check Is in the Ether," *Datamation* (April 1999): http://www.datamation.com/e-comm/04bill1.html.

[End Technology Application 11.1 box here]

[Start Technology Insight 11.2 box here]

TECHNOLOGY INSIGHT 11.2

Solutions for the Float Problem

One of the earliest initiatives in the realm of **electronic funds transfer (EFT)** is the **automated clearing house (ACH).** If you have ever had your paycheck deposited directly to your checking account, you have been a party to an ACH transaction. Over 40,000 companies use ACH, most of them for direct deposit. In addition, the government is a big user of ACH. For instance, each month millions of senior citizens have social security checks deposited electronically through the ACH banking network. The idea of the ACH system is similar to that of a debit card. Through a prearranged agreement between trading parties, the collector's bank account is credited and the payer's account is debited for the amount of a payment. This transaction might happen at specified recurring intervals as in the case of direct deposit, or it might be initiated by the payer—a so-called customer-initiated payment (CIP)—via a touch-tone or operator-assisted phone call or through a personal computer.

Another solution is the use of a lockbox for processing customer payments. A **lockbox** is a postal address, maintained by the firm's bank, which is used solely for the purpose of collecting checks. A firm selects a variety of banks with lockboxes across the country so that customer mail arrives quickly at the lockbox. The bank constantly processes the lockbox receipts, providing a quick update to the firm's bank balance. To provide the collecting company with the information to update customer accounts, the lockbox bank traditionally sends the company the remittance advices (RAs), photocopies of the checks, and a listing of the remittances, prepared by scanning the RAs. Many banks now offer an **electronic lockbox** service, by which the lockbox bank scans the payer's remittance advice details into its computer system and then transfers the remittance advice data electronically to the collector's accounts receivable computer system. Obviously, the electronic lockbox allows the company to post cash receipts more rapidly, at reduced cost, and with more accuracy.

Two other technologies of interest relate to emerging payment methods for e-business. A major problem for e-business concerns payment by individual customers. Many people are hesitant to transmit personal credit card information across the Web, and others do not have sufficient credit card funds available to use. An alternative is to use either an **electronic check** or **electronic cash.** An *electronic check* closely resembles a paper check with the inclusion of the customer's name, the seller's name, the customer's financial institution, the check amount, and a *digital signature.* Public key cryptography is used to protect the customer's account. With *electronic cash,* a financial institution issues cash that is placed into an electronic wallet. The cash is issued in an electronic form much the way it would be in paper form. Cash is loaded onto the wallet and spent in a manner similar to a phone card. The wallet may be a card or it may be data stored on a server or the individual's computer. However, unlike using a check, the individual making the cash transfer is generally not traceable. Electronic cash has been a little slower to catch on, as banks are only beginning to support the cash form, and accessibility to customers for use is still limited.

[End Technology Insight 11.2 box here]

[Start Technology Insight 11.3 box here]

TECHNOLOGY INSIGHT 11.3

Enterprise System Support for the Billing Process

The main effect of the introduction of an enterprise system into the billing process depicted in Figure 11.6 is the integration of the processing programs and the various data stores into a single unified processing system with a single underlying database. In terms of the diagrams, the primary impact is therefore on the activities depicted within the "data center." These changes are demonstrated in the diagram on page 389. Note that the systems flowchart has significantly simplified, but the consolidation of all of the processes and databases shown in Figure 11.6 to the single process and database in the figure shown on page 389 is indicative of the complexity within an enterprise system. You should also recognize that for clarity and comparability the diagram shows the use of batch totals and batch comparisons. In many enterprise-wide environments, traditional batch control procedures as depicted on page 389 might not be retained, depending on how much the organization decides to change its business processes upon implementation of the enterprise system.

[Insert UNF-p.389-1 here]

[End Technology Insight 11.3 box here]

[Start Technology Insight 11.4 box here]

TECHNOLOGY INSIGHT 11.4

Enterprise System Support for the Cash Receipts Process

The main effect of the introduction of an enterprise system into the M/S process depicted in Figure 11.8 is the integration of the processing programs and the various data stores into a single unified processing system with a single underlying database. In terms of the diagrams, the primary impact is therefore on the activities depicted within the "data processing department." These changes are demonstrated in the diagram below.

[Insert UNF-p.397-2]

[End Technology Insight 11.4 box here]

12

THE "PURCHASE-TO-PAY" (PTOP) PROCESS

Kraft Foods, Inc., recently received an excellence award from Giga Information Group for its new automated Purchase-to-Pay Information System.[1] Kraft, similar to most organizations, was concerned over the cost and inefficiencies of processing purchases and related payments. One of the big efficiency problems arose whenever a purchase invoice was in question. An associate would have to search through mounds of paper to reconcile the invoice with old invoices, paid and unpaid. Application of a consistent set of controls over the process was difficult because of variations in purchase invoices and vendor requirements. Further complicating matters, another department had to calculate the related taxes manually by analyzing the invoice and identifying the most advantageous method.

1 Barb Cole-Gomolski, "Oh I Wish I Had a Better Invoice System," *Computerworld* (May 18, 1998).

Kraft's solution was to implement a new accounts payable system that used advanced workflow technologies to eliminate paper, cut unnecessary steps, and automatically route high-priority tasks to key employees. The workflow technologies automatically capture purchase invoice data and facilitate business process activities by electronic routing of invoices through the required approval procedures for signature validation, audit control, and tax compliance. The system also automatically arranges invoices according to due dates and allows Kraft to negotiate discounts with vendors based on payment date. The results include improved process control, reduction in invoice processing cost from an average of $7 to $4, and improved productivity of 30%.

In this chapter, we will explore the processes, systems, and controls that should be in place to ensure that the Purchase-to-Pay process operates efficiently and effectively. Additionally, we will examine specific control procedures that help ensure all payments are made in a timely fashion.

Synopsis

This chapter presents our second business process, Purchase-to-Pay (PtoP), also known as procurement. By now, you are familiar with the overall structure of these business process chapters, but note the sections on Managing the PtoP Process, Physical Process Description, and the Applications of the Control Framework to General Expenditures. These sections also cover material on current and evolving technologies.

LEARNING OBJECTIVES

- To describe the business environment for the Purchase-to-Pay (PtoP) process
- To analyze the effect of enterprise systems and other technologies on the PtoP

process

- To describe the PtoP process logic, physical characteristics, and support of management decision making
- To describe and analyze controls typically associated with the PtoP process

Introduction

We begin by reviewing how the PtoP process combines with other processes within a company. Figure 12.1 depicts the PtoP process.

[Insert Figure 12.1 here]

Note that the PtoP process interacts with inventory (in the Order-to-Cash process) as the ordering, receipt of goods, and updating of inventory data takes place. The PtoP process also interacts with the general ledger (Chapter 14). We examine those relationships later in the chapter. Let's take a closer look at the PtoP process.

Process Definition and Functions

The **Purchase-to-Pay process** is an interacting structure of people, equipment, methods, and controls that is designed to accomplish the following primary functions:

1. Handle the repetitive work routines of the purchasing department, the receiving department, the accounts payable department, the payroll department, and the cashier[2]

[2] To focus our discussion, we have assumed that these four

departments are the primary operating units related to the PtoP process. For a given organization, however, the departments associated with the process may differ.

2. Support the decision needs of those who manage the departments listed in item 1

3. Assist in the preparation of internal and external reports

Review Question

What primary functions does the PtoP process perform?

First, the PtoP process handles repetitive work routines by capturing and recording data related to the day-to-day operations of affected departments. The recorded data then may be used to generate source documents (such as purchase orders and receiving reports) and to produce internal and external reports.

The PtoP process prepares a number of reports that personnel at various levels of management use. For example, the manager of the purchasing department might use an open purchase order report to ascertain which orders have yet to be filled. The cash disbursements manager might use a cash requirements forecast to help her decide which invoice(s) to pay next.

Finally, the PtoP process assists in the preparation of external reports such as financial statements. The process supplies the general ledger with data concerning various events related to the procurement activities of an organization.

Before leaving this section, we need to clarify two terms that we will be using throughout the chapter: *goods* and *services. Goods* are raw materials, merchandise, supplies, fixed assets (e.g., buildings, machinery), or intangible assets (e.g., patents, copyrights, franchises). *Services* are tasks performed by outside vendors, including contractors, catering firms, towel services, consultants, auditors, and the like. Employee activities feeding the payroll process are a specialized form of *services.*

Review Question

How, in your own words, would you define the PtoP process?

Organizational Setting

Figure 12.2 presents a generic organization chart for the PtoP process. You are already familiar with some of the roles shown in the figure. We will concentrate on the managers or the supervisors of the accounts payable, payroll receiving, and purchasing departments.

[Insert Figure 12.2 here]

A Vertical Perspective

The *accounts payable department* is responsible for processing invoices received from vendors, preparing payment vouchers for disbursement of cash for goods or services received, and recording purchase and disbursement events. Responsibility for all cash disbursements lies with *accounts payable,* except payroll, which is handled separately by the *payroll department.*

Review Question

How does the PtoP process relate to its organizational environment?

The *receiving department* is responsible for receiving incoming goods, signing the bill of lading presented by the carrier or the supplier in connection with the shipment, reporting the receipt of goods,[3] and making prompt transfer of goods to the appropriate warehouse or department.

[3] In this section and the section describing the logical PtoP process, we assume that the receiving supervisor also is responsible for indicating that *services* have been received. In practice, the receipt of services might well be reported by various operating departments instead.

The chief purchasing executive assumes various titles in different companies, such as manager of purchasing, director of purchasing, or purchasing agent. We use the term *purchasing manager.* The purchasing manager usually performs major buying activities as well as the required administrative duties of running a department. In many organizations, professional buyers do the actual buying.

Review Question

What are the fundamental responsibilities of each position: accounts payable supervisor, receiving supervisor, purchasing manager, and buyer?

A Horizontal Perspective

Figure 12.3 presents a horizontal view of the relationship between the PtoP process and its organizational environment. They show various information flows generated or captured by the process. After reviewing Figure 12.3, read Technology Insight 12.1 (page 424), which discusses how horizontal information flows in an enterprise system become automated and therefore more efficient in terms of supporting the PtoP process.

[Insert Figure 12.3 here]

[Insert Table 12.1 here]

[Insert Technology Insight 12.1 box here]

Goal Conflicts and Ambiguities in the Organization

As discussed in Chapter 5, the goals of individual managers may conflict with overall organizational objectives. For instance, some of the managers and supervisors shown in the organization chart (Figure 12.2 on page 421) might very well be "marching to different drummers." As one specific example, the purchasing manager may well want to buy in large quantities to take advantage of quantity discounts and to reduce ordering costs. Receiving, inspecting, and storing large quantities of inventory, however, likely presents problems for the receiving department supervisor and the warehouse manager.

In addition to goal conflicts between managers, ambiguity often exists in defining goals and defining success in meeting goals. For instance, one of the purchasing goals might be *to select a vendor who will provide the best quality at the lowest price by the promised delivery date.* But what does this goal mean precisely? Does it mean that a particular vendor must satisfy all three conditions of best quality, lowest price, and timely delivery? Realistically, one vendor probably will not satisfy all three conditions.

Recall from Chapter 5 that prioritizing goals is often necessary to choose the *best* solution given the various conflicts and constraints placed on the process. This necessity implies that trade-offs must be made in prioritizing among goals that conflict. For example, if a company operates in an industry that is extremely sensitive to satisfying customer needs, it may be willing to incur excessive cost to ensure that it is procuring the best quality goods and obtaining them when needed.

Logical Process Description

This section expands on the PtoP process. Once again, logical data flow diagrams present the basic composition of a typical process. We consider the relationship between certain goals of the process and the process' logical design. The section includes brief discussions of the interfaces between the PtoP and Inventory processes. We also examine the process' major data stores.[4]

[4] As we have in several earlier chapters, we remind you once again that the data stores in the logical DFDs and systems flowchart might well be the PtoP process's view of an *entity-wide database.*

Discussion and Illustration

Figure 12.4 (page 426) reflects the level 0 data flow diagram for a typical PtoP process. To focus our discussion, we have assumed that the PtoP process performs four major subprocesses, represented by the four bubbles in the DFD.

[Insert Figure 12.4 here]

Note that purchase requisitions are initiated by entities outside the context of the PtoP process. The purchasing process begins with each department identifying its need for goods and services. These needs are depicted by one of two data flows entering bubble 1.0: *inventory's purchase requisition* or *purchase requisition—supplies and services.*

Review Question

What major *logical* processes does the PtoP process perform?

Figure 12.5 is an example screen for an electronic **purchase requisition,** which is an internal request to acquire goods and services. Observe the various items included in the header and body of the requisition, including company data and items to be ordered. The requisitioning department supervisor usually approves the requisition.

[Insert Figure 12.5 here]

At first glance, the processes involved in preparing a purchase requisition may appear to be quite simple and straightforward. However, a closer analysis reveals that the techniques and methods involved in determining *what* inventory to order, *when* to order it, and *how much* to order are considerably more intricate and complex than we might first imagine. The processes associated with reordering inventory involve several important concepts and techniques, such as cyclical reordering, reorder point analysis, economic order quantity (EOQ) analysis, and ABC analysis. We discuss each of these methods in Technology Insight 12.2 (page 428).

[Insert Technology Insight 12.2 box here]

Each of the four process bubbles shown in the level 0 diagram are exploded in Appendix A, along with a discussion of the handling of *exception routines.*

Review Question

Why is the process of identifying the need for goods and services not technically considered part of the PtoP process?

Vendor selection can have a significant impact on the success of an organization's inventory control and manufacturing functions. For example, goods must arrive from vendors when needed and must meet required specifications.

After selecting a vendor, the buyer prepares a **purchase order**, a request for the purchase of goods or services from a vendor. Typically, a purchase order contains data regarding the needed quantities, expected unit prices, required delivery date, terms, and other conditions. Figure 12.6 displays a requisition record with the necessary information to release the associated purchase order.

[Insert Figure 12.6 here]

The purchase order notification could take a number of forms—including paper or electronic. It is not uncommon for the copy available for the receiving department to be a **blind copy**, meaning that certain data are blanked out (i.e., blinded) or simply not included in an electronic replica. For instance, the quantities ordered might be blanked out so that the receiving personnel will not be influenced by this information when counting goods. Price data may also be blinded because receiving personnel have no need to know that information.

At some point, the vendor uses a notification known as a **vendor acknowledgment** to inform the purchaser that the purchase order has been received and is being processed. In the case of inventory, the **vendor packing slip**, which accompanies the purchased inventory from the vendor and identifies the shipment, triggers the receiving process. Once annotated with the quantity received, the PO receiving notification becomes a **receiving report**, which is the form used to document and record merchandise receipts.

As in the case of the receipt of goods, services received also should be documented properly. Some organizations use an **acceptance report** to acknowledge formally the satisfactory completion of a service contract. The acceptance report data supports the payment due to the vendor in the same way as the receiving report.[5]

[5] For simplicity in drawing the DFDs, we intend that the single data flow labeled *receiving report* represents either a receiving report (goods) or acceptance report (services).

The accounts payable process is triggered by receipt of the **vendor invoice**, a business document that notifies the purchaser of an obligation to pay the vendor for goods or services that were ordered by and shipped to the purchaser. (Figure 11.5, on page 384, shows a typical invoice screen).

Review Question

In designing vendor records to be incorporated into the vendor master data, what specific data elements would you include to help you select the best vendor? Be specific as to the nature of the data stored and how it will be used in the selection process.

Logical Data Descriptions

The general PtoP process entails several different data stores. The **accounts payable master data** contain all unpaid vendor invoices. The design of the accounts payable master data should consider how data are processed when the cash manager is deciding what payments to make. For example, the manager may want to merge vendor invoices so that the total amount due each vendor can be accumulated. Alternatively, the manager might want to select specific invoices for payment.

The **vendor master data** contain a record of each vendor from whom the organization is authorized to make purchases. Purchasing personnel when selecting an appropriate vendor usually accesses the data. During processing, vendor data are retrieved to prepare purchase orders and to issue payments. In addition to storing identification data, vendor data are used by management to evaluate vendor performance and to make various ordering decisions.

The **purchase order master data** are a compilation of open purchase orders and include the status of each item on order. To keep track of a purchase, the purchasing department generally creates an entry in the purchase order master data. The data are a compilation of open purchase orders, including information about the status of each item on order. The order is closed only on receipt and acceptance of all goods detailed on the order.

Other data stores appearing in the data flow diagrams are the:

- **Inventory master data**, which contain a record of each inventory item that is stocked in the warehouse or is regularly ordered from a vendor. These records are used to manage the inventory and to support the inventory balance in the general ledger.
- **Receiving report data**, which contain a record of each receipt. These data combine purchase order data with the quantity received and date goods were received.
- **Cash disbursements event data**, which show, in chronological sequence, the details of each cash payment made.

Technology Trends and Developments

Recall from Chapter 4 the rapid movement toward electronic document interchange (EDI) to improve the business processes between two organizations exchanging goods. The PtoP process is the primary candidate for EDI in major organizations (although they certainly may use this technology in the Order-to-Cash process as well). As noted in Technology Application 12.1, several major companies have implemented EDI systems into the PtoP process, resulting in significant cost savings. An increasing trend among some of these major companies is to require all vendors to use EDI in their business processes with the company.

[Insert Technology Application 12.1 box here]

You may also recall in Chapter 4 that we discussed the emergence of electronic marketplaces that create a more competitive purchasing market. The introduction of these marketplaces into the business processes of major business organizations is usually the Purchase-to-Pay process. Accordingly, we explore several examples of such marketplaces arising in certain industries as described in Technology Application 12.2. Recall from Chapter 4, however, that there are many risks also involved in the move towards electronic marketplaces that may limit success in the short-term.

[Insert Technology Application 12.2 box here]

Physical Process Description

As the name implies, **paperless systems** eliminate documents and forms as the medium for conducting business. In a truly paperless system, printed reports are replaced with screen displays of requested information. With the increasing use of EDI, *electronic funds transfer (EFT), digital image processing, electronic mail, workflow software, enterprise systems,* and similar technologies, is the paperless office at hand? A growing number of organizations operate the bulk of their business processes using *paperless systems.*

The major roadblocks are more likely to be organizational and behavioral/psychological than technological in nature. Over time, these cultural barriers to the paperless office continue to disintegrate as a new generation of managers—who have grown up with the computer as a fact of their daily lives—emerges. Online billing is one area wherein widespread acceptance is beginning to be noted. See Technology Excerpt 12.1 for a discussion of the benefits of online bill presentment and payment.

[Insert Technology Excerpt 12.1 box here]

The physical model of the PtoP process presented in this section employs *electronic payments* and *data communications* technology. Although the process is not completely *paperless*, hard copy documents are held to a minimum.

Discussion and Illustration

Figure 12.7 (pages 434–437)presents a systems flowchart of the process. At several points in the flowchart, you see notations that *exception routines* are not flowcharted. They are also omitted from the discussion in the following paragraphs.

[Insert Figure 12.7 here]

Requisition and Order Merchandise As shown in the first column, the purchasing process begins when a cost center employee establishes a need and completes a requisition form on the computer system. When a requisitioner calls up the system, the system automatically supplies a four-digit requisition number. The requisitioner designates the items desired, as well as information about the cost center making the request.

The completed requisition is routed via the system to a cost center supervisor for approval. Depending on the amount and nature of the requisition, several approvals may be required. Approval is granted in the system by forwarding the requisition to the next person on the list; approval codes are attached to the record along the way and are displayed in the appropriate boxes on the requisition form. The approved requisition is automatically recorded to the audit data and routed to the purchasing department.

In the purchasing department, a buyer checks the requisition for proper approval by matching the codes against “authorized approver” data. Then, vendor candidates are chosen by consulting the inventory and vendor master data. Final vendor selection and price determination may require contact with the potential vendor. When the vendor choice is settled, the buyer updates the requisition by adding any necessary details.

Next, the system displays the purchase order (see the second page of the flowchart), and the buyer or the purchasing manager checks the purchase order data on the screen against the requisition data on the screen. The manager then approves the purchase order, a system confirmation is made available to the requisitioner, a record is created in the purchase order master data, and the inventory records are updated to reflect the quantity on order. The purchasing process releases the PO to the EDI translator, where it is converted to the appropriate EDI format. The translation software also *encrypts* the EDI message and appends a *digital signature* to it (as discussed in Chapter 9).

Receive Merchandise On the third page of the flowchart, we see that receiving department personnel receive and count the merchandise sent by the vendor. They compare the items and item quantities received to those on the open purchase order master data.[6] If the shipment is correct, they enter the receiving data into the computer. This information creates a record in the receiving report data, updates the status field in the purchase order data, and records the receipt in the inventory master data. The shipping documents are filed in chronological sequence for *audit trail* purposes. Alternatively, an image of the shipping documents might be stored on the computer.

[6] The database software prevents receiving personnel from accessing price data in the purchase order master data. In this way, the process implements the *blind copy* concept explained earlier.

Establish Accounts Payable The organization's system picks up the vendor's invoice from the Value-Added Network (VAN) and routes it to the EDI translator. The EDI translator converts the invoice to the appropriate format and records it in the incoming invoice data. Triggered by the receipt of a batch of EDI invoices, the accounts payable application accesses the purchase order and receiving report data and compares the items, quantities, prices, and terms on the invoice to comparable data from the PO and receiving report data. If the data correspond, a payable is created, and the general ledger is updated. The purchase order, receiving report, and invoice data must be marked so that it cannot be used to establish another payable.

Make Payments The physical model depicted on the fourth flowchart page utilizes EDI to make the payment. Banks that are members of the National Automated Clearing House (ACH) Association combine EDI and electronic funds transfer (EFT) standards to transmit electronic payments between companies and their trading partners.

As shown in Figure 12.7, the accounts payable master data are searched each day for approved vendor invoices due that day. The cash disbursements application prepares the payment order and remittance advice, updates the accounts payable master data and the general ledger for the payment, and sends the data on to the EDI translator. The translator converts the data to the appropriate format, encrypts the message, adds a digital signature, and sends the EDI payment order and remittance advice on to the communications network.

If the bank is acting as a VAN for the payment order, the communications network sends the data to the bank. Otherwise, the system sends the payment order to a VAN for pickup by the bank. The bank debits the account and then sends the payment order to an automated clearinghouse for processing. Next, the automated clearinghouse sends the data to the vendor's bank, where it is automatically credited to the vendor's bank account. Finally, the vendor's bank transmits the RA and payment data to the vendor. If the electronic remittance advice does not accompany the payment order through the banking system, it would be forwarded directly (via VAN) to the supplier.[7]

[7] You should be aware that using electronic funds transfer (EFT) to wire funds between banks and employing EDI to transmit remittance data from the payer's to the vendor's computer system do *not* necessarily go hand in hand. For instance, a company could utilize EFT to make payments but still rely on paper remittance advices to notify the vendor of the details of what is being paid.

Consider how this process might change in an enterprise systems environment. After you have thought through the impact and the resulting changes to Figure 12.7, read Technology Insight 12.3, which provides an overview of how a fully implemented enterprise system affects the PtoP process discussed in this chapter.

[Insert Technology Insight 12.3 box here]

Application of the Control Framework to General Expenditures

In this section, we apply the control framework from Chapter 9 to the PtoP process. Figure 12.8 (pages 442–443)presents a completed *control matrix* for the annotated systems flowchart shown in Figure 12.7. After briefly discussing the control goals shown as column headings in the matrix, we then consider in Exhibit 12.1 (pages 444–445) each of the recommended control plans listed in the first column. As you study the control plans, be sure to see where they are located on the systems flowchart.

[Insert Figure 12.8 here]

[Insert Exhibit 12.1 here]

Control Goals

The following control-goal categories are presented in the matrix. Those for the operations process are:

- *Effectiveness of operations* relative to four example operations process goals. The first goal, mentioned earlier, might be *to select a vendor who will provide the best quality at the lowest price by the promised delivery date.* When goods arriving at the receiving department are inspected, counted, and compared to the vendor packing slip, the receiving clerk is helping to achieve a second operations process goal: *to ensure that the right goods in the correct amount are received in acceptable condition.* To help achieve a third operations process goal, *to optimize cash discounts,* the responsibility for ensuring savings through cash discounts includes (1) seeing that proper cash discount terms are incorporated in the order, (2) securing invoices promptly from vendors, (3) processing invoices promptly and getting them to the disbursing office within the discount period, and (4) when unavoidable delays are encountered because of some fault of the seller, making sure that the discount privilege is not waived and that the vendor is notified to this effect.

Most cash managers attempt to optimize cash balances to help achieve a fourth operations process goal: *to ensure that the amount of cash maintained in demand deposit accounts is sufficient (but not excessive) to satisfy expected cash disbursements.* To accomplish this goal, many banks offer to their commercial customers a cash management service by which the bank transfers from the customer's money market or other investment account into its checking account the exact amount needed to cover the checks that clear each day.

- *Effectiveness of operations* in respect to complying with the organization's code of conduct concerning conflicts of interest, accepting illegal or improper payments, and like matters. Recall from Chapter 8 that one of the three categories of control objectives is compliance with applicable laws, regulations, and contractual agreements. For each process to which it applies, we have elected to include COSO's "compliance" objective under our operations goals.

- *Efficiency* of the purchasing, receiving, payables, and cash disbursement processes.
- *Resource security;* note that the resources include assets, cash, inventory, and the information resources represented by the purchase order and accounts payable master data.

Controls for the information system are:

- Input validity (IV) of input events[8]
- Input completeness (IC) and input accuracy (IA)
- Update completeness (UC) and update accuracy (UA)

Input validity for each input event type can be summarized as follows:

- *Purchase requisitions.* Those that have been properly approved and that utilize existing (real) and approved vendors.
- *Vendor packing slips.* Those that are supported by authorized purchase orders and that represent existing (real) receipts of goods and services.
- *Vendor invoices.* Those that bill the company for goods that were

actually ordered and actually received (i.e., the invoices are supported by proper purchase orders and receiving reports).

- *Payment vouchers.* Those that are documented by *validated, unpaid* vendor invoices. Note that in this case, part of ensuring validity is to prevent paying for an item twice.

[8] In the matrix, please note that the inputs and master data vary for each of the processes. These variations can be summarized as follows:

Process	**Nature of inputs**	**Updated master data**
purchasing	purchase requisition	purchase order
receiving	vendor packing slip	purchase order
payables	vendor invoice	accounts payable
cash disbursements	payment voucher	accounts payable

Review Question

What are four operations process goals of the PtoP process?Provide an example illustrating each goal.

Recommended Control Plans

Before analyzing control plans for the PtoP process, let's begin by summarizing some plans that are *not* listed in the control matrix nor discussed in Exhibit 12.1. First, in the interest of simplicity, we exclude those plans that are related to the information processing method (see Chapter 9), such as preformatted purchase requisition screens, online prompting, digital signatures, and programmed edit checks.[9]

[9] As we mentioned in earlier applications of the control framework, the controls enumerated here should be included, wherever appropriate, in your list of "recommended control plans" (step 3 in "Steps in Preparing a Control Matrix," Exhibit 9.1 on page 287).

Second, certain control plans simply aren't appropriate to the procedures used in the process that we are reviewing. However, you might very well encounter them in practice. The following are a few examples:

- Where paper documents are the basis for making disbursements, paid invoices (and supporting purchase orders and receiving reports) are often marked "void" or "paid" to prevent their being paid a second time. In paperless systems, the computerized payable records would be "flagged" with a code to indicate they had been paid and to prevent duplicate payment.
- Where payments are by check, appropriate physical controls should exist over supplies of blank checks and signature plates that are used for check signing.
- It is not uncommon to have more than one authorized signature required on large-dollar checks.
- Most companies have standing instructions with their banks not to honor checks that have been outstanding longer than a certain

number of months (e.g., three or six months).

- To prevent alteration of (or misreading of) check amounts, many businesses use check-protection machines to imprint the check amount in a distinctive color (generally a blue and red combination).

Finally, another control plan not presented in the control matrix is to have the firm's internal audit staff conduct periodic *vendor audits.* In a vendor audit, the purchasing organization's internal auditors periodically visit a vendor's office and examine its records. At a minimum, the site visit and inspection of the vendor's facilities *validates* the existence of the vendor. The vendors chosen for audit could be those doing large volumes of business with the company, those with peculiar names or names very similar to one another, those whose invoices are in tight sequential order, or other characteristics that might flag the vendor's relations to a firm as peculiar or unusual. The on-site audit program generally covers vendor disbursements for entertainment, promotion, commissions, travel, donations, payroll, and the like.

Now turn to Exhibit 12.1 and study the explanations of the cell entries appearing in the control matrix. As you know from similar studies in prior chapters, understanding how the recommended control plans relate to specific control goals is the most important aspect of applying the control framework.

Review Question

Select three application control plans presented in the chapter. How does each relate to the PtoP process presented in Figure 12.7?

Conclusions

This chapter has covered the PtoP process that accounts for most of a company's expenditures. Like the Order-to-Cash process, the purchasing component of the PtoP process fills a central coordinating role as it supports the supplies and inventory components of an organization's operations.

The physical process implementation presented in this chapter evidences many attributes of the paperless office of the future. Are these visions of a paperless society that farfetched? Hardly. The technology exists today, and many companies have availed themselves of some, if not all, of that technology.

Appendix 12A

Lower-Level DFDs

Order Goods and Services Figure 12.9, a lower-level view of bubble 1.0 in Figure 12.4 (page 426), provides a look at the logical functions involved in ordering goods and services. The first process involves vendor selection (bubble 1.1). A buyer generally consults the vendor master data to identify potential suppliers and then evaluates each prospective vendor.

[Insert Figure 12.9 here]

Buyers often attempt to combine as many orders as possible with the same vendor by using *blanket orders* and/or *annual agreements*. If large expenditures for new or specially made parts are involved, the buyer may need to obtain *competitive bids* by sending a *request for quotation (RFQ)* to prospective vendors.

Process bubble 1.2 of Figure 12.9 depicts the process of preparing a purchase order. Process 1.2 first checks the inventory master data to obtain additional information with which to prepare the purchase order. The purchase order data flow out of process 1.2 is sent to the vendor. At the same time, the inventory master data are updated to reflect the goods on order. The purchase order information is distributed to several departments as shown by the four other data flows out of process 1.2.

The data flow "Vendor acknowledgment" into bubble 1.3 informs the purchaser that the purchase order has been received and is being processed. As a result of the vendor acknowledgment, process 1.3 updates the "Purchase status" in the purchase order master data.

Receive Goods and Services Figure 12.10 is the lower-level diagram for process 2.0 in Figure 12.4. As indicated by bubble 2.1 of the figure, goods arriving at the receiving department are inspected, counted, and compared to the vendor packing slip. Nonconforming goods are denoted by the *reject* stub out of process 2.1.

[Insert Figure 12.10 here]

Notation of rejected goods is added to the vendor service record in the vendor master data.

Once the condition of the goods has been approved, process 2.2 completes the receiving report by noting the quantity received on the approved PO receiving notification. Process 2.3 compares the receiving report to the information stored in the purchase order master data—a process that often is automatically completed by the information system. Bubble 2.3 also reflects the following activities:

- Data about vendor compliance with the order terms (product quality, meeting promised delivery dates, etc.) is linked to the vendor master data.
- Receiving report data may be accessed by the accounts payable department (i.e., the receiving report) and the warehouse (i.e., the stock notice).
- The inventory master data are updated to reflect the additional inventory on hand.
- Finally, the purchase order master data are updated to reflect the receipt of the goods, and the receiving report data are stored.

Establish Payable Figure 12.11 (page 450)presents a data flow diagram for establishing accounts payable. As shown by bubble 3.1, the first step in establishing the payable involves validating the vendor invoice. Process 3.1 comprises a number of steps. First, the vendor invoice is compared against data for the purchase order (PO accounts payable notification) to make sure that (1) the purchase has been authorized and (2) invoiced quantities, prices, and terms conform to the purchase order agreement. Next, the invoice is matched against the receiving report data to determine whether the goods or services actually have been received. Finally, the invoice is checked for accuracy of computed discounts, extensions, and total amount due.

[Insert Figure 12.11 here]

If the data items do not agree, the invoice is rejected and follow-up procedures are initiated (see the reject stub emanating from bubble 3.1). If the data items agree, the invoice is approved, and the validated invoice is then used to record the payable. Note that the vendor master data are also updated at this point to reflect purchase history data.

Bubble 3.2 in Figure 12.11 depicts the process of recording the payable in the accounts payable master data. A payable is recognized and recorded by simultaneously:

- Creating a record in the accounts payable master data.
- Updating the inventory master data for the cost of the items received.

- Notifying the general ledger of the amount of the payable that was recorded (see the data flow “GL payable update”).

Make Payment Figure 12.12 presents a data flow diagram of the cash disbursements process. Remember that the payment process is *triggered* by payment due-date information residing on the accounts payable master data (i.e., a temporal event).

The payment schedule adopted depends on the availability of any favorable discounts for prompt payment and on the organization’s current cash position. Some companies pay multiple invoices with one check to minimize the cost of processing invoices.

[Insert Figure 12.12 here]

Exception Routines

In the data flow diagrams, you saw a number of *reject* data flows; they occur for a number of reasons. **Purchase returns and allowances** frequently arise with respect to purchases. This *exception routine* usually begins at the point of inspecting and counting the goods (bubble 2.1 of Figure 12.9) or at the point of *validating* vendor invoices (bubble 3.1 of Figure 12.10).

To initiate an adjustment for returned goods or for a price allowance in the case of otherwise nonconforming goods, someone usually prepares a *debit memorandum* and transmits it to the vendor; the vendor commonly acknowledges by returning a *credit memorandum.* The debit memo data are also transmitted to the accounts payable department. In the case of a return, data are also made accessible to the storeroom and shipping department. The merchandise to be returned is then released from the storeroom and sent to the shipping department. There the items to be returned are counted, recorded to the debit memorandum, and shipped. The shipping department's recording of the debit memo data is also made available to the accounts payable department.

Appendix 12B

Logical Database Design

As in the prior two chapters, this section focuses on a *database approach* to data management. In Figure 12.13, we first portray the data model for the PtoP process in an *entity-relationship (E-R) diagram.*

[Insert Figure 12.13 here]

In examining the figure, you'll notice that the *events* of preparing purchase orders, receiving merchandise, recording vendor invoices, and paying those invoices are depicted by four of the entity boxes. The other two entities reflect how these four events relate to an *agent* (VENDOR) and to a *resource* (INVENTORY). To simplify the figure, we have:

- Ignored the event of preparing the *purchase requisition.*

- Assumed that all purchase orders are for merchandise inventory items (i.e., purchases of other goods and services are ignored).

From Figure 12.13, we move to the relational tables shown in Figure 12.14 (page 453). Note that the relations in Figure 12.14 are similar to those shown in Figures 10.14 (page 363) and 11.14 (page 407) (e.g., VENDORS is similar to CUSTOMERS, PURCHASE_ORDERS resembles SALES_ORDERS, PO *line item* INVENTORY is like SALES_ORDER *line item* INVENTORY, and so forth).

[Insert Figure 12.14 here]

REVIEW QUESTIONS

RQ12-1 What primary functions does the PtoP process perform?

RQ12-2 How, in your own words, would you define the PtoP process?

RQ12-3 How does the PtoP process relate to its organizational environment?

RQ12-4 What are the fundamental responsibilities of each position: accounts payable supervisor, receiving supervisor, purchasing manager, and buyer?

RQ12-5 What major *logical* processes does the PtoP process perform?

RQ12-6 Why is the process of identifying the need for goods and services not technically considered part of the PtoP process?

RQ12-7 In designing vendor records to be incorporated into the vendor master data, what

specific data elements would you include to help you select the best vendor? Be specific as to the nature of the data stored and how it will be used in the selection process.

RQ12-8 What are four operations process goals of the PtoP process? Provide an example illustrating each goal.

RQ12-9 Select three application control plans presented in the chapter. How does each relate to the PtoP process presented in Figure 12.7 (pages 434–437)?

DISCUSSION QUESTIONS

DQ12-1 Refer to the four operations process goals shown in the control matrix (goals A–D in Figure 12.8 on pages 442–443). For each activity (purchasing, receiving, accounts payable, and cash disbursements), describe an operations goal other than the one discussed in the chapter.

DQ12-2 Explain why ambiguities and conflicts exist among operations process goals, and discuss potential ambiguities and conflicts relative to the system goals you described in DQ12-1.

DQ12-3 Discuss how a "year-to-date purchases" field in the vendor record might be of use in selecting a vendor.

DQ12-4 Without redrawing the figures, discuss how Figures 12.4 (page 426)and 12.9 through 12.12 (pages 448–451)would change as a result of the following independent situations (be specific in describing the changes):

a. Purchasing a technical product that could not be inspected in the receiving department but had to undergo quality control testing before being accepted.

b. Purchasing goods through an online auction site, so that the price changes each time a purchase is made.

c. Making payments twice per month, on the fifth and twenty-fifth of the month, and taking advantage of all cash discounts offered.

DQ12-5 a. Figure 12.10 on page 449 (the DFD depicting the receipt of goods and services) shows an update to the vendor master data from bubble 2.1 and another update to that same data from bubble 2.3. Discuss the *difference(s)* between these two updates. Be specific as to the nature of the data being updated in each case. How would your answer to this question be affected by your assumption about whether the purchase order receiving notification entering bubble 2.1 was “blind”as to quantities? Explain.

b. Figure 12.11 on page 450 shows still a third update to the vendor master data from bubble 3.1. Speculate as to the nature of this update. Be specific.

DQ12-6 In terms of effectiveness and efficiency of operations, as well as of meeting the generic Information System control goals of validity, completeness, and accuracy, what are the arguments for and against each of the following? Does it matter if the copy is paper or electronic?

a. Sending a copy of the purchase order from the purchasing department to the receiving department.

b. Having the "quantity ordered" field "blinded" on the receiving department copy of the purchase order.

c. Sending a copy of the vendor invoice to the purchasing department for approval of payment.

d. Sending a copy of the vendor invoice to the requisitioning department for approval of payment.

DQ12-7 "Auditors will never allow an organization to adopt a paperless system, so why do we waste our time bothering to study them?" Do you agree? Why or why not?

DQ12-8 Refer to Figure 12.7 on pages 434–437 (the systems flowchart for the PtoP process). After all necessary approvals have been added to the purchase requisition, it is routed to the buyer and "is automatically sent to the audit data." Speculate about the nature and purpose of the "requisition audit data." Who might access this data and for what purposes? *Hint:* You might want to consider the purposes that such data could serve in a completely paperless system.

DQ12-9 In the physical implementation depicted in Figure 12.7, the computer updated the accounts payable data upon receipt of a vendor invoice (a clerk handled any exceptions). Describe the procedures that you believe should control that process.

DQ12-10 In the physical implementation depicted in Figure 12.7 (pages 434–437), the payment order and the remittance advice were either sent together through the banking system, or the remittance advice was sent directly to the vendor. Which is better? Why?

DQ12-11 With an EDI system, a customer's order may be entered directly into the Order-to-Sales system without human intervention. Describe control concerns under these circumstances.

PROBLEMS

Note: As in Chapters 10 and 11, the first few problems in the business process chapters are based on the processes of specific companies. Therefore, the problem material starts with case narratives of those processes.

CASE STUDIES

CASE A: Klassic Grocers, Inc.

Klassic Grocers is an online grocery service that provides home delivery of groceries purchased via the Internet. Klassic operates in the greater Tulsa area and provides delivery to precertified customers. Because of the perishable nature of many grocery products, the bulk of orders must be handled similarly to processes used for just-in-time processes.

To facilitate the process, Klassic uses a variation of *vendor-managed inventory* to monitor inventory levels closely. The purchasing process is triggered by a vendor (via an extranet portal) accessing Klassic's inventory system to check current inventory levels of goods they provide. If additional grocery stocks (i.e., inventory) are needed, the vendor initiates a purchase requisition within Klassic's purchasing system. The requisition is entered into the purchasing database. Periodically, throughout the day, Klassic's purchasing manager accesses the purchasing database and reviews vendor-initiated purchase requisitions. The purchasing manager keys in either an acceptance or denial of the purchasing requisition (which is entered into the purchasing database) and the vendor is notified electronically through a transmission from the purchasing system. If the order is accepted, this transmission takes the form of an electronic purchase order; if it is rejected, the transmission is simply an electronic mail message of denial.

When goods are received from the vendor, a printout of the authorized purchase order is attached. The receiving department keys in the purchase order information to retrieve electronic authorization from the purchasing database. Accepted goods are recorded in the purchasing database as received, bar codes are automatically printed in the receiving department to label the crates/boxes received, and the goods are stored in the warehouse. Rejected goods are returned to the vendor along with the purchase order stamped "unauthorized—shipment refused."

At the beginning of the following day, the cash disbursements officer connects to the purchasing database to review the received goods that automatically update the accounts payable balances. Per agreement with suppliers, all payments are due within 10 days after receipt of shipped grocery stocks. Thus, the cash disbursements officer connects to Klassic's electronic banking system via the bank's Web site and initiates payments to all vendors via electronic transfers the day after receipt of goods, as the bank requires five business days to complete all transactions. The bank sends a confirmation number instantaneously in response to the transaction and the cash disbursements officer enters the confirmation number into the purchasing database, serving to confirm completion of the payment to the vendor.

Case B: Lifeline Medical Supplies

Lifeline Medical Supplies makes a variety of medical supplies such as test tubes, thermometers, and disposable surgical garments. Lifeline employs the following procedures for purchases and accounts payable.

The supplies manager orders goods and maintains perpetual inventory records. The records include reorder points for all regularly used items. The supplies manager prepares a requisition on a two-part prenumbered form. After signing the requisition, he files one copy by requisition number and sends the other copy to the purchasing department. The production manager also must approve requisitions for items that cost over $100 and are not covered by a blanket order.

Some supplies that are used in large quantities come under “blanket” purchase orders. Blanket orders are based on agreements between Lifeline and different vendors to buy a *minimum* amount of supplies over a specified period of time at a guaranteed price. Purchase requisitions against these orders do not require the production manager’s approval, as long as the agreed minimum is not surpassed. The purchasing department keeps the blanket orders filed by item name.

The purchasing department checks a requisition for proper approval and selects a vendor. A five-part prenumbered purchase order is prepared. Copies are sent to the vendor, receiving department, accounts payable, and the supplies manager. The purchasing agent records the current purchase on the blanket order if applicable and files its purchase order and requisition copies by purchase order number in the open order file. The receiving department files its copy in a file by purchase order number. The supplies manager files his copy with its corresponding requisition.

The receiving department counts the goods when they are received, compares the count to the packing slip, and prepares a four-part receiving report. Copies of the receiving report are sent to the supplies manager, the purchasing department, and accounts payable. The receiving department files its copy of the receiving report and the packing slip with its copy of the purchase order. The supplies manager updates the perpetual inventory records when he receives the receiving report and then files the purchase order, purchase requisition, and receiving report by purchase order number. The purchasing department files its copy with the order in the open order file.

The purchasing department receives two-part invoices from the vendors. The invoices are compared by a clerk to the purchase order and the receiving report from the open order file. The clerk initials them if they are accurate. The purchasing agent must approve any price or quantity variances that are more than 5 percent over the price or quantity quoted on the purchase order. One copy of the approved invoice is sent to accounts payable. The purchase order, purchase requisition, invoice, and receiving report are then filed in the closed order file by purchase order number.

The accounts payable department receives purchase orders and approved invoices from the purchasing department and receiving reports from the receiving department. As each one is received, it is filed in the pending file by vendor name. When all the documents for an order are received, a clerk posts the payable amount to the payable voucher for the particular vendor. A disbursement voucher is then prepared and attached to the order, receiving report, and invoice. This package is then given to the accounts payable manager for review and approval. The manager gives the approved disbursement vouchers to a second clerk. This clerk batches and totals the approved vouchers and prepares a batch summary. The batch summary is sent to the accounting department. A third clerk completes a two-part, prenumbered check/remittance advice form for each disbursement voucher. The check/remittance advices and the disbursement vouchers are sent to the cashier.

The cashier totals the checks and compares that total to the total of all the batches. She then signs the checks with the treasurer's signature using a check-signing machine that she has in her office. She then places in envelopes the first copies of the check/remittances and sends them to the vendors. The second copy is sent to the accounting department.

P12-1 For the company assigned by your instructor, complete the following requirements:

a. Prepare a table of entities and activities.

b. Draw a context diagram.

c. Draw a *physical* data flow diagram (DFD).

d. Prepare an annotated table of entities and activities. Indicate on this table the groupings, bubble numbers, and bubble titles to be used in preparing a level 0 logical DFD.

e. Draw a level 0 *logical* DFD.

P12-2 For the company assigned by your instructor, draw a systems flowchart. If any exception routines are described in the narrative, they should be shown on a separate page (referenced through an off-page connector), so that the exception routines will not clutter the flowcharting of *normal* activities.

P12-3 For the company assigned by your instructor, prepare a control matrix for the *purchasing* and/or the *receiving* functions *only*, as appropriate for the case in question. Observe the following specific instructions:

a. Your choice of recommended control plans should come from this chapter plus any other control plans from Chapters 9 through 11 that are germane to your company's process.

b. Annotate the systems flowchart (either prepared by you in P12-2 or distributed by your instructor) to show the points where control plans are "present" (codes P-1 . . . P-*n*) or where they are "missing" (codes M-1 . . . M-*n*).

c. Because your explanations of the cell entries are as important as the cell entries themselves, pay particular attention to step 5 in "Steps in Preparing a Control Matrix," Exhibit 9.1 (page 287).

d. In the appropriate control goal columns of the matrix, (1) identify the specific resources of this process, for which we want to ensure security of resources, and (2) indicate the master data, for which we want to ensure update accuracy (UA) and update completeness (UC).

P12-4 For the company assigned by your instructor, prepare a control matrix for the *accounts payable* and the *cash disbursements* functions *only*, as appropriate for the case in question. Observe the specific instructions listed in items (a) through (d) of P12-3.

P12-5 The following capsule cases present short narratives of processes used by three actual organizations whose names have been changed for the purpose of this problem. You will use the cases to practice the mechanics of drawing data flow diagrams.

Capsule Case 1: Rock of Gibraltar Insurance Co.

Rock of Gibraltar Insurance Co. (ROG) is one of the largest automobile insurance companies in the country. Each year, ROG receives more than 30,000 claims billings from Plexlite Glass Corp. (Plex), the country's largest auto glass replacement chain and a leading manufacturer of replacement windshields. Recently the two companies entered into an agreement to abandon paper invoices and adopt EDI for the processing of claims. The new process works as follows:

An insured party calls ROG to report glass damage. The ROG representative taking the call gives the insured an authorization number and opens a claim record on ROG's claims processing system. The insured party takes the automobile to a Plex shop to have the glass repaired, gives Plex the authorization number, and pays the deductible amount required by the insurance policy. After the Plex store replaces the glass, the store manager enters the authorization number and other data into its computer system via a point-of-sale (POS) terminal, and the data are recorded to the receivables data.

Plex's computer system collects the invoice data from the individual Plex stores and transmits the data each week to ROG in EDI format through IVANS, a value added network owned by the insurance industry. Thus, the data is received by ROG's computer system without the need for human intervention.

After the data are checked electronically against the open claim data for proper authorization number, auto make and model, proper insurance coverage, and correct pricing by Plex, the claims invoice is written to the validated claims data, and an EDI message informs Plex which claims will be paid. Claims rejected by ROG's system are processed manually; description of the exception routines is beyond the context of this case. Once a week, ROG's treasurer accesses the validated claims data and sends a single check to Plex for all claims approved that week.

Capsule Case 2: Baby Bell Telephone Co.

Baby Bell Telephone Co. uses a computer-assisted PtoP process called PRP (purchasing, receiving, payables) that includes an EDI function. An abbreviated description of the *purchasing* portion of PRP follows. (The description covers only the purchase by field technicians of items to be delivered by suppliers directly to the technicians in the field.)

The company's field technicians continually need to replace items such as small hand tools, wire, and power tools. (*Note:* Assume that an external entity called "Field Inventory System" triggers the PRP system by identifying a "Field inventory replacement need.") They do so by using handheld computers to log into the PRP system. Users have login IDs and passwords that allow them access only to information for which they have clearance. Once logged in, a technician enters the requested item's stock number. PRP presents the user with a display showing the item's description, size, and so forth. Information on price, brand, or supplier is not provided to most users because it is information they don't need to know. To complete the order request, the user visually verifies the information shown in the display, keys in the quantity ordered, and presses the "enter" key.

PRP records the order in the purchase order master data (disk). The order is routed through a wide area network to the workstation of an available order entry clerk in the purchasing department. The clerk enters a code that requests PRP to match the item's stock number with the supplier code in the inventory master data. The system then retrieves the supplier's *standing data* (e.g., name, address, whether or not an EDI vendor, and so forth) from the vendor master data and displays it on the workstation screen. The purchasing clerk next enters another code that either transmits the order electronically to the vendor through an EDI VAN or prints a hard copy purchase order document that is mailed to the vendor, in the case of a supplier that does not have EDI capability. In either case, the purchase order master data are updated to show that the PO has been issued. Hard copy purchase orders are put in envelopes and mailed.

Capsule Case 3: Big 3, Inc.

Big 3, Inc. (BIG), is a major manufacturer of automobiles. This narrative gives an abbreviated description of the procedures used by BIG in buying original equipment windshields from its only supplier of windshields, Akron Glass Co. (AGC). When BIG's inventory system requests the purchasing department to reorder windshields, the order information is recorded to the purchase order data store and transmitted electronically directly from BIG's computer to AGC's computer via the Internet. AGC returns an electronic acknowledgment to BIG.

When AGC is ready to ship the order, it transmits an electronic invoice to BIG and prints a paper bill of lading that is given to the trucker who transports the goods. BIG's computer records the invoice to the pending invoices data. The receiving department at BIG keys in the goods received. The keying operation creates a receiving record in the receiving data and updates the purchase order master data store to reflect the receipt. Each morning, a clerk in BIG's accounts payable department accesses the electronic invoices received from all EDI suppliers the previous day. He audits the invoice by checking it against data from the purchase order master data store (e.g., descriptions, quantities, prices, and purchase terms) and from the receiving data. The clerk then enters the date to be paid and a code to authorize payment of each invoice.

The payment authorization is transmitted electronically to BIG's bank where it is stored in the authorized payments data until the specified payment date. The evening before the payment date, BIG's bank forwards the payment—with remittance data electronically "attached" to it—to AGC's bank. The payment data are in encrypted, authenticated form. BIG's bank account is debited for the payment. The next morning, AGC's bank account is credited for the payment.

BIG's remittance data are translated to a standard lockbox format, integrated with AGC's other lockbox remittances, and reported online to AGC for automatic posting to its accounts receivable database.

REQUIRED: For the capsule case assigned by your instructor, complete the following requirements:

a. Prepare a table of entities and activities.

b. Draw a context diagram.

c. Draw a *physical* data flow diagram (DFD).

d. Prepare an annotated table of entities and activities. Indicate on the table the groupings, bubble numbers, and bubble titles to be used in preparing a level 0 logical DFD.

e. Draw a level 0 *logical* DFD.

P12-6 Figure 12.3 (page 422)presents only the "normal" horizontal flows for the PtoP process. In other words, that figure intentionally ignores flows related to exception routines.

REQUIRED: Using Figure 12.3 as the model, create a figure that shows all the horizontal data flows related to handling purchase returns to vendors. Observe the following specific requirements:

a. At the top of the figure, draw triangles to show the functional entities involved in processing purchase returns. Enter the titles of the specific managers that are involved, including any *new* managers not shown in Figure 12.3.

b. Near the right margin, draw a vertical line to demarcate the PtoP process from the “environment.” As you draw the horizontal flows, insert any necessary external entities to the right of the vertical line.

c. Draw all of the horizontal flow lines (and their directions) needed to process purchase returns. Number each flow, starting with 1.

d. List the numbers 1 . . . *n* to correspond to each flow line added to the diagram in part (c). Provide a brief description of each information flow number.

P12-7 Draw a DFD to reflect the exception routine of handling purchase returns and allowances.

P12-8 *Note:* If you were assigned DQ12-4, consult your solution to it. Modify the DFDs in Figures 12.4 (page 426)and 12.9 through 12.12 (pages 448–451), as appropriate, to reflect the following *independent* assumptions:

a. Purchasing a technical product that could not be inspected in the receiving department but had to undergo quality control testing before being accepted.

b. Purchasing goods through an online auction site, so that the price changes each time a purchase is made.

c. Making payments twice per month, on the fifth and twenty-fifth of the month, and taking advantage of all cash discounts offered.

Note: Because the three assumptions are independent, your instructor may assign only some of them.

P12-9 Modify the DFDs in Figures 12.4 and 12.9 through 12.12, as appropriate, to reflect that the purchase from our vendor was "drop-shipped" to one of our customers instead of being shipped to us.

P12-10 Assume that Pyrotechnics, Inc., has the following departments (plus others not to be considered in this problem):

A. Storeroom (including inventory control)

B. Purchasing

C. Accounts payable

D. Receiving

E. Treasurer

F. General ledger

The following documents/forms are to be considered in this problem:

1. Purchase requisition

2. Purchase order

3. Receiving report

Gelinas 12-52

The following information system control goals are to be considered in this problem:

IV. Purchase events are valid.

IC. All valid purchase events are input to the system.

IA. Purchase events are accurately input to the system.

UC. Recorded events are completely updated to the proper master data.

UA. Recorded events are accurately updated to the proper master data.

REQUIRED:

a. List the numbers 1 through 3 on your solution sheet. Each number represents a document from the second list. In column 1, opposite each of the three document numbers, insert a *single* capital letter (A through F) to indicate the department in the first list that would originate (initiate) that document.

b. In column 2, opposite each of the three document numbers, insert *one or more* capital letters (A through F) to indicate every department that you want to receive a copy of that document (i.e., the destination departments). Include the letter of the originating department if you want it to keep a copy of the document.

c. From your solution to requirement b, select *only one* department from column 2 for *each* document (obviously, the department could be different for each document). Circle the letter of that department in column 2. Then in column 3, describe how that department could use the document in question to serve a control purpose. In other words, describe a control procedure (control plan) related to the document in question. Limit each description to two or three sentences.

d. In column 4, insert a code from the third list above (IV, IC, IA, UC, or UA) to show the control goal that you believe is best served by the procedure described in column 2. Limit your answer to one procedure performed in one destination department for *each* document.

The format of your solution will appear as follows:

Doc.	Col. 1	Col. 2	Col. 3	Col. 4
#	Originating	Destination	Description	Control
	Department	Department	of control	goal
			procedure	
1				
2				
3				

P12-11 Listed below are 12 process failures that indicate weaknesses in control.

Process Failures

1. A cash disbursements event was updated on the wrong record in the accounts payable master data because the data entry clerk transposed digits in the vendor identification number.
2. Several scanned invoice documents were lost and did not get recorded.
3. The amount of a cash disbursement event was erroneous, resulting in a negative balance in the accounts payable master data.
4. Supplies were purchased from a vendor found on an auction site. The supplies arrived late, and were of poor quality.
5. A purchasing agent ordered unneeded inventory items from a supplier company of which he is one of the officers.
6. The total shown on a vendor's invoice was greater than the sum of the invoice details, resulting in an overpayment to the vendor.
7. The vendor invoiced for goods that were never delivered. The invoice was paid in its full amount.
8. The vendor shipped goods that were never ordered. The invoice for those goods was paid.
9. The unit prices the vendor charged were in excess of those that

had been negotiated. The invoice rendered by the vendor was paid.

10. Goods were stolen by storeroom personnel. When the shortage was discovered, the storeroom personnel claimed that the goods had never been delivered to them from the receiving department.

11. A vendor submitted an invoice in duplicate. The invoice got paid twice.

12. Because of several miscellaneous errors occurring over a number of years, the total of the outstanding vendor payable balances shows a large discrepancy from the balance reflected in the general ledger.

REQUIRED: List the numbers 1 through 12 on your solution sheet. For each of the 12 process failures described above, provide a two- to three-sentence description of the control plan that you believe would *best* address that deficiency. Obviously, there could be more than one plan for a particular situation. However, select *only one* plan for each of the 12 process failures and include in your description a justification of why you believe it is *best.* When in doubt, opt for the plan that is *preventive* in nature, as opposed to plans that are *detective* or *corrective.*

P12-12 In applying the control framework to the physical PtoP process in the chapter, we intentionally omitted from the control matrix (see

Figure 12.8 on pages 442–443) certain technology-related and other control plans introduced in Chapters 9 and 10. While we did so in the interest of simplifying the discussion, we acknowledged that such control plans—to the extent that they are germane to the process—should be included in the matrix and should be discussed in Exhibit 12.1 (page 445).

REQUIRED:

a. Prepare a continuation of the control matrix of Figure 12.8 (pages 442–443) that includes any additional control plans that you believe are relevant to the process depicted in the systems flowchart in Figure 12.7 (pages 434–437).

b. Annotate the systems flowchart (distributed by your instructor) to show the points where the additional control plans are "present" (codes P-8 . . . P-*n*) or where they are "missing" (codes M-1 . . . M-*n*).

c. Because your explanations of the cell entries are as important as the cell entries themselves, pay particular attention to step 5 in "Steps in Preparing a Control Matrix," Exhibit 9.1 (page 287).

P12-13 (Appendix 12A) Use the data flow diagrams in Figures 12.4 (page 426)and 12.9 through 12.12 (pages 448–451) to solve this problem.

REQUIRED: Prepare a 4-column table that summarizes the PtoP processes, inputs, and outputs. In the first column, list the four processes shown in the level 0 diagram (Figure 12.4). In the second column, list the subsidiary functions shown in the four lower-level diagrams (Figures 12.9 through 12.12). For *each* subsidiary process listed in column 2, list the data flow names or the data stores that are inputs to that process (column 3) or outputs of that process (column 4). (See Note below.) The following table has been started for you to indicate the format for your solution.

Note: To simplify the solution, do *not* show any reject stubs in column 4.

SOLUTION FORMAT

Summary of the PtoP inputs, outputs, and data stores

	Subsidiary		
Process	**Functions**	**Inputs**	**Outputs**
1.0 Order	1.1 Select	Inventory's	Purchase
goods and	vendor	purchase	requisition
services		requisition	
		Purchase	
		requisition—	
		supplies and	
		services	

Gelinas 12-58

		Vendor master	
		data	
	1.2 Prepare	Purchase	Continue
	purchase	requisition	solution...
	order	Inventory	
		master data	

TABLES

Table 12.1 Description of Information Flows*

Flow No.	Description
1	Purchase requisition sent from inventory control department to purchasing department
2	Purchase requisitions from various other departments sent to purchasing department
3	Purchase order sent to vendor
4	Purchase order notification sent to various other departments or to inventory control department
5	Purchase order notification sent to receiving department
6	Purchase order notification sent to accounts payable department
7	Goods and services received from vendor
8	Receiving notification sent to accounts payable department
9	Receiving notification sent to purchasing department

10	Invoice received from vendor
11	Approved voucher sent to cashier
12	Accounts payable notification and inventory cost information sent to general ledger
13	Check sent to vendor by cashier
14 .	Paid voucher returned to the accounts payable department
15	Notification of the cash disbursement sent from the cashier to the general ledger

* Many of these steps may be automated. See Technology Insight 12.1 for a description of these steps in an enterprise systems implementation.

BOXES

[Start Technology Insight 12.1 box here]

TECHNOLOGY INSIGHT 12.1

Enterprise System Support for Horizontal Information Flows

The information flows presented in Figure 12.3 (page 422) are very similar to what we would expect if the organization were using an enterprise system. However, many of the tasks outlined for that figure would occur quite differently because of the messaging capabilities embedded in contemporary enterprise systems. Let us take a quick look at each of the information flows for Figure 12.3.

1. When the inventory control department enters the purchase requisition, the requisition is automatically entered into the database for processing by the purchasing department.

2. Similarly, as purchase requisitions are entered into the system by various other departments, the requisitions are automatically entered into the database to await processing by the purchasing department.

3. Purchase orders are transmitted to vendors. Usually, these purchase orders are transmitted via EDI transmission either automatically by the enterprise system or upon a release (i.e., an authorization) keyed in by the purchasing department.

4. When the purchase order is released, the release is recorded in the database and instantly available for the initiating department's review, should a department want to check on the status of a purchase order.

5. The recording of the purchase order release also makes the necessary portions of the purchase order information available to the receiving department for review when the vendor delivers the goods or services.

6. Recording the purchase order release also places the data on the authorized purchase order list for review by the accounts payable department.

7. Goods and services are received from vendor.

8. When the receiving department enters information upon receipt of the goods and services, the purchase order is automatically flagged for receipt and, therefore, for processing by accounts payable department.

9. This entry to the system (in step 8) also notifies the purchasing department that the goods and services have been received. These data become part of the vendor's history.

10. Invoice is received from vendor—this normally arrives as an EDI transmission from the vendor.

11. Approval of voucher is recorded to the database, flagging the purchase for payment by the cashier. This approval may be automatically performed by embedded rules in the enterprise system.

12. Accounts payable information is automatically flagged for inclusion in the general ledger and inventory costing information.

13. Cashier sends check to vendor. Again, this step may be an authorized electronic funds transfer (EFT), either by the cashier or automatically per embedded rules in the enterprise system.

14. Payment is entered into the database and immediately made available for viewing by the accounts payable department.

15. The entry of the cash disbursement authorization flags the database and creates the source of the update in the general ledger.

[End Technology Insight 12.1 box here]

[Start Technology Insight 12.2 box here]

TECHNOLOGY INSIGHT 12.2

Inventory Reordering Processes

- **Cyclical reordering** is a *time-based* approach to reordering inventory. In practical terms, cyclical reordering assesses an organization's total inventory (on a periodic basis) to determine the status of individual inventory items. If the stock levels for a given inventory item appear to be insufficient to meet customer needs for the upcoming period, a purchase requisition is prepared.

- **Reorder point (ROP) analysis** recognizes that each item of inventory is unique with respect to the rate at which it is sold. Based on each inventory item's sales rate, a reorder point is determined. Thus, when the on-hand level for an item falls to its specified reorder point, the item is reordered.

- **Economic order quantity (EOQ)** is a technique of analyzing all incremental costs associated with acquiring and carrying particular items of inventory. *Inventory carrying costs* are composed of five cost elements: (1) opportunity cost of investment funds, (2) insurance costs, (3) property taxes, (4) storage costs, and (5) cost of obsolescence and deterioration.

- **ABC analysis** is a technique for ranking items in a group based on the output of the items. ABC analysis can be used to categorize inventory items according to their importance. A given organization, for example, may have a situation where 15% of its inventory items accounts for 70% of its total inventory investment. Let's call this portion group A. Furthermore, an organization may find that an additional 10% of its inventory items account for an additional 20% of its total inventory investment. Let's call this portion group B. From this assessment, we can now deduce that the remaining 75% of the organization's inventory items constitute only 10% of its inventory investment. With this information in hand, the warehouse manager or the supervisor of inventory control can decide which items of inventory are relatively more important to an organization and, consequently, require more attention and control. For instance, category C items might be ordered on a *cyclical* basis, whereas categories A and B might be ordered using *reorder point* analysis.

[End Technology Insight 12.2 box here]

[Start Technology Application 12.1 box here]

TECHNOLOGY APPLICATION 12.1

Uses of Electronic Data Interchange for the PtoP Process

Case 1

Kaiser Permanente of Southern California is a pioneer in trying to cut medical costs. One more way to do that is through the accounts payable and cash disbursements process. The Southern California region alone processes more than 1 million invoices and 800,000 claims with over 500,000 payments. A small cut in the cost of processing each transaction adds up quickly. The solution was to move to EDI for its patient care providers—both inside and outside the managed care program. Kaiser implemented the ANSI X12 837 healthcare claims standard specifically designed for the detailed health care information required for claims processing. In cases where the provider only accepts a check, check processing has been outsourced at a savings of 35%–40%. For vendors who accept electronic funds transfers (EFT), the savings are even greater.

Case 2

John Hancock Mutual Life Insurance Co. spent $337 million in 1997 on supplies needed to run its business. Only 8% of these purchases went through the central purchasing department, though. The result was huge cost compared to prices that could have been negotiated on bulk purchases. Armed with a new intranet system, Hancock Mutual now processes 85% of those purchases through central processing while maintaining zero growth in staffing of the purchasing department. The key is to run all small ticket items such as office supplies and business cards through central purchasing along with big ticket items such as personal computers and contract labor. Employees simply point and click to select items from the intranet Web page displaying available goods and services. Orders route through an automatic electronic approval process based on the individual's purchasing privileges. Authorized purchases are transferred electronically to central purchasing. Another key to the system is that the intranet is also integrated into the enterprise system to make sure orders pass through back-end processing and to facilitate payment through the EDI system, which further minimizes transaction costs.

Case 3

Cummins Engine Co. is a leader in using EDI to make advances in global markets to sell its products. It shouldn't come as a big surprise that Cummins also uses EDI extensively to make its own purchases, since the same economies are garnered on both sides of the transaction. The company has found on average that suppliers receive their orders two to three days earlier than they would under the old process. Additionally, the electronic form of the order generally triggers a faster response by the supplier because any manual data entry steps are generally avoided. These small changes in timing allow for more efficient inventory and supplies management, while also providing major costs savings in processing purchases.

Sources: Sharon Watson, "Kaiser Taking Advantage of EDI to Process Claims Online," *Computerworld* (August 8, 1997); Carol Sliwa, "Purchasing Via Web to Save Big Bucks," *Computerworld* (July 20, 1998): 1, 14; Suruchi Mohan, "Engine Manufacturer Cuts Costs Worldwide," *Infoworld* (April 6, 1998).

[End Technology Application 12.1 box here]

[Start Technology Application 12.2 box here]

TECHNOLOGY APPLICATION 12.2

Uses of B2B Marketplaces for the PtoP Process

Case 1

A trend in the B2B electronic marketplaces environment has been a move toward consolidation of the numerous marketplaces that popped up quickly in the early 2000s. One example is the merger between MyAircraft and AirNewco—two early entrants into the electronic marketplaces for supplying aviation-related supplies and materials. MyAircraft was a joint venture by supplier organizations such as United Technologies Corp., Honeywell International, Inc. (which at the time of this writing is in the process of merging with General Electric), and BF Goodrich Co. On the other hand, AirNewco was a joint venture by buyer organizations, including eight major international airlines and the United Parcel Service of America, Inc. The result of the merger is a single major exchange that represents the interests of both suppliers and buyers.

Case 2

In one of the earliest major marketplaces to arise, Covisint quickly gained the attention of the Federal Trade Commission (FTC) for possible limitations on fair trade. Covisint is a joint venture of the Big Three U.S. automakers and so has the potential to change radically the pricing and partnering structures of the three automakers with numerous automotive parts suppliers. The FTC ultimately gave its blessings to the new electronic marketplace in September 2000 after apparently recognizing the enormous cost savings and efficiencies that would likely result from such a venture through sharply reduced sales and distributions costs and through streamlining of purchasing operations at the automakers.

Case 3

An alternative to the creation of a public electronic marketplace such as Covisint is the creation of a private network such as the approach used by Toyota Motor Sales USA Inc. Toyota hopes to decrease about $175 million from inventory levels (roughly 50%) by using a private electronic marketplace to replenish necessary automotive parts supplies from its established suppliers. The reduction in inventory may save $30 million per year once the exchange is operating fully. Toyota is not the only company turning to private exchanges with their own supplier networks. While there are an estimated 600 planned or operating public electronic exchanges, about 30,000 such private exchanges are planned. These exchanges may link as few as a half-dozen suppliers in some cases, but are still expected to provide most of the benefits of larger public exchanges without many of the risks.

Sources: Todd R. Weiss, "Two Aviation Industry B2B Marketplaces Agree to Merge," *Computerworld Online* (October 26, 2000); John R. Wilke, "Green Light Is Likely for Auto-Parts Site," *The Wall Street Journal* (September 11, 2000): A3; Steve Ulfelder, Members Only Exchanges—Building a Private Business-to-Business Exchange Has its Benefits—and Challenges," *Computerworld Online* (October 23, 2000).

[End Technology Application 12.2 box here]

[Start Technology Excerpt 12.1 box here]

Technology Excerpt 12.1

Online Bill Presentment and Payment

Although most of the hype in online billing is for business-to-consumer billing (such as utilities and communication companies), more than half of the 20 billion electronic bills issued each year are to businesses. New bill payment service providers let companies receive electronic bills and pay them directly from their bank account.

How This Saves Money

- *Lower cost per bill payment.* Traditional paper-based payments including stamps, checks, and envelopes cost about $0.50–$1.50 each. For about 25 monthly online payments, the cost per payment ranges from $0.24 to $80, depending on the vendor and additional services selected.

- *Save time* by receiving e-mail notification of new bills and paying them online instead of offline. The time it takes to manually open envelopes and print checks is significantly reduced. Helpful features like receiving e-mail reminders of bills due and designating bills for automatic payment also save time.

- Companies can even *make interest off the float* in their bank accounts by controlling exactly when payments are made.

Source: www.dotcomadvisor.com, September 20, 2000.

[End Technology Excerpt 12.1 box here]

[Start Technology Insight 12.3 box here]

TECHNOLOGY INSIGHT 12.3

Enterprise System Support for the PtoP Process

The main effect of the introduction of an enterprise system into the PtoP process depicted in Figure 12.7 (pp. 434–437) is the integration of the processing programs and the various data stores into a single unified processing system with a single underlying database. The major change to the diagrams is in the activities depicted within the "Information Systems Function." These changes are depicted in the diagrams included with this Technology Insight. Note while studying these diagrams, that while the systems flowchart has been significantly simplified, the consolidation of all of the processes and databases shown in Figure 12.7 may be misleading. The single process and database in the figure shown here is indicative of the complexity within an enterprise system. In essence, all of the diverse information needed for the different activities performed in the PtoP process are interlinked and share a common data source.

[Inset UNF-p. 440-1 here]

[Inset UNF-p. 441-2 here]

[End Technology Insight 12.3 box here]

14

The Business Reporting (BR) Process

FW Murphy, a privately held company, is the leading manufacturer of gauges used by a variety of major companies such as Caterpillar. When the youngest son of the founder took over the organization, he had a vision of creating an efficient, state-of-the-art manufacturer. But the information systems were not able to support the management practices the junior Murphy was bringing to the organization. He soon learned, for example, that the current set of business processes and information systems were unable to even determine the manufacturing costs for specific goods. As the new CEO, he quickly pushed the organization to implement first a new integrated manufacturing system, and subsequently the JD Edwards enterprise system, to provide integration of enterprise-wide information. These new systems provided them with a wealth of new information. For example, they discovered that they were selling gauges to Caterpillar, a company that represented a major portion of their business, at a price below the cost of manufacturing. At first it seemed that they would be better off not selling to Caterpillar. Instead, they teamed up with Caterpillar to adjust pricing to an appropriate level and to coordinate manufacturing in a manner that was mutually beneficial to the two organizations. In this chapter, we focus on the value of integrated systems to providing efficient generation of business information, as well as supplying key management reports needed for effective decision making and organizational management.

Synopsis

For many years, business reporting was synonymous with periodic historical reports that drew on the general ledger for their content. These financial reports were the main source of business information for both internal (e.g., management) and external (e.g., investor) decision making. They still are a critical component of a company's business reporting process, and the general ledger remains a major source of data for decision-making support.

The general ledger is the repository where all financial data comes together for reporting purposes, which is why it is included in this chapter on business reporting. However, more than just general ledger-based reports are needed for most business decisions. Rather, the business reporting that supports an organization's decision making must synthesize business information on operational and strategic performance derived from a multitude of sources. Successful managers also make use of a broad range of sources of nonfinancial information, which differ with the decision to be made and the circumstances in which the firm finds itself. The data needed to support such business reporting are captured through various business processes as discussed in previous chapters. Easy-to-use, flexible business intelligence tools are frequently adopted to analyze and synthesize the aggregated data in order to support performance measurement, alternatives evaluation, and competitive analysis needs within this broader view.

This chapter begins by defining the boundaries of business reporting including the general ledger activities, explaining its functions, and examining its organizational context. Then we proceed to a discussion of the *logical* general ledger system features. Sections on extended business reporting processes and technology follow.

Learning Objectives

- To describe how business processes feed data required for general ledger updates and business reporting
- To explain how the general ledger and business reporting capabilities support an organization's external and internal reporting functions
- To analyze the limitations of the traditional general ledger approach in contemporary systems
- To describe the extensive business reporting capabilities enabled by enterprise systems, the Internet, and business intelligence software
- To explain the applicability of business reporting to both operational and strategic planning

Process Definition and Functions

Similar to the business processes covered in Chapters 10 through 13, the **business reporting process (BR)** is an interacting structure of people, equipment, methods, and controls designed to accomplish both operations and information process functions. Unlike other business processes, the BR process has fewer *operational* functions; it focuses mainly on *information* functions. While the other processes perform important functions related to their "work" of providing goods and services to customers, the processing and communicating of *information* is the work of the BR process.

Review Question

What, in your own words, is business reporting?

Periodic financial reports are one of the many kinds of reports that result from the BR process. Their importance lies not only in their critical value for internal decisions, but also in the fulfillment of regulatory and other fiscal requirements. The major source of data for financial reporting is the general ledger (GL). Because financial reporting is so vital to every firm, the general ledger updating and reporting process will appear in detail in the following sections. This detailed example illustrates the issues and complexities of the more inclusive BR process, which itself relies on the general ledger as well as many other database updates first covered in Chapters 10 through 13.

What are the important Information Systems functions of the

business reporting process?

- Accumulating data, classifying data, and recording data
- Providing for the generation of both ad hoc and predetermined business reports that support operational and strategic decision making
- Preparing general-purpose, external financial statements from data accumulated by other business processes that flow into the general ledger
- Generating Web-based forms of key business reporting information for dissemination via the Internet.

Before beginning your exploration of the BR process, it may be useful to revisit Figure 1.6 (page 18) and think about the competing values of information. Ponder these values as you explore the various types of internal and external information that organizations have and choose to make available to decision makers.

Review Question

What are the primary functions the business reporting process performs?

Business Reporting: The Special Case of the General Ledger

While many BR functions support a wide range of managers and decision makers in an organization, some financially oriented business-reporting activities remain in the purview of the finance function. Information Systems typically support **ad hoc** (i.e., on demand) business reporting for the benefit of all decision makers who access data through easy-to-use business intelligence software. **Periodic** (i.e., regularly scheduled) business reports, such as the financial reports produced by the financial function from the data stored in the general ledger, are also supported by the Information Systems function. In this section we focus on the role of the general ledger in the BR process and the interactions between the general ledger and its relevant environment.

Before we begin, we should define a term that is used in this section and throughout the chapter. A **feeder process** is any business process that accumulates *business event* data that are then communicated to and processed within the enterprise system database (and to the general ledger within that database). Accordingly, the feeder processes include all those discussed in the earlier business process chapters, as shown in Figure 14.1. Business event data flow into the enterprise database, from which both periodic and ad hoc reports are produced. The general ledger comprises the accumulation of *financially related* business event data, providing summary-level data to the financial functions.

[Insert Figure14.1 here]

Consider how the information flows in Figure 14.1 are affected by integrated enterprise systems. The flows from feeder processes to the integrated database permit the consolidation of data, without creating separate physical copies of this data. For example, the general ledger data flows directly from the business processes along with nonfinancial business event data and does not have to be stored separately in its own file or database. The output side from the enterprise systems is much the same, providing information that can be extracted by the respective departments or managers using either pre-established reporting forms or queries of the enterprise system data. Because financial and nonfinancial data are truly integrated, analysts can focus on the provision of more complex and interesting information that can be used to increase the effectiveness and efficiency of the organization's operations and strategies. We will explore some of the possibilities within this extended business reporting capability later in this chapter.

As we look to emerging capabilities, we should also consider how the external reporting model is changing. Increasingly, organizations are deciding to make financial information available on the Internet. Currently, there is little standardization to this information between companies. Figure 14.2 (page 498)provides a diagram that synthesizes these various financial information flows in what is labeled the "financial information chain." Note that the "operational data stores" are the central enterprise system database or other business reporting system data storage. From this data store(s), information is extracted for internal reporting (i.e., the reports on the left hand side of the diagram). Note that for external reporting, however, the information must be first filtered through the chart of accounts and the general ledger. Additional formatting may be required for special-purpose reports, such as those submitted to the Securities and Exchange Comission (SEC) or publication of the statements on the Web. Later in this chapter, we will discuss current efforts to improve the standardization and quality of this information to improve the efficiency and effectiveness of business reporting.

[Insert Figure14.2 here]

Budgets and Financial Reporting

The finance function provides the oversight needed for preparation of required financial reports. Other business reports and analysis, both financial and nonfinancial, are easily accessed by technology supporting business intelligence capabilities. In addition, companies often employ budget analysts to assist managers in the identification and preparation of special reports containing financial plans. Examples of these include departmental budgets and performance reports.

The **budgeting department** advises and assists managers in preparing their budget. The budgeting department should not actually prepare the budget estimates; it should offer technical advice to the operating line managers as they develop the budgets for their centers. Good participative management practice argues that the responsibility for budget preparation should fall to the operating center managers who later will be held accountable for budget variations.

Some budget assessment reports are called **performance reports** because they compare actual performance with budgeted expectations. In a hierarchically organized company, as information is reported upward, the level of detail is filtered, meaning that figures are aggregated (summarized) as they are reported to successive management levels. Figure 14.3 shows a specimen *performance reporting* flow for the production arm of an organization.

Review Question

What are the fundamental responsibilities of the budgeting department?

As we will discuss later in this chapter, major enterprise system vendors support much of this additional business reporting demand for performance reporting. The integration of this functionality allows these reports to be generated easily from information captured by business processes and maintained at the business event level in the enterprise-wide database. Technology Application 14.1 (page 501)gives examples of successful budgeting and reporting systems.

[Insert Technology Application 14.1 box here]

Review Question

In your own words, what is a performance report?

Horizontal and Vertical Information Flows

In Figure 1.5 (page 14), the distinction between horizontal and vertical information flows was introduced at a conceptual level. Perhaps now is a good time to review the concepts shown in Figure 1.5 and enhance that figure based on our study of information systems. Figure 14.4 (page 500)is designed to do exactly that.

Along the bottom of Figure 14.4, we can trace the horizontal business event data flows as they progress from left to right through the various *operations processes,* culminating in the general ledger or BR databases, and resulting in external business reporting. We also see the vertical reporting dimension (in the form of internal performance reports prepared from information supplied by the general ledger, the BR database, and through budgeting) flowing upward in each of the principal functional columns. Again, note that in an enterprise system environment, the distinction between the general ledger and BR databases vanishes, and all business event data can be used as the basis of managerial reports in support of vertical information flows.

Logical System Description

Once again in this chapter, we use DFDs to explain the *logical* features of the business reporting process. This section focuses specifically on the general ledger update and financial reporting pieces of the process, which are fairly standardized in business today due to extensive government regulation. Business reporting is frequently an ad hoc process, making it difficult to portray in a generic diagram. However, a good understanding of the general ledger update activity will give you the foundation to recognize the potential and widespread usefulness of business reporting.

Discussion and Illustration

We start with the highest-level view of the general ledger reporting process; namely, the *context diagram,* shown in Figure 14.5 (page 502).

[Insert Figure 14.5 here]

Note the *business event* data flows from the business processes discussed in Chapters 10 through 13. If you are uncertain about the nature and timing of any of these updates, go back to the appropriate business process chapter and review them.

Logically, each business event from a feeder process can be posted *directly, individually,* and *immediately* to the general ledger. As a practical matter, *physical* implementations vary. For example, the flows from the feeder processes could comprise *summaries* of a number of business events posted *periodically* at the end of a day, week, or month. For example, the RC process may collect data related to sales and send it to the general ledger. The resulting summarized entry to the general ledger would include postings to sales and accounts receivable.

In an enterprise system, these business event data are recorded separately for each sale within the module designed for that business process (e.g., sales). In some enterprise system implementations, these business event data could be batched during sales processing and then used to update the general ledger database at one point. However, the enterprise system maintains data for each individual business event in the underlying business process database, which, for sales, corresponds to the Order-to-Cash process. At this point, however, let's continue to concentrate on the logical connections of the individual feeder processes with the general ledger.

Review Question

What major *logical* processes does the business reporting process perform?

Figure 14.6 (page 504) shows the general ledger/business reporting process level 0 DFD. Let's take a moment to talk about bubble 1.0, "Validate business event updates." What might be involved here? Here are some examples:

[Insert Figure 14.6 here]

- We would want to check business event updates to make sure that they come from the correct feeder process. Do you agree that this check addresses the information system goal of ensuring event data *input validity?*
- We also want to make sure that no business event updates have been overlooked (recall the discussion of *input completeness* in each business process chapter).

Bubbles 4.0, 5.0, and 6.0 are also worth examining more carefully in this figure.

- For general distribution, the business reports in bubble 4.0 and related information are often posted to the entity's Web site. Frequently, at this stage, the financial statements are reformatted to take advantage of embedded links that can be placed into the Web page. For instance, some companies provide hot links in the financial statements directly to the financial statement notes to make it easier for users to tie the notes with specific financial statement accounts.
- Process 5.0, "Record budget," provides one example of how the business reporting process can fuel reporting systems that rely on information that has been aggregated in the system—in this case, providing information related to both budgeted and actual results.
- Process 6.0, like some that you encountered in previous chapters,

is *triggered* by a temporal event (i.e., the data flow into the process from the general ledger master data), rather than by a data flow from another process or from an external entity. Specifically, at an appropriate time, the condition of the general ledger accounts indicates that the accounts should be closed before repeating the accounting cycle for the next accounting period.

The General Ledger Master Data

The **general ledger master data** contain summarized information of all company event data. The main inputs to the general ledger consist of totals, extracted by event type, from the business event data captured in the various feeder processes discussed earlier.

One piece of data on each general ledger entry is a code that identifies the source of the entry and provides a beginning point of reference for developing a proper **audit trail**. The code gives the auditor a means of tracing back to the individual business events that have been aggregated into the general ledger balances. Note that in addition to storing the entries of the current period (both monthly and yearly activity are usually maintained in general ledger systems), beginning-of-period and year-to-date balances also are available.

In an enterprise system, the user can select any beginning and ending date to accumulate information for a period of time of interest, because the source business event data are maintained.

Thus, if a manager wants to examine sales over a two-week period or a three-month period or any other period, the information can be aggregated through a query to provide the manager the precise information of interest.

Limitations of the General Ledger Approach

Recall in Chapter 3 the discussion regarding the limitations of traditional file processing approaches and the emerging focus on event-driven systems. The discussion focused on the limitations that come from having disjointed files for financial and nonfinancial information. The traditional general ledger approach has been a primary suspect as the source of many of these problems.

While other business event information may be captured in separate systems operated by other departments, such as marketing, any such nonfinancial information becomes separated from the financial information. Once the end-of-period closings are completed for the general ledger, the detailed business event-level data are eventually purged from the general ledger system—the interest being only in maintaining correct current balances for each account. It is at this point that, even if there were a link between financial and nonfinancial information in the business event data, the relationships are lost as soon as the periodic closings are completed and the financial data discarded. From that point on, information for decision making is limited to only that information captured in the account files. If you decide you want more detailed information than these accounts provide, historical business events usually cannot be reconstructed.

You will recall that in Chapter 3 we noted the evolution toward database-driven systems—and in particular, event-driven systems. This discussion explains why the rapidly expanding information needs of management created conflict with traditional general ledger structures. The move toward enterprise systems accelerated because of the frustration of managers who needed access to integrated financial and nonfinancial data.

Technology-Enabled Initiatives in Business Reporting

We begin with three topics related to enterprise systems. The first is simply a brief look at the financial reporting module in an enterprise system, while the second and third topics relate to contemporary extensions of enterprise systems to accommodate recent business reporting interests—i.e., balanced scorecard and business intelligence (as discussed in Chapter 5). The fourth topic is also related in some ways to enterprise systems (i.e., major vendors are currently working to build in the functionality), but it is more specifically focused on business reporting via the Internet and the standardization of this reporting for all entities.

Enterprise System Financial Module Capability

Although we discussed earlier in this chapter the integration of business reporting in enterprise systems (as well as integration of information from other business process activities), conceptually this integration may still be a bit foggy. For purposes of clarification, let's take a closer look at integration within several modules.

Figure 14.7 shows the entry level screen for JDEdwards OneWorld enterprise software. We have exploded the menu options for the financial section to show you the wide range of options that are available in the software just for the financial module. Note that the software interface looks like a very typical Microsoft Windows-based application. Indeed, the "JDEdwards OneWorld Explorer" interface screen works very similarly to Microsoft's "Windows Explorer." Pointing and clicking with the mouse on higher-level options drills down to lower level menu options.

[Insert Figure 14.7 here]

Note on the left hand side that the "Financials" option is highlighted. Directly above the "Financials" option, you see another option at the same level. The "Foundation Systems" option allows the user to set security options, change the way in which information flows through the system, and many other such systems' management- and maintenance-related activities. Other options that fall off the bottom of the screen include "Human Resources and Payroll" (which relates to business process activities discussed in

Chapter 13), "Distribution/Logistics" (activities in Chapters 10, 11, and 13), and "Manufacturing" (activities in Chapter 13). These options are shown in more detail in Figures 14.8, 14.9, and 14.10.

[Insert Figure 14.8 here]

[Insert Figure 14.9 here]

[Insert Figure 14.10 here]

With the "Financials" option highlighted on the left side of the screen, note on the right side of the screen that all of the first-level menu options for the financials module appear. These options include information processing capabilities related to all of the business processes we have discussed in this text. Note also that these options clearly go beyond just general ledger activities to include a variety of other information processing and business reporting issues such as cost accounting, billing options, and expense reimbursements. If you think back to the situation at FW Murphy in the opening vignette, it becomes apparent how this functionality would help FW Murphy better monitor their cost processes.

Back on the left side of the screen, see that all of the menu options for accounts receivable have been exploded out and are visible. The main processing activities take place in the sub-menus of daily and periodic processing. However, there are also options for configuring the processing of accounts receivable. You may see that the last few menu options in the accounts receivable area include set-ups for European community countries for value-added tax issues ("EC VAT Processing") and Italian tax-related issues ("Italian IVA Processing"). These options facilitate the operations of multinational corporations. Most large multinational corporations have instituted enterprise systems, in part because of the ease by which cross-border and multi-currency issues can be facilitated within the systems. While we have not exploded the further menus for the other areas beyond accounts receivable, you can see on the left side of Figure 14.7 that the sub-menu options for "Daily Processing," "Periodic Processing,""Advanced and Technical Operations," and "System Set-up," are consistent for all of the areas (i.e., Accounts Payable, General Accounting, etc.)

Review Question

In your own words, how do enterprise system financial modules facilitate the business reporting process?

Figures 14.8, 14.9, and 14.10 show the equivalent detailed reporting options provided to support several other business processes. Take some time to check over the options provided, to see how completely the functionality covers the types of operational business event processing and reporting within each area. Figure 14.8 (page 508)depicts the menu for the distribution and logistics functions offered by JD Edwards. Traditional inventory and procurement processes are augmented by e-commerce capabilities. Business event transactions as well as reporting are supported by the menu items on this initial screen. In Figure 14.9 (page 509), payroll and human resource management activities are listed along with the many reports needed by the government, unions, and internal management. Manufacturing activities are provided by the menu choices in Figure 14.10 (page 510), in which manufacturing processes are tracked, forecasts are generated, and planning is supported.

This multitude of options should give you some feel for the complexity and magnitude of enterprise systems. For security reasons, as well as ease of use, you limit access to menu items to only those needed by a given user to perform his or her responsibilities. You may want to allow a given user to have different privilege levels for different information—i.e., view access, write access, entry access, and/or change access. All of these choices must be carefully specified in the user's profile to set up the system limitations for that specific user. Normally, this profile is set up with the user's ID automatically initiated at log-on.

Balanced Scorecard

The **balanced scorecard** is a methodology for assessing an organization's business performance via four components:

(1) *Financial.* The financial aspect focuses on more traditional

measures of business performance related to how shareholders view the organization's performance.

(2) *Internal business processes.* The internal business processes relate to the organization's ability to identify its core competencies and to assess how well it performs in these identified areas of competency.

(3) *Customers.* The customer component focuses on identifying how customers perceive an organization.

(4) *Innovation and improvement activities.* Innovation and improvement activities are monitored to assess how the organization is continuing to improve and how it is creating additional value.

The concept of *balanced scorecard* has been around for several years, but it has been only within the last few years that enterprise system vendors have focused on integrating this functionality and in turn making assessment a reasonable possibility. Fundamental to incorporating effective *balanced scorecard* assessment is the aggregation of varied data in a *data warehouse* (discussed in Chapter 3) that can then be analyzed using powerful analytical tools—i.e., *business intelligence* tools as discussed in the next section. Because an enterprise system provides the ability to aggregate the necessary data in its underlying database, linking this data with other data to create the *data warehouse* is a logical and efficient way to provide *balanced scorecard* capabilities. In the past two years, all of the major enterprise system vendors have announced new product integration to provide the *balanced scorecard* functionality. Consider how data captured in the various business processes could be used to support assessment in each of the four areas underlying the *balanced scorecard.*

Business Intelligence

Fundamental to providing *balanced scorecard* functionality is the development of *business intelligence* functionality within enterprise systems. Business intelligence, as presented in Chapter 5, is the integration of statistical and analytical tools with decision support technologies to facilitate complex analyses of *data warehouses* by managers and decision makers. In short, the ideal *business intelligence* solution within an enterprise system should provide the right tools, the right interface, and access to the right kind of data for effective business decision making.[1] Some examples of successful applications of business intelligence are found in Technology Application 14.2.

[Insert Technology Application 14.2 box here]

[1] Cognos, "Enterprise Reporting in an ERP Environment," *Quest Technical Journal* (Fall 1999): 27–29.

In addition to the prespecified reports outlined by Figures 14.8

through 14.10, JD Edwards supports a generic business intelligence tool to permit the user easy access to ad hoc reporting and analysis. Figure 14.11 (page 512) shows how this functionality is divided into several sections. The report writer permits the user to produce ad hoc reports. Predefined user-specified reports are available through the Executive Information System section, and the OnLine Analytical Applications area supports more complex analysis. Finally, the user can analyze trend data through the historical database comprising the Data Warehouse.

[Insert Figure 14.11 here]

Business Intelligence Systems for Aiding the Strategic Planner

Many of the reporting options discussed so far center around ensuring the effective and efficient operations of a company's business processes. The information system supporting the BR process can play an important role in the development of a company's strategic plan in addition to monitoring ongoing operations to measure attainment of the plan. This section discusses the upfront and ongoing assistance that the strategic planner obtains from the information system.

During the strategic planning process, data from the *entity-wide database* or *data warehouse* can be compared to data about the competition to determine an organization's relative strengths and weaknesses. For example, these data might include sales trends, gross margin on sales, age of capital assets, skills of existing personnel, and so on. These data can be presented in reports from the existing IS applications, such as sales/marketing, human resources management, fixed assets, finance and inventory, or via the OLAP models incorporated in the *BI system.* Recall from Chapter 5 that data from the environment can also be incorporated into the BI system output. Strategic planners can combine environmental data with those obtained internally to assess the organization's competitive position.

In addition to assisting in the planning phase, the IS can be used to follow up by reporting certain *key performance indicators* that illustrate the status of processes and critical success factors. For example, the number of customers along with the level of sales and number of customer complaints for each should indicate the status of an organization's sales network. Other key performance indicators might be the number of new products, the cost to manufacture the products, and their selling price. If the *data warehouse* is developed in light of the strategic plan, many of the data for the key performance indicators should be readily available. Clearly, business intelligence tools are invaluable for companies like FW Murphy (discussed at the beginning of the chapter) as they work to manage relationships with key customers like Caterpillar.

Review Question

How is business intelligence used to support strategic planning?

eXtensible Business Reporting Language (XBRL)

Perhaps the most exciting technology-driven advancement to hit business reporting in its history is that of *XBRL*. **eXtensible Business Reporting Language (XBRL)** is an *XML*-based language consisting of a set of tags that are used for business reporting to provide a single, underlying format that can be read by XML-equipped software packages and can be searched by XML-enabled Web browsers. Recall from Chapter 4 that *XML* (eXtensible Markup Language) is a generic Web-based programming standard that interprets a set of user-defined tags to determine the context of information on a Web site and to provide a key to the tags that can be applied by Web users to search a given site easily. XBRL is a specialized business-reporting taxonomy that is based on XML, where the tags are predefined for users so each have a common understanding of the tag's meaning. In this case, *XBRL* provides uniformity for users of financial statements and other business reporting information. Such uniformity simplifies delivery of information via the Web, enhances the searchability of information, and enables easy uploading, downloading, and comparison of the information within other software packages for mandated reporting, analysis, and so forth.[2]

[2] We should note that there are not, as yet, universal data

definitions, making it difficult to compare XBRL- tagged data between organizations.

Review Question

Why is XBRL so important to efficient Web-based business reporting?

XBRL has been developed by an international consortium of accounting bodies, software vendors, providers of information, and information-intensive industry representatives in a united effort towards uniformity of business reporting information. Participants in the consortium include many of the international professional accounting bodies, the Big Four professional service firms, Microsoft, IBM, Oracle, SAP, Fidelity, Moody's, and many business intelligence software vendors.

The intent is that with a unified format, enterprise system vendors (and other BR software vendors) can add functionality that will automatically generate *XBRL*-based reports as well as any other business report. This feature eases the cost and complexity of delivering business information via the Web. Thus, accessibility of information increases for external users of business reports, the information is easier to decipher and analyze, and the information can easily be downloaded for use by other software packages such as spreadsheets, database packages, or data analysis packages. In Technology Excerpt 14.1 we present an article that describes how you can generate your own *XBRL* statements now if you wish. This article should give you some sense of how XBRL works and how it can facilitate the reporting, reading, and analysis of business information.

[Insert Technology Excerpt 14.1 box here]

Conclusions

The good news is that the integration that makes enterprise systems so vital for organizations has the embedded side benefit of supporting automatic updates through the feeder processes that combine to make the electronic inputs work. There is very little need for human-generated inputs to the general ledger or other BR components.

But what about system outputs? We've come a long way from the days where mandated financial reports were the only "business reporting" application emitting from the IS function. Now, decision makers have access to a wide range of information generated within the organization as well as external data found over the Internet. Will we ever see the day when business reporting will do away with paper reports and use only "electronic reports?" The answer is an emphatic "Yes!" The advent of XBRL is one clear indicator that major changes are on the way. Some companies are already there; recall the paperless company described in Technology Application 5.6 (page 163).

REVIEW QUESTIONS

RQ14-1 What, in your own words, is business reporting?

RQ14-2 What are the primary functions the business reporting process performs?

RQ14-3 What are the fundamental responsibilities of the budgeting department?

RQ14-4 In your own words, what is a performance report?

RQ14-5 What major *logical* processes does the business reporting process perform?

RQ14-6 In your own words, how do enterprise system financial modules facilitate the business reporting process?

RQ14-7 How is business intelligence used to support strategic planning?

RQ14-8 Why is XBRL so important to efficient Web-based business reporting?

DISCUSSION QUESTIONS

DQ14-1 Do companies still need a general ledger if they have an enterprise system? Why or why not?

DQ14-2 "Published financial reports are useless as an investing tool because they are so out of date." Do you agree? Why or why not?

DQ14-3 "I don't need to study accounting because computers do all the debits and credits automatically these days." Do you agree? Why or why not?

DQ14-4 With the advent of the Internet, business intelligence, data warehouses, and other technologies, the strategic planner has access to far more data than any one person can effectively analyze. What are the costs and benefits of all this access?

DQ14-5 How do you measure your success in college (i.e., your university *performance measurement factors)*? Design your personal *balanced scorecard* that covers academic, personal, and professional progress.

DQ14-6 In your own words, how do E-S distribution/logistics modules facilitate the business reporting process?

DQ14-7 In your own words, how do business intelligence systems facilitate the business reporting process?

DQ14-8 In your own words, how do enterprise systems facilitate *balance scorecard* and *business intelligence?*

PROBLEMS

P14-1 Search for "Balanced Scorecard" software on the Web using your favorite search engine (e.g., Altavista, Yahoo!, Lycos, google). Try a demo if you can find one. What are the four dimensions of the balanced scorecard and how might it help in a strategic planning process? How would it help in monitoring day-to-day operations?

P14-2 Refer to the level 0 data flow diagram shown in Figure 14.6 (page 504).

Draw a lower-level DFD for process 4.0 shown in Figure 14.6. Make sure that each lower-level DFD is *balanced* with its parent.

P14-3 Visit the XBRL Web site at www.xbrl.org. Discuss how XBRL reports could be used to (a) communicate with the investment community, (b) apply for a loan, (c) file with the SEC or other governmental reporting agency, (d) report to a corporate parent, and (e) communicate with a business partner.

P14-4 Search for business intelligence software on the Web using your favorite search engine (e.g., Altavista, Yahoo!, Lycos, google). Try a demo if you can find one. Who are the intended users of this software? How could it be useful for running a college or university?

P14-5 Take a set of financial statement information that you have available or can find in the library and implement the process discussed in Technology Excerpt 14.1 (page 514).

BOXES

[Start Technology Application box 14.1 here]

TECHNOLOGY APPLICATION 14.1

Budgeting and Reporting

Case 1 Vivendi is a French company that provides media, communications, and environmental services in more than 100 countries. The success of its business units is based on predetermined key performance indicators. The company recently implemented a management reporting system to support budgeting, forecasting, legal decisions, and operational management to replace its older budgeting and reporting systems. It uses Cartesis OLAP technology to analyze 20 analytical dimensions in a flexible way over the Web. Cartesis also supports corporate planning, performance management, and financial consolidation. The system combines five years of historical data with budget information to quickly support a wide range of decision makers.

Case 2 Before installing a business intelligence product called Cognos Finance 5.1, Standard Pacific Homes had to consolidate many Excel spreadsheets to be able to provide quarterly reports and budgets to its financial decision makers. Using Cognos' tool to streamline financial processes has cut almost a

week from the time it previously took to provide these reports, resulting in more time for reviewing the

budget and making informed decisions. Financial data is now available real-time, so that analysis of the margins for each housing project underway at the firm can be reviewed before the end of the quarter.

Sources: http://www.cartesis.com/cartesis.htm, as of June 2001;

http://www.cognos.com/news/releases/2001/0730.html as of September 2001.

[End Technology Application 14.1 box here]

[Start Technology Application 14.2 box here]

TECHNOLOGY APPLICATION 14.2

Business Intelligence

Case 1

Faced with declining game attendance and lower television ratings, the National Basketball Association (NBA) has reacted swiftly in applying business intelligence tools to facilitate customer relationship management. The NBA currently assembles information about fans who purchase tickets from a number of sources around the world, including Ticketmaster, the Home Shopping Network, All-Star nominating ballots, New York's NBA Store, databases of individual teams, and the NBA.com Web site. Each NBA team will soon be able to access the combined data in a data warehouse and use business intelligence applications to analyze the data. Teams will be able to tell if a customer prefers to purchase tickets when a particular opposing team is in town or at specific times of the year. The data analysis will also be used to market sports merchandise directly to select customers through a customer relationship management capability.

Case 2

In 1998, the Malaysian currency crisis resulted in the collapse of the Malaysian stock market and internal asset values. U.S. banks and financial institutions with offices in the area needed to assess quickly the risk they faced because of the sudden drop in their investment value, and report it immediately to the Federal Reserve. The Chase Manhattan Global Investment Bank was able to produce daily reports as the crisis unfolded because it had recently implemented a business intelligence system. The system provided highly detailed reports to its internal users as well as to the Federal Reserve. The software allows the company to adapt quickly when facing imminent risk.

Sources: Marc L. Songini, "NBA Shoots for Data Analysis," *Computerworld,* May 28, 2001; Talila Baron, "Chase Stays Ahead of Its Rivals," *InformationWeek,* October 11,

1999, 104–108.

[End Technology Application 14.2 box here]

[Start Technology Excerpt 14.1 box here]

Technology Excerpt 14.1

Run XBRL Right Now

If your accounting software doesn't include XBRL—and few, if any, products have it now—it doesn't mean you can't start applying the feature immediately.

I've created a method that gives you the opportunity to try XBRL now. Once you understand the process, you can use it with your own accounting software until XBRL is added eventually to your system.

Many software vendors are working to incorporate XBRL. For example, SAP will include ready-to-use XBRL templates for reporting, financial consolidation, modeling, simulation and planning, and budgeting. FRx Software, financial accounting/reporting software that works with some 50 accounting packages, will incorporate the function later this year. And 11 major accounting software vendors are members of the XBRL working group—a further indication of the industry's interest in XBRL.

Do It Now

To see how XBRL works, go to www.xbrl.org/demos/demos.htm. You can download the demo or run it off the Web site. You will need Microsoft Access 2000. The demo shows you how to publish your general ledger trial balance in XBRL. Here's a summary of the steps:

Gelinas 14-34

Step 1. Get a copy of your chart of accounts. Note that although this demo (see Exhibit 1, below) was prepared at the account level, you can present information in more detail, such as the type of transaction (invoice, payment, credit, debit entries to accounts receivable), or at a more summarized level, such as a financial statement line item.

[Insert UNF-p. 514-1]

Although it's possible to enter this chart of accounts manually, it's better to copy one of your own and use it in the demo.

Step 2. Get a copy of the appropriate XBRL taxonomy (template), which in this case is on the XBRL Web site. Note that this demo already includes the commercial and industrial taxonomy within the Access database table.

Step 3. Create a database table and map (assign or cross-reference) each general ledger account to the appropriate XBRL taxonomy element. If no available XBRL tag (technically called an element) meets your need, simply type in your own. It's the ability to customize that makes the program extensible—capable of being extended to your individual needs. Again, the demo Access application provides this functionality, as you see in Exhibit 2 and Exhibit 3.

[Insert UNF-p. 515-2]

This demo Access application provides the functionality to select one of your accounts and then assign an XBRLelement to it.

[Insert UNF-p. 515-3]

This demo chart of accounts, which is in the Access database, contains XBRLelements assigned to each account line.

Step 4. Summarize your trial balance by the general ledger account for the period you wish. This provides you with an account number and a total by account for a given period, as shown in Exhibit 4.

[Insert UNF-p. 516-4]

This is the trial balance summarized by account for the period you select.

Step 5. Apply the map to the trial balance. What the map says, in effect, is: "When I use this general ledger account, replace it with this XBRL element." Note Exhibit 2, which shows the map, and Exhibit 5, which shows the result of the mapping. Also note that the general ledger account is assigned to the "id" attribute (as shown in Exhibit 2). This is done only in the demo to help you see what is going on; it isn't required.

[Insert UNF-p. 516-5]

This is the segment of the general ledger chart of accounts and the XBRLelement plus all the other information needed to create a valid XBRLinstance document.

Exhibit 6 shows the XML file called an XBRL instance document.

[Insert UNF-p. 517-6]

And finally, in less than 25 lines of code, the database query generates a file that is XML-compliant with the XBRL specification. This XMLfile is called an XBRLinstance document.

That's all there is to it. Once the XBRL function is added to your software, these steps will occur automatically.

But the fact that your accounting software isn't XBRL-compliant yet should not dissuade you from manually doing the job in the interim. It's going to take a little knowledge about databases or, if you're more comfortable in Excel, it can be done with that application, too.

Although this demonstration shows how to transform general ledger trial balance information into XBRL, the concept applies to literally any data—trial balance, other accounting system data, and even nonaccounting system data.

Some things to note:

- If the available taxonomies don't work for you, you can easily modify a taxonomy or create your own.
- The data in the XBRL document you created are accessible from any of the most popular office productivity tools: Excel, Access, Word, or PowerPoint. XBRL still will work accurately if someone adds additional information to the document without your knowledge. It's as if someone added a row of data to an Excel spreadsheet: It does not affect your spreadsheet.

Source: Charles Hoffman, "Run XBRL Right Now," *Journal of Accountancy* (August 2000): 28–29.

[End Technology Excerpt 14.1 Box here]

GLOSSARY

A

ABC analysis A technique for ranking items in a group based on the output of the items. Can be used to categorize inventory items according to their importance. (p. 428)

Acceptance report A formal acknowledgment that a service contract has been satisfactorily completed. (p. 429)

Acceptance test A user-directed test of the complete system in a test environment. (p. 226)

Accounts payable master data A repository of all unpaid vendor invoices. (p. 430)

Accounts receivable adjustments data A file, normally keyed by date, of data related to business events such as sale returns, bad debt write-offs, estimated doubtful accounts, or similar adjustments. In addition to date, the typical data elements include journal voucher number, customer identification, adjustment type, account(s) and amount(s) to be debited, account(s) and amount(s) to be credited, and authorization indicator (i.e., approval code, signature, or the like). (p. 385)

Accounts receivable master data A repository of all unpaid invoices issued by an organization and awaiting final disposition. (p. 384)

Accuracy The correspondence or agreement between the information and the events or objects that the information represents. (p. 19)

ACH *See* Automated clearing house. (p. 381)

Activity Any action being performed by an internal or external entity. (p. 39)

Ad hoc (business reporting) A term that means on demand. (p. 496)

Agents Something buyers can send over the Internet to browse through electronic catalogs or Internet portals to compare prices and product specifications. (p. 357)

Application service provider (ASP) An organization that hosts, manages, and provides access to application software and hardware over the Internet to multiple customers. (p. 211)

ASP *See* Applicaton service provider. (p. 211)

Attribute An item of data that characterizes an entity or a relationship. (p. 83)

Audit trail A means of tracing back to the individual business events that have been aggregated into the general ledger balances. (p. 503)

Automated clearing house (ACH) A method of electronic funds transfer in which the collector's bank account is credited and the payer's account is debited for the amount of a payment, and the paid amount is captured and transmitted electronically between banks through the ACH network. (p. 381)

Availability Relates to information being available when required by the business process now and in the future. It also concerns the safeguarding of necessary resources and associated capabilities. (p. 17)

Available to promise The accumulation of the data on current inventories, sales commitments, and planned production to determine whether the production of finished goods will be sufficient to commit to additional sales orders. (p. 487)

B

Balanced When two DFDs have equivalent external data flows. (p. 29)

Balanced scorecard A methodology for assessing an organization's business performance via four components: (1) financial, (2) internal business processes, (3) customers, and (4) innovation and improvement activities. (p. 507)

Bar code readers Devices that use light reflection to read differences in bar code patterns in order to identify a labeled item. (p. 117)

Batch control plans Control plans used in batch processing systems to regulate information processing by calculating control totals at various points in a processing run and subsequently comparing these totals. (p. 302)

Batch processing A type of data processing in which groups, or batches, or transactions are collected and processed together. (p. 109)

Batch sequence check A type of batch control plan in which the serial numbers of the documents comprising a batch are checked by the computer against a sequence number range entered by the operator. (p. 305)

Bill of lading A shipping document that represents a contract between the shipper and the carrier in which the carrier agrees to transport the goods to the shipper's customer. (p. 340)

Bill of materials A form that shows the standard raw material quantities (i.e., component parts, subassemblies, and the like) that are required to produce one unit of finished goods. (p. 474)

Biometric security systems Identify authorized personnel through some unique physical trait such as fingerprints, voice, eyes, face, writing dynamics, and the like. (p. 269)

Blind copy A paper or electronic document on which selected data are blanked out (i.e., blinded) so that persons receiving that copy will not have access to those data. (p. 429)

Bubble symbol Depicts an entity or a process within which incoming data flows are transformed into outgoing data flows. (p. 27)

Budgeting department The department that advises and assists managers in preparing their budget. (p. 497)

Business continuity planning *See* Contingency planning. (p. 265)

Business event data stores Stores of data that represent the "books of original entry" used for recording most business events. (p. 11)

Business intelligence (BI) systems Information systems that assist managers with unstructured decisions by retrieving and analyzing data in order to identify, generate and interpret useful information. (p. 149)

Business interruption planning *See* Contingency planning (p. 265)

Business process A set of business events that together enable the creation and delivery of an organization's products or services to its customers. (p. 7)

Business process reengineering (BPR) The fundamental rethinking and radical redesign of business processes to achieve dramatic improvements in critical contemporary measures of performance, such as cost, quality, service, and speed. (p. 180)

Business reporting process (BR) An interacting structure of people, equipment, methods, and controls that is designed to accomplish both operations and information system functions. The work of the BR process is to process and communicate information including the generation of business reports and general purpose, external financial statements. (pp. 495–496)

C

Capability Maturity Model for Software (SW-CMM®)A model that helps organizations evaluate the effectiveness of their software development processes and identify the key practices required to increase the maturity of those processes. (p. 178)

Capable to promise The accumulation of the data on current inventories, sales commitments, planned production and excess production capacity or other planned production capacity that could be quickly converted to production of the desired finished goods necessary to fulfill a sales order request. (p. 487)

Capacity requirements planning (CRP) The process that translates materials requirements into detailed machine- and labor-utilization schedules, and releases purchase orders to vendors and manufacturing orders to the factory. (p. 478)

Cardinality constraint The specification of how many occurrences of an entity can participate in the given relationship with any one occurrence of the other entity in the relationship. (p. 91)

Cash disbursements event data A file that shows, in chronological sequence, the details of each cash payment made. Each record typically contains the date the payment is recorded, vendor identification (or other account to be debited), disbursement voucher number (if a voucher system is used), vendor invoice number(s) and gross invoice amount(s), cash discounts taken on each invoice, net invoice amount(s), check amount, and check number. (p. 430)

Cash receipts data A file that contains the details of each payment received. Each record in this file normally would show the date the payment is recorded, customer identification (or other account[s] to be credited), invoice number(s) and gross invoice amount(s), cash discount(s) taken on each invoice, net invoice amount(s), check amount, and check number. (p. 385)

Character The basic unit of data such as a letter, number, or special character. (p. 72)

Check digit verification A type of programmed edit check in which an extra digit is included in the identification number of entities such as customers and vendors. Through mathematical formulae, the computer uses the check digit to verify whether the identification number is input correctly. (p. 292)

Client-server The physical and logical division between user-oriented application programs that are run at the client level (i.e., user level) and the shared data that must be available through the server (i.e., a separate computer that handles centrally shared activities between multiple users). (p. 118)

Cold site A recovery strategy commonly included in contingency planning. A facility usually comprising air-conditioned space with a raised floor, telephone connections, and computer ports into which a subscriber can move equipment. (p. 266)

Comparability The quality of information that enables users to identify similarities and differences in two pieces of information. (p. 19)

Compare input data with master data Input data is compared to data previously entered. Includes input/master data dependency checks and input/master data validity and accuracy checks. (p. 298)

Completeness The degree to which information includes data about every relevant object or event. (p. 19)

Compliance Deals with complying with those laws, regulations, and contractual obligations to which the business process is subject (i.e., externally imposed business criteria). (p. 17)

Computer virus A program that can attach itself to other programs (i.e., "infect" those programs) and that operates to alter the programs or to destroy data. (p. 247)

Computer-based training (CBT) Provides learning via computer directly to the trainee's computer screen. (p. 225)

Computer-integrated manufacturing (CIM) A production strategy that uses computer technology to link people, equipment, policies, procedures, information, and business strategy into an integrated manufacturing system. (p. 470)

Confidentiality Concerns the protection of sensitive information from unauthorized disclosure. (p. 17)

Consistent When we can compare information about the same object or event collected at two points in time, the information is consistent. (p. 19)

Context diagram A top-level diagram of an information system that describes the data flows into and out of the system and into and out of the external entities. (p. 26)

Contingency planning A process or methodology designed to provide backup facilities, equipment, and personnel that will allow an organization to survive and recover from a major calamity with a minimum disruption to its operations. (p. 265)

Control environment A state of control consciousness that reflects the organization's (primarily the board of directors' and management's) general awareness of and commitment to the importance of control throughout the organization. (p. 249)

Control goals Business process objectives that an internal control system is designed to achieve. (p. 249)

Control matrix A tool used to analyze a systems flowchart (and related narrative) to determine the control plans appropriate to that process and to relate those plans to the process' control goals. (p. 282)

Control plans An information processing policy or procedure that assists in accomplishing control goals. (p. 253)

Corrective control plans Control plans that are designed to rectify problems that have occurred. (p. 253)

Cost accounting A production subsystem that is responsible for tracking the cost of work in process. The subsystem accumulates cost information for the purposes of product costing, inventory valuation, performance evaluation, cost control, and decision making. (p. 473)

Cost/benefit analysis *See* Cost/benefit study. (p. 193)

Cost/benefit study Determines which design alternative accomplishes the user's goals for the least cost (or greatest benefit). (p. 193)

Cost/effectiveness study Provides quantitative and certain qualitative information concerning alternative physical designs. (p. 193)

CRM *See* Customer relationship management. (p. 338)

Cumulative sequence check A type of batch control plan in which document numbers are checked by the computer against a file containing all possible numbers. (p. 305)

Customer acknowledgment A sales order confirmation that is sent to the customer as notification that an order has been accepted and to inform the customer of the expected shipment date. (p. 340)

Customer master data A data store—usually indexed by a unique code number assigned to each customer—that contains data identifying the particular characteristics of each customer, such as name, address, telephone number, credit data, and other standing data. (p. 342)

Customer relationship management systems (CRM) Systems designed to manage all the data related to customers. (p. 338)

Customer self-service system An information systems extension that allows a customer to complete an inquiry or perform a task within an organization's business process without the aid of the organization's own employees. (p. 378)

Cyclical reordering A time-based approach to reordering inventory in which an organization's entire inventory is assessed on a periodic basis to determine the status of individual items. (p. 428)

D

Data Facts or figures in raw form. Data represent the measurements or observations of objects and events. (p. 16)

Data encryption A process that employs mathematical algorithms and encryption keys to change data from plain text to a coded text form so that it is unintelligible and therefore useless to those who should not have access to it. (p. 309)

Data flow diagram (DFD) A graphical representation of a system. A DFD depicts a system's components; the data flows among the components; and the sources, destinations, and storage of data. (p. 26)

Data flow symbol Represents a pathway for data. (p. 27)

Data maintenance Includes activities related to adding, deleting, or replacing the standing data portions of master data. (p. 11)

Data mining The exploration, aggregation, and analysis of large quantities of varied data from across the organization to better understand an organization's business processes, trends within these processes, and potential opportunities to improve the effectiveness and/or efficiency of the organization. (p. 82)

Data store symbol Represents a place where data are stored. (p. 27)

Data warehousing The use of information systems facilities to focus on the collection, organization, integration, and long-term storage of entity-wide data. Data warehousing provides users with easy access to large quantities of varied data from across the organization for the sole purpose of improving decision-making capabilities. (p. 82)

Database A collection of files that is independent of application programs and is available to satisfy a number of different processing needs. (p. 77)

Database and files review Review of an organization's database and paper files related to events processing. (p. 197)

Database approach to data management Concept to decouple the data from the system applications (i.e., to make the data independent of the application or other users). (p. 77)

Database management system A set of integrated programs designed to simplify the tasks of creating, accessing, and managing a database. (p. 76)

Data-structured development A method of systems development that entails analysis of the data to determine the nature of the system from the point of view of the data. From the analysis, computer programs are designed based on the structure of the data that the programs are processing. (p. 174)

Decision making The process of making choices. (p. 142)

Deliverables Reports and other documentation that must be produced periodically during systems development to make development personnel accountable for faithful execution of systems development tasks. (p. 171)

Denial of service attack When a web site is overwhelmed by an intentional onslaught of thousands of simultaneous messages, making it impossible for the attacked site to engage in its normal activities. (p. 268)

Destination *See* External entitity symbol. (p. 27)

Detective control plans Control plans that are designed to discover that problems have occurred. (p. 253)

DFD *See* Data flow diagram. (p. 26)

Digital image processing systems Computer-based systems for capture, storage, retrieval, and presentation of images of real or simulated objects. (p. 118)

Digital signatures A technology that validates the identity of the sender and the integrity of an electronic message. (p. 259)

Digital signatures A technology that validates the identity of the sender and the integrity of an electronic message. (p. 298)

Direct approach The riskiest method for systems implementation in which at time *x* the old system is stopped and the new system is begun. (p. 221)

Disaster recovery planning *See* Contingency planning. (p. 264)

Distributed denial of service attack Uses many computers that unwittingly cooperate in a denial of service attack by sending messages to the target web sites. (p. 268)

Distribution requirements planning (DRP) A component of manufacturing resource planning. (p. 470)

Document design A control plan in which a source document is designed in such a way as to make it easier to prepare the document initially and later to input data from the document. (p. 291)

Document/record counts A type of batch control total. A simple count of the number of documents entered. (p. 303)

Document/record hash totals A summarization of any numeric data field within the input document or record. (p. 292)

Dollar totals A type of batch control total. A summation of the dollar value of items in the batch, such as the total dollar value of all remittance advices in a batch. (p. 303)

E

E-Business *See* Electronic business. (p. 4)

E-commerce The business events associated with the Order-to-Cash and Purchase-to-Pay business processes, which encompass electronically ordering goods and services, and often the associated electronic payments. (p. 107)

Economic feasibility A problem solution has this if the costs seem reasonable and the benefits of the solution compare favorably to competing uses for the organization's resources. (p. 186)

Economic order quantity (EOQ) A technique that calculates the optimum quantity of inventory to order which will minimize the total cost of acquiring and carrying particular items of inventory. (p. 428)

EDI *See* Electronic data interchange. (p. 121)

Effectiveness (a control goal) An operations process control goal that describes a measure of success in meeting one or more goals. (p. 250)

Effectiveness (a quality of information) Deals with information being relevant and pertinent to the business process as well as being delivered in a timely, correct, consistent, and usable manner. (p. 17)

Effectiveness analysis *See* Effectiveness study. (p. 193)

Effectiveness study Determines which alternative best accomplishes the user's goals for the system being developed. (p. 193)

Efficiency (a control goal) An operations process control goal that describes a measure of the productivity of the resources applied to achieve a set of goals. (p. 250)

Efficiency (a quality of information) Concerns the provision of information through the optimal (most productive and economical) use of resources. (p. 17)

Electronic business (E-Business) The application of electronic networks (including the

Internet) to undertake business processes between individuals and organizations. (p. 4)

Electronic cash A financial institution issues an individual cash that is placed into an electronic wallet. The cash is issued in an electronic form much the way it would be in paper form. Cash is loaded onto the wallet and spent in a manner similar to a phone card. The wallet may be a card or data stored on a server or on an individual's computer. (p. 381)

Electronic check Similar to a paper check, the electronic version includes the customer's name, the seller's name, the customer's financial institution, the check amount, and a digital signature. (p. 381)

Electronic data interchange (EDI) Computer-to-computer exchange of business data (i.e., documents) in structured formats that allow direct processing of those electronic documents by the receiving computer system. (p. 121)

Electronic document management (EDM) The capture, storage, management, and control of electronic document images for the purpose of supporting management decision making and facilitating business event data processing. (p. 120)

Electronic funds transfer (EFT) A general term used to describe a variety of procedures for transmitting cash funds between parties via electronic transmission instead of using paper checks. (p. 381)

Electronic lockbox A banking service in which the lockbox bank scans the remittance advice details into its computer system from the payer's paper remittance advice and then transfers the remittance advice data electronically from the bank's computer to the collector's accounts receivable computer system. (p. 381)

Enterprise systems Integrated software packages designed to provide complete integration of an organization's business information processing systems and all related data. (p. 4)

Entity Any object, event, or agent about which data are collected. (p. 83)

Entity-relationship diagram (E-R diagram) A diagram that reflects the system's key entities and the relationships among those entities and is commonly used to represent a data model. (p. 37)

Entitywide database The central repository for all the data used by the organization. (p. 15)

Environmental test *See* Operations test. (p. 226)

EOQ *See* Economic order quantity. (p. 428)

E-R diagram *See* Entity-relationship diagram. (p. 37)

Error routine *See* Exception routine. (p. 49)

Event data processing The process whereby event-related data are collected and stored. (p. 67)

Event-driven systems Information systems that capture a complete description of each event and permanently store the individual descriptions of each event. These systems facilitate use by multiple information users with very differing needs for information about the events that have occurred within business processes. (p. 70)

Events Activities that occur as a result of the various business processes in which an organization engages. (p. 67)

Exception and summary report A computer-generated report that reflects the events—either in detail, summary total, or both—that were accepted by the system and those that were rejected by the system. (p. 300)

Exception routine Processes for out-of-the-ordinary (exceptional) or erroneous transactions (p. 49)

Expert system (ES) An information system that emulates the problem-solving techniques of human experts. (p. 152)

Exploding the BOM A process in which mrp determines the standard raw material quantities required to produce the number of output units shown in the MPS. (p. 474)

eXtensible Business Reporting Language (XBRL) An XML-based language consisting of a set of tags that are used to unify the presentation of business reporting information into a single format that can be easily read by almost any software package and can be easily searched by web browsers. (p. 512)

Extensible Markup Language (XML) A Web-based data format that enables information to be shared over the Web. (p. 128)

External entity symbol Portrays a source or a destination of data outside the system. (p. 27)

External entities Those entities (i.e., persons, places, or things) outside the system that send data to, or receive data from, the system. (p. 27)

External interviews Those interviews conducted with personnel outside the organization. (p. 216)

External literature review Gathering information from documentation outside the organization (e.g., industry statistics). (p. 196)

Extranets Used to link together a set of users through use of the Internet rather than a private communication network. Access to the extranet is restricted, so that private activities using internal data can be securely supported as part of the organization's business processes. (p. 119)

Extreme Programming (XP) A deliberate and disciplined approach to software development that emphasizes customer involvement and promotes teamwork. (p. 175)

F

Feasibility study *See* Systems survey. (p. 184)

Feedback value *See* Predictive value. (p. 17)

Feeder process Any business process that accumulates business event data that are then communicated to and processed within the enterprise system database (and the general ledger within that database). (p. 496)

Fidelity bond A type of insurance protection that indemnifies a company in case it suffers losses from defalcations committed by its employees. (p. 261)

Field A collection of related characters, such as a customer number or a customer name. (p. 72)

File A collection of related records, such as a customer file or a sales business event data file. (p. 72)

File management Comprises the functions that collect, organize, store, retrieve, and manipulate data maintained in traditional file-oriented data processing environments. (p.

71)

Firewall A technique to protect one network from another "untrusted" network. (p. 269)

Flexible manufacturing system (FMS) A highly automated CIM system whose goal is to make a plant more flexible. (p. 472)

Float When applied to cash receipts, float is the time between the customer tendering payment and the availability of good funds. (p. 380)

Forced vacations A personnel policy that requires an employee to take leave from the job and substitutes another employee in his or her place. (p. 261)

Fraud A deliberate act or untruth intended to obtain unfair or unlawful gain. (p. 245)

Freedom from bias See Neutrality. (p. 19)

Functional decomposition The term used to describe a design approach which focuses on a system's functions and utilizes top-down, hierarchical simplification to derive the new system's design. (p. 174)

G

General ledger master data A data repository that contains summarized information of all company event data. (p. 503)

Group support systems (GSS) Computer-based systems that support collaborative intellectual work such as idea generation, elaboration, analysis, synthesis, and decision making. GSS use technology to solve the time and place dimension problems associated with group work. (p. 151)

Groupware Software identified with GSS that focuses on such functions as e-mail group scheduling, and document sharing. (p. 151)

GSS *See* Group support systems. (p. 151)

H

Hardware plan Summarizes how the recommended vendor proposal will fulfill the physical requirements specified in structured systems analysis. (p. 217)

Hash totals A type of batch control total that is calculated for control purposes only. A summation of any numeric data existing for all documents in the batch, such as a total of customer numbers or invoice numbers in the case of remittance advices. (p. 303)

Hot site A recovery strategy commonly included in contingency planning. A fully equipped data center, often housed in bunker-like facilities, that can accommodate many businesses and that it is made available to client companies for a monthly subscriber's fee. (p. 266)

I

Immediate mode The data processing mode in which there is little or no delay between data processing steps. (p. 114)

Information Data presented in a form that is useful in a decision-making activity. (p. 16)

Information process That portion of the overall IS related to a particular business process. (p. 12)

Information processing Includes data processing functions related to economic events such as accounting events, internal operations such as manufacturing, and financial statement preparation such as adjusting entries. (p. 11)

Information processing activities Activities that retrieve data from storage, transform data, or file data. (p. 40)

Information system A man-made system that generally consists of an integrated set of computer-based and manual components established to collect, store, and manage data and to provide output information to users. (p. 10)

Information Systems function The department that develops and operates an organization's information system. (p. 255)

Information technology Any hardware, software, or communications technology that might be adopted by an organization to support or control a business process, enable management decisions, or provide a competitive advantage. (p. 5)

Input accuracy An information process control goal which requires that events be correctly captured and entered into a system. (p. 250)

Input completeness An information process control goal which requires that all valid events or objects be captured and entered into a system. (p. 250)

Input data Data received by the information system from the external environment or from another area within the information system. (p. 11)

Input validity An information process control goal which requires that input data be appropriately approved and represent actual economic events and objects. (p. 250)

Input/master data dependency checks These edits test whether the contents of two or more data elements or fields on an event description bear the correct logical relationship. (p. 298)

Input/master data validity and accuracy checks These edits test whether the master data supports the validity and accuracy of the input. (p. 298)

Integrity Relates to the accuracy and completeness of information as well as its validity in accordance with business's values and expectations. (p. 17)

Intelligent agent A software component integrated into a business intelligence system or other software tool that provides automated assistance and/or advice on the use of the software, factors that should be considered when using a system for decision making, or supplying of common responses by other users. (p. 156)

Interactive feedback check A control plan in which the data entry program informs the user that input has been accepted and recorded. (p. 292)

Internal control A system of integrated elements—people, structure, processes, and procedures—acting together to provide reasonable assurance that an organization achieves business process goals. (p. 248)

Internal entity A person, place, or thing within the system that transforms data. Internal entities include accounting clerks (persons), departments (places), and computers (things). (p. 27)

Internal literature review The examination of documentation maintained within the organization. (p. 196)

Internet A massive interconnection of computer networks worldwide that enables communication between dissimilar technology platforms. (p. 119)

Internet assurance A service provided for a fee to vendors in order to provide limited assurance to users of the vendor's web site that the site is in fact reliable and event data security is reasonable. (p. 132)

Internet auction markets An Internet base for companies to place products up for bid or for buyers to put proposed purchases up for bid. (p. 136)

Internet market exchanges Exchanges that bring together a variety of suppliers in a given industry with one or more buyers in the same industry to provide Internet commerce through organized markets. (p. 136)

Interviews A method of gathering information through direct contact, either face-to-face or via telephone. (p. 196)

Intranets Smaller versions of Internet technology that are used to link an organization's internal documents and databases into a system that is accessible through web browsers or internally developed software designed to maximize the benefits from utilization of organizational information resources. (p. 119)

Inventory master data A repository of inventory-related data that contains a record of each inventory item that is stocked in the warehouse or is regularly ordered from a vendor. (p. 430)

IS *See* Information system. (p. 10)

ISO 9000-3 A set of standards developed by the International Organization for Standards (ISO), that describe what an organization must do to manage their software development processes. (p. 178)

IT *See* Information technology. (p. 5)

Item or line counts A type of batch control total. A count of the number of items or lines of data entered, such as a count of the number of invoices being paid by all the customer remittances. (p. 303)

J

Just-in-time (JIT) An approach to production planning and control that is predicated on pull manufacturing. (p. 472)

K

Key attribute The attribute whose value is unique (i.e., has a different value) for every entity that will ever appear in the database and is the most meaningful such attribute for identifying each entity. (p. 84)

Key verification A control plan in which documents are keyed by one individual and then rekeyed by a second individual. The data entry software compares the second keystroking against the results of the first keystroking. (p. 223)

Knowledge management The process of capturing, storing, retrieving, and distributing the knowledge of the individuals in an organization for use by others in the organization to improve the quality and/or efficiency of decision making across the firm. (p. 159)

L

LAN *See* Local area network. (p. 118)

Library controls A combination of people, procedures, and computer software that restricts access to stored data, programs, and documentation to authenticated users with authorized requests. (p. 268)

Limit checks *See* Reasonableness checks. (p. 291)

Local area networks (LANs) Communications networks that link several different local user machines with printers, databases, and other shared devices. (p. 118)

Lockbox A postal address, maintained by the firm's bank, that is used solely for the purpose of collecting checks. (p. 381)

Logical data flow diagram A graphical representation of a system showing the system's processes and the flows of data into and out of the processes. (p. 28)

Logical database view The manner in which the data appear to the user to be stored. It represents the structure that the user must interface with in order to extract data from the database. (p. 77)

M

Management control point A place in the systems development process requiring management approval of further development work (i.e., a go/no go decision). (p. 187)

Management process A human-made system consisting of the people, authority, organization, policies, and procedures whose objective is to plan and control the operations of the organization. (p. 12)

Manufacturing firm A firm that acquires raw materials, converts those materials into finished goods, and sells those goods to its customers. (p. 69)

Manufacturing order And order sent to manufacturing departments to initiate the physical manufacturing operations in the factory. (p. 478)

Manufacturing resource planning (MRP) A process that has the following five main parts: master production schedule, materials requirements planning, shop floor control, distribution requirements planning, and capacity requirements planning. (p. 470)

Marketing and sales (M/S) process An interacting structure of people, equipment, methods, and controls designed to support repetitive work routines of the sales order department, the credit department, the warehouse, and the shipping department; to support decision needs of those who manage various sales and marketing functions; and to support information flows and recorded data in support of the operations and management process. (p. 327)

Master data Data related to entities—persons places and things. (p. 11)

Master data stores Repositories of relatively permanent data maintained over an extended period of time. (p. 11)

Master data update An information processing activity whose function is to incorporate new master data into existing master data. (p. 11)

Master production schedule (MPS) The anticipated "build schedule" for selected items that serves as the set of planning numbers that "drives" the materials requirements planning process. (p. 470)

Materials requirements planning (MRP) A process that is driven by the MPS and that also uses bills of materials, inventory status data, and open order status data from the manufacturing order and open purchase order. (p. 470)

Mathematical accuracy checks This edit compares calculations performed manually to those performed by the computer to determine if a document has been entered correctly. (p. 292)

Merchandising firm An organization that buys good from vendors and resells those goods to customers. (p. 68)

Mirror site A site that maintains copies of a company's primary site's programs and data. During normal processing activities master data is updated at both the primary and mirror sites. (p. 265)

Modular approach A method for systems implementation in which the new system is either implemented one subsystem at a time or is introduced into one organizational unit at a time. (p. 222)

Module A box on a structure chart representing a collection of program statements. (p. 219)

Move tickets Record completed assembly line activities. (p. 478)

N

Network providers Companies that provide a link to the Internet by making their directly connected networks available for access by fee-paying customers. (p. 132)

Neural networks (NN) Computer-based systems of hardware and software that mimic the human brain's ability to recognize patterns or predict outcomes using less than complete information. (p. 155)

Neutrality (freedom from bias) The quality of being not biased. Bias is the tendency of information to fall more often on one side than on the other of the object or event that it represents. (p. 19)

O

Object-oriented (OO) development Method for creating systems that think of the world as a set of objects that are related to and communicate with one another. Object-oriented systems consist of objects that contain data and the procedures, or methods, for manipulating the data. (p. 174)

Object-oriented database model A database that allows both simple and complex objects (including such things as video, audio, and pictures) to be stored using abstract data types, inheritance, and encapsulation. (p. 87)

Observations A technique used by a systems analyst to gather current information about how a system operates or to corroborate other information, such as that gathered in an interview. (p. 196)

OCR *See* Optical character recognition. (p. 118)

Offline A computer device that is not directly connected to the processing computer. (p. 111)

One-for-one checking A type of application control plan that entails the detailed comparison of the individual elements of two or more data sources to determine that they agree. (p. 307)

Online A computer configuration in which certain equipment is directly connected to the processing computer. (p. 112)

Online prompting A control plan that asks the user for input or asks questions that the user must answer. (p. 291)

Online real-time (OLRT) Systems that gather transaction data at the time of occurrence, update the master records essentially instantaneously, and provide the results arising from the transaction within a very short amount of time—i.e., real time. (p. 114)

Online transaction entry (OLTE) The use of data entry devices to allow business event data to be entered directly into the information system at the time and place that the transaction occurs. (p. 112)

Online transaction processing (OLTP) A real-time system that performs all or part of the processing activities at the data entry terminal location. (p. 116)

Operational feasibility A problem solution has this if it uses the organization's available (already possessed or obtainable) personnel and procedures. (p. 185)

Operations process A human-made system consisting of the people, equipment, organization, policies, and procedures whose objective is to accomplish the work of the organization. (p. 12)

Operations process goals Operations process control goals that describe the criteria used to judge the effectiveness of an operations process. (p. 250)

Operations test Runs a subset of the system in the actual production environment to determine whether new equipment and other factors in the environment—such as data entry areas, document and report deliveries, telephones, and electricity—are satisfactory. (p. 226)

Optical character recognition (OCR) Devices that use light reflection to read handwritten or printed characters. (p. 118)

Order requirements schedule A schedule that outputs materials requirements for an order. (p. 474)

Outsourcing The assignment of an internal function to an outside vendor. (p. 209)

P

Packing slip A shipping document—generally attached to the outside of a shipping container—that identifies the customer and the contents of the package. (p. 340)

Paperless systems A system that eliminates documents and forms as the medium for conducting business. (p. 433)

Parallel approach A method for systems implementation in which both the old and new systems operate together for a time. (p. 221)

Participation constraint A specification of both the minimum and maximum number of occurrences of one entity that can participate in the given relationship with any one occurrence of the other entity in the relationship. (p. 92)

Performance reports Managerial accounting reports that compare actual performance with budgeted expectations. (p. 498)

Periodic (business reporting) A term that means regularly scheduled. (p. 496)

Periodic mode A data processing mode in which there is some delay between data processing steps. (p. 109)

Personnel termination policies Personnel policies that require an employer to deal with employees who leave an organization. (p. 261)

Pervasive control plans Control policies or procedures that relate to a multitude of control goals and processes; they provide a climate or set of surrounding conditions in which the various business processes operate. (p. 253)

Physical data flow diagram A graphical representation of a system showing the system's internal and external entities, and the flows of data into and out of these entities. (p. 27)

Physical database storage The manner in which data are actually physically stored on the storage medium used in the database management system. This has little relationship to how the data appear to be stored to the user. (p. 77)

Picking ticket Authorizes, often via a paper document, the warehouse to "pick" the goods from the shelf and send them to shipping. (p. 340)

Populate inputs with master data Upon entry of an entity's identification code the computer populates the input with data about that entity from existing master data. (p. 298)

Postbilling system A billing system in which invoices are prepared after goods have been shipped and the sales order notification has been matched to the shipping's billing notification. (p. 385)

Post-implementation review An examination of a working information system, conducted soon after that system's implementation, to determine whether the user's requirements have been satisfied and whether the development effort was efficient and conducted in accordance with the organization's systems development standards. (p. 228)

Prebilling system A billing system in which invoices are prepared immediately on acceptance of a customer order—that is, after inventory and credit checks have been accomplished but before the goods have been shipped. Master data are updated when the invoice is prepared, but the customer copy of the invoice is not released until the goods have been shipped. (p. 385)

Predictive value (Feedback value) The ability of feedback information (such as past inventory shortages and overages) to improve a decision maker's capacity to predict, confirm, or correct earlier expectations. (p. 17)

Preformatted screens Computer screens designed to control the entry of data by defining the acceptable format of each data field, automatically moving to the next field, requiring that certain fields be completed, and by automatically populating fields. (p. 291)

Preliminary feasibility study *See* Systems survey. (p. 184)

Prenumbered documents Documents that are numbered sequentially with a number that is preprinted on the document. (p. 305)

Preventive control plans Control plans that are designed to stop problems from occurring. (p. 253)

Preventive maintenance A hardware control plan in which all computer equipment is periodically cleaned, tested, and adjusted to ensure continued efficient and correct operation. (p. 270)

Procedures for rejected inputs A control plan designed to ensure that erroneous data—not accepted for processing—are corrected and resubmitted for processing. (p. 292)

Process A series of actions or operations leading to a particular and usually desirable result. (p. 248)

Process control plans Controls that are particular to a specific process or subsystem, such as inventory or human resources, or to a particular mode of processing events, such as online or batch. (p. 253)

Production planning and control A production subsystem that is concerned with the orderly and timely movement of goods through the production process and that comprises activities such as planning material, people, and machine requirements; scheduling; routing; and monitoring the progress of goods through the factory. (p. 473)

Production process A manufacturing firm's process which includes recording activities related to the manufacture of goods for sale. (p. 69)

Production schedule Authorizes the factory to begin manufacturing specific products. (p. 479)

Program change controls Policies and procedures designed to ensure that programs that have been developed in-house or purchased externally are not surreptitiously modified. Program change controls provide assurance that all modifications to programs are authorized, tested, properly implemented, and adequately documented. (p. 263)

Programmed edit checks Edits that are automatically performed by data entry programs upon entry of the input data. (p. 291)

Project plan A statement of a project's scope, timetable, resources required to complete the project, and the project's costs. (p. 187)

Pull manufacturing An approach to manufacturing management in which an idle machine pulls the next part from the previous machine as soon as that part is available. (p. 469)

Purchase order A request for the purchase of goods or services from a vendor. (p. 428)

Purchase order master data A compilation of open purchase orders that includes the status of each item on order. (p. 430)

Purchase requisition An internal request to acquire goods and services. (p. 427)

Purchase returns and allowances An exception routine that occurs where purchased goods (or services) received do not conform to those ordered. The goods are either returned to the vendor or a price reduction (an allowance) is made by the vendor. (p. 450)

Purchase-to-Pay process An interacting structure of people, equipment, methods, and controls that is designed to handle the repetitive work routines of the purchasing department, the receiving department, the accounts payable department, the payroll department, and the cashier; to support the decision needs of those who manage these departments; and to assist in the preparation of internal and external reports. (p. 420)

Push manufacturing An approach to manufacturing management in which the sales forecast drives the production plan, and goods are produced in large batches (or jobs). (p. 468)

Q

Quality assurance (QA) Addresses the prevention and detection of errors, especially defects in software that may occur during the system development process. (p. 177)

Query language Language used to access a database and to produce inquiry reports. Allows a nontechnical user to bypass the programmer and access the database directly. (p. 78)

Questionnaires Forms containing a standardized list of questions. (p. 197)

R

Rapid applications development (RAD) A management approach to systems development that employs small teams of highly skilled developers using higher order development tools, such as ICASE, PowerBuilder or even Visual Basic, to develop the system iteratively. (p. 174)

Raw materials requisition An authorization that identifies the type and quantity of materials to be withdrawn from the storeroom. (p. 478)

Reasonableness checks A type of programmed edit check that tests whether the contents (e.g., values) of the data entered fall within predetermined limits. (p. 291)

Receiving report The business document used to record merchandise receipts. (p. 429)

Receiving report data A record of each receipt. (p. 430)

Record A collection of related data fields pertaining to a particular entity (person, place, or thing, such as a customer record) or event (sale, hiring of a new employee, and so on). (p. 72)

Record layout Depicts the fields comprising a record. (p. 72)

Recursive relationship A relationship between two different entities of the same entity type. (p. 91)

Referential integrity A specification that for every attribute value in one relation that has been specified in order to allow reference to another relation, the tuple being referenced must remain intact. (p. 89)

Reject Stub A data flow assigned the label "Reject" that leaves a bubble but does not go to any another bubble or to a data store (p. 49)

Relation A collection of data representing multiple occurrences of an object, event, or agent. (p. 88)

Relational database model A logical model for a database in which data are logically organized in two-dimensional tables. Each table is referred to as a relation. (p. 85)

Relationships Associations between entities. (p. 85)

Relevance Information capable of making a difference in a decision-making situation by reducing uncertainty or increasing knowledge for that particular decisions. (p. 17)

Reliability of information Relates to the provision of appropriate information for management to operate the entity and for management to exercise its financial and compliance reporting responsibilities. (p. 17)

Remittance advice (RA) A business document used by the payer to notify the payee of the items being paid. (p. 385)

Reorder point (ROP) analysis A technique for determining when to reorder inventory that establishes a reorder point for each inventory item based on that item's unique rate of sale or use. (p. 428)

Request for proposal (RFP) A document sent to vendors that invites submission of plans for providing hardware, software, and services. (p. 213)

Revenue collection (RC) process An interacting structure of people, equipment, methods, and controls designed to support the repetitive work routines of the credit department, the cashier, and the accounts receivable department; to support the problem-solving processes of financial managers; to assist in the preparation of internal and external reports; and to create information flows and recorded data in support of the operations and management processes. (p. 374)

Risk The possibility that an event or action will cause an organization to fail to meet its objectives (or goals). (p. 243)

Rotation of duties A personnel policy that requires an employee to alternate jobs periodically. (p. 261)

Route sheet A sheet showing the sequence of operations to manufacture an end item and the standard time allowance for each operation. (p. 478)

S

Sales event data A file comprised of one or more invoice records, analogous to a sales journal in a manual bookkeeping system. Each file record normally would contain the invoice date, invoice number, customer identification, and invoice amount. (p. 385)

Sales order master data A repository of "open" sales order records, created upon acceptance of a sales order and kept open until the order has been shipped. (p. 343)

Sales order notification A notification that is sent to the billing department to notify it of a pending shipment. (p. 340)

Scanner Input device that captures printed images or documents and converts them into electronic digital signals that can be stored on computer media. (p. 118)

Schema A complete description of the configuration of record types and data items and the relationships among them. Defines the logical structure of the database. (p. 78)

Security module A form of access control software embedded within an operating system. (p. 268)

Security of resources An operations process control goal directed toward protecting an organization's resources from loss, destruction, disclosure, copying, sale, or other misuse. (p. 250)

Segregation of duties An organizational control plan that consists of separating the four basic functions of event processing—authorizing events, executing events, recording events, and safeguarding resources resulting from consummating events. (p. 258)

Server clustering Use of clustered servers to disperse the processing load among servers so that if one fails, another can take over. (p. 266)

Service bureau A firm providing information processing services, including hardware and software, for a fee. (p. 209)

Service firm An organization that sells services, rather than merchandise, to its customers. (p. 68)

Shop floor control (SFC) A process that monitors the status of manufacturing orders as they move through the factory. (p. 470)

Signoffs Provided during systems development by users, managers, and auditors to signify approval of the development process and the system being developed. (p. 171)

Software plan Documents how the logical specification will be implemented, using in-house development, vendor purchase or Lease, ASP, or a combination of these. (p. 217)

Source *See* External entity symbol. (p. 27)

Standing data Relatively permanent portions of master data, such as the credit limit on customer master data and the selling price and warehouse location on inventory master data. (p. 12)

Structure chart A graphic tool for depicting the partitioning of a system into modules, the hierarchy and organization of these modules, and the communication interfaces between the modules. (p. 218)

Structured decisions Decisions for which all three decision phases (intelligence, design, and choice) are relatively routine or repetitive. (p. 144)

Structured systems analysis A set of procedures conducted to generate the specifications for a new (or modified) information system or subsystem. (p. 189)

Structured systems design A set of procedures performed to convert the logical specification into a design that can be implemented on the organization's computer system. (p. 217)

Subschema A description of a portion of a schema. (p. 78)

Subsystem A part of a system. (p. 9)

Supply chain All of the business processes that are involved in obtaining components and materials from suppliers and producing the goods that are ultimately sold to customers. (p. 466)

Supply chain management software Software that provides support for the planning and/or execution of the complete integrated production process. (p. 487)

System A set of interdependent elements that together accomplish specific objectives. A system must have organization, interrelationships, integration, and central objectives. (p. 9)

System test Verifies the new system against the original specifications. (p. 226)

Systems analysis The methodical investigation of a problem and the identification and ranking of alternative solutions to the problem. (p. 189)

Systems development Comprises the steps undertaken to create or modify an organization's information system. (p. 170)

Systems development life cycle (SDLC) (1) A formal set of activities, or a process, used to develop and implement a new or modified information system (the systems development methodology); (2) The documentation that specifies the systems development process (the systems development standards manual); (3) The progression of information systems through the systems development process, from birth, through implementation, to ongoing use. (p. 170)

Systems development methodology A formalized, standardized, documented set of activities used to manage a systems development project. It should be used when information systems are developed, acquired, or maintained. (p. 171)

Systems flowchart A graphical representation of the information processes (activities, logic flows, inputs, outputs, and a data storage), as well as the related operations processes (entities, physical flows, and operations activities). (p. 30)

Systems implementation A set of procedures performed to complete the design contained in the approved systems design document and to test, instill, and begin to use the new or revised information system. (p. 221)

Systems integrators Consulting/systems development firms that develop systems under contract. (p. 210)

Systems maintenance The modification (e.g., repair, correction, enhancement) of existing applications. (p. 229)

Systems selection A set of procedures performed to choose the computer software and hardware for an information system. (p. 207)

Systems survey A set of procedures conducted to determine the feasibility of a potential systems development project and to prepare a systems development plan for projects considered feasible. (p. 184)

T

Technical feasibility A problem solution has this if it uses available (already possessed or obtainable) hardware and software technology. (p. 185)

Throughput Quantity of work performed in a period of time. (p. 215)

Tickler file Any file that is reviewed on a regular basis for the purpose of taking action to clear the items from that file. (p. 307)

Timeliness Information that is available to a decision maker before it loses its capacity to influence a decision. (p. 17)

Top-down partitioning The successive subdividing, or "exploding," of logical DFDs that, when properly performed, leads to a set of balanced DFDs. (p. 29)

Total quality control (TQC) A subset of JIT that places responsibility for quality in the hands of the builder rather than in those of the inspector. (p. 472)

Transaction processing system A system that records data that reflect the minimal information needed to represent each transaction. (p. 69)

Transactions Particular events that have an economic impact on a firm. (p. 69)

Tuples Sets of data that describe an instance of an entity represented by the relation. (p. 88)

Turnaround documents Documents—printed by the computer as an output of one process—that are then used to capture and input subsequent event data. (p. 303)

U

UML^{TM} *See* Unified Modeling Language^{TM}. (p. 175)

Understandability Enables users to perceive the information's significance. Valued from the point of view of the user, understandable information is presented in a form that permits its application by the user in the decision-making situation at hand. (p. 17)

Unified Modeling Language^{TM} (UML^{TM}) A tool often associated with object-oriented development that is used to specify, visualize, and document models of software systems, including non-object oriented applications. (p. 175)

Unstructured decision One for which none of the decision phases (intelligence, design, and choice) are routine or repetitive. (p. 144)

Update accuracy An information process control goal which requires that data entered into a computer are reflected correctly in their respective master data. (p. 250)

Update completeness An information process control goal which requires that all events entered into a computer are reflected in their respective master data. (p. 250)

V

Validate To determine whether a system meets the requirements of the RFP. (p. 215)

Validity Information about actual events and actual objects. (p. 19)

Value-added network (VAN) A network service that provides communication capabilities for organizations not wishing to obtain their own dedicated communication links. (p. 125)

Vendor acknowledgment A notice by which the vendor acknowledges that a purchase order has been received and is being processed. (p. 429)

Vendor invoice A business document that notifies the purchaser of an obligation to pay a vendor for goods and services that were ordered and shipped to the purchaser. (p. 430)

Vendor master data A repository of data about approved vendors. (p. 430)

Vendor packing slip A business document that accompanies the purchased inventory from the vendor and identifies the shipment and triggers the inventory receiving process. (p. 429)

Verifiability A piece of information has verifiability when there is a high degree of consensus about the information among independent measurers using the same measurement methods. (p. 17)

W

Walkthrough Procedure in which the analyst follows a transaction as it is processed, observing and documenting what happens at each processing stage. (p. 196)

Waterfall method An alternative to the SDLC that derives its name from the fact that the output of each step in the process becomes input for the next step. (pg. 174)

Web browsers Software programs designed specifically to allow users to browse various documents and data sources available on the Internet. (p. 119)

Wide area networks (WANs) Communications networks that link distributed users and local networks into an integrated communications network. (p. 118)

Written approval A control plan in which a business document is checked to see that it contains an authorized signature indicating that the event has been authorized by that person. (p. 291)

X

XBRL *See* eXtensible Business Reporting Language. (p. 512)

XML *See* Extensible Markup Language (XML). (p. 128)

INDEX

A

B

C

D

E

F

G

H

I

J

K

L

M

P

Q

R

S

T

U

V

W

CPSIA information can be obtained
at www.ICGtesting.com
Printed in the USA
BVHW010206030120
568428BV00008B/58/P